Je t'aime… moi non plus

Je t'aime… moi non plus

Franco-British Cinematic Relations

Edited by
Lucy Mazdon and Catherine Wheatley

Berghahn Books

New York • Oxford

First published in 2010 by
Berghahn Books
www.berghahnbooks.com

Library of Congress Cataloging-in-Publication Data

Je t'aime… moi non plus : Franco-British cinematic relations / edited by Lucy
Mazdon and Catherine Wheatley.
    p. cm.
Includes bibliographical references and index.
ISBN 978-1-84545-749-5 (alk. paper)
1. Motion pictures, French–Great Britain. 2. Motion pictures–France–
History–20th century. 3. Motion pictures, British–France. 4. Motion
pictures–Great Britain–History–20th century.
I. Mazdon, Lucy. II. Wheatley, Catherine.
PN1993.5.F7J34 2010
791.43'750944–dc22
                                        2010018549

The project 'French Cinema in Britain' which enabled the
research at the heart of this book was funded by

Arts & Humanities
Research Council

British Library Cataloguing in Publication Data

A catalogue record for this book is available from the British Library

Printed in the United States on acid-free paper.

ISBN: 978-1-84545-749-5

Contents

List of Illustrations

List of Tables

Acknowledgements

A number of individuals and organisations have benefitted the production of this collection of essays. In particular the editors would like to thank the Arts and Humanities Research Council whose funding of Lucy Mazdon's 'French Cinema in Britain' project in 2006 enabled the research which lies at its heart. An early event in the lifespan of that project was a major conference on Franco-British cinematic relations held at the University of Southampton in 2007. The editors would like to thank all those who participated in that conference for their enthusiasm and inspiration. Thanks must also go to colleagues and students in Film Studies at the University of Southampton whose encouragement and interest has been much appreciated. The editors would also like to express their gratitude to staff at the BFI library and stills department, at the *Bibliothèque de film* in Paris and at the viewing department of the *Centre national de la cinématographie*. Their expertise and advice has been invaluable. Finally thanks must also go to Mark Stanton at Berghahn Books. His patience, efficiency and support for the project have been welcome indeed.

INTRODUCTION

Franco-British Cinematic Relations: An Overview

Lucy Mazdon

The title of this book will no doubt be familiar to many readers. Perhaps the most notorious of all Franco-British collaborations, the song 'Je t'aime, moi non plus' was written by French singer/songwriter Serge Gainsbourg and originally recorded in 1968 with Brigitte Bardot. Bardot vetoed the release of her recording and Gainsbourg set about producing a new version which was recorded at London's Marble Arch Studio and which featured the then relatively unfamiliar English actress Jane Birkin. As Robert and Isabelle Tombs remark, the contrast with the 'pouting, pneumatic Bardot' was striking (Tombs and Tombs 2006: 634). Birkin was a skinny English girl with an unmistakable accent and a breathy, childlike vocal style which 'gave the record more than a hint of perversity – for the French knew that if the British were not much good at straight sex, kinkiness was their forté' (ibid.). Gainsbourg in contrast seemed to epitomize the heavy drinking, Gauloise-smoking Parisian artiste and as Leila Wimmer reveals in her contribution to this volume, this combination of stereotypes (the cynical French seducer, the English *ingénue*) would prove highly fruitful in the establishment of Birkin as a major French star. The song itself was a huge *succès de scandale*, its Europe-wide record sales indubitably bolstered by the controversy it provoked. While French radio permitted broadcasting of the song after eleven pm, the BBC banned it outright, placing it firmly within a tradition of licentiousness which has long defined British reactions to French culture. Despite this ban the song reached number two in the British pop charts in 1969. It is noteworthy that in a country in which French pop music has traditionally held a very minor presence, this song is still recognisable to many, its iconic status underlined by a 1986 cover version recorded by none other than Gorden Kaye and Vicki Michelle, René and Yvette of British television sitcom *'Allo 'Allo!*, described here by Ginette Vincendeau as a veritable hotbed of British stereotypes of France.

So *Je t'aime... moi non plus* seems an entirely fitting title for this collection of essays. The Gainsbourg/Birkin collaboration emerges of course from a very specific moment (the 'swinging 60s' detailed here by Wimmer) but makes a significant if controversial contribution to broader Franco-British cultural exchange. The particular French and British stereotypes embodied by the two performers, along with the notable contrast between Birkin and Gainsbourg's initial singing partner, Bardot, recall a much more extensive history of stereotypes and images of the cross-Channel 'other'. Moreover, the song, its mixed British reception (moral outrage and popular acclaim) and the complex nature of the relationship between its two performers recall only too well the contradictory ('I love you, me neither'), often fraught and not infrequently hostile nature of the relationship between France and Britain. The two countries are close, geographically and culturally, and for this reason they have many affinities and much to share, yet they are also very far apart indeed, frequently at loggerheads. Birkin and Gainsbourg, like many other performers and artists before and since, played an important role in reflecting their own nation to the other in a manner that ultimately confirmed existing expectations and desires (Tombs and Tombs 2006: 635). In so doing they made visible the complex reality of exchange and collaboration between these 'sweet enemies', Britain and France.[1]

So Near Yet So Far: Franco-British Relations

Birkin and Gainsbourg followed their infamous song with a film of the same title (Gainsbourg 1976), providing a striking example of the cinematic exchange which plays an important role in Franco-British dialogue and which is the focus of the essays gathered in this collection. However, before looking more closely at film I would like to say a few words about Franco-British relations more broadly. Any attempt to understand cinematic exchange must be located within the broader networks of social and cultural exchange which surround and penetrate it. I have already noted the cultural and geographical proximity of Britain and France and it is undeniable that the two countries are closely intertwined. There is, for example, a long tradition of British love for a certain image of France. Over 600,000 Britons now own homes in (often rural) France, many of them inspired by Peter Mayle's bucolic but somewhat patronising account of his life in the Luberon in *A Year in Provence* (1989) and its various sequels and television and film adaptations. Robert and Isabelle Tombs suggest that this British devotion to rural France dates back to the nineteenth century (2006: 406); while, writing in *Sight and Sound* in 1953, Jean Queval remarks upon British affection for the Provençal films of Marcel Pagnol: 'He is ... vastly over-estimated in Hollywood and Hampstead, for obvious reasons of exoticism' (Queval 1953: 106). This British love for an 'exoticized' version of France, often depicted via film, continues to this day. Although *Le Fabuleux Destin d'Amélie Poulain* (2001) replaces an idealized version of southern France with a nostalgically kitsch Montmartre, its success with British audiences can surely be attributed to a similar taste for a picture postcard version of French life.[2]

French people have also flocked to the United Kingdom over the past twenty years or so, a particularly striking migration as 'for the first time ever there were more French in Britain than British in France' (Tombs and Tombs 2006: 654). As Robert and Isabelle Tombs point out, while the extent of this migration was perhaps unprecedented, its patterns can once again be traced back, this time to the eighteenth century: 'Most French came to Britain to make money; most British went to France to spend it' (2006: 655). While there are of course many exceptions to this rule, this general pattern of a French cross-Channel journey motivated by economics and a British journey propelled by leisure has an enduring history. And it is a pattern which is not without interest in terms of the cinematic exchanges that concern us here. As we shall see, the association of British cinema with industry and/or economics and French cinema with art and culture has long dominated the Franco-British filmic dialogue.

The history of cross-Channel relationships is then one of admiration and affection, a desire for that which the other is perceived to offer (idyllic lifestyle, financial opportunity) frequently figured through cultural, particularly cinematic, representations. But it is also a relation of suspicion and hostility. Before 1815 France and Britain were declared enemies and yet various forms of Anglophilia and Francophilia could be found alongside this open enmity. In the last one hundred or so years the two countries have become allies and yet Anglophobia and Francophobia go hand in hand with this unity. France and Britain have acted as models for one another but also as polar opposites, and stereotypes, negative and positive, have a long and enduring history:

> Fairly searching studies in the 1990s and for the centenary of the *entente cordiale* in 2004 showed much continuity and some change. Ancient stereotypes were alive and well. The British associated the French with elegance, refinement, culture, talkativeness, gastronomy, seductiveness and arrogance. The French associated the British with humour, eccentricity, insularity, coldness, principle, egotism, drunkenness, tradition and snobbery, and thought that 'five o'clock tea' was a universal British custom. These notions would have been familiar to Dr Johnson and Abbé le Blanc, and to Flora Tristan and William Makepeace Thackeray. They are deeply rooted in literature, memory and language. Reality was often bent to fit them: hence the durable popularity of the puerile comedian Benny Hill in France, regarded as a brilliantly surrealist manifestation of British humour, or the belief in Britain that French footballers talk philosophy (Tombs and Tombs 2006: 661–2).

'*Je t'aime... moi non plus*' indeed. We should of course add film to the list of sources for these stereotypes cited here. Moreover, we can perhaps extend their longevity and their constant vacillation between truth and fiction by remarking that Benny Hill is now considered by many in Britain as well as France as a highly skilled comic performer while Eric Cantona has become a respected film actor.

New Waves and Ooh Ah Cantona!

I shall come back to Cantona in a while but first let us look more closely at Franco-British cinematic relations which, as we shall see, emerge from and mirror the broader discourses mapped out briefly above, but which at the same time posses their own particularities. Two articles from *The Observer* are, I think, extremely suggestive here. In a piece published on 16 November 2008, Jason Solomons discusses the relative success of recent French films in the United Kingdom (Solomons 2008: 8–9). He points out that French films currently dominate foreign language releases in Britain, stating that forty-two French films given a British release in 2008 earned receipts of over £15 million. He goes on to claim, 'What we are seeing, in other words, is a new wave of commercialism in French cinema' (2008: 8). He quotes director Agnès Jaoui who bemoans the impact of the *Nouvelle Vague* and the *snobisme* of the *Cahiers du cinéma* critics. And yet, despite his avowed celebration of this new commercial success, Solomons to some extent buys into the longstanding dominance of the New Wave and myths of French cinephilia decried by Jaoui. The very title of the article, 'France on the Crest of a New Wave', clearly references that influential cinematic moment/movement, while his attempts to prove the new prominence of French film in the U.K. seem to depend largely on the discourses of auteurism: 'the names of French directors are once again rolling off the tongues of cinephiles: [Laurent] Cantet, Abdellatif Kechiche, Olivier Assayas, Agnès Jaoui. Is this the start of a new New Wave?' (2008: 9). In other words, Solomons appears to celebrate a new commercial success for French cinema while simultaneously reinforcing the tropes of auteurism, art-cinema and above all the powerful status of the *nouvelle vague* that have largely structured British perceptions of French cinema since the 1960s.

In a second piece in *The Observer*, published on 1 March 2009, David Smith asks, 'Is this a New Golden Age for British Cinema?' (Smith 2009: 10–11). Prominent among the films he cites as part of what he sees as a clear revival in the fortunes of British cinema are: Ken Loach's *Looking for Eric* (2009), a Franco-British coproduction in competition at the 2009 Cannes festival and starring the aforementioned Eric Cantona; Jackie Oudney's *French Film* aka *A Frenchman's Guide to Love* (2008), a comedy which also stars Cantona (here playing a film director) and which explores the differences between French and British attitudes to relationships; Rachid Boucharib's *London River* (2009), a Franco-British-Algerian coproduction starring Brenda Blethyn and Sotigui Kouyaté and which recounts the endeavours of a British mother (Blethyn) and a Malian father (Kouyaté) to trace their children in the aftermath of the terrorist attacks in London in July 2005. In other words, three of the films which constitute this *British* revival are Franco-British collaborations at the level of production, narrative and/or performance. When we consider this alongside Solomons's account of the growing presence of French cinema in the United Kingdom it would seem that in the field of contemporary cinema the 'sweet enemies' are currently quite close indeed. And yet just as the broader relationships between Britain and France continue to recycle age-old stereotypes, the cinematic dialogue is bound up with discourses and perceptions which have an enduring history – the overweening influence of the *Nouvelle Vague*, footballer-cum-philosopher Eric Cantona as the 'archetypal' Frenchman.

High Brow or Low Brow?
Ice Creams, Sausages and Cricket

Despite this clear evidence of collaboration and shared interests, there has long been a tendency to see French and British cinematic cultures as polar opposites. While France is consistently described as a highly cinephilic nation, Britain is a country in which cinema is at best not taken seriously and at worst dismissed as entirely moribund. I shall not repeat once more Truffaut's infamous dismissal of British cinema (discussed here by Robert Murphy); however, suffice to say that his take on the films of *la perfide Albion* was not a solitary perspective. Interviewed by Caroline Lejeune in *The Observer* in 1939, René Clair gives an account of British cinema which seems uncannily prescient:

> But I tell you, it is very difficult to find dramatic stories in the English life. I have lived here for four years, and I love England, but I am beginning to understand your problems. It is a quiet life, the English. Night after night, I found myself reading the evening paper, drinking a whiskey-soda, and going off to bed at 9.30 because there was nothing else to do. If you are to give a true picture of England today you cannot be dramatic. That is why the best English films and plays deal with historical subjects. Life was robust then, before the Victorian age killed its vigour… Oh yes, I know it makes for good homes and happy children. But it is very hard on the poor dramatist. Perhaps that is another reason why you find the French films so refreshing today (Lejeune 1939).

Writing in France eight years before Truffaut, Alain Tanner gave an equally bleak account of British film culture (Tanner 1958: 30–38). While Tanner certainly did not share Truffaut's apparent contempt for the very notion of a British cinema – indeed he codirected the British Free Cinema short *Nice Time* in 1957 – he was extremely critical of its state at the time of writing. A central problem, according to Tanner, was British reluctance to take cinema seriously: 'The philistinism of the British has deep roots even in cultured circles and among those working in the cinema these attitudes are so deep set that it would be considered an obscene joke to even mention the word "art" in front of a film producer' (Tanner 1958: 31).[3] Tanner went on to condemn the British mode of film production and exhibition:

> A director's job is to make sure that the film is finished in the time allowed by the budget. The producers of these 'quota quickies' … are for the most part small-time business men who have chosen to work in the movies rather than in the sausage industry. These sixty or seventy minute films are shown

before the main feature in the hope that they will sell more ice-creams. In English cinemas, usherettes dressed in white like nurses wander around during the film selling snacks. At one point Rank actually admitted that only these sales were keeping their cinemas afloat! (1958: 32).

While Tanner is clearly referring specifically to the British 'quota quickies' here, his account of British cinema as an industry with a distinctly antiartistic prejudice is typical of French accounts of British film culture and it was an account which had its roots firmly in reality. As Rachel Low has remarked, from the outset film was taken much more seriously in France than in the United Kingdom: 'In France and Italy the film might be a younger sister of the arts, in America art itself. In England it was a poor relation, and, moreover, not a very respectable one' (Low 1971: 137–8). Writing in *Sight and Sound* in spring 1963 Penelope Houston bemoans the 'monotony' of comparisons between the young cinema of Britain and France (Houston 1963: 55). She goes on to declare that it is a 'delusion' that French audiences are more sophisticated and intellectually alert than others and suggests that British audiences, given the opportunity, could be just as adventurous. She notes that the French 'young cinema' is now being hampered by economic difficulties but points out that the need to adapt to financial constraints, to treat cinema as an industrial rather than a creative process, has always bedevilled British filmmakers who 'have been compelled, all along the line, to think and act as economic realists' (1963: 55). In other words this British critic more or less echoes the vision of British film culture holding sway on the other side of the Channel and although she decries this state of affairs it could be argued that she unwittingly slips into the very philistinism decried by Tanner when she states: 'On the grounds of originality and sheer creative volume of work there can be no real argument: by comparison with a cinema headed by Truffaut, Godard, Resnais, Demy, Rivette, etc. we are fielding a second eleven and that is all there is to it' (1963: 55). By reducing British cinema to a sporting metaphor this writer seems to undermine the very 'art culture' she is avowedly advocating.

Writing only a year earlier in *Films and Filming*, Raymond Durgnat states 'the French enjoy culture as the English enjoy cricket', anticipating the slippage expressed by Houston in *Sight and Sound* (Durgnat 1962: 48–55). While Durgnat takes pains in this article to unpack some of the preconceptions which dominate French and British accounts of their cross-Channel cinematic other, he does acknowledge that the French 'ace-in-the-hole' is that theirs is an 'industry of artists'. Strikingly he locates these very different attitudes to culture in each country's political traditions. French volatility may not make for a stable economy but it can enable diversity and experimentation; 'England, by comparison, is a land of uniformity, of stiff upper lips and stiff upper minds; every Briton his own bobby; somewhere, in the depth of his being, where lesser breeds have a soul, the average Briton has, if not an Arnold of Rugby, then a Dixon of Dock Green' (1962: 48). Durgnat does not despise this middle-class fortitude but makes a connection between these attitudes and the rigid distinctions between 'low-brow' and 'high-brow' culture in Britain. 'The difference between the French and the Anglo-Saxon cinema is not that there's no French trash, it abounds, but that low-brows also enjoy a "serious" approach' (1962: 50).

So it would seem that there is a long critical tradition in both Britain and France that draws very clear distinctions between the two cinematic cultures. According to this discourse, Britain is a country which sees film as an industry like so many others (recall Tanner's reference to sausage makers!), where the films of Hollywood are allowed, indeed encouraged, to dominate, where the director is just a figure on a budget-driven conveyor belt and where state support for film is unreliable and often more or less nonexistent. France, on the other hand, is a nation of cinephiles, a country in which cinema is taken seriously, where film professionals are not in thrall to Hollywood, where the director/auteur is taken seriously and where the state has long provided significant support for an art form that is seen to play a vital role in disseminating national culture. In the words of Lindsay Anderson: 'One of the most delightful features about a visit to France – apart from food, sunshine, etc. – is that civilized attitude toward living that finds its most obvious expression in the way people talk about the arts' (Anderson 1954: 105), adding an admiration for French cultural life to the affection for climate and cuisine discussed earlier in this Introduction.

Of course even this British admiration occasionally found itself caught up in the very reluctance to take culture seriously identified by Tanner et al. Anderson himself, while praising the French critical writing he reviews, criticizes the 'dithyrambic', overly literary style of the young *Cahiers* critics and their 'perverse cultivation of the meretricious' (1954: 105). Writing a few years earlier in 1948, D.A. Yerrill reveals a similar ambivalence:

> Over there [in France], they really go to town with criticism and every kind of film news. The result is that the French public are really film conscious and acutely aware of their own country's efforts. One hesitates to advocate a bringing about of the French attitude, which can be a bit of a bore, over here, but it would be useful to take a small step in that direction. (Yerrill 1948: 98–9).

What is perhaps most striking about these accounts is both their repetition of long-held assumptions about the French and British film cultures and the fact that these assumptions are far from nationally specific. The British Durgnat, the French-based but Swiss-born Tanner and the French Truffaut can, in different ways and different measures, criticize British cinema from their different national perspectives. Anderson can simultaneously exalt the new French cinema and the young French critics while criticising the style and focus of some of their work (and of course embarking on a revivification of British cinema via his own films). In other words, attitudes towards the 'other' cinema are not always nationally specific and no account of Franco-British cinematic relations should be reduced to a simple set of binary oppositions. Rather it is vital to understand the complex and shifting nature of these discourses and, despite the longevity of certain stereotypes and assumptions, the various ways in which they are shaped by the broader cultural and historical discourses in which they are embedded.

Special Films for Special Audiences?
French Films in Britain, British Films in France

British perceptions of French cinema, in particular those of British cinemagoers, are to a great extent shaped by the relative scarcity of French cinema in the United Kingdom. This book is part of a wider project tracing the history of French cinema in Britain which I am currently researching alongside Catherine Wheatley. While French cinema has long been the most visible non-English language cinema in Britain, its presence is still relatively limited. Various factors contribute to its growth and dwindling at certain times. However, it has long been and remains a 'niche' cultural form to all intents and purposes. As Vincent Porter demonstrates in his chapter in this collection, the 1930s was a boom time for French cinema in the United Kingdom as political events led to the falling away of Soviet and German film, and the establishment of the 'Continental' cinemas and the growth of the film society movement established new venues and new audiences for these 'foreign' films. The Second World War put paid to this growth but French film returned to the forefront in the 1950s as it provided material to fill the gap left by dwindling Hollywood product and, as Catherine Wheatley suggests in her chapter, distributors took advantage of the advent of the X certificate in 1951 to market it as a 'risqué' and daring alternative to Anglo-American fare.[4] A French Film Festival sponsored by Unifrance, supported by the French Embassy and attended by the Queen was held in London in February 1953 and the event trumpeted the 'mainly adult but seldom highbrow' nature of recent French cinema. In the words of Ingram Fraser, then Managing Director of distributors Films de France: 'Among Continental productions, those from France enjoy special box-office advantages. France is the Englishman's most favoured tourist haunt and ten people speak French for every one who speaks another language. The very differences between French and English life can be turned to advantage' (Fraser 1953). Clearly we are back here to that British passion for France as holiday/leisure destination and Fraser seizes on this as another means of selling French films in the U.K. And yet this attempt to increase the visibility of French film and position it as an intelligent but commercially viable alternative to Hollywood was to prove short lived. As we have noted, the advent of the films of the New Wave on British shores had a huge impact on the country's critics and by extension its audiences. The films were admired by many, emulated by others, but they also set in stone a vision of French cinema as 'specialized' which had been in circulation to varying degrees for many years. Writing in *Picturegoer* in 1946, Eric Goldschmidt argues that Continental films would sell far more tickets if they were not described as 'special'

> Probably the most pernicious factor blocking the wider showing of specialized films is the very word 'special'. So long as the legend persists – misleading and useless though it is – that foreign films should be roped off and filed away for the benefit of a handful of lost souls, the inhabitants of Portsmouth, Putney and Perth won't get a chance of taking sides in this argument (Goldschmidt 1948: 17)

Despite Goldschmidt's pleas or the efforts of Fraser and his ilk in the 1950s, this is a term which did not disappear. Indeed it is still used today by the U.K. Film Council to denote all films which do not 'sit easily within a mainstream and hugely commercial genre'. Not surprisingly this includes all foreign-language, subtitled films. One result of this 'specialization' of foreign-language films has been the tendency to designate them as 'art-house', clearly positioned in opposition to the 'commercial' or 'mainstream' offering of Hollywood and, to a great extent, Britain. These terms are of course far from straightforward and as the essays in this book begin to suggest, they need to be handled with some care. The very journey from one culture to another can significantly alter the identity of a given film – a light-hearted genre film from France becomes a 'French specialized' feature when it is renamed, subtitled and distributed via a British art-house circuit. In other words, when thinking about the Franco-British cinematic relationship it is vital to consider the varying modes of exhibition, distribution and reception to which they are subject as they move between cultures.[5]

While British perceptions of French cinema can then to a great extent be seen to have been shaped by critical esteem but a limited visibility with audiences, the opposite is broadly true of France. British films have had a relatively wide presence on French cinema screens and many have proved highly successful – the cross-Channel appreciation of the films of Ken Loach is an oft-cited example. However, French critics have proved rather less welcoming and, to a great extent, have either ignored or worse, condemned *le cinéma d'outre-manche*. In her recently published history of the French reception of British cinema (2009), Leila Wimmer relates the critical neglect which for many years typified this reception:

> [Early] French film histories shared a more or less consensual view of the low achievements of British cinema, in that it was largely ignored and overshadowed by the artistic achievements of the American, French, Soviet, Italian and Swedish cinema that were taken much more seriously as examples of film art. The critical neglect of British cinema was endemic and when we then turn to French historiography on British cinema in the post-war period, there is a surprising dearth of material up until the late 1960s (Wimmer 2009: 18).

This rejection of British cinema reached a peak in the 1950s when it was vilified by Truffaut and his fellow *Cahiers* critics. As Wimmer demonstrates, these writers condemned British cinema that, like the French *cinéma de qualité*, spurned formal innovation in favour of solid scripts and well crafted adaptations, and this rejection became a central tool in the establishment of the *politique des auteurs* and of course the French New Wave (2009: 75–149). It is striking that these negative discourses still dominate our understanding of French accounts of British cinema today (remember that oft-cited Truffaut dismissal). And yet, as Wimmer suggests in her book, while British cinema did not perhaps receive the critical attention accorded to the films of other nations, it has certainly not always been condemned by French critics. The 1940s, for example, now often described as a British 'Golden Age', saw many French critics praising films such as *Brief Encounter* (Lean 1945) for their 'truth' and 'authenticity' (Wimmer 2009: 63). An admiration for the films of Michael Powell, discussed in detail here by Ian Christie, sparked a new interest in British film in the 1970s and the shifts in the British film industry in the 1980s, largely due to the innovative funding policies of Channel Four, drew huge admiration, much of it centred on the social-realist works of British auteurs Mike Leigh, Stephen Frears and, of course, Ken Loach: as French writers envied the filmmakers working in Britain, things seemed to have come a long way from those ice cream-selling film producers by default condemned by Alain Tanner.

So it would seem that there have been and indeed continue to be some very positive French critical takes on British film culture, and yet just as British filmgoers' perceptions of French cinema tend to be dominated by the equation French film equals art-house fare, so it is the negative accounts of British cinema which tend to override all other French critical voices. Perhaps not surprisingly both sets of perceptions have their roots in that seminal cinematic moment, the French *Nouvelle Vague*, indisputably a high point in the development of film art yet arguably a cause of a rather limiting ossification in the Franco-British cinematic dialogue. As opprobrium for British cinema gathered pace among the writers/directors of the French New Wave so it became the negative model against which they defined their own conception of what cinema should be. While Hollywood provided the good model of vibrancy and excitement, British films were the bad model of stultifying respectability to be rejected at all costs (Wimmer 2009: 110). Just as wider Franco-British relations have long been bound up with ongoing stereotypes, so the cross-Channel cinematic nexus depends upon some rather rigid perceptions which can be traced back to the early days of film production but which were to a great extent set in stone in the 1950s and 1960s. The complete absence of any British films in *Cahiers*'s 2008 list of its one hundred best films testifies to the endurance of the French critical establishment's ongoing dismissal of British cinema, while Jason Solomon's previously cited description of a new 'French New Wave' constructed through the tropes of auteurism bears witness to an ongoing alignment of French film with art cinema. Writing in *Kinematograph Weekly* in 1953, Jacques Flaud, then director of the *Centre national de la cinématographie française*, remarks upon the limited presence of French films in Britain: 'France is Great Britain's nearest neighbour, and yet Great Britain is the only country of all France's neighbours into which it is difficult for French films to penetrate' (Flaud 1953: 5). He urges closer cooperation between the two nations and concludes by stating: 'I have no fear of contradiction by my English friends when I say that British films encounter no difficulty or antagonism in their attempts to penetrate the French market. I hope that after this London film week French producers may be able to detect an equally encouraging state of affairs on your side of the Channel' (ibid.). How ironic then that Flaud's impassioned plea should come just as the vilification of British cinema espoused by Truffaut and his colleagues was beginning to hit its stride in France, leading to a cinematic movement which in many ways would nip in the bud the green shoots of commercial potential for French films in the British cultural landscape of the 1950s.

Not Just the New Wave:
Franco-British Cinematic Relations

Figure I.1: Ken Loach and Eric Cantona on the set of *Looking for Eric* (2009).
Image courtesy of the BFI stills department.

The aim of this collection is to unpack, historicize and indeed move beyond the
rather limiting definitions which have tended to define the Franco-British cinematic
relationship to date. As the essays gathered here reveal, there is much more to this
than simple oppositions between British critical esteem for the films of France and
French dismissal of '*le cinéma British*', or the success of Ken Loach et al. at the French
box office and the relative dearth of French movies on British screens. There has long
been a rich and productive dialogue between these two cultures in which both their
clear differences and their shared concerns have played a vital role and while the
focus of this book is Franco-British cinematic relations, this particular process of
conversation and/or rejection must always be positioned within a much more fluid
network of exchange. As Cristina Johnson demonstrates here in her analysis of David
Niven's movement between performances of Britishness and Frenchness in a number
of U.S. films, the presence of Hollywood in the Franco-British relationship is
primordial. Just as each 'national' cinema necessarily defines itself to a great extent in
relation to (or against) that dominant U.S. 'other', so any understanding of the cross-
Channel dialogue must also acknowledge the impact/influence of Hollywood.
Beyond this the wider context of what is after all a global film industry should also
not be ignored. It is striking that two recent films which have placed some form of

journey between France and Britain at the heart of their narratives have explicitly positioned that journey within a much broader context of international relations. Rachid Bouchareb's *London River* sees Malian immigrant Mr Ousmane (Sotigui Kouyaté) travel from France to London in search of his son lost in the aftermath of terrorist bombings provoked by global political events. Philippe Lioret's *Welcome* (2009) recounts a young Kurdish refugee's (Firat Ayverdi) attempt to swim across the Channel in a desperate attempt to reach England. The film is set in Calais with frequent shots of the grey sea and the distant image of British shores on the horizon. In other words the film represents the geographical closeness of the two countries while stressing their impossible distance from the point of view of the displaced and dispossessed victims of global politics. The cinematic relationship between Britain and France is rich and fascinating, but its location within a far broader network of cultural, cinematic and political exchange is absolutely crucial.

The essays are divided into three parts which map out some of the key areas of exchange and collaboration which structure the Franco-British cinematic dialogue. These distinctions are of course somewhat artificial as there is evidently a great deal of overlap between each, however we intend them to serve as an organizing tool rather than as a prescriptive set of divisions. Part I examines 'Industry and Institutions'. Vincent Porter begins the section with a detailed account of the distribution and exhibition of French films in the United Kingdom in the 1930s, a golden moment for the 'Continental' cinema and for the growth of a 'serious' film culture in Britain more generally. Charles O'Brien provides a fascinating study of the different versions of Hitchcock's *Waltzes from Vienna / La Chant du Danube* (1934) made for release in the French and British markets and the impact this particular form of export had on British film culture. His focus on one of Hitchcock's British-made films is also striking in the context of this collection's broader scope when we recall the *Cahiers* critics' adulation of Hitchcock and the necessary concomitant denial of his 'Englishness'. Justin Smith addresses another significant moment in the history of Franco-British cinematic relations as he traces the history of the Anglo-French coproduction agreement from 1965 to 1979. As Smith reveals, debates over this agreement said much about differing attitudes to cinema and indeed to European integration more broadly and the filmic results were, to say the least, mixed. Cécile Renaud discusses another example of active collaboration at the level of industry in her account of the French Film Festival U.K. and the *Festival du film britannique* in Dinard. Here again Hitchcock provides a somewhat ironic focus as the French event awards a '*Hitchcock d'or*' to the festival's favourite film – ironic given that earlier denial of Hitch's Englishness. Finally Catherine Wheatley analyses the British marketing campaigns for three French film versions of D.H. Lawrence's *Lady Chatterley's Lover*. As Wheatley demonstrates, in varying ways and to different degrees the films' distributors played upon the novel's controversial reputation and a well established association between French cinema and the risqué in the minds of cinemagoers to sell these French versions of an English text back to British audiences.

Part II concerns itself with 'Reception and Perceptions' – how was the cinema from across the Channel perceived? What responses and reactions did it provoke?

Geoffrey Nowell-Smith turns his attention to that seminal and, as we have seen, highly influential moment in the history of Franco-British cinematic relations, the *Nouvelle Vague*. He traces the early critical and commercial reception of the French New Wave in Britain and its impact on British art film culture. Daniel Biltereyst extends this analysis by looking at the differing reactions of censors in Britain and France to the films of the *Nouvelle Vague*. Drawing on numerous censors' files he provides a suggestive account of the rather different attitudes towards the cinematically acceptable in the two countries at this moment of great social and cultural change. Sarah Street also focuses upon the New Wave, arguing that in many ways its critical reception in Britain created problems for domestic cinema as it introduced a set of criteria or comparisons which led to misunderstandings of some of the central aspects of contemporary British films. Via a detailed study of Simone Signoret's performance in *Room at the Top* (Jack Clayton 1959), Street reveals a far more complex internationalization of many of the films of the period than these comparisons may tend to suggest. Ian Christie moves away from the New Wave to look at the reappraisal of the works of Powell and Pressburger in France. He argues that long-standing doubts about the role and function of cinema in Britain have meant that the view from France has always played a vital role in defining and distinguishing domestic film culture. Melanie Selfe and Ingrid Stigsdotter both turn their attention to actual British audiences watching French films. While Selfe focuses on responses to the so-called French 'extreme' cinema, Stigsdotter looks at British receptions of Erick Zonca's realist drama *La Vie rêvée des anges / The Dreamlife of Angels* (1998). Both chapters unpack the various ways in which films are transformed as they journey from one culture to another – the addition of subtitles, differing censorship practices, shifts in exhibition venues and so on – and analyse the complex ways in which British viewers' interpretive strategies make sense of these French films.

Part III turns to the performers and personnel who have engaged with Franco-British exchange. Jonathan Driskell looks at an early French émigré, Annabella, analysing the shifts and transformations brought to bear on her star persona as she moved across the Channel. Cristina Johnston engages in a similar study of David Niven, Annabella's costar in *Dinner at the Ritz* (Harold D. Schuster 1937), looking closely at the ways in which Niven embodied varying notions of Englishness and/or cosmopolitan glamour across a range of French, British and American films of the 1950s and 1960s. Robert Murphy turns his attention to François Truffaut, a figure who perhaps cannot be ignored in a collection such as this. However, Murphy moves beyond that infamous anti-British remark to demonstrate, via an account of Truffaut's shooting of *Fahrenheit 451* (1966) in London, a far more nuanced relationship with *la perfide Albion*. Leila Wimmer's chapter discusses the transformation of Jane Birkin from 'English rose' to the iconic figure of French stage and screen whose ongoing mobilization of her very 'Englishness' would remain so central to her cross-Channel success. Ginette Vincendeau looks at a rather different set of representations in her study of British accounts of the French Resistance in the highly successful television series *'Allo 'Allo!* and Gillian Armstrong's film *Charlotte Gray* (2001). Vincendeau skilfully reveals the relationship between the long-running television series and its televisual and cinematic predecessors and followers and underlines their continuing negotiation of a limited and limiting set of stereotypes. Finally Jim Morrissey provides a detailed comparative study of two films which offer British and French versions of 'ghettoized' or marginal lifestyles, Mathieu Kassowitz's *La Haine* (1995) and Saul Dibb's *Bullet Boy* (2004). Morrissey unpacks variations between French and British critical receptions of Kassowitz's film and analyses the different ways in which these two films represent urban space and ethnic difference, arguing that these differences speak volumes about contrasting French and British attitudes towards identity and integration.

The diversity of these essays says much about the complex ways in which French and British film cultures interact. Those enduring stereotypes – French cinephilia and art versus British philistinism and formal caution – are clearly not the whole story. And yet their very longevity suggests they should be reconsidered but not perhaps entirely discredited as a last look at Eric Cantona and his new collaborator, Ken Loach, reminds us. In an article in *The Guardian* on 9 May 2009, Simon Hattenstone discusses the relationship between the two men and their work on *Looking for Eric*: 'While Loach has spent most of his career revered in France and ignored at home, Cantona is still revered in England 12 years after he stopped playing. But in France he tends to be regarded as an underachieving maverick [but since retiring] he has worked consistently as an actor in French cinema' (Hattenstone 2009: 21). To paraphrase Raymond Durgnat, 'the French enjoy cinema like the English enjoy football'. However, in this particular case that very difference in attitude and taste has led to a *Palme d'Or* nominated, critically acclaimed, cross-Channel cinematic collaboration. *Je t'aime... moi non plus.*

Notes

1. *That Sweet Enemy* is the title given to Robert and Isabelle Tombs' magisterial work on Franco-British relations. The phrase is taken from Sir Philip Sidney's *Astrophel and Stella* (1591), Sonnet XLI, 'that sweet enemy, France'.
2. See Mazdon and Wheatley (2008).
3. All translations from the French are my own unless otherwise stated.
4. I discussed this in more detail in a seminar paper delivered at the University of Stirling in November 2008. A version of the paper entitled, 'Vulgar, Nasty and French: Selling French Films to British Audiences in the 1950s' will be published in *The Journal of British Cinema and Television* in 2010.
5. It is worth pointing out that due to the title changes mentioned here, we have endeavoured to provide French and English titles throughout. One exception is Vincent Porter who has given French titles only, as in the early 1930s films screened at the Film Society and the Academy were shown with French titles and no subtitles.

Bibliography

Anderson, L. 1954. 'Book Reviews: French Critical Writing', *Sight and Sound* 24(2): 105.

Durgnat, R. 1962. 'A Mirror for Marianne', *Films and Filming* November: 48–55.

Flaud, J. 1953. 'This Golden Opportunity', *Kinematograph Weekly* 19 February: 5.

Fraser, I. 1953. 'Appetite Grows with Eating', *Kinematograph Weekly* 19 February: 9–15.

Goldschmidt, E. 1948. 'What's So Special About All These Foreign Films?', *Picturegoer* 18 December: 17.

Hattenstone, S. 2009. 'The Awkward Squad', *The Guardian*, 9 May, 18–23.

Houston, P. 1963. 'The Front Page', *Sight and Sound* 32(2): 55.

La Lettre de la Maison Française, 11, Trinity-Michaelmas 1999.

Lejeune, C.A. 1939. 'René Clair on France's Cinema Industry', *The Observer*, 22 January.

Low, R. 1971. *The History of the British Film, 1906–1914*. London: Allen and Unwin.

Mazdon, L. and C. Wheatley. 2008. 'Intimate Connections', *Sight and Sound* 18(5): 38–40.

Queval, J. 1953. 'French Films Since the War', *Sight and Sound* 22(3): 102–108.

Solomons, J. 2008. 'France on the Crest of a New Wave', *The Observer*, 16 November, 8–9.

Smith, D. 2009. 'Is This a New Golden Age for British Cinema?', *The Observer*, 1 March, 10–11.

Tanner, A. 1958. 'L'Impossible cinéma anglais', *Cahiers du cinéma* November: 30–38.

Tombs, R. and I. Tombs. 2006. *That Sweet Enemy: The French and the British from the Sun King to the Present*. London: William Heinemann.

Yerrill, D.A. 1948. 'On Film Critics', *Sight and Sound* 17(56): 98–99.

Wimmer, L. 2009. *Cross-Channel Perspectives: The French Reception of British Cinema*. Oxford: Peter Lang.

Filmography

Brief Encounter. 1945, David Lean, U.K.

Bullet Boy. 2004, Saul Dibb, U.K.

Charlotte Gray. 2001, Gillian Armstrong, U.K./Australia/Germany.

Dinner at the Ritz. 1937, Harold D. Schuster, U.K.

Fabuleux Destin d'Amélie Poulain, Le / Amelie. 2001, Jean-Pierre Jeunet, France.

Fahrenheit 451. 1966, François Truffaut, U.K.

French Film aka *A Frenchman's Guide to Love*. 2008, Jackie Oudney, U.K.

Haine, La. 1995, Mathieu Kassowitz, France.

Je t'aime, moi non plus / I Love You. I Don't. 1976, Serge Gainsbourg, France.

London River. 2009, Rachid Bouchareb, France/U.K./Algeria.

Looking for Eric. 2009, Ken Loach, U.K./France.

Nice Time. 1957, Claude Goretta/Alain Tanner, U.K.

Room at the Top. 1959, Jack Clayton, U.K.

Vie rêvée des anges, La / The Dream-life of Angels. 1998, Erick Zonca, France.

Waltzes from Vienna / La chant du Danube. 1934, Alfred Hitchcock, U.K.

Welcome. 2009, Philippe Lioret, France.

PART I

Industry and Institution

CHAPTER 1

The Exhibition, Distribution and Reception of French Films in Great Britain during the 1930s

Vincent Porter

Introduction

The exhibition of French films in Great Britain expanded dramatically during the 1930s, and by the outbreak of the Second World War a Francophile cinemagoer living in London could have seen approximately 110 feature films, and some twenty shorts and documentaries. By 1939, French films could be seen in up to seven London cinemas, two of which were repertory cinemas, and six of which were located only a short walk from Oxford Circus. Outside London, screenings of French films were far more limited, and people living in Scotland and the English regions had to rely on their local film society to see a French film, although by 1939, it was estimated that there were over one hundred of them (Grierson 1939).

Building an Audience for Continental Films

The first performance of London's Film Society, on 25 October 1925, was in the New Gallery Kinema in Regent Street, when the audience consisted mainly of 'the beau monde of Bohemia, including some of the more adventurous members of society and official circles. Chelseaites and Bloomsburyians were in evidence – young men with beards and young women in homespun cloaks' (Brunel 1949: 113). The society screened *Feu Mathias Pascal*, at its seventh performance on 11 April 1926, but few people saw it as the society's membership fee was expensive and it was impossible for the ordinary cinemagoer to buy a ticket for a single performance.

By 1930, virtually the only commercial cinema where continental films were regularly screened was the 750-seat Avenue Pavilion in Shaftesbury Avenue. For about eighteen months, its owners, the Gaumont-British Picture Corporation, allowed its previous owner, Stuart Davis, to programme American, German and Swedish classics. Davis then launched a season of French films with a white-tie opening in the presence of the French Ambassador. He screened *Finis Terrae, Un Chapeau de paille en Italie, Les Deux timides, En rade, Rien que les heures* and *La Chute de la Maison Usher*. But Davis' greatest success was *Thérèse Raquin*, which had been made with a Franco-German cast for quota purposes, and subsequently obtained many provincial bookings (Rotha 1958: 63).

The audience at the Avenue Pavilion consisted of roughly three different classes: 'the intelligentsia, the intellectual amateur who likes to follow new art movements, and the ordinary average middle-class business man who doesn't go to the cinema as a rule because he does not like the fare provided for "the masses"' (Davis 1929). But despite Davis' success in finding a new audience, Gaumont decided to convert the Avenue Pavilion into a newsreel cinema, although before it finally closed they allowed him to screen revivals of *Feu Mathias Pascal, Maldone* and *Un Chapeau de paille en Italie* (*The Times*, 6 January 1930, p. 10; 15 January 1930, p. 12).

Film critic Paul Rotha and his friends struggled to find a replacement for the Avenue Pavilion, but they failed. Despite having access to Davis' mailing list of 12,500 Londoners, four-fifths of whom said that they would support a similar venture, they were unable to find a new venue (Rotha 1958: 63–4). The next cinema to show continental films was the smaller, and recently modernized, 534-seat Academy Cinema in Oxford Street. Its owner, Eric Hakim, allowed Elsie Cohen, who had previously shown German and Soviet films at the Palais de Luxe Cinema in Windmill Street, to programme the films for him (Eyles 2000). In order to encourage students and other film aficionados to patronize the cinema, the Academy kept several rows of the stalls at very cheap prices. Moreover, the feature films at the Academy were generally longer than average, and Cohen supported them with a three-reel documentary, or perhaps two good shorter documentaries (Cohen 1971: 9).

To excite people's curiosity, Cohen initially programmed one film per week, and gave weekly press shows to which she invited all the London press. Her first season was a six-week series of French films, which included *Le Roi des resquilleurs, Jean de la Lune, Dreyfus* and *La Douceur d'aimer* (*The Times*, 25 March 1931, p. 12; 20 April 1931, p. 12; and 25 May 1931, p. 8). In June, the Academy announced that the experiment had been a success, and advertised itself as 'The home of real French talkies' (Eyles and Skone 1991: 35). During the 1930s, Cohen premiered over thirty French feature films at the Academy.

The arrival of the talkies meant increased expenditure to launch a foreign language film. The preparation of a subtitled print, plus the cost of import and other duties, could easily cost an exhibitor several hundred pounds before the film opened (Oakley 1947: 4). Because all the press came to the Film Society's screenings, Cohen realized that a preview of one of her films at one of the society's screenings could offer a further opportunity for publicity. Accordingly, she became friendly with the members of the society's council, and when she acquired the British rights to the German film, *Mädchen in Uniform*, a proto-Lesbian tale directed and acted entirely by women, Cohen allowed the Film Society to screen it first (Cohen 1971: 10).

For the initial screening of the film at the Film Society, its members, who were peppered with ladies in tweeds and monocles, were asked to hold a synopsis on translucent paper up to the light from the screen. The organizers had also inserted roll-up titles between the sequences in the film, which summarized the facts which had gone before and hinted at those to come (Dickinson 1975). Cohen then engaged Miss J.M. Harvey, the Secretary of the Film Society, to subtitle the print, which required two hundred and thirty titles (Harvey 1936: 168). The film subsequently ran at the Academy for six months, and brought a great number of people to the cinema who had not been before (Cohen 1971: 10). French films presented Harvey with further difficulties, however. This was partly because 'the quality of the dialogue in French films was seldom outstanding', but also because 'some of the very natural acting in French films was often dialogue which was filled with broken sentences and small words or ejaculations which could not be translated' (Harvey 1936: 169).

In order to recoup her higher launch costs, Cohen had to build a substantial new audience for each film. To do this, she switched to a policy of premieres and longer runs. She also informed potential patrons about important aspects of each picture, such as the director, the technical staff, the country and place of origin, and above all, its artistic aim, by circulating this information to people on her mailing list. By 1933, Cohen's list ran into the thousands. A good many of those on the list were people who lived far away, but who liked to know what was going on so that they could come up to London for a particular film (Coxhead 1933: 135–6).

To enhance the social standing of her films, Cohen solicited the patronage of royalty and the aristocracy at her premieres (Cohen 1971: 10). On average, she premiered two French films a year, at which she combined establishment patronage with charitable giving. In October 1933, March 1934 and March 1935, she gave the proceeds from her premieres of *Paris Méditerranée*, *La Robe rouge* and *Lac aux dames* to the Westminster, Belgravia and Pimlico Associations for Women's Welfare; and in November 1934 those from the premiere of *Le Dernier Milliardaire* went to the Shoreditch Infants Welfare Society (*The Times*, 6 October 1933; 15 March 1934; 15 November 1934; 16 March 1935).

Cohen's early success at the Academy led to an invitation to programme continental films at the 1200-seat Cambridge Theatre in Cambridge Circus, but the building was too large for her enterprise, and after six months she abandoned it (Cohen 1971: 10). Another short-lived venue for continental films was the 684-seat Rialto Theatre in Coventry Street, which screened a number of French films between 1931 and 1933, notably *The Erl King*, which was made in France by a German company with French dialogue, followed by *Un Soir de rafle* and *A nous la liberté*, both of which an anonymous correspondent of *The Times* considered to be 'first class' (29 July 1932, p. 10). But in March 1933, the Rialto was converted to a news theatre (Eyles and Skone 1991: 37). Hakim also invited Cohen to programme the Cinema House, another Oxford Street cinema which he owned and where, during

January 1934, she premiered *Prenez garde à la peinture* and the documentary *Ombres sur l'Europe*. But two months later Hakim sold the Cinema House to the D.J. James circuit, which converted it into a double cinema. It reopened in March 1936 as Studios One and Two, with *Veille d'armes* in Studio One, and a newsreel programme in Studio Two. Although Cohen subsequently claimed that she continued to programme the cinema between 1934 and 1937, it is unclear whether she was actually closely involved after 1935, for Studio One advertised itself as 'the distinguished temple of continental screen craft', which had 'no connection with any other continental cinema in London' (Cohen 1971: 10; Eyles and Skone 1991: 25).

Competition for the Continental Film Audience

Cohen's pioneering programming of continental films led to both imitation and direct competition. The first new venue was the small Everyman Cinema opposite Hampstead underground station, which had previously been a repertory theatre. It was opened by the solicitor J.S. Fairfax-Jones, who was also Secretary and Treasurer of the Southampton Film Society. But the next cinema to open was a direct competitor to the Academy: the luxurious 492-seat Curzon Cinema, which was situated in Mayfair's Curzon Street and backed by Captain H.G. Morrison and the affluent architect, the Marquis of Casa Maury. With the arrival of the Curzon, the Academy began to lose its position as the principal venue for continental films (Cohen 1971: 12). As competition between the Academy, the Curzon and Studio One increased, so did the advances which they had to pay for the best films. In order to recoup their investments, they held over the more popular films for ever-longer runs, and looked to students and to commuters from London's expanding suburbs to boost their revenues.

The competition to screen good French films became more intense in the middle of the decade, as the political situations in Russia and Germany began to change. The Russian doctrine of Soviet socialist realism put an end to classical Soviet cinema; and in 1937 Cohen stopped showing German films because she didn't like the way things were going there (Cohen 1971: 12). French films were held over for longer and longer. Studio One screened *La Kermesse héroïque* for eight months between October 1936 and May 1937; and *Carnet de bal* for four months between December 1937 and March 1938. The Curzon followed suit, playing *Pépé le Moko* for seven weeks during April and May 1937. Not to be outdone, Elsie Cohen responded by holding over *La Grande Illusion* for three months at the Academy during the spring of 1938. She replaced it with *Le Roi s'amuse*, which she proudly claimed as enjoying 'London's longest continental run'. By 1938, when Cohen had to pay £5,000 for the British rights of *Le Quai des brumes* in order to match Casa Maury's offer to screen it at the Curzon, she concluded that the cinema had become like a stock market, and that it was the beginning of the end (Cohen 1971: 12).

Despite the febrile competition between the Academy, the Curzon and Studio One, even more cinemas switched to showing continental films. In March 1937, the County cinema circuit asked Cohen to programme the films at their revamped

277-seat subterranean Berkeley Cinema in Mayfair's Berkeley Street. She subsequently screened there *Nitchevo*, *La Belle Èquipe* and *L'Homme du jour*, plus *Le Quai des brumes*, which she transferred from the Academy. Cohen also programmed two more French films at the Berkeley, which had previously been screened by the Film Society: *La Femme du boulanger*, which enjoyed a good run, and the Fernandel comedy *Ignace*, which was the last film to be screened there before the government took the cinema over for war purposes in November 1939.

In June 1939, after failing to buy the freehold to the Academy cinema for £28,000, the Marquis de Casa Maury opened the aptly named Paris Cinema in Lower Regent Street (Cohen 1971: 12). His first choice was *Hôtel du Nord*, followed a month later by *Les Ôtages*, and on 30 October by a comedy, *Les Rois du sport*. Finally, on 25 September, three weeks after the outbreak of the Second World War, Montague, Cohen and Arnold Michaels opened the 580-seat Embassy Theatre in Tottenham Court Road. But the cinema's programmes quickly became very eclectic, with weekly changes of foreign revivals and Hollywood double bills (Eyles and Skone 1991: 92). Moreover, with the advent of war, the supply of French films soon started to dry up, and a golden decade for London's Francophile cinemagoers soon came to an end.

The Distribution of French Films to Provincial Film Societies

Cinemagoers living outside London normally had to rely on their local film society in order to see a French film. The first of these were established in Glasgow (1929), in Edinburgh (1930), and in Birmingham, Leicester and Southampton (all 1931). Distributors of continental films who tried to obtain commercial bookings by means of trade shows, dinner parties and other inducements achieved only meagre and ephemeral results (Oakley 1947: 6). The only continental films which were distributed outside London in dubbed versions were *Paris Méditerranée*, which was exhibited as *Into the Blue*, and *Le Roman d'un tricheur*, which was shown in the London suburbs during January 1939 as *The Cheat*, with a voice-over by Norman Shelley (Low 1985: 99; *The Times*, 24 October 1938, p.12).

The distribution of French films premiered by the Film Society was more complicated. Immediately after the enactment of the 1927 Cinematograph Film Act, the Society announced that it would distribute the films which it screened to provincial film societies (The Film Society 1936: 139). However, the Act also required all distributors to distribute a quota of British films. In subsequent discussions, the Film Society told the Board of Trade that, when there was a general demand for a film such as *Mädchen in Uniform*, it would transfer the distribution to a commercial distributor. The Board of Trade therefore indicated that it would not prosecute the Society for infringing the 1927 Act, because, 'the Society did not propagandise the films for which it acted as a formal distributor, but await[ed] applications for them'. Moreover, the Board regarded, 'a single showing in London at a specialised theatre' as analogous to a trade show (The Film Society 1936: 140). Although *Le Rosier de Madame Husson*, *Crainquebille* and *Marchand d'amour* were subsequently shown in commercial cinemas, several other French films, which had been premiered by the Film Society, were only screened by provincial film societies. Initially, the provincial film societies found it difficult to obtain copies of films that they wanted to screen, and it was not until 1933 that good films became available (Oakley 1947: 8). Three days before its first meeting in the autumn of 1932, the Film Society of Glasgow had literally nothing to show, although several of its members believed that many good films would soon become available, because the renters had obtained so few commercial bookings in the city (Oakley 1947: 6). Many films could rarely be seen after they had completed their runs, however, as they had been packed away in cellars – or scrapped (Oakley 1947: 14). There was also the question of cost. The commercial distributors wanted to charge commercial rates, but the embryo film societies couldn't afford them. Although one renter tried to charge the Film Society of Glasgow £250 for a single showing of a film, Charles Oakley managed to negotiate a rental of £10 with UFA for *Le Chemin du paradis*, which became a standard rental fee throughout the 1930s (Oakley 1947: 6; Oakley 1975).

By 1936, the supply of worthwhile films had again diminished because there were fewer from Germany and the cinematic merit of the Russian films was perceived to have fallen off (Cottrill 1951: 16). Two surveys showed how few French films were available for hire by the film societies. Nearly all of Réné Clair's French films, with the exception of *Sous les toîts de Paris* and *Le Dernier Milliardaire*, had been withdrawn from circulation. *Poil de carotte*, *Le Petit Roi* and *La Crise est finie* were available from British Lion; *La Maternelle* was available from Gaumont; *La Dame aux camélias* was available from Exclusive, and New Realm distributed *Charlemagne* (*World Film News* 1936: 42; Fairfax-Jones 1937a). Otherwise, film societies had to rely on three specialist distributors – each of which was linked to a London cinema –which had barely a dozen French titles between them. They were Denning Films (Fairfax-Jones / Hampstead Everyman), Reunion Films (Hakim / Academy Cinema), and Tobis Film Distributors, whose parent company, Tobis Maatschapij NV, had a long-term arrangement with the Curzon Cinema (*The Times*, 28 December 1934, p. 8; 19 September 1934, p. 8).

The distribution of continental films was economically precarious, however. In July 1936, Denning Films, which distributed *Le Rosier de Madame Husson, Remous, Marchand d'amour, Bonne chance* and *Le Dernier Milliardaire*, doubted whether it could continue in business; and a year later, Eric Hakim's Reunion Films, which distributed *Son Autre Amour* and *Sans famille*, went into liquidation (Denning Films 1936; *The Times*, 16 June 1937, p. 15). Tobis continued in business nonetheless, with *Crime et châtiment, Merlusse* and *Veille d'armes*; and it later boosted its coffers with the rentals from the very popular *La Kermesse héroïque*. The other supplier of continental films was, of course, the Film Society itself, which retained the rights to *Zéro de conduite* and *L'Atalante*, which it had screened in November 1934 and December 1935, along with those for *Itto*, which lay forgotten in its vaults until 1941 (Hardy 1941).

At the other end of the distribution chain, most film societies relied heavily on the judgements of a few individual members of their committee, many of whom turned to the sometimes unreliable film critics of the broadsheet newspapers. In 1932, when the well connected Film Society of Glasgow booked *Jean de la lune* on the strength of an enthusiastic review in *Punch*, it discovered that the print was not subtitled, and therefore proved incomprehensible to many members of the society (Oakley 1947: 6). Committee members from other film societies were also members of the Film Society in London. E. Irving Richards of the Leicester Film Society used to see every major continental film and most of the important shorts brought to London; and in April 1936, on the second day of a conference held in Leicester by the embryonic Federation of Film Societies, many of the forty delegates left early for London in order to attend that evening's performance of Film Society (Richards 1951: 16; Fairfax-Jones 1937b). Personal contacts with the film trade also helped. Fairfax-Jones was able to screen a print of the long-awaited *La Kermesse héroïque* to the Southampton Film Society on Sunday 16 January 1938, the day before he revived the film at the Everyman. In Glasgow, C.A. Oakley had personal contacts with the management of the Curzon Cinema, although few members of the society realized that he had booked *Amphitryon* against the advice of the cinema's management, as it had proved such a failure there (Oakley 1947: 15–16).

The Relative Popularity of French Films during the 1930s

Not everybody shared the same taste in French films. Indeed, few members of the Film Society were devoted cinephiles. Between November 1929 and March 1930, its council frequently had to ask its members not to talk during the screening of a film (Amberg 1972: 33rd to 38th performances). Even then, the problem persisted for a further fifteen months, and the members still had to be asked to arrive on time in order to be prepared to see the short films which opened each performance (Amberg 1972: 41st to 52nd performances). These problems gradually disappeared, however, when the less devoted members of the society were able to watch continental films in the growing number of continental cinemas.

Outside London, some film societies adopted populist policies, while others catered for a more specialist membership. Both the Glasgow and the Edinburgh societies grew apace. The Glasgow waiting list became so long that by May 1939 the 825-seat Cosmo Cinema was able to open with a special inaugural screening of *Carnet de bal* for the society's members; and by the spring of 1940 it had already screened twenty-five French films (Oakley 1947: 16; *Sight and Sound* 1940: 9). By 1934, the Edinburgh Film Guild had 440 members, and its membership steadily increased until 1939, before reaching a record 2,500 in 1948 (Wilson 1950: 4). Birmingham's membership rose from 543 to 738 between 1934 and 1939, but Southampton never reached 400, even though it also recruited its members from nearby Winchester (Knight et al. 1948: 10; Fairfax-Jones 1952: 8). Leicester's membership, on the other hand, steadily declined from a peak of 341 in 1933 to 239 in 1938–39 (Richards 1951: 9 and 11; Cottrill 1951: 13–18).

During the early 1930s, Réné Clair's films were extremely popular. His lightweight and deliberately artificial satires, which allowed him to explore the stylistic possibilities of the film medium to manipulate movement and later sound, captured the imagination of both popular and specialist audiences alike. *Un chapeau de paille en Italie, Sous les toits de Paris, Le Million, A nous la liberté, Le Quatorze juillet* and *Le Dernier Milliardaire* were all shown and reshown in London. Even mainstream cinemas, like the Alhambra and the Phoenix, screened them during the depression years (*The Times*, December 1930 and April 1931). From late 1931, however, all Clair's subsequent French films opened at the Academy, and they were widely shown by film societies throughout the country. In June 1931, the Hampstead Film Group mounted an exhibition of designs and models from Clair's films at the Chris Moffat Gallery; and in November 1934, the Everyman mounted an exhibition of original designs and photographs from Clair's films to accompany a season of his films (*The Times*, 6 June 1931, p. 10; 23 November 1934, p. 12). But by 1936, the Clair mini-boom was over as, with the exception of *Le Dernier Milliardaire*, the British rights had expired.

In 1933, a more popular strand of French talkies emerged, which were revived at both the Everyman and the Forum and screened by all five provincial film societies for which complete records have survived: namely those in Glasgow, Edinburgh, Birmingham, Leicester and Southampton. They were *La Maternelle* (also screened by the film societies in Colne, Maidstone, Manchester and Salford and Tyneside); *Ces Messieurs de la santé* (also screened by the societies in Ayrshire, Maidenhead, Merseyside and Tyneside); *Remous* (also screened in Ayrshire, East Kent, Manchester and Salford, and Tyneside); *Bonne chance* (also screened in Ayrshire, Billingham, Dundee and St Andrews, Ipswich, Oxford and Tyneside); *Merlusse* (also screened in Ayrshire, Dundee and St Andrews, Merseyside, Tyneside and Wimbledon); and of course *La Kermesse héroïque*, the most popular film screened by the Tyneside Film Society during its 1937/38 season (*Sight and Sound* 1933–1937; Dyer 1938: 78–9). Two more popular films were *Le Rosier de Madame Husson* and *La Belle Équipe*, although neither was booked by the elitist Southampton Film Society.

Close examination of these films, which include comedies and historical epics, fantasy and social realism, reveals that many of them explore the ambiguous relations between the individual behaviour of their principal characters and the social norms of the French milieu where they live. Consider the comedies. Both *Le Rosier de Madame Husson* and *La Kermesse héroïque* lightheartedly explore the apparent acceptability for socially respectable French women to lose their virginity, or to cast aside their chastity. In *Le Rosier de Madame Husson,* which J.R. Cottrill of the Leicester Film Society considered to be 'immortal', the committee of *Ville-les-Roses* decides to make the gross Isidore (Fernandel) the Queen of the May, as none of the eligible village girls is still a virgin (Cottrill 1951: 12). But by the end of the film, Isidore has also lost his virginity. In *La Kermesse héroïque*, set in the seventeenth century, when the Spanish soldiers invade the Flanders town of Boom, the defensive strategy of the town's mayor is to pretend to be dead. However, the women of the town, led by his wife (Françoise Rosay), decide that flattery, flirtation, and possibly sexual acquiescence, are better ways in which to placate their Spanish conquerors. By so doing, they save the mayor's life and earn the town a year's remission of taxes. Jacques Feyder's direction won first prize at the Venice Film Festival, and both Lazare Meerson's art direction and Harry Stradling's photography evoke the paintings of the

Flemish masters. But beneath the film's glossy and exuberant surface lies a sobering meditation on the relative unimportance of female chastity in times of war.

Similarly, *Ces Messieurs de la santé* plays on the ambivalent attitudes among the audience towards racketeering. In between two spells in La Santé prison, financier M. Gédéon (Raimu) sells machine guns from a corset shop. Although he is spineless, cunning and genially seductive, he is authoritarian in his exercise of power. *The Times* considered the film to be a satire on the French world of finance (23 August 1934, p. 8). But writing in 1983, French film historian Jean-Pierre Jeancolas argued that the film was a profound critique of the corrupt French petit-bourgeoisie, which allowed Gédéon to take the corsetiere and her son for a ride (Jeancolas 1983: 134). Most British audiences missed the social satire, however. For them, the film was little more than a lighthearted comedy. There was more laughter when Gédéon walked out of prison than at any other meeting of the Film Society of Glasgow (Oakley 1947: 10).

It was not until the mid-1930s that French filmmakers were able to merge successfully their theatrical and cinematic traditions. Two of the earliest were Marcel Pagnol and Sacha Guitry (Jeancolas 1983: 147). A theme common to both *Merlusse* and *Bonne chance*, which were widely shown in Britain during 1936, is their ambivalent attitude to social authority. In Guitry's *Bonne chance*, an artist who wins the lottery takes on holiday with him a girl who gave him half her ticket. Some British audiences considered the film to be too frivolous. Although Guitry's disregard of social convention impressed the members of the Glasgow society, it brought a howl of protest from audiences in Edinburgh who wanted sterner stuff (Oakley 1947: 13: Hardy 1950: 8). They got it from Pagnol's *Merlusse*, which revealed how a sensitive human being can often be concealed behind an apparently authoritarian figure. *Merlusse* [Cod-fish], a sad-looking and bad-tempered schoolmaster, is left in charge of a French boarding school over Christmas. He gradually starts to respect the boys, rather than to despise them. They slowly realize that their authoritarian master is human after all, and not the ruthless tyrant that they originally thought. Once again, the film explores the differences between personal appearance and individual character. Although more serious than *Bonne chance*, *Merlusse* also has a positive ending.

La Belle Équipe (starring Jean Gabin), which opened at the Berkeley in January 1938 and was shown by four of the five principal film societies during their 1938/39 season, is equally optimistic. A group of unemployed men win some money in the lottery, and decide to build a small restaurant by the river. After some minor misfortunes, their enterprise succeeds. Another fable with a positive message: unemployment can be overcome with a little mutual tolerance (and, of course, a lot of money).

Attempts to Censor French Films

The British Board of Film Censors (BBFC), which was set up by the film trade to censor films screened in commercial cinemas, was worried about films which tackled serious subjects, but failed to offer a positive outcome. In 1933, it banned *Poil de carotte* because the producers refused to remove scenes showing a child driven to suicide. A Brighton exhibitor was fined £5 for showing it. His defence was that he was catering for an intelligent audience, and that the film had been recommended by the British Film Institute (Low 1985: 70). The film subsequently received a certificate from the London County Council (LCC), but the Liverpool magistrates prevented the Merseyside Film Institute from screening it. Nevertheless, the local authorities in Billingham, Birmingham, Southampton and Tyneside all allowed their local film society to show it (*Sight and Sound* 1933–1937). *La Maternelle*, a similarly disturbing film about the attempt by the unhappy child of a prostitute to commit suicide, was withdrawn from circulation after only a short period, and was never available for revival (Oakley 1947: 10). The BBFC also banned *Zéro de conduite*, screened by the Film Society in November 1934, as it feared that the behaviour it depicted might encourage British schoolboys to follow suit. Wiser counsels prevailed in the LCC, however, which allowed it to be shown in London.

Many film critics were concerned about the overt expression of erotic passion. *Remous*, directed by the Anglo-French filmmaker Edmond T. Gréville, which was essentially about eroticism and nothing else, opened at the Curzon in January 1935, and most film societies booked the film for their 1936 season. The screening in Glasgow was a notable success, although the Tyneside Society decided to omit the film from their programme as they thought it would probably soon be shown locally (*Sight and Sound* 1936a: 55; *Sight and Sound* 1936b: 57). But for the critic of *The Times*, it was only Gréville's directorial touch which saved the film from being dull. 'In any other idiom than the Gallic,' he opined, 'there would be something, if not actively unpleasant, at least positively tedious about *Remous*. It is absorbed in the physical attraction the sexes have for each other and allows nothing to interfere with its absorption' (7 January 1935, p. 10).

Competing Cultural Tendencies

As the flow of French films into Britain increased, many French filmmakers began to turn to generic forms, such as the thriller and the *policier*, in order to make their films more accessible to the ordinary cinemagoer. The critics writing for the broadsheet press therefore had to establish ways of maintaining their cultural distinction, by establishing rules about the cinematic representation of France and French society, which would enable them to distinguish the good from the critically poor and the indifferent. They developed three sets of cultural criteria for French films being shown in London: the residual, the oppositional, and an emerging realist culture.

It was from the films of Sacha Guitry, the Russian-born, polymath dramatist, actor and all-round *boulevardier*, that British audiences might have learned about the glories of French history, or the traditional eloquence of the French stage. Although Guitry's first two films to be shown in London were pleasant and witty, they did not break much fresh ground stylistically. Neither did *Pasteur*, which did not reach London until November 1938, although it was premiered in Paris at the same time as *Bonne chance* (*The Times*, 22 November 1938, p. 12).

In 1936, Guitry gradually developed a more didactic approach towards French history; and in the closing years of the decade, London audiences were able to see *Le*

Roman d'un tricheur, Les Perles de la couronne, Le Mot de Cambronne and *Remontons les Champs-Elysées*. In March 1937, the Film Society screened *Le Roman d'un tricheur*, in which Guitry told the story in his own words, illustrated by a series of dumb-shows. When a subtitled version of the film opened at the Academy six months later, *The Times* was ecstatic about Guitry's success in breaking through the language barrier: 'The spoken dialogue is in French, but the sub-titles are in English and, with M. Sacha Guitry at his best in a delightful part, the barriers of language need present no terrors to the film-goer', it enthused. 'Not only can we delight in M. Guitry's merit as a raconteur, but we can also enjoy the novelty of his approach to the subject' (20 September 1937, p. 10). A year later, a dubbed version opened at the Gaumont, in which Norman Shelley stood in for Guitry (*The Times*, 24 October 1938, p. 12).

Guitry deployed a similar approach in his anglophile *Les Perles de la couronne*, which opened at the Curzon in October 1937. He proceeded first to regale his wife, and then the audience, with a half-factual, half-fictional history of the pearls in the Crown of England. But this time, he illustrated his mini-lectures with short polyglot scenes from the lives of the owners of the pearls, which were spoken in French, Italian and English. But the narrative complexities of Guitry's plot annoyed *The Times*, which considered it to be a 'curious, at times moving, and at times interesting, and usually exasperating film' (14 October 1937, p. 12). None of the film societies booked it.

Guitry's next film, *Le Mot de Cambronne*, which the Film Society screened in January 1938, was a flop. Nobody wanted a one-act film in verse about the English wife of General Cambronne, who was devoured with curiosity about a rude word which he once used. In all three films, Guitry tried to marry the glories of French history with the traditional eloquence of the French stage, by opening up a didactical space between the images and the words. But since most of the scenes were little more than family charades, their success depended almost entirely on Guitry's verbal wit. Although he sought to transcend the barrier of language which arrived with the sound film, Guitry's stylistic innovations ultimately failed to marry the image track and the sound track. Their historical topics and their often fragmented narratives revealed Guitry to be a culturally anachronistic filmmaker. This was confirmed by *Remontons les Champs-Elysées*, which opened at the Academy in December 1939, and was the last French film to be screened in London before the decade closed. It was another residual fantasy about the life of a French family during the previous two hundred years, in which Guitry acted as many parts as possible. For *The Times* it was 'a wonderful *tour-de-force*' and 'a lesson to all of us in how to be patriotic without losing good manners'. Guitry's secret, its critic claimed, was 'irony' (18 December 1939, p. 6). To be successful, however, irony requires a culturally shared convention between the speaker and the listener, against which the ironic statement can resonate. But by December 1939, this was no longer possible. Britain was at war with Germany, and despite the encomiums of *The Times*, none of the film societies in Birmingham, Glasgow, Leicester or Southampton had booked any of the films made by Sacha Guitry after *Bonne chance*. The sole exception was the Edinburgh Film Guild, which screened *Remontons les Champs-Elysées* on 20 October 1940 as the Battle of Britain was drawing to its close.

The critical establishment, like the BBFC, disliked the mixture of schoolboy revolution and surrealism in Jean Vigo's *Zéro de conduite*. *The Times* was withering: 'If one had already suspected a resemblance between *surrealisme* and the elaborate inconsequence of schoolboy humour,' it wrote, 'the suspicion was amply confirmed by *Zéro de conduite*' (26 November 1934, p. 10). Commercial exhibitors ignored the film, and the Film Society became its distributor by default. Critical scorn did not deter the film societies in Edinburgh and Birmingham, however, both of whom screened it during the following season, as did the societies in Ayrshire, North London, Tyneside and Wolverhampton. Indeed, the Tyneside Film Society screened it twice (*Sight and Sound* 1933–1937).

Thanks to the film's LCC Certificate, the Everyman was able to show *Zéro de conduite* in December 1936, as part of a 'unique programme of surrealist and avant-garde films'. 'Neither Jean Vigo's film nor any of the supporting films', *Sight and Sound* commented with obvious relief, 'contain those elements of horror, perversion or morbidity which have become associated with the word Surrealist' (*Sight and Sound* 1936–1937: 119).

The film critics of both *The Observer* and *The Evening Standard* decided to trash the film. 'Nought for direction. Nought for acting. Nought for story. Nought for continuity. Five for trying', Caroline Lejeune dismissively asserted in *The Observer*; and Ian Coster followed suit in *The Evening Standard*. But John Grierson, Alberto Cavalcanti and Maurice Jaubert took Lejeune to task for 'a distempered and ugly critical performance'. 'Much that was great and fine could have been discovered in *Zéro de conduite*', they wrote, and '*Zéro* will still be alive when some of the films which now secure the fervent attention of Miss Lejeune are as dead as mutton and [it] will have ample opportunity to register among the classics of film expression.' (Grierson, Cavalcanti and Jaubert 1937).

The audiences at the Everyman were no more appreciative. Roderic Pepineau astringently noted how the sociopolitical message of *Zéro de conduite* had been neutered by the atmosphere in which it had been screened at the Everyman. 'No less maudlin', he wrote 'is the atmosphere in which Vigo's work is being shown in Hampstead, making a play for the naughty surrealist element and the *bourgeois enragé* at the same time.' He left the cinema 'boiling with hatred against … the arty audience which mistakes a sincere and heroic treatment for fashionable comic attire' (Pepineau 1937).

Vigo's last film, *L'Atalante*, which the Film Society screened in December 1936, was similarly dismissed. *The Times* considered that its simple story was 'embroidered with a mass of eccentric detail which at times seems slightly mad from excess of sophistication', and concluded that 'the garish and improbable amusements of the poor and the extraordinary tastes of the simple-minded provide an excuse for making the film into a positive museum of curiosities' (16 December 1935, p. 12). Needless to say, none of London's continental cinemas screened the film. The film societies in Birmingham, Edinburgh, Glasgow and Leicester all booked it, however, as did those in Ayrshire, Manchester and Salford, North London and Stirlingshire (*Sight and Sound* 1933–1937). Although *L'Atalante* was a notable success when it was screened in Glasgow, not everyone in Edinburgh agreed, and the atmosphere in which the film was shown became tenser than in previous screenings (*Sight and Sound* 1936: 55; Hardy 1950: 8).

Jean Vigo's surrealism was ahead of its time, therefore, and it exposed divisions within the membership of some provincial film societies. Some were interested in all types of film art, including the experimental and the avant garde. Others were more conservative, and only prepared to listen to French dialogue provided it was clearly subtitled and they were pleasurably entertained while doing so. They may also have reflected on the differences between the social and sexual values of Britain and France.

The film critic of *The Times* considered that the best French films were those which offered a realist view of France and French society. But that view had to be suitably distanced both aesthetically and socially. Reviewing Siodmak's *Mister Flow* in June 1937, he highlighted the cultural significance of vocal timbre and physical gesture at the expense of the subtitles. 'The charms of the spoken language and of the negligent Gallic shrug', he opined, 'incline one at times to tolerate the *longeurs* in a French film that would be inappropriate in a British one' (10 June 1937, p. 14).

What he especially admired, however, was financial prudence. Reviewing Allégret's *Gribouille*, which was set in a bicycle shop, he linked the alleged frugality of the French people to the modest nature of the film's principal setting. 'Perhaps the greatest advantage enjoyed by French films is that they are not expected to have luxurious settings …[;] the consequence is that their films are at once more convincing and give more varied pleasure to the eye than most of the productions of other countries' (17 January 1938, p. 10). French frugality, he averred a few months later, stood in opposition to the portrayal of extravagance in British films, and had enlarged the scope of films which were available to the cinemagoer. 'The French', he suggested,

> seem to dislike seeing money wasted as much as they dislike wasting it. With a public thus enlightened by parsimony, the cinema has become a worthy successor to the impressionist movement in painting, and its detached accurate vision of everyday people in their natural surroundings, quite apart from the intrinsic interest of such scenes, has greatly enlarged the scope of the films. It has allowed them to present situations and characters that could never exist in the marble halls of which our cinema so persistently dreams (16 August 1938, p. 10).

He returned to his analogy with impressionist painting in his review of Prévert's *Quai des brumes*. The film's visual style, he argued, placed the [British] viewer at exactly the right distance from the real milieu of Le Havre. '[T]he characters move both literally and metaphorically in shadow … [and] … here the shadows put the characters, episodes and scenes at the right distance from reality and make possible that oblique treatment for which the medium is so exactly suited' (16 January 1939, p. 10).

The Times's Special Correspondent in Paris went even further, and sought to elevate the oblique realism in French feature films above that in British documentaries. The realist aesthetic of the British documentary film, he alleged, had left the British fiction film, 'putting forth its shoots in an unhealthy climate of costume piece, police romance, and adapted theatre'. 'In France', he continued, 'what we may call the documentary talent – the power to study truly a milieu and a way of life – has remained at the service of the fictional film: and it is that, more even than the fine acting, which has made so many recent French films an arresting experience' (20 June 1939, p. 12).

Conclusion

The 1930s was the decade during which the French film established its presence in Britain, even though the film trade and British society also structured and shaped that presence in a number of economic, geographic, linguistic and aesthetic ways. Although the first screenings of French films had been mounted during the late 1920s by the Film Society, as the 1930s progressed, French films flourished most strongly in London, where they were screened in six cinemas situated within half a mile of Oxford Circus, to a growing number of Francophile cinemagoers, many of whom were students or had travelled in from the suburbs. People living outside London, however, had, for the most part, to rely on their local film society.

By the middle of the decade there was intense, although ultimately unstable, competition between the principal London cinema owners to acquire the most popular French films. However, this also allowed the owners of repertory cinemas and the provincial film societies to choose the most popular titles which the London cinemas, and their associated distributors, had already imported and subtitled. Although one or two French films were dubbed into English, they were not especially popular at the box office, and so Francophile audiences soon became accustomed to watching subtitled prints.

A taste for watching French films was also a marker of cultural distinction in a decade in which popular taste was dominated by screenings of American films, the music of popular dance bands and the radio broadcasts of the BBC. Initially, the comedy films of René Clair were extremely popular, but as talkies became more widespread, it soon became clear that the social values and structures in France were different from those in Britain. During the middle of the decade, British audiences appear to have enjoyed several French films which offered an insight into social and sexual mores which differed from those which permeated 1930s Britain, even though they occasionally upset the BBFC and some broadsheet film critics.

As the decade came to an end, it became clear that two parallel markets for French films were developing in Britain. There was a primary market of London's continental cinemas, backed up by the critics writing for the broadsheet press. But there was also a growing secondary market of the major provincial film societies, whose members generally consisted of members of the local cultural elite and free thinkers, who were often associated with a local university or technical college. A cultural and commercial struggle began to emerge both within and between the primary and secondary markets for French films. There were three competing tendencies. First, there was the residual style and content of Sacha Guitry's later films, which looked back to French history and to the glories of the French theatrical tradition. Second, there was the slightly surrealist and socially oppositional tendency of Jean Vigo's films. And third, there was an alternative tendency of a socially critical, but often impressionist or poetic, realism, which could be seen in the films of Marc Allégret or the writer-director team of Jacques Prévert and Marcel Carné. It was this category of films which ultimately became popular in both the primary and secondary markets for French films. And it was this group of films which would be screened and rescreened as French film classics after the Second World War.

Note

The author would like to thank Janet McBain of the Scottish Screen Archive at the National Library of Scotland, Yvonne Wattam from the Record Office for Leicestershire, Leicester and Rutland, and Christopher Butler from the Edinburgh Film Guild for their help in locating ephemeral material published by the Film Society of Glasgow, the Leicester Film Society and the Edinburgh Film Guild respectively.

Bibliography

Amberg, G. (ed.). 1972. *Film Society Programmes 1925–1939*. New York: Arno Press.

Brunel, A. 1949. *Nice Work*. London: Forbes Robertson.

Cohen, E. 1971. 'Elsie Cohen talks to Anthony Slide about the Academy Cinema, Political Censorship and the British Cinema Scene in the Thirties', *The Silent Picture* 11/12(Summer–Autumn): 9–13.

Cottrill, J.R. 1951. 'Later Years: 1934–51', in *Leicester Film Society One Hundred Programmes 1931–1951*. Leicester: Leicester Film Society, pp. 12–31.

Coxhead, E. 1933. 'Towards a Co-operative Cinema. The Work of the Academy, Oxford Street', *Close-Up* 10(2): 133–37.

Davis, S. 1929. 'Making Repertory Pay', *The Bioscope*, 27 February, p. 25.

Denning Films. 1936. 'Memorandum by Denning Films Ltd.', in Great Britain: Board of Trade, *Minutes of Evidence Taken Before the Departmental Committee on Cinematograph Films Together with Appendices and Index*, Fifth to Eighth Days. London: HMSO, p. 146.

Dickinson, T. 1975. 'There was a time when…', *50 Years of Film Societies. Film* (second series), October/November: 8–9.

Dyer, E. 1938. 'What Do They Like?', *Sight and Sound* 7(26): 78–79.

Eyles, A. 2000. 'Elsie Cohen', in *The Oxford Dictionary of National Biography*. Oxford: Oxford University Press.

———. and K. Skone. 1991. *London's West End Cinemas*. Sutton: Keytone.

Fairfax-Jones, J.S. 1937a. 'Foreign Films Available for Film Societies', *World Film News* 1(11): 45.

———. 1937b. 'Film Federation Reborn', *World Film News* 2(7): 45.

———. 1952. 'The Early Days: Southampton Film Society', in *One Hundred Programmes of the Southampton Film Society, 1931–1952*. Southampton: Southampton Film Society, pp. 6–8.

Grierson, J. 1939. 'Letter to Gilbert McAllister', in New Zealand Public Relations Council, *Memorandum on Films*. New Zealand: New Zealand Public Relations Council, April–May, Appendix.

Grierson, J., A. Cavalcanti and M. Jaubert. 1937. '*Zéro de Conduite*', in *World Film News* 1(11): 5.

Hardy, F. 1941. 'An Open letter to Film Societies', *Sight and Sound* 10(38): 29.

———. 1950. 'Twenty-one Years Films', in *Twenty-one Years of Cinema*. Edinburgh: Edinburgh Film Guild, pp. 7–10.

Harvey, J.M. 1936. 'The Presentation of Foreign Films', *Life and Letters* (autumn): 166–70.

Jeancolas, J-P. 1983. *15 ans d'années trente: Le Cinéma des Français, 1929–1944*. Paris: Stock/Cinéma.

Knight, R.C. et al. 1948. *Flashback: A Hundred Shows of the Birmingham Film Society, 1931–1948, with a Souvenir Programme of the 101st Meeting*. Birmingham: Birmingham Film Society.

Low, R. 1985. *The History of the British Film, 1929–1939: Film-making in 1930s Britain*. London: George Allen and Unwin.

Oakley, C. 1947. *The Film Society of Glasgow: A Review Published on the Occasion of the 150th Meeting*. Glasgow: Film Society of Glasgow.

———. 1975. 'How It Began in Glasgow', *50 Years of Film Societies. Film* (second series), October/November: 10.

Pepineau, R. 1937. 'Continental Films: *Zéro de conduite* (Nought for Conduct)', *World Film News* 1(11): 28.

Richards, E. 1951. 'The First Years: 1930–34', in *Leicester Film Society. One Hundred Programmes 1931–1951*. Leicester: Leicester Film Society, pp. 6–12.

Rotha, P. 1958. 'The "Unusual" Film Movement', in P. Rotha (ed.), *Rotha on the Film*. London: Faber and Faber, pp. 61–64.

———. 1933–1937. 'News from BFI Branches / Scotland / Film Societies', *Sight and Sound* 2(8) (1933–34) to 6(21) (1937): passim.

———. 1936–1937. 'Imagination at the Everyman', *Sight and Sound* 5(20): 119.

———. 1936a. 'Scotland: Progress 1935–36', *Sight and Sound* 5(18): 55.

———. 1936b. 'Film Societies: Season 1935–36', *Sight and Sound* 5(18): 57.

———. 1940. 'Mister Cosmo Takes a Bow', *Sight and Sound* 9(33): 9.

The Film Society. 1936. 'Memorandum of the Film Society', in Great Britain: Board of Trade, *Minutes of Evidence Taken Before the Departmental Committee on Cinematograph Films Together with Appendices and Index*, Fifth to Eighth Days. London: HMSO, pp. 139–43.

The Times. 1930–1939. Passim.

Wilson, N. 1950. 'History and Achievement', in *Twenty-one Years of Cinema: A Twenty-first Anniversary Retrospect of the Work of the Edinburgh Film Guild*. Edinburgh: Edinburgh Film Guild, pp. 3–6.

World Film News. 1936. 'Films Available for Society Programmes', *World Film News* 1(7): 42.

Filmography

A nous la liberté / Freedom for Us. 1931, René Clair, France/Germany.
Amphitryon / Happiness from the Clouds. 1935, Reinhold Schünzel, Germany.
Atalante, L'. 1934, Jean Vigo, France.
Belle Équipe, La / They Were Five. 1936, Julien Duvivier, France.
Bonne chance! / Good Luck. 1935, Sacha Guitry and Fernand Rivers, France.
Carnet de bal. 1937, Julien Duvivier, France.
Ces Messieurs de la santé. 1933, Pierre Colombier, France.

Chapeau de paille en Italie, Un / *An Italian Straw Hat.* 1928, René Clair, France.

Charlemagne. 1934, Pierre Colombier, France.

Chemin du paradis, Le / *The Road to Paradise.* 1930, Wilhelm Thiele and Max de Vaucorbeil, France/Germany.

Chute de la Maison Usher, La / *The Fall of the House of Usher.* 1928, Jean Epstein, France.

Crainquebille. 1933, Jacques de Baroncelli, France.

Crime et châtiment / *Crime and Punishment.* 1935, Pierre Chenal, France.

Crise est finie, La. 1934, Robert Siodmak, France.

Dame aux camélias, La / *Lady of the Camellias.* 1934, Abel Gance and Fernand Rivers, France.

Dernier Milliardaire, Le / *The Last Millionaire.* 1934, René Clair, France.

Deux Timides, Les / *Two Timid Souls.* 1929, René Clair, France.

Douceur d'aimer, La / *The Sweetness of Loving.* 1930, René Hervil, France.

Dreyfus / *The Dreyfus Case.* 1930, Richard Oswald, France/Germany.

Erl King, The / *Le roi des aulnes.* 1930, Marie-Louise Iribe, France/Germany.

En rade / *Sea Fever.* 1927, Alberto Cavalcanti, France.

Femme du boulanger, La / *The Baker's Wife.* 1938, Marcel Pagnol, France.

Feu Mathias Pascal / *The Late Matthew Pascal.* 1925, Marcel L'Herbier, France.

Finis Terrae. 1929, Jean Epstein, France.

Grande Illusion, La / *The Grand Illusion.* 1937, Jean Renoir, France.

Gribouille. 1937, Marc Allégret, France.

Homme du jour, L' / *The Man of the Hour.* 1935, Julien Duvivier, France.

Hôtel du Nord. 1938, Marcel Carné, France.

Ignace. 1937, Pierre Colombier, France.

Itto. 1934, Jean Benoît-Levy and Marie Epstein, France.

Jean de la lune. 1931, Jean Choux and Michel Simon, France.

Kermesse héroïque, La / *Carnival in Flanders.* 1935, Jacques Feyder, France/Germany.

Lac aux dames / *Ladies' Lake.* 1934, Marc Allégret, France.

Mädchen in Uniform / *Girls in Uniform.* 1931, Leontine Sagan, Germany.

Maldone / *Misdeal.* 1928, Jean Grémillon, France.

Marchand d'amour. 1935, Edmond T. Gréville, France.

Maternelle, La / *Children of Montmartre.* 1931, Jean Benoît-Levy and Marie Epstein, France.

Merlusse. 1935, Marcel Pagnol, France.

Million, Le / *The Million.* 1931, René Clair, France/Germany.

Mister Flow / *Compliments of Mister Flow.* 1936, Robert Siodmak, France.

Mot de Cambronne, Le. 1937, Sacha Guitry, France.

Nitchevo. 1936, Jacques de Baroncelli, France.

Ombres sur l'Europe / *Shadows Over Europe.* 1933, Louis Cottard and René Brut [camera], France.

Otages, Les / *The Mayor's Dilemma.* 1938, Raymond Bernard, France/Germany.

Paris Méditerranée / *Into the Blue.* 1932, Joe May, France/Germany.

Pasteur. 1935, Sacha Guitry, France.

Pépé le Moko. 1937, Julien Duvivier, France.

Perles de la couronne, Les / *Pearls of the Crown.* 1937, Sacha Guitry and Christian-Jaque, France.

Petit Roi, Le / *The Little King.* 1933, Julien Duvivier, France.

Poil de carotte / *Gingerhead.* 1932, Julien Duvivier, France.

Prenez garde à la peinture / *Mind the Paint.* 1933, Henri Chomette, France.

Quai des brumes, Le / *Port of Shadows.* 1938, Jacques Prévert, France.

Quatorze juillet, Le / *Fourteenth July.* 1932, René Clair, France/Germany.

Remontons les Champs-Elysées / *Champs-Elysees.* 1938, Sacha Guitry, France.

Remous / Whirlpool. 1934, Edmond T. Gréville, France.

Rien que les heures / The Book of Hours. 1926, Alberto Cavalcanti, France.

Robe rouge, La / The Red Dress. 1933, Jean de Marguenat, France.

Roi des resquilleurs, Le / The Gatecrasher. 1930, Pierre Colombier, France.

Roi s'amuse, Le / The King. 1936, Pierre Colombier, France.

Rois du sport, Les. 1937, Pierre Colombier, France.

Roman d'un tricheur, Le / The Cheat. 1936, Sacha Guitry, France.

Rosier de Madame Husson, Le / The Virtuous Isidore. 1931, Bernard Deschamps, France.

Sans famille. 1934, Marc Allégret, France.

Soir de rafle, Un. 1931, Carmine Gallone, France.

Son Autre Amour. 1933, Alfred Machard and Constant Remy, France.

Sous les toits de Paris / Under the Roofs of Paris. 1930, René Clair, France/Germany.

Thérèse Raquin. 1930, Jacques Feyder, France/Germany.

Veille d'armes / Sacrifice of Honour. 1935, Marcel L'Herbier, France.

Zéro de conduite / Nil for Conduct. 1933, Jean Vigo, France.

CHAPTER 2

The 'Cinematization' of Sound Cinema in Britain and the Dubbing into French of Hitchcock's *Waltzes from Vienna* (1934)

Charles O'Brien

The project of investigating the history of interaction between British and French cinema brings out important film-historical phenomena ordinarily occluded in much film studies research, in which national cinemas are studied in isolation from one another. In examining British and French film together, it becomes possible to see how national film cultures entail a significant transnational dimension enabled by the circulation of films made elsewhere and then imported in. In the preceding chapter, for example, Vincent Porter details how French films became the major foreign-cinema presence in Britain in the 1930s, thereby altering the aesthetic context for some British movie audiences. Other cases in which French films provided a key reference for British audiences are discussed in chapters by Geoffrey Nowell-Smith and Melanie Selfe, for example. This chapter on the French-dubbed version of Hitchcock's *Waltzes from Vienna* can be said to consider the other side of the equation, as it were: the presence of British films in France. Its emphasis, however, is not on how British films affected cinema in France but rather on a different facet of the transnational film trade, whereby the export of films changes not only the cinema of the target country but that of the source country as well. My concern, in short, is with how the endeavour in Britain of producing films for export affected the British film style itself. The following analysis of *Waltzes from Vienna* focuses on the specifics of the dubbed version and how the anticipation of its making conditioned Hitchcock's work on the original British film.

The emphasis on the details of style and technique is animated by a broader hypothesis concerning how the project of preparing films for foreign-language export in the early 1930s shaped film style generally, and in Britain specifically. This hypothesis concerns a basic factor behind the style of *Waltzes from Vienna*: the producer's intent with respect to distribution. Sound films made for export in the early 1930s, in many cases, were made differently from films intended for domestic release, thus affecting film style generally, and in ways commonly recognized in the transatlantic film community at the time. In 1930 an editorialist for *The Bioscope* captured the dynamic of the situation by proposing that as long as British films were made mainly for domestic release, a theatre-inspired aesthetic would endure as the British cinema's main style option; on the other hand, insofar as British producers aimed for export, the 'cinematization' of British film style would result (Lipscombe 1930). The editorialist doubted that the British film industry would become a film exporter at the level of the industries in the United States and Germany, but the cinematization to which he referred soon began as the latest American and German multitrack technologies and methods were adopted in British film studios such as the Shepherd's Bush facility of Gaumont British where *Waltzes from Vienna* was planned and shot (Anon. 1932a).

Dubbing as a Transnational Practice

The use of multitrack technology in the shooting of *Waltzes from Vienna* enabled preparation of an 'international version' of the film, whose dialogue track could be manipulated apart from its music and ambient effects. The separation of sound into separate tracks not only let Hitchcock explore new possibilities with respect to film music, it also facilitated the film's life as an export commodity by allowing the crew at Jacques Haïk's studio in Courbevoie, where the dubbing of *Waltzes from Vienna* was undertaken, to preserve the intricacies of the film's music track while otherwise changing the film substantially – changes extensive enough to reduce the film's running time by one-third. Beyond replacing English with French speech, the changes included eliminating certain shots, scenes and song sequences, as well as rearranging the order of scenes. In addition, to match exactly the actors' lip movements to the duration of the dubbed speech, frames were extracted from, and probably added into, numerous shots.

But the analysis cannot stop at what occurred in France at Courbevoie since much of that was contingent on work undertaken months earlier in England at Gaumont British's Shepherd's Bush facility, where *Waltzes* was scripted and filmed. Moreover, *Waltzes from Vienna*, though not itself a dubbed film, exhibits a host of stylistic peculiarities linked to dubbing practice in the early 1930s. One can begin with decisions in framing and cutting consonant with recent dubbing-related changes in American filmmaking, as in the dozens of shots in *Waltzes from Vienna* in which actors' lip movements are concealed in ways designed to ease the voice-synchronization work undertaken months later in Courbevoie. In this respect *Waltzes from Vienna* was typical of dubbing practice at the time. Though nominally a postproduction activity, dubbing depended crucially on decisions made in planning and shooting (Le Verrier 1931). Complicating the situation was the fact that by 1933 dubbing of sufficient quality typically took place in a country other than the one where the film was planned and shot, thus requiring the film's producers to anticipate modifications that might or might not be performed later on by agents operating independently in other countries. In assessing dubbing's stylistic impact, at least two phases of work on the dubbed version of *Waltzes from Vienna* require analysis – one of which occurred in England and the other in France – and both of these invite contextualization relative to film-technical developments in the United States and Germany, the two film-producing countries at the time most oriented toward the making of films for export.

Waltzes from Vienna as a Sound-film Experiment

The sophisticated soundtrack of *Waltzes from Vienna* merits emphasis in light of the film's low status in critical writing on Hitchcock. Nearing the end of his long and productive career, Hitchcock, in a famous interview with François Truffaut, disparaged *Waltzes from Vienna* as a low point, labeling the film 'a low-budget "musical without music" that had nothing to do with my usual work' (Truffaut 1975: 91). Anyone searching for information on *Waltzes from Vienna* will encounter Hitchcock's damning comment, which still echoes through much of the critical writing on the director. One exception to this critical trend has been Charles Barr, who regards *Waltzes from Vienna* as a breakthrough film in Hitchcock's use of music. Hitchcock had adopted recorded music effectively in earlier sound films, Barr observes, 'but it is not until *Waltzes from Vienna* that music becomes a serious structural element' (Barr 1999: 127–31), deeply integrated into the film's visuals and narrative logic. Echoing Barr's assessment is critic Jack Sullivan, who details how the film's use of music – its narrativization of music, one might say – anticipates many features that would come to define the soundtracks of Hitchcock's later and more celebrated films (Sullivan 2006: 20–30). The positive evaluation of *Waltzes from Vienna* advanced by Sullivan and Barr finds corroboration in a 1934 interview with the director, who stressed the film's value as a film-music experiment: '*Waltzes from Vienna* gave me many opportunities for working out ideas on the relation of film and music. Naturally every cut in the film was worked out in the script before shooting began. But more than that, the musical cuts were worked out too' (Hitchcock 1995: 244).

The film's music track is indeed complex and carefully edited, the preplanned use of multitrack technology allowing Hitchcock to achieve a variety of effects difficult if not impossible to reach otherwise. Exemplifying music-image integration are scenes showing stages in the composition of the 'Blue Danube Waltz' in which Hitchcock and Gaumont's British music director, Louis Levy, extract from the great Strauss tune myriad narrative implications for the film's image track. One such scene, singled out for praise by critics at the time for its use of music to suggest a character's thoughts, depicts Schani's visit to the pastry kitchen, where the film's nondiegetic score suggests that Schani hears in the bustle of the bakers' activity the rhythm needed for his waltz-in-progress. Also notable are the many moments when orchestral music provides mickey-mouse mimicry of the narrative action – as when Prince Gustav, dreaming he is fighting a duel, tosses and turns in bed, his wild gesticulations punctuated by the orchestra's violin section. In mobilizing music for dramatic and comic effect, Hitchcock's collaboration with Louis Levy, the film-savvy musical director responsible for the score for *Waltzes from Vienna*, was essential (Levy 1949). With Levy involved in the project from the planning stage, Hitchcock was able to design the image track with a clear knowledge of what would happen musically, thus making possible the tight synchronization of sound and image needed for the film's stylistic embellishments.

The music technique of *Waltzes from Vienna* thus inclines in the direction not of theatre-affiliated films made for the home market – "'musicals" which interpolate "numbers" rather than employ music', as Hitchcock put it – but of the sophisticated cinematic operetta (Hitchcock 1995: 242). The top export genre of the time, the operetta included the Chevalier-MacDonald vehicles directed by Lubitsch for Paramount, as well as many European-made films – from the films produced by Erich Pommer in multiple languages for Ufa in Germany to the musicals directed by René Clair at the Tobis studio near Paris. These music-defined films required special technical expertise as well as careful planning. A related attribute of the film operetta, likewise evident in *Waltzes from Vienna*, was a sophisticated self-awareness regarding its own artifice, manifest in comic moments when the material conditions of the film's making, ordinarily a subliminal force, surface in the film's story-world in the form of jokes and gags alluding to the technology behind the film. Pertinent to the topic of dubbing is the scene in *Waltzes from Vienna* featuring the comic, long-take performance of the servants playfully translating a conversation between the Countess and Prince Gustav. The latter remain off screen, on opposite sides of the room supposedly, while the amorous servants in between, framed in a two-shot, kiss and fondle each other while mockingly 'dubbing' their masters, mistranslating each line of speech.

Figure 2.1: *Waltzes from Vienna* (1934). This shot shows servants in the act of translating their off-screen masters and is among several in *Waltzes from Vienna* that seem to allude to the ultimate production of a dubbed version of the film.

Dubbing Practice in France

Waltzes from Vienna marks a crucial dubbing-related change in sound-film technique: the adoption of multitrack sound technologies. The change began in 1930 as Hollywood shifted away from foreign-language versions and towards dubbing as the main means of preparing films for export. The change would have been difficult to predict in early 1930, when dubbing was often characterized as useless for preparing films for foreign-language release. In February a British journalist reporting from Hollywood commented as follows: '"Dubbing" is becoming more and more a thing of the past [for foreign-market distribution], and after experience with the showing of "dubbed" versions all over the world it is becoming recognized that this is merely a makeshift method' (Belfrage 1930). Change was underway, however, and dubbing technique, spurred by work at Metro Goldwyn Meyer (MGM) and Paramount, was evolving rapidly. By the summer of 1930 these Hollywood studios, soon joined by others, began phasing out the making of separate foreign-language versions in favour of exporting the Hollywood originals in dubbed form. The new dubbed movies, moreover, were received well in France, a country where they had done poorly previously (Lehmann 1931; M. 1931; Morienval 1931). French audiences in the provinces, in fact, were reported to prefer dubbed imported films over subtitled (Anon. 1933b).[1] Paramount's studio in St-Maurice-Joinville had previously been used to make French-language shorts and features; however, in 1932 it was also given over to the dubbing of films shot in the United States.

In 1932, the 496 films distributed in France included sixty-six that had been dubbed (Anon. 1932b). At the end of 1933, as American films were increasingly released in dubbed form, the number of dubbed films circulating in France had doubled, and would continue to climb over the next years: 'The import [into France] of dubbed films has increased from 143 in 1933 to 251 in 1935', reported *Sight and Sound* (Anon. 1936, p. 5).[2] The increase followed a French law passed in October 1932 requiring that the dubbing of films for the French market take place in France. The law had a significant impact on the French cinema by stimulating the quick development in Paris of a thriving dubbing industry. In the summer of 1933 dubbing-related work was estimated to provide employment to some 4,000 French people, including some 1,200 dubbing '*artistes*' (T. 1933; Anon. 1933a; Anon. 1934a). During the summer of 1934, the trade journal *La Cinématographie française* reported that fourteen studios devoted solely to dubbing and postsynchronization were operating in the Paris area (Anon. 1934b).

At this point, with dubbed imports more popular in France than subtitled original versions, dubbing acquired new status as a form of employment – notwithstanding hostility in France towards dubbed movies from critics and film producers. A report on the Paris situation in the German publication *Film-Kurier* characterized 1933 as a turning point in dubbing's history in France, where until very recently, dubbing had been seen as the lowest sort of film work; now, however, '[i]t has suddenly become fashionable for popular, recognized actors to do the dubbing. The wages for this work, of course, have increased' (Anon. 1933b). With name actors performing the dubbing, it had become possible at this point, a French journalist noted (Richard 1935), to speak of 'dubbing stars' ['*vedettes du doublage*'], actors who enjoyed a modest celebrity from their work dubbing imported films. Dubbing's improved status is reflected in the credits of *La Chant du Danube*, which lists the French actors who did the dubbing in the same font size used for the original English actors. An additional title page lists the technical crew, identifying prominently the authors of the French continuity, song lyrics and dialogue along with the sound engineer and editor.

Cross-Atlantic Connections

The producer responsible for the French-dubbed version of *Waltzes from Vienna* was Jacques Haïk, a key figure in the French dubbing industry of the time (Anon. 1932d) and also a frequent collaborator with British film companies. Haïk's business connections in England dated back to 1910, when he first entered the film industry as a teenage employee of British companies (Anon. 2008a). In 1929 Haïk established himself as a leader in France's nascent sound-film industry by financing the making of one of the first French-language talking films: the shipwreck epic *Atlantic* (dir. Jean Kemm, 1929), filmed in England at the Elstree studio of British International Pictures in separate versions in French, English and German (Clarrière 1930a). Besides coproducing British films Haïk also dubbed various British films for French release (Anon. 1932d). In 1931 Haïk and Adolph Osso were described in the London-based trade weekly *Bioscope* as the two French producers who had made 'serious efforts' since the coming of sound 'to cooperate with British production firms and studios' (Clarrière 1931).

Haïk's role as a leading French producer, exhibitor and distributor of sound films ended in 1933 when he was unable to sustain his costly luxury theatres in the face of a steep decline in ticket sales. In March 1933, Haïk turned over the management of the theatres to Gaumont-Franco-Film-Aubert (Choukroun 2007: 172). Haïk soon secured new bank loans, however, and in 1934 formed Régent Film, a smaller firm whose principal production activity during its five years of existence was the shooting of some one dozen films as well as the dubbing of various foreign films into French. In mid 1940 Haïk, a Jew targeted by fascists and Nazis, fled France after producing the anti-Hitler film *Après Mein Kampf mes crimes* (dir. Alexandre Ryder, 1940), returning to his native Tunisia where he hid during the war (Anon. 2008a).

The majority of the dubbed films prepared by Régent Film were probably from the U.S.A., since in the mid-1930s U.S. films made up over 70 per cent of the dubbed films circulating in France. All the same, the number of dubbed films from England increased during this time, climbing from eleven in 1933 to nineteen in 1935 (Choukroun 2007: 190–1). *Waltzes from Vienna* offered significant commercial potential for the making of a French version since it was based on a major stage production that had opened in Paris in October 1933 (Anon. 2008b) after successful runs in other European cities including Vienna (1930), where it had premiered, and London (1931). A French stage adaptation, called *Valses de Vienne*, opened in Paris in October 1933 while Hitchcock was shooting *Waltzes from Vienna* in England. By purchasing Hitchcock's film for French adaptation Haïk stood to benefit from publicity related to the current stage production in Paris.

Haïk's project as a producer of dubbed films was contingent on double-bill exhibition, which became common in France in 1932 as the economic depression cut deeply into the movie box office, and the large cinemas – including the Rex and the Olympia, two major Parisian houses owned by Haïk until his financial crash in 1933 – began struggling to draw people in (Morel 1932; Choukroun 2007: 157, 163–5). The prevalence of the double-bill format in France over the following years explains the peculiar running time of *La Chant du Danube*, which clocks in at a mere fifty-one minutes versus the seventy-six minutes of *Waltzes from Vienna*. In France dubbed films were typically slotted into the opening half of the double bill, a purpose for which '*films de moyenne métrage*' – medium-length films such as *La Chant du Danube* – were more useful than conventional features (Anon. 1932c; Rose 1937: 73–4).

What Was Removed from the French Version?

The question of how the French dubbers managed to chop from *Waltzes from Vienna* an entire twenty-five minutes – roughly one-third of the film's total running time – involves considering how Haïk had sized up the commercial potential of Hitchcock's film for the French market. The availability of both the English and French versions of the film allows for the identification of the cuts, which fall into two basic categories: whole scenes and sequences, on the one hand, and individual shots, or bits thereof, on the other. The scenes and sequences come in two blocks. The first begins in the orchestra's rehearsal hall, where Rasi (short for Teresa), played by music-revue star Jessie Matthews, tries to help Schani by delivering to Johann Strauss Sr her copy of Schani's 'Blue Danube' score. When Rasi's claims for Schani's greatness are dismissed out of hand by Strauss Sr, she bursts from the rehearsal hall in tears. In the next shot Rasi runs up to the camera and freezes in close-up just as Schani can be overheard performing his waltz-in-progress for the Countess, Rasi's rival for Schani's affections. Rasi next confronts the couple and learns that Schani has dedicated the waltz to the Countess. This sequence of three scenes, pivotal to the romantic triangle of the British film, is omitted entirely from the French version.

The second deleted section lasts a full eleven and a half minutes and makes up almost the entire ending of *Waltzes from Vienna*. This section begins almost where the French film ends: at the conclusion of Schani's victorious 'Blue Danube' performance at the St Stephen's festival. It then continues through several short scenes leading to a clandestine meeting between Schani and the Countess, interrupted once more by jealous Prince Gustav. Next comes Rasi's reconciliation with Schani, and a short coda featuring the older Strauss, who adds 'Sr.' when signing his autograph for a young fan, thus acknowledging for the first time his son's achievement as a musician. This block of scenes, the coda excepted, is entirely missing from the French version, in which the festival performance leads immediately to Strauss Sr's act of signing the autograph.

Making sense of these two massive cuts requires factoring in a further editorial choice by Haïk's team: a rearrangement of the plot via a shift in the placement of a sequence of three scenes: (1) the rehearsal hall scene in which Strauss Sr humiliates Schani in front of the musicians; (2) the scene at the Countess' when she and Schani sing the pop tune 'Like a Star in the Sky', intercut with Rasi, telepathically singing the same tune in a distant garden; and (3) the first of the scenes where the Countess and Schani are confronted by the sudden arrival of Gustav. The same three-scene sequence occurs in the French film, too – but much later. In the English film, it begins roughly one-quarter of the way into the film's running time, whereas in the French version it occurs almost halfway into the film. In stressing the filial conflict at the expense of subplots involving secondary characters such as the Countess, Haïk's team approached the editing of *La Chant du Danube* in line with the prevalence in French films of the 1930s of narratives centered on powerful fathers or father-like figures (Vincendeau 1989).

Besides the excised and reshuffled scenes, the French film differs from the English one in a further respect: its scenes are often shorter as a consequence of the removal of whole shots as well as pieces of shots. Intriguing from the standpoint of dubbing technique are the partial excisions, as in the sequence of three scenes beginning with Schani's squabble with his father in the rehearsal hall, which ends with Schani quitting the orchestra. In *Waltzes from Vienna* these scenes add up to some eight minutes and forty seconds of screen time, whereas in *La Chant du Danube* they work out to seven minutes twenty seconds – almost one minute-and-a-half less.[3] Sequences in both versions contain the same thirty-three shots. In the French version, however, the shots are often shorter. The insert of Jessie Matthews performing 'Like a Star in the Sky' counts as an extreme case: the shot lasts forty-five seconds in the English film but only five in the French version. This excision is consonant with the handling of Matthews' other singing performance, the early music-lesson scene when Rasi sings 'With All My Heart' while Schani accompanies on the piano, which was cut entirely from the French version. A rising star in Britain, Jessie Matthews was at this point apparently unknown in France – a circumstance *La Chant du Danube* probably did little to change.

A further dubbing-related stylistic quirk is the many jump cuts in *La Chant du Danube* resulting from the removal of a piece of a shot. The extraction of frames from, as well as their addition to, dubbed films was common practice in the 1930s for fixing synchronization errors. As explained in the London-based *The Bioscope*: 'If a player takes nine frames to pronounce a word and the actual speaker takes eleven, two extra frames are spliced in and vice versa' (Anon. 1930b). Close-ups especially raised difficult synchronization problems (Autré 1932; Turpin 1935). To bring dialogue into synch in a feature film could involve shuffling ten thousand frames or more. A report in *Variety* noted that '[i]n one experiment by RCA 16,000 different frames were shifted, it is understood, in getting the desired result' (Anon. 1930a). This figure works out to over eleven minutes of screen time – roughly 13 per cent of the total running time for an average feature film of the time.[4] Haïk, a few years before founding Régent Film, had contracted with RCA to outfit his studio, which

Figure 2.2: *Waltzes from Vienna* (1934). This shot is among numerous shots in the film whose compositions are contrived to conceal the actors' lip movements and hence facilitate the film's eventual dubbing.

raises the possibility that the RCA people had introduced the frame-shifting technique to Haïk's team.

La Chant du Danube includes at least six dubbing-related jump cuts, by my count. Certain of the cuts involve enough frames to be easily detected by the viewer. An example occurs in the scene in the Countess' bedroom, in the two-shot showing the maid, angled toward the camera on frame left, and the Countess on frame right, visible in silhouette only. The dubbers reduced this shot's duration by more than half – from fourteen seconds down to six. Also noteworthy is the shot's peculiar mise en scène, whereby the Countess, the main speaker, is hidden behind the curtain through the entire shot. This sort of framing, whereby the speaker's lips are concealed, surfaces in dozens of shots in *Waltzes from Vienna*. In the early scene showing Schani's arrival at the dance school, for instance, a shot depicts the faces of the women peering silently through the window and toward the camera. In the next, reverse-angle shot, however, in which the women are seen from behind, they chatter away. Later, Gustav's short conversation with the servant he has thrown down the stairs is depicted in a shot in which Gustav is shown at the stairway's top, visible below the knees only, while the servant is at the bottom, the back of his head peaking into the frame. Recall, too, the strange shot of the servant at the St Stephen's festival who speaks while concealed behind a massive beer barrel.

Such shots are easy to dub and they prepare the viewer for other moments when voices come untethered from lip movement, thus naturalizing the technique. Filmmakers other than Hitchcock had already gone down this path, as is suggested in a report in 1933 in the *New York Times* on Fritz Lang's work on his film *M* (1931) in anticipation of the eventual making of an English-language version:

> In making this picture Fritz Lang, believing that it would have a wide circulation in English-speaking countries, took into consideration the fact that the English voices would have to be dubbed, therefore he avoided close-ups of actors talking to the audience, and some scenes were produced

specially for the dubbed version. The characters in speaking sometimes hide the movements of their lips, either by lighting a cigar or by turning their heads (Hall 1933).

What Lang had done in 1931 with *M* could be said to have become standard practice in transnational cinema by 1933 and the shooting of *Waltzes from Vienna*: as multitrack technologies and techniques became standard in studios in Britain and other countries, films were shot in ways which would ease the dubbing later on at other studios in other countries.

In crafting their films in light of an eventual dubbed version, Lang and Hitchcock acted in accord with methods of framing and scene construction that became standard in Hollywood in 1931 when multitrack sound was introduced throughout the studio system. Before then American films routinely depicted speaking actors in ways emphasizing the legibility of lip movement, with speech always sourced in the image. Once the Hollywood majors switched to dubbing as the main means of preparing films for foreign-market release, however, a new approach was instituted. At MGM, for instance, it was decided for the 1930–1931 film season that '[l]ong and medium shots will be tricked so that at no time will the lip movement be discernible' (Anon. 1930b).

French journalists in the summer of 1931 noted in recent dubbed films from Hollywood the new approach to shots with synchronous speech. An article in *La Cinématographie française* reported that American filmmakers now favoured 'shots depicting actors whose lip movements were not visible' (Anon. 1931). Exemplifying the '*nouvelles versions européenes*' was *Cœurs brûlés*, the dubbed version of Paramount's *Morocco*: 'when one hears an actor speak one is shown not this actor but the actor who listens and whose demeanor is necessarily mute' (Morienval 1931). Whatever Hitchcock's intent regarding his work on *Waltzes from Vienna*, the peculiar framings were consonant with current export-film practice.

Conclusion

The project of investigating British and French cinema in terms of their interaction with one another can entail encountering phenomena, such as dubbed films, that are difficult to grasp within the familiar national cinema framework of film studies. With respect to the preceding examination of the dubbed version of *Waltzes from Vienna*, two concluding remarks suggest themselves. The first remark concerns obstacles to research stemming from the difficulty of finding dubbed films for examination. My analysis of *La Chant du Danube* together with reports on dubbing in the contemporary film-industry press concern what I take to be typical dubbing practice. But despite dubbing's great importance to movie culture worldwide, where dubbed cinema is the norm for hundreds of millions of filmgoers, copies of dubbed films are extremely hard to come by. Archives do not make it a priority to restore them, it seems, and DVD producers, who have created wonderful multiple-version editions, appear uninterested in including dubbed versions on DVD releases. I have examined some four hundred feature films of the early 1930s so far and *Waltzes* was among the tiny handful I could find in both original and dubbed form. If DVD copies of dubbed films were readily available it would be very helpful, though better yet would be original 35mm prints. Working from my bootleg DVD copy of *La Chant du Danube*, I found six dubbing-related jump cuts. But viewing the film on DVD allows one to detect only examples involving blatant excisions. Slight editing jumps or instances in which frames have been added into a shot are likely to be detectable only through examining a 35mm print of the film on an editing table. In sum, until more dubbed films from the period turn up and are examined, the study of the history of dubbing practice must rest content with findings based on a few rare films.

The second concluding point pertains to methodological challenges deriving from the dispersal of dubbing-related activity across two studios in different countries, so that the dubbing occurred in a country other than where the film was planned and shot. This dispersion of activity across national borders raises complications for the historian of style, who traces a film's style and technique back to causes and conditions in specific places and times. What complicates the study of a dubbed film such as *La Chant du Danube* is that in investigating causes it can be difficult to know where to stop. Important aspects of the style of *La Chant du Danube*, to be sure, trace directly to work undertaken at Courbevoie, where the dubbing was performed, the scenes rearranged, and so on. But to make sense of *that* requires looking into work months earlier in the Shepherd's Bush studio of Gaumont British, where Hitchcock's film was planned and shot in a manner allowing its dubbing later on in France. These activities of planning and shooting in turn appear to have been anticipated in U.S. practice over the preceding few years, when multitrack technologies were introduced, adapted and standardized in Hollywood for dubbing purposes. One can also cite the contemporaneous commercialization of dubbing-related synchronization devices in Germany such as the Rhythmograph (Wedel 2002). In any case, dubbed films such as *La Chant du Danube* amount to transnational phenomena and as such require the exploration of how they affected – and were affected by – circumstances in at least two countries, both source and target.

Notes

1. This piece reports on the findings of a poll of French film viewers taken by a 'large regional daily'.
2. These figures can be compared to those cited in the Carmoy Report and quoted in Choukroun (2007).
3. The figures are as follows. For the English version: 3.45 for the rehearsal-hall scene, 3.17 for 'Like a Star in the Sky' and 1.45 for the scene with Gustav, the Countess and Schani. For the French version: 3.45, 2.10 and 1.35. In both films, the first scene contains seventeen shots, the second five and the third thirteen. The performance of 'Like a Star in the Sky' runs 2.10 in the English version and 1.06 in the French.
4. This figure derives from an examination I made of sixty-seven synch-sound feature films from Britain, France, Germany and the U.S. released in 1930.

Bibliography

Anon. 1930a. 'Patented "Dubbing" Device Makes Foreign Films 100% Synchronized', *Variety* 99(9): 4.

———. 1930b. 'Scientific Dubbing', *The Bioscope* 84(1,240): i.

———. 1931. 'Les Nouvelles méthodes américaines de "dubbing"', *La Cinématographie française* 13(655): 65.

———. 1932a. 'New British Film Studios', *The Times*, 24 May: 12.

———. 1932b. '1932', *La Cinématographie française* 14(739): 7.

———. 1932c. 'Le Doublage, ses nécessités et ses limites', *Le Cinéopse* 14(152): 158.

———. 1932d. 'La Question du doublage', *La Cinématographie française* 14(712): 65.

———. 1933a. 'American Films Lead in France', *Wall Street Journal*, 18 April: 8.

———. 1933b. 'In Frankreich: Große Tätigkeit im Dubbing', *Film-Kurier* 15(93): 5.

———. 1934a. 'French Film Groups Meet', *New York Times*, 26 May: 12.

———. 1934b. 'Studios de doublage et de synchronisation', *La Technique cinématographique* 5(43–44): 204.

———. 1936. 'News of the Quarter', *Sight and Sound* 5(18): 3–6.

———. 2008a. 'Jacques Haïk'. Retrieved 2 December 2008 from http://www.lips.org/bio_Haik_GB.asp

———. 2008b. 'Johann Strauss II'. Retrieved 30 November 2008 from http://pagesperso-orange.fr/anao/composit/strauss.html

Autré, P. 1932. 'Attention au dubbing!' *La Cinématographie française* 14(691): 22.

Barr, C. 1999. *English Hitchcock*. Moffat, Scotland: Cameron and Hollis.

Belfrage, C. 1930. 'Hollywood's Multi-lingual Quandary', *The Bioscope* 82(1,217): 20.

Choukroun, J. 2007. *Comment le parlant a sauvé le cinéma français : une histoire économique, 1928–1939*. Perpignan: AFHRC/Institut Jean Vigo.

Clarrière, G. 1930a. '"Atlantic" French Version', *The Bioscope* 82(1,225): 30.

———. 1930b. 'Dubbing's Comeback on the Coast', *Variety* 100(4): 4.

———. 1931. 'Osso to Commence British Production', *The Bioscope* 88(1,299): 24.

Hall, M. 1933. '"M" in English', *New York Times*, 16 April: X3.

Hitchcock, A. 1995. 'On Music in Films', in S. Gottlieb (ed.), *Hitchcock on Hitchcock: Selected Writings and Interviews*. Berkeley and Los Angeles: University of California Press, pp. 241–45.

Lehmann, R. 1931. 'A propos de "dubbing"', *Pour vous* 133: 2.

Le Verrier, T. 1931. 'Le Problème de la synchronisation de la parole de la musique et des bruits "après coup" semble être définitivement résolu', *Comoedia* 25(6,850): 6.

Levy, L. 1949. *Music for the Movies*. London: Sampson Low, Marston.

Lipscombe, W. 1930. 'Saving the "Talkies" from Talk', *The Bioscope* 85(1,265): 95.

M., L. 1931. 'Il faut mettre au point la question du "dubbing"', *Pour vous* 129: 2.

Morel, F. 1932. 'Directeurs, attention à votre nouvelle "programmation"', *La Cinématographie française* 14(717): 11.

Morienval, J. 1931. 'Films françaises synchronisés U.S.A.', *Le Cinéopse* 13(141): 224.

Richard, A. 1935. 'Le Mille et un métiers du film parlant', *Pour vous* 343: 14.

Rose, F. 1937. 'The French Cinema, 1936', *Sight and Sound* 6(22): 71–74.

Sullivan, J. 2006. *Hitchcock's Music*. New Haven: Yale University Press.

T., H. 1933. 'The French Film Decree', *Wall Street Journal*, 17 August: 3.

Truffaut, F. with H. Scott. 1975. *Le Cinema selon Hitchcock*. Paris: Seghers.

Turpin, R. 1935. 'Le Doublage des films', *La Technique cinématographique* 6(57): 459.

Vincendeau, G. 1989. 'Daddy's Girls, Oedipal Narratives in 1930s French Films', *Iris* 8: 70–81.

Wedel, M. 2002. 'Vom Synchronismus zur Synchronisation: Carl Robert Blum und der frühe Tonfilm', in J. Polzer (ed.), *Aufstieg und Untergang des Tonfilms*. Potsdam: Polzer Media Group, pp. 97–112.

Filmography

Après Mein Kampf mes crimes / My Crimes After Mein Kampf. 1940, Alexandre Ryder, France.

Atlantic / Atlantis. 1930, Ewald André Dupont and Jean Kemm, England.

Chant du Danube, La / Waltzes from Vienna. 1934, Alfred Hitchcock, England/France.

Cœurs brûlés / Morocco. 1931, Josef von Sternberg, United States.

M: Dein Mörder sieht dich an / M. 1931, Fritz Lang, Germany.

CHAPTER 3

Une Entente Cordiale? – A Brief History of the Anglo-French Film Coproduction Agreement, 1965–1979

Justin Smith

One of the most obvious ways in which one might consider the formalization of Franco-British cinematic relations is in respect of trade agreements. Yet Anglo-European treaties with France (1965), with Italy (1967) and with West Germany (1974), proved relatively ineffectual in promoting coproduction. Recourse to the archives offers an explanation as to why. During the 1970s, as Britain continued to equivocate over full membership of the European Community, so the domestic interests of the British film trade increasingly diverged from those of her closest continental film ally, France. Department of Trade files at the National Archives reveal the nature of the split and the way in which it mirrored, in microcosm, larger divisions over financial commitment and cultural provision between Britain and her new European partners. Meanwhile, the Anglo-French treaty gave rise to a coproduction slate which, if limited in number, was eclectic and, occasionally, successful. This chapter considers the policies, the puddings and the odd plum.

The Treaty of Rome, Free Trade and Harmonization

The Treaty of Rome (1957), whose articles set the parameters for establishing a Free Trade Area between states within the 16-member Organization for European Economic Cooperation (OEEC), did not address the cinema specifically at all. However, this did not deter the principal continental film-producing nations (France, Italy and West Germany) from preparing a tripartite pact for film coproduction as a first step on the road to the prospective integration of their film industries, and the French quickly established themselves as the principal architects of cinematic harmonization.

Jacques Flaud, Director-General of the *Centre Nationale de La Cinématographie* (CNC) spoke optimistically to Henry Kahn of the British trade journal *Kinematograph Weekly*: 'The present differences existing between the Italian, French and German film industries are sufficiently flexible to make it quite possible to bring them into harmony. But', he admitted, 'there are three problems to be resolved before the Common Market can be a working organization: taxation, charges for social services, and aid to the industry within each country must be brought into line as far as possible' – no small task, as it turned out. As far as British involvement was concerned, M. Flaud was adamant that 'the whole question of collaboration between the European Common Market countries and Britain will have to be carefully examined'. While he was 'working hard on a plan for a wider exchange of films between France and Britain' and was confident that 'by 1960 Franco-British coproduction will be a possibility', he warned that 'the free zone must not open a continental door for the United States' (Kahn 1957).

Despite cautious encouragement for Britain to be included in the tripartite pact, the Board of Trade had reservations of its own:

Officials and a good part, though by no means the whole, of the British film industry are doubtful whether the inclusion of films within the Free Trade Area would substantially increase the earnings of United Kingdom films in Europe or would substantially diminish their earnings in the United Kingdom because of the competition of films from other Free Trade Area countries (Knight 1957a: 1).

But certain sectors of the British film trade had already nailed their colours to the mast. In a phone call on 26 November 1957, Victor Finney of the Rank Organization told G.S. Knight of the Film Branch that Rank were 'taking active steps to make British films more acceptable on the Continent and vice versa by an exchange of artistes' (Knight 1957b).

Aside from a small import duty of 1d. per foot on exposed film stock (designed to protect the British film processing industry), Britain herself had no import restrictions on foreign feature films. Following the *ad Valorem* débâcle of 1947, which saw the threat of a U.K. tax on U.S. film imports countered by a temporary U.S. film embargo, the Board of Trade (with Harold Wilson then as its President) had been forced to concede to the United States generous terms in the Cinematograph Films Act of 1948, which established an Anglo-American film treaty offering a liberal definition of what constituted a British film (Harper and Porter 2003: 5–6). That, coupled with the devaluation of sterling in September 1949, meant that by the early 1950s Hollywood's premier overseas market permitted the repatriation of up to 70 per cent of a film's U.K. earnings, provided those monies were reinvested in film production on British soil (thus guaranteeing work to British studios and technicians). This apparently sensible measure opened the door to the major Hollywood studios to set up production offices in the U.K. and to make American films on British soil which could count, under the terms of Britain's quota system (by now reduced to 30 per cent), as British films, thus benefiting also from the Eady levy which returned a percentage of box-office revenue to the film's 'American' producers. In other words, U.S. films, long predominant in the U.K. market, could, by these means, receive the full benefits of British state aid. This anomaly arose out of the fact that British protectionist measures were primarily motivated by the desire to defend British labour, rather than British culture. Yet in cultural terms, with the Act about to come up for review in 1960, some saw the nascent European Free Trade Area as an opportunity to gather collective opposition to Hollywood's hegemony. Mr S. Golt of the Board of Trade wrote sceptically:

> Some leading figures in the film industry itself profess to believe that the creation of a Free Trade Area would in some mystic way create a unified European film industry which would wrest from Hollywood its dominating position in the European and (in their more visionary moments) the world market (Golt 1957).

But this idealistic ambition was more complex than it appeared. Paradoxically, while the definition of what counted as a British film for the purposes of her three instruments of financial support (the Eady levy, the British Film Production Fund and the quota system) created favourable loopholes for the U.S. to exploit, they presented barriers to European coproduction. R.C. Bryant of the Film Branch judged that:

> If films are included in the Free Trade Area it will raise some very difficult technical problems for the United Kingdom. It may very well entail the throwing open of the United Kingdom screen quota to films made in the Free Trade Area. Will a film be eligible then on the basis of something on the lines of the present labour cost provisions but allowing Free Trade Area nationals to count for this purpose on the same footing as British nationals, or will it simply mean that a film will be eligible for quota provided it complies with the nationality rule in the country of origin? Another difficulty may well be the applicability of the film levy to such films (Bryant 1957: 2).

Meanwhile, across the Atlantic, the European initiatives received a polite, if cool, endorsement from the Motion Picture Association of America: of course you can do what you like, ran the argument, providing you do nothing to jeopardize Hollywood's European export market. Those Californian voices were right to remain cool. Britain, for her part, waited in the wings, observing a Whitehall policy of masterly inactivity, while her major European neighbours debated a means by which parity across the various state subsidies might be achieved, once the barriers to free trade were lifted. The following Board of Trade memorandum sums up the British position: 'The proper course seems to be to ask our Delegation in Paris to endeavour by informal discussion to ascertain what is proposed by the Common Market countries, and in the light of this consider our attitude to the Free Trade Area' (Knight 1957a: 1). What exactly was proposed remained unclear until the eleventh hour. But when it came into force, under the terms of the Stockholm Convention, which established the Free Trade Area, import duties on films from other countries within the area were to be reduced by 20 per cent from 1 July 1960, as part of a progressive phasing out of protection tariffs. And at the same time, the British government made a significant amendment in the 1960 Films Act, which allowed that films made in accordance with agreements between the U.K. and other countries might, in certain circumstances, be registered as British for quota purposes.

However, on 31 May 1961, negotiations between the French and West German representatives on moves towards fiscal harmonization broke down. It was, according to the French, 'the most serious cinematographic event since the Liberation' (Anon. 1961). Two months later, the British prime minister, Harold Macmillan, announced the government's intention formally to apply to join the Common Market. While the immediate implications for the film industry remained unclear, the Federation of Film Unions (FFU) issued an unequivocal statement via their mouthpiece, the *Film and Television Technician*, to the effect that no further discussion should be held on 'coproductions until the implications of the Common Market were fully known' (Elvin 1961a). A month later, their tone had softened somewhat, endorsing the government's intention to join, while keenly searching for the devil in the detail (Elvin 1961b).

As the heady 1960s gathered momentum, it was U.S. investment in British 'runaway' production that increasingly controlled the British market. In 1960, forty-one of Hollywood's 158 films produced were made overseas, while in the same year eighteen of the U.K.'s 86 films made were Anglo-American coproductions (BT 258/495). By 1966 all the Hollywood majors had production offices in London, MGM had a permanent base at Borehamwood and, by 1968, 80 per cent of British film production was American funded.

Nonetheless, the mandarins at the Board of Trade's Film Branch remained exercised by precisely how EEC law would adjudicate on national film subsidies, and what threat, if any, Britain's membership would pose to its quota system and Eady levy. In fact, they considered that concerns about parity of aid (the French cinema was by far the most fortunate beneficiary in this) and union fears about unequal labour conditions (especially in Italy) might both be addressed in a more manageable and equitable manner through the negotiation of individual coproduction treaties with those countries who remained keenest on cinematic collaboration. As Andrew Filson, Secretary of the Federation of British Film Makers, shrewdly predicted, 'My guess is that the gradual transition [towards free trade conditions] will be effected not by dramatic fiscal reforms, but gradually by measures of controlled reciprocity' (Filson 1959). His forecast was soon borne out by similar noises from the Board of Trade:

The best hope of cooperation with Community members lies in coproduction of films. Government-recognized coproduction is a system of bilateral reciprocation of the benefits accorded national films. It has been used successfully on the Continent to break down the barriers imposed by individual countries' systems of protection of their film industries and generally to widen film-makers' markets. We are about to open negotiations with France, Italy and Germany with a view of governmental agreements which would accord dual 'nationality' to films made jointly by British producers and producers in those countries.

Coproduction will reinforce the existing links between the British and Continental film industries and could give each direct interests in the success of the others. Moreover, since the double state-aid on coproduction films is one of the main attractions to participants, coproduction seems likely to encourage a certain amount of automatic harmonisation of support. Coproduction should at least provide a means of ensuring that we have a recognized interest in any Community proposals relating to state-aids on films and hence that our European partners would listen to our views on them. This would provide a partial substitute for exclusion from the deliberations at Brussels (BT 258/496: 83).

This view was diplomatically astute, politically shrewd and, as events turned out, prescient in the extreme. It made the right noises, employed the right buzz-words and embraced the right spirit, while maintaining, unequivocally, that Britain's best way of contributing to European integration was from the sidelines. All in all, it was a measured civil service response in the best traditions of Whitehall. All the more so when, in February 1963, negotiations for Britain's entry into the Common Market abruptly came to a halt. From that point talks began in earnest between the Board of Trade, the Film Producers Association (FPA), the FFU and other interested parties towards the formulation of a draft coproduction treaty. Copies were duly sent to France, Italy and West Germany, with only the Germans failing to respond. Later that year, a British delegation met representatives from the French and Italian governments and the process was set in motion, which resulted in coproduction agreements with France (in 1965) and Italy (in 1967).

Coproduction

Having cleared the ground politically, we are now in a position to focus on coproduction itself. Anne Jäckel reminds us that France and Italy had been the first European countries to sign a coproduction agreement as early as 1949, as a means of mutual benefit to protect their respective native film industries from a postwar European market bombarded with the backlog of U.S. product (Jäckel 1996: 87). Because of this threat also, both countries maintained tight restrictions on Hollywood imports.

The chief advantage of such treaties was that, providing a project met the criteria laid down, a film could count as home-produced and thus qualify for state aid (such as the U.K.'s quota and Eady levy or the French *Fonds de Soutien*) in each partner country. At the same time, if the logistics of such arrangements could be agreed under the terms of the treaties, there were divisions of labour and a spread of risk, which made such alliances, at least potentially, safer prospects.

As Vincent Porter has suggested, 'In any coproduction agreement there are essentially three areas for negotiation: the division of production finance between the coproducers; the division of revenue and (sometimes) copyright; and the question of editorial and creative control' (Porter 1977: 206). Usually the party supplying the greater investment share (or who has taken the greatest risk in advancing capital) retains creative control and, in turn, enjoys the greatest share of revenues. This major/minor stakeholder scenario is characteristic of most coproductions. And it determines key creative decision-making in the production process, in respect of, for example: script approval, casting, proportion of location scenes, use of studio facilities, original language and so on.

The Anglo-French partnership was finally ratified in 1965 for a cautious trial period of eighteen months, with the possibility of extension for further periods of eighteen months thereafter, subject to the approval of the Mixed Commission of the Competent Authorities of both partner countries, which was required to meet every six months. There followed, in 1970, an 'Exchange of Notes' between the two governments, which somewhat relaxed and prolonged the terms of the original agreement, and required the Mixed Commission only to meet annually. In the first five years of the agreement, while U.S. 'runaway' investment in British film production continued to escalate, an average of one film a year resulted from the Anglo-French partnership.

In several respects, these titles were typical not only of the formulaic product which coproduction is maligned for promoting, but also of late-1960s cultural exploitation. *La Nuit des géneraux / Night of the Generals* (Anatole Litvak, 1966), a big-budget wartime thriller about a plot to assassinate Hitler, boasted an international star cast including Peter O'Toole, Omar Sharif, Tom Courtney, Donald Pleasance and Philippe Noiret. Omar Sharif appeared again in Terence Young's *Mayerling* (1968), a lavishly expensive romantic costume drama, whose international star cast also included Catherine Deneuve, James Mason and Ava Gardner. The stage was set for the kind of coproduction property which might draw on a common European cultural history and boast big-budget values and all-star casts to earn wider international (American) appeal. Between these two pillars of continental heritage were two films of the 1960s probably best forgotten. One starred the haplessly chic Marianne Faithful as *La Motocyclette / Girl on a Motorcycle* (Jack Cardiff, 1968); the other, *A cœur joie*, which predated it, was an even more unlikely Brigitte Bardot vehicle about a French model who falls in love in Scotland. Directed by Serge Bourguignon, its English title is *Two Weeks in September* (which is probably as long as it ran). It is now only statistically famous as having been the first film made under the Anglo-French treaty in 1966.

By 1970 the Films Division of the Department of Trade took stock. The new decade brought recession and saw a rapid withdrawal of American funding from British film production. Several of the Hollywood majors had suffered heavy losses through over-zealous speculation at the end of the 1960s. In 1969 MGM lost $35.4m and Warner Bros $42m. And in 1970 United Artists lost $45m and Fox $76.4m. In 1971 Columbia had debts of $28.8m. By 1974, total U.S. funding for British subsidiaries had fallen to £2.9m (Street 2002: 190).

British film producers were further alarmed at the incoming Conservative Government's decision to renege on Labour promises to extend support to the

National Film Finance Corporation. In 1971 the new Tory film minister, Nicholas Ridley, insisted it was not the 'Government's policy to put money into industry of this sort. In the long term it should be able to stand on its own feet in the market' (Page 1971: 1). In the same year the FPA and the FFU produced a guide for filmmakers to the Anglo-French and Anglo-Italian treaties. Writing in 1972, Neville Hunnings sounded a gloomy note of warning: 'Paradoxically, the British film industry anticipates less difficulty from the EEC than from the policies of the British government' (Hunnings 1972: 82). In 1973 representatives from these industry bodies formed a Working Group constituted by the Department of Trade to discuss ways of encouraging applications under the agreements.

Specifically, representatives of the FPA lobbied to relax certain conditions of the Anglo-French agreement. First, there was a stipulation that no film made under the terms of the agreement could be handled by the same distributor in both partner countries. Second, the director of any coproduction film had to be a native of, or legally domiciled in, either British or French territory. Finally, Morris Dyson, the head of the Department of Trade's Films Division, himself craved leniency of his French opposite number in respect of the strict need to balance financial investment between the partners. For in respect of the first five features produced under the agreement by 1970, the balance of investment was heavily in favour of the French, as the Department's own figures show (Table 3.1).

Indeed, the nature of the relative contributions of the partners, and the benefits received, were already, and largely remained, unequal. For while the French side consistently invested more in production resources and benefited from more lucrative state incentives than their British partners, English language and actors became the lingua franca of international appeal to the American market which remained so impenetrable to French-speaking film exports in all but the narrow realms of art-house fare.

Concessions were obtained on the matter of financial equilibrium, however, and it was agreed that the terms of the balance be calculated over a longer timescale, to allow British partners to catch up. As the figures produced in 1975 show, there was some improvement in this aspect, though the inherent inequality of the relationship remained (Table 3.2).

Table 3.1: Anglo-French Coproduction Equilibrium, 1965–70 (5 Films).

	UK	France
Production Costs (£m)	2.6	3.8
Exp on Studios & Labs (£)	102,000	293,000
Leading Artists (days)	378	430
Other Artists	42	127
Other Personnel (ex crowd & musicians)	413	770

(*Source*, DTI, FV 81/32)

Table 3.2: Anglo-French Coproduction Equilibrium, 1965–75 (12 Films).

	UK	France	Balance
Production Costs (£)	5,246,799	5,666,000	Fr +419,201
Exp on Studios & Labs (£)	321,643	376,752	Fr +55,109
Leading Artists (days)	709	689	UK +20 days
Other Artists	153	271	Fr +118
Other Personnel (ex crowd & musicians)	755	1034	Fr +279

(*Source*, DTI, FV 81/32)

Upon the other matters of concern to British film producers, there were exceptions permitted to the rule on distribution (under an amendment to Annex [xi], paragraph two of the Anglo-French agreement made in July 1971), though the Department of Trade resisted its outright waiver (despite the fact that the 1967 Anglo-Italian and 1974 Anglo-West German treaties contained no such restriction). Thus, independent producer John Woolf successfully gained exemption to enable Cinéma International Corporation (CIC) to distribute his Frederick Forsyth adaptation *Chacal / The Day of the Jackal* (1973) in Britain and in France which, with the backing of its Hollywood parent Universal, successfully marketed the film on both sides of the Atlantic. It did very well, being the third-highest grossing British film of 1973, and earning $8.6m in U.S. rental earnings. However, neither the Department of Trade nor the Association of Cinematograph Television & Allied Technicians (ACTT) would compromise on the director's nationality issue. Fortunately for Woolf, his director of choice (the Austrian-born Hollywood veteran Fred Zinnemann) was able to claim U.K. residency. Other American exiles living in Britain (Joseph Losey and Robert Parrish) enjoyed similar immunity to pursue Anglo-French projects in this period.

Woolf and the Jackal – a Case Study

I now want to pursue *The Day of the Jackal* in some detail, as an Anglo-French case study. After the war, Woolf felt himself at odds with Rank's parochialism and branched out with his brother James, to form Romulus, an independent production company. They immediately capitalized on Hollywood's disillusionment during the McCarthy era of the early 1950s and their second feature, *The African Queen* (1951), won international acclaim. Also famed for backing Jack Clayton's *Room at the Top* (1958), which did much to usher in the British New Wave of social realist films, the partnership ended with the death of James Woolf in 1966. John Woolf cofounded Anglia Television in 1959 and, in 1968, bought British & American Film Holdings. At the end of the 1960s he produced the Oscar-winning Lionel Bart musical *Oliver!* He was riding high on the wave of that particular success, therefore, when he chose to purchase the rights on the first novel by the then unknown journalist Frederick Forsyth, about a failed 1962 plot to assassinate French president Charles De Gaulle. The film itself is admittedly a modest thriller, yet it represents a rare mark of achievement in international coproduction for a number of reasons, which are worth exploring.

First, Woolf recognized, when he read the proofs, three important qualities: its semidocumentary foundations, its European location appeal and its exploitation of contemporary European fears about the dissident resurgence of the far Right. This despite the fact that the pretext of this thriller made it an unlikely prospect – a suspense story, set a decade earlier, the outcome of which is not only known, but is known to be a fiction. Undaunted by this apparent lack of promise, Woolf set Kenneth Ross to work on a screenplay. The producer told the British trade journal *Cinema TV Today*: 'In making use of the Anglo-French coproduction treaty … the point is that the subject has to be absolutely right …. [I]t is no use just writing in a French scene or two. The story itself has to have France as an integral part' (Lewin 1972: 13).

Second, Woolf was canny in securing a majority French-funded deal, while effectively retaining artistic control. This crucial arrangement is evident in the Department of Trade figures relating to the production under the terms of the treaty (Table 3.3). We can see, from these figures for the first ten years of the Anglo-French treaty, that the balance in U.K. control was somewhat restored in the second half of the period, *The Day of the Jackal* being, with Lewis Gilbert's *Paul et Michelle / Paul and Michelle* (1974), one of only two French majority-funded pictures. In explaining the advantages of coproduction, Woolf also betrayed the lack of parity between the British and French systems:

We will qualify for aids in both countries and I must say that of the two I think I prefer the French system because it is paid out to the producer specifically on the understanding that it must be used for future film production and therefore the money stays in the industry.

In Britain on the other hand the money doesn't go directly to the producer and it can leave the industry because there is no special commitment that it has to be applied to making more films (Lewin 1972: 13).

Third, Woolf was shrewd in appointing two established coproducers, one British (David Deutsch), the other French (Julien Derode). They made an early decision to retain from the novel the key British, French and Italian locations, and to employ British and French crews respectively, using studios in London and in Paris. Although the French and English scenes employed different set designers, French cinematographer Jean Tournier photographed the entire shoot. The small, mobile outfit (fewer than forty in number) journeyed across Europe for location scenes in Vienna, Rome, Genoa, Nice, Menton, Tourtour, Gap, Paris and, finally, London.

Despite Universal Studios' pressure, the lead roles were all taken by (then relatively unknown) British stage actors (including Edward Fox, Derek Jacobi, Ronald Pickup and Timothy West), and the ensemble was supported by key French personnel (see Table 4.3). Indeed, in casting the English assassin, 'both Zinnemann and Woolf agreed that it would be a mistake to use a well known actor whose face

Table 3.3: Anglo-French Coproduction Statistics, 1970–75.

Title	Year	Financial Participation (%) UK	France	Majority Country	Production Costs Split (£) UK	France	Prod Cost Total (£)	Exp on Studios & Labs (£) UK	France	Total
Catch Me a Spy	1971	70	30	UK	304,706	130,589	435,295	23,024	4,815	27,839
Day of the Jackal	1973	40	60	F	577,813	866,719	1,444,532	70,600	56,899	127,499
A Doll's House	1973	70	30	UK	258,453	110,766	369,219	22,493	0	22,493
Paul & Michelle	1974	36	64	F	110,228	199,202	309,430	37,597	9,320	46,917
Caravan to Vaccares	1974	70	30	UK	455,000	195,000	650,000	12,715	9,662	22,377
The Marseille Contract	1974	59	41	UK	354,272	242,091	596,363	27,198	2,753	29,951
The Romantic Englishwoman	1975	70	21	UK	599,002	161,956	760,958	25,599	0	25,599

Title	Director	Employment Leading Artists (days) UK	France	Other artists UK	France	All other personnel (musicians) UK	France
Catch Me a Spy	Dick Clement	22	45	37	3	89 (50)	2
Day of the Jackal	Fred Zinnemann	74	29	39	48	121 (46)	166 (2)
A Doll's House	Joseph Losey	41	14	6	1	39 (36)	2 (1)
Paul & Michelle	Lewis Gilbert	113	84	5	17	10 (71)	33 (2)
Caravan to Vaccares	Geoffrey Reeve	39	67	24	39	62 (61)	20
The Marseille Contract	Robert Parrish	42	20		36	21 (75)	41
The Romantic Englishwoman	Joseph Losey	74		44	4	65 (25)	8

(*Source*, DTI, FV 81/32)

was instantly recognizable to audiences. When they saw Edward Fox in *The Go-Between* (1971) they knew they had got their man' (Lewin 1972: 13).

The director Fred Zinnemann's return to fortune (following MGM's cancellation of *Man's Fate*, the André Malraux adaptation on which he had been working following the Oscar-winning *A Man for All Seasons* [1966]), was also a return to his finest work, as exemplified in the western *High Noon* (1952). Like *Noon*, *The Day of the Jackal*'s narrative is a sustained exercise in observational montage, researched with painstaking precision, and photographed with documentary detachment. Yet each film is driven by a portentous rhythm worthy of classical tragedy and, not insignificantly, clocks are a recurrent motif in both. Zinnemann's dismissal of the picture as 'just a technical exercise in suspense' is telling, because it also points to the director's own investment in the project (Michaud 2005: 31). Zinnemann's dogged pursuit of authenticity was aided by the coproduction arrangements; the French coproducer Julien Derode was privileged to gain the cooperation of the Parisian authorities to film inside the Ministry of the Interior and behind the barricades at the 1972 14 July parade (Zinnemann 1992: 212).

Finally, as Lloyd Michaels points out in an article which does much to rehabilitate this rather neglected genre piece, 'at least one sequence deserves closer scrutiny ... when the would-be assassin ... takes his specially designed rifle to a bucolic meadow and fine tunes the scope by firing at a melon he has hung from a distant tree'.

> The scene, based on four pages in Forsyth's novel and consisting of seventeen shots in two minutes and fifteen seconds, serves most obviously to anticipate the intended result of the conspirators' plot – the sniper's attack against de Gaulle – and to define the cold-hearted precision of the professional assassin .... [But] moreover, as a rehearsal of the film's aborted climax, it satisfies the audience's desire to see, at least in symbolic form, the ultimate act of violence denied in this case by history (Michaels 1994: 102).

Furthermore, as Michaels sets out, it is no accident that our point-of-view glimpse through the killer's telescopic sight mimics that of the cinematographer's. And while this potential moment of self-reflexivity brooks no indulgence from the self-effacing director of this modest thriller, it is perhaps significant that:

> Zinnemann's awareness of the connection has been memorialised in a special photograph he chose to include in his recent photographic memoir, showing his head posed in profile in front of the melon and between the cross hairs of the scope. Zinnemann's caption reads: 'I wonder if someone would have liked to pull the trigger?' (Michaels 1994: 104).

Woolf's keen eye for an appropriate property and his shrewd sense in exploiting the provisions of the Anglo-French coproduction agreement did much to boost the modest fortunes of the British international thriller well into the 1970s. And it promoted what might be described, if the term is not too inflated, as a European

Figure 3.1: Border Crossing: directed by Fred Zinnemann, *The Day of the Jackal* (1973) was a rare success for the Anglo-French Coproduction Agreement.
Copyright Universal / The Kobal Collection.

tourist aesthetic in terms of cinematography. As *Newsweek* magazine's critic Paul D. Zimmerman wrote of *The Day of the Jackal*: 'Zinnemann serves up handsome prospects, rococo edifices, sweeping coastlines and towering mountain scenery – a kind of cinematic coffee table book' (Zimmerman 1973: 85).

Conclusion

The film titles for which I have Department of Trade figures in the first half of the 1970s reveal a typically eclectic mix, bearing many of the much maligned hallmarks of Anglo-European coproduction. And across the decade, this diversity is pretty much the only constant.

During this period, when British domestic film production was at a particularly low ebb, a number of filmmakers returned to this production formula: Jack Gold and Joseph Losey each directed two Anglo-French pictures, while Lewis Gilbert managed three. These films range in nature from Gold's First World War flying adventure *Le Tigre du ciel / Aces High* (1976) starring Malcolm McDowell and Christopher Plummer, and his lamentable Richard Burton psychic-thriller *La Grande Menace / The Medusa Touch* (1978), to Losey's studied domestic dramas in both a contemporary and a literary vein: *Une Anglaise romantique* / *The Romantic Englishwoman* (1975) with Glenda Jackson and Michael Caine, and *Maison de poupée* (Ibsen's *A Doll's House*, 1973), starring the unlikely Jane Fonda opposite David Warner. Gilbert's Anglo-French projects were even more varied, including a French student romance (*Paul et Michelle*, 1974), an exotic far-eastern historical adventure (*Seven Nights in Japan*, 1976) and the Bond offering *Moonraker* (1977).

But these Anglo-French ventures and adventures, enjoying varying degrees of popular success, also exemplify the essentially pragmatic facility which coproduction treaties offer. As such, they have little to do with cultural exchange and everything to do with economic exigency. Note how the balance of majority funding shifted during the 1970s from French to British investment. This was not simply a matter of redressing the disequilibrium of the late 1960s. It was indicative of the shared awareness that prudent funding of medium-to-large-budget pictures with international appeal could be of mutual benefit to both partners. These were essentially British international pictures, in which the French (with their more lucrative state aid schemes) had a useful stake, in exchange for access to the English language market – conditions which pertained even with the advent of a European Coproduction Fund in the early 1990s (Jäckel 2003: 61). Yet in the great scheme of things, they amounted to little more than a drop in *la Manche*.

In 1975, the then Chairman of the British Film Producers' Association, Michael Relph, blamed the relative dearth of coproductions on British producers' tendency 'to be somewhat insular in their attitude' (Falk 1975: 1). By the end of the 1970s, British industry views had changed little. Relph's successor at the FPA, Ken Maidment, warned: 'It is only if you have the right sort of subject that coproductions should be sought' (Falk 1981: 15). Such caution from the enthusiasts for joint European ventures is an expression of deeper diplomatic rifts beneath the surface of Anglo-French cinematic relations. Quentin Falk, writing in the British trade journal *Screen International*, condemned what he called 'uneasy hybrids – often bastardized beyond recognition to fulfil the conditions necessary to bring home the bacon. And the truth is', he continued, 'that in the main, the bacon has resolutely remained on the counter' (Falk 1981: 15). But this value-for-money argument frequently aired in public was, in fact, something of a commercial smoke screen.

Government files at the National Archives show that the triumvirate of the FPA, the Department of Trade's Films Division and the FFU shared a fundamental mistrust of, and resistance to, Anglo-European cooperation. When, in 1973, French representatives of the CNC contacted their British counterparts to seek a meeting of the Mixed Commission (which had not been convened since 1970 – remembering that under the terms of the agreement they were obliged to meet annually), a Department of Trade internal memo reveals that the Films Division did not even know who their own representative was, the civil servant originally appointed to the role having changed jobs. Eventually, as a result of a protracted correspondence and several postponements, the Mixed Commission met in London on 27 April 1976, ostensibly to review the operation of the agreement thus far, and to discuss ways of improving its working. What Morris Dyson of the Films Division didn't anticipate were very clear French proposals to take advantage of European Commission directives, which relaxed trade barriers and employment laws, to pursue a much more radical vision of multilateral film collaboration – in fact, a revival of their original vision for film under the Treaty of Rome. Pierre Viot of the CNC proposed an international coproduction agreement between all nine member states, the harmonization of state film aid, and the establishment of a European film fund (to be underwritten by the banks of member states). Needless to say, by now this was a bridge too far for the British delegation. Government, film producers and trade union representatives were unanimous in rejecting the French proposals. Officially, they agreed to pursue multilateral European talks on these matters; privately, however, the government and industry feared deterring U.S. investment and offending Hollywood distributors. M. Boxall, a civil servant at the Department of Trade's Film Branch, wrote in an internal memo: 'While the benefits of such an alternative may be great for the industry in most European countries, they are more dubious for the British industry, given that its primary orientation (outside the home market) is not towards Europe, but towards North America'. He feared that 'the schemes proposed may prove counter-productive if it jeopardizes sales to English-speaking markets, for example by antagonizing the US majors who dominate those markets' (Boxall 1976: 4). The antipathy of the unions was far simpler: they resisted any initiatives which might 'lead to a deterioration in labour conditions and the integrity of national culture' (Mixed Commission 1976: 46).

The failure of this largely Franco-Italian-inspired, pan-European initiative hampered cooperation until the advent of the single market and the passing of the European Convention of Cinematographic Coproduction in 1992. And it led Britain's European partners, in the meantime, to pursue selective, rather than automatic, aid schemes to assist specific project funding, alongside their own bilateral agreements. By the late 1970s the Anglo-French treaty was effectively ignored by the handful of producers who ventured to market British-French projects with limited commercial appeal: for example, Roman Polanski's *Tess* (1979) and Merchant/Ivory's *Quartet* (1981). Writing in 1985, Vincent Porter summarized the sceptical views of many in wondering whether we were not

> destined to a future diet of Euroschlock where rootless characters pass through sanitized and anonymous environments of international expense-account hotels, airport lounges and offices, make love in anonymous golden cornfields as the Eurowheat waves gently in the breeze and speak to one another in any one of half a dozen badly dubbed tongues (Porter 1985: 6).

If Anglo-French film culture was largely saved from this dystopic future it was only because, as Anne Jäckel reports:

> After 1985, cultural, institutional and political differences prevailed. With, on the British side, a producer/scriptwriter approach, close links with Hollywood and a lack of incentives under a Conservative government which

appointed a new Minister for the Arts almost every year, and, on the French side, a directorial approach and the introduction of a new system of tax-shelter by a socialist government whose flamboyant Minister of Culture, Jack Lang, was openly committed to a programme of state intervention in the film industry, little wonder coproductions between France and Britain came to a halt for three years (Jäckel 1996: 88).

So much for the *entente cordiale*! One wonders whether – despite further European integration – post-unification, British cultural policy today remains as Janus-faced as ever, ambivalent in its views across both the Channel and the Atlantic. If so, this is a situation which, arguably, remains as detrimental to British film culture as it does to wider economic and political concerns.

Bibliography

Anon. 1961. 'Franco-German Rupture', *Le Film Français* 890, 9 June. Board of Trade library translation service, 3045/61/EL/French, BT/258/495: 52.

Boxall, M. 1976. 'Minute', 7 June. FV 81/100.

Bryant, R.C. 1957. 'Memorandum', 20 August. BT 258/495.

Elvin, G. 1961a. 'Editorial: European Coproduction', *Film and Television Technician* September, BT/258/495: 74.

———. 1961b. 'General Council in Session: European Common Market', *Film and Television Technician* October, BT/258/495: 99.

Falk, Q. 1975. 'UK Production Back into Gear', *Screen International*, 6–13 September: 1.

———. 1981. 'Whatever Happened to Coproduction?' *Screen International*, 21–28 February: 15.

Film Production Association of Great Britain and Federation of Film Unions. 1971. *Coproduction: A Guide to the Anglo-French and Anglo-Italian Coproduction Treaties*.

Filson, A. 1959. 'Prospects in the European Common Market', *Kinematograph Weekly*, 29 January: 3 and 10.

Golt, S. 1957. 'Films, the Treaty of Rome and the Free Trade Area'. 25 July. BT 258/495.

Harper, S. and V. Porter. 2003. *British Cinema of the 1950s: The Decline of Deference.* Oxford: Oxford University Press.

Hunnings, N. 1972. 'The Film Industry and the EEC', *Sight and Sound* 41(2): 82–85.

Jäckel, A. 1996. 'European Coproduction Strategies: The Case of France and Britain', in A. Moran (ed.), *Film Policy: International, National and Regional Perspectives.* London: Routledge, pp. 85–97.

———. 2003. *European Film Industries.* London: British Film Institute.

Kahn, H. 1957. 'Coproduction With Britain by 1960', *Kinematograph Weekly*, 12 December: 5.

Knight, G.S. 1957a. 'Memorandum'. 30 July. BT 258/495.

———. 1957b. 'Note'. 26 November. BT 258/495.

Lewin, D. 1972. 'Excitement: That's the Key to Success', *Cinema TV Today*, 2 September: 12–13.

Michaels, L. 1994. 'Shooting a Melon: The Target Practice Sequence in *The Day of the Jackal*', *Film Criticism* 18/19/(3/1): 101–107.

Michaud, P.R. 2005. 'The Lone Wolf and the Jackal', in G. Miller (ed.), *Fred Zinnemann: Interviews.* Jackson: University of Mississippi Press, pp. 31–36.

Mixed Commission. 1976. 'Notes of a Meeting of the France-United Kingdom Coproduction Agreement Mixed Commission Held in London on 27 April'. FV 57/28.

Page, R. 1971. '"Stand On Your Own Feet" Film Row', *Today's Cinema*, 2 July: 1.

Parmentier, E. (ed.). 1973. 'Day of the Jackal', *Filmfacts* 16(4): 81–85.

Porter, V. 1977. 'Television and Film Production in Europe', *Sight and Sound* 46(4): 205–207 and 251.

————. 1985. 'European Co-productions: Aesthetic and Cultural Implications', *Journal of Area Studies* 12(Autumn): 6–10.

Street, S. 2002. *Transatlantic Crossings: British Feature Films in the USA*. New York/London: Continuum.

UNESCO. 'Films and Cinema Statistics', *Motion Picture Almanac*. Films Branch files. BT 258/495.

Zimmerman, P.D. 1973. 'Film Review', *Newsweek*, 28 May, in E. Parmentier (ed.), 'Day of the Jackal', *Filmfacts* 16(4): 84–85.

Zinnemann, F. 1992. *An Autobiography*. London: Bloomsbury.

Filmography

A coeur joie / Two Weeks in September. 1967, Serge Bourguignon, U.K./France.

Anglaise romantique, Une / The Romantic Englishwoman. 1975, Joseph Losey, U.K./France.

Chacal / The Day of the Jackal. 1973, Fred Zinnemann, U.K./France.

Grande Menace, La / The Medusa Touch. 1978, Jack Gold, U.K./France.

High Noon. 1952, Fred Zinnemann, U.K.

Maison de poupée / A Doll's House. 1973, Joseph Losey, U.K./France.

Man for All Seasons, A. 1966, Fred Zinnemann, U.K.

Mayerling. 1968, Terence Young, U.K./France.

Moonraker. 1979, Lewis Gilbert, U.K./France.

Motocyclette, La / Girl on a Motorcycle. 1968, Jack Cardiff, U.K./France.

Nuit des géneraux, La / Night of the Generals. 1966, Anatole Litvak, U.K./France.

Paul et Michelle / Paul and Michelle. 1974, Lewis Gilbert, U.K./France.

Quartet. 1981, James Ivory, U.K./France.

Seven Nights in Japan. 1976, Lewis Gilbert, U.K./France.

Tess. 1979, Roman Polanski, U.K./France.

Tigre du ciel, Le / Aces High. 1976, Jack Gold, U.K./France.

CHAPTER 4

Channel-crossing Festivals: The Cases of the French Film Festival U.K. and Dinard's *Festival du Film Britannique*

Cécile Renaud

With the past twenty years having seen an unprecedented worldwide boom in the number of film festivals, events in Britain and France devoted to the national cinemas of the country across the Channel have emerged and, in some cases, flourished. In the last decade alone, British festivals focusing on French cinema have included the Martell French Film Tour of 1999 and 2000, the Renault French Film Season, the Rendez-Vous with French Cinema sponsored by Unifrance – the French organization responsible for promoting French cinema abroad – and the ephemeral London Carte Noire French Film Festival, which occurred only in 2002. Amongst these events, the French Film Festival U.K., which began in 1992, asserts a unique position as arguably the only British festival devoted exclusively to French cinema, a claim legitimized by its programming choices and longevity. Meanwhile in France two festivals have been created with a similarly exclusive focus on British cinema. In 1990, the small Brittany resort of Dinard hosted its inaugural *Festival du film britannique*, presented in the press as the first film festival in France devoted entirely to British cinema – despite the fact that the British Film Festival in Cherbourg was actually in its sixth year by this point (*Screen International*, 21 September 1990, p. 12).

There were fears that British film production, not at its healthiest at the time of the festival's inception (with only seventeen British films coming to completion in 1991 (Heymann 1992)), might not be sufficient to sustain two film festivals in the same month in such geographical proximity (Dobson 1991);[1] sure enough, Dinard quickly imposed itself as the main event, while the Cherbourg festival dwindled. Like the French Film Festival U.K., the *Festival du film britannique de Dinard* has strengthened its identity as an independent festival over the years, enduring and even expanding where many other events disappeared. For this reason, the two events will constitute the primary focus of this chapter, which will examine and compare the histories, identities and marketing strategies of the two festivals in order to elucidate the manners in which each focuses on the national cinema of their cross-Channel neighbours, and investigate what this might be able to tell us about contemporary attitudes to French cinema in Britain, and to British cinema in France.

Origins and Audiences

Although both festivals were set up to broaden the range of access that domestic audiences have to the national cinematic product of the other country, the two events have developed in very distinct manners. Neither, it must be admitted, has undertaken any thorough audience research; nonetheless it is possible to identify some of their target audiences through their organization and the discourses surrounding both events.

The French Film Festival U.K. is a multicity festival destined to show primarily French films which might not otherwise find distribution in Britain. It presents a selection of films which, having in many cases travelled the international festival circuit, have not been picked up by British distributors. Its stated remit is not to find distributors for these films, rather to offer a wide range of films to audiences who would otherwise have a more limited view of French cinema. As we will see over the course of this chapter, the French Film Festival U.K. caters to a large extent for existing Francophile and cinephile audiences: it is these groups, rather than mainstream audiences, who are targeted via the strategy of advertising the festival primarily in French cultural centres and art-house venues. Nonetheless, it has attempted over the years to broaden the appeal of French films shown in Britain, albeit in a limited capacity, notably by introducing popular comedies to its programming and screening them to audiences in cities such as Aberdeen or Dundee, outside the restricted circuit of London and the selected cities often adopted for releases of French films. Moreover, despite not featuring any industry-specific events (such as exclusive screenings, round tables or meeting spaces), the festival presents an opportunity to test out French films on British audiences and to gauge whether or not a specific film could find an audience on British territory, sometimes proving the appeal of the film to hesitant distributors.

Dinard's *Festival du film britannique*, on the other hand, was set up by the town mainly as a means to boost its cultural reputation and tourist appeal. With a much larger budget from its inception, and a link to the British film industry cemented by the chartering of a plane to bring the British delegation to the festival from its first year on, Dinard can appear to be significantly more industry-oriented than the French Film Festival U.K. Its appeal for local audiences, however, remains strong, with a total attendance of 27,000 in 2008, amongst which number only some five hundred were professionals from the cinema industry.[2] For both industry insiders and local star-spotters, one of Dinard's main points of appeal is the concentration of actors, directors and producers over four days in this small resort on the coast of

Brittany. In this respect, its tightly circumscribed location plays an important role: as producer Andreas Bajohra claims, 'because it is such a small place, you can see everyone at the same time' (Gallen 2001). While Bajohra is one of the British industry delegates drawn to the festival by the networking opportunities it provides, the hysterical crowds in the beach-front bars in 2000 for the French premiere of *Bridget Jones's Diary* (2001) were also mobilized by the opportunity to come into contact with key figures in the film industry, namely its stars. In this case, it was the much-publicized presence of Hugh Grant that served as a lure for the masses; his visit is one of several such occasions which have become part of the 'official' history of the festival, recounted in numerous newspaper articles (see for example *Ouest-France*, 1 August 2006, p. I).

The French Film Festival U.K. similarly claims to have included in its guest list over its seventeen years 'some of the starriest names in French cinema', as the 2006 programme states. However, Antoine de Caunes in 1998 and Jean Reno in 2006 aside,[3] the star status of most of those French celebrities within Britain is questionable: Josiane Balasko, Gérard Jugnot and Arnaud Despleschin in 1992; Jean-Paul Rappeneau in 1993; Agnès Varda in 1996; Pascale Ferran in 1997; Patrice Leconte, Olivier Dahan and Patrice Chéreau in 1998; Bertrand Blier in 2000; Sabine Azéma and Bertrand Tavernier in 2006; Sylvain Chomet and Christian Vincent in 2007 and Mevil Poupaud and Jean-Pierre Darroussin in 2008 – these are but a few figures who, while holding a distinct appeal for French audiences, might not be instantly recognisable as celebrities to the general British public. Their appeal may be stronger for Francophiles and cinephiles of course; but in this case, the deployment of 'celebrity' in service of publicity serves to only reinforce predominant discourses surrounding French cinema in the U.K., which take it as an esoteric, if not outright elitist, art form, accessible only to those 'in the know'. In any case, because the French Film Festival U.K. is set up to run in multiple cities simultaneously, the celebrity effect might be said to be somewhat diluted in this instance. With appearances scattered across the country, the concentration of stars which contributes to creating the 'buzz' of Dinard and other festivals is effectively eliminated.

Spatial Identities

Such geographical splitting necessarily affects the identity of a festival. In *Film Cultures,* Janet Harbord emphasizes 'the significance of the spatial for understanding festival events' (2002: 68), and demonstrates how, despite being transnational spaces of flow, film festivals are deeply rooted in locality, their identity linked to the location in which they are situated. In the case of Dinard, British culture and cinema were already an integral part of the town's identity even before the Festival's inception: Dinard owes much of its architecture and its wealth to nineteenth century British aristocrats who took to holidaying in the small resort, where Agatha Christie is said to have learned to swim (French 1999), and where Hitchcock used to spend his summers (Gritten 2006). The festival's national remit seems a natural fit for the location then; indeed, although Dinard is also the host of three other festivals – one for young fashion designers, one for stand-up comedians, and another for classical music in the summer – none of them are as visible as the British Film Festival. The first editions were organized by the Town Council itself, seeking glamour by association, and from the outset, the town contributed half of the £200,000 budget (Winn 1993). The statue of Hitchcock erected in 1993 on the beach-front promenade, a larger version of the prize statuettes, with birds on its shoulders in homage to his 1963 film, has subsequently become a permanent reminder of the link between the town's history and the festival.

As the issue of celebrity (non)presence suggests, unity of space – or rather its lack – is a more problematic point for the French Film Festival U.K. Although the festival has expanded steadily, some of its locations have come and gone over the years with sponsor changes. The festival started simultaneously in Edinburgh and Glasgow in 1992; it then spread to Aberdeen and Dundee in 1996, and extended beyond the borders of Scotland to London in 1999, and Manchester in 2003. In 2006, it joined up with the Renault French Film Season and spread to three further cities: Cardiff, Birmingham and Leeds. Those three new venues disappeared with the sponsor in 2007, although Birmingham and Cardiff rejoined the festival in 2008.

This geographical split makes for a somewhat amorphous identity; however, it is part of the remit of the French Film Festival U.K., the direct consequence of its organizers' aim to bring French films to audiences who would otherwise be unable to see them. In spreading the event as far and wide as possible, they maintain, a more diverse range of British cinema audiences can potentially be reached. Richard Mowe states that he and Alan Hunter cofounded the French Film Festival U.K. when they realized, after attending the European Cinema Awards in 1992, how underrepresented European cinema as a whole was in the U.K., especially outside London (Renaud 2007). They therefore decided to create their own festival in Scotland, highlighting one single national European cinema.[4] The organizers settled on French cinema since they knew there were sufficient audiences for French films in both Glasgow and Edinburgh.

The festival was therefore set up in two different cities with two very distinct identities, both with a strong cinematic tradition: while Edinburgh hosts the world's longest-running film festival, Glasgow harboured the first Scottish film society. Although the organizers' aim was to eventually extend the Festival further so as to reach the broadest audience possible, their decision to commence by showing French cinema, a national product described by Mazdon and Wheatley as 'the stalwart of foreign-language distribution' in the U.K. (Mazdon and Wheatley 2008: 39) to the highly cine-literate audiences of Scotland's two major cities belies to some extent their stated intentions. At the very least, in order to reach new audiences for French cinema in Britain, they were starting by engaging with the existing ones.

Be that as it may, the will to create a festival that would cater primarily to audiences outside the London area, in regions where audiences for foreign-language film, both existing and potential, were less well catered for, was at the core of the French Film Festival U.K. This might explain why the British capital city only joined the festival in its eighth year and why, today, the festival remains much more visible in its Scottish venues than in London, with extensive targeted advertising in venues associated with French culture, such as the *Alliance française* in Glasgow and the French Institute in Edinburgh, as well as posters and flyers placed in the universities and art-house venues. In London, where audiences for French cinema have at their disposal the widest range of films available in Britain, the festival, split between three venues, disappears in a myriad of more widely publicized events, and does not generate the same sense of anticipation as it does in the Scottish cities. Richard Mowe claims nevertheless that the growing presence of the French Film Festival U.K. in London is essential to its financial survival: having a London showcase for the festival is particularly important to the festival's sponsors, who are mainly based in the London area and whose contribution can be substantially enhanced by the presence of the festival in the capital city (Renaud 2007).

If location defines a festival, the French Film Festival U.K. was, then, at risk of lacking a clear identity from its very inception. This issue has affected other French cinema-oriented events in the United Kingdom. In fact, the identity of the Martell French Film Tour, for instance, cannot be dissociated from its eponymous sponsor, so much so that it might not be obvious that the Martell French Film Tour did not exactly disappear in 2001 but was merely carried on by a different sponsor and with a different name as the Renault French Film Season. It might also have gone unnoticed that after a brief alliance with the French Film Festival U.K. in 2006, the Renault event continued the following year under the name Rendez-Vous with French Cinema and sponsored by Unifrance. These events cannot be considered to have a stable identity, as their names and shape have changed many times over the years, none of them claiming the legacy of their predecessors. In this respect, the French Film Festival U.K. has managed to keep its identity distinct from those of its sponsors, with the exception of the 2006 event, which saw the programme foreground the main sponsor and announce the Renault French Film Festival.

That year, the festival also took the decision to change the time of year that it ran, moving from autumn to spring, a format it kept for two years before reverting to an autumn slot for its 2009 edition. This decision was taken to suit Unifrance's desire to couple the French Film Festival U.K. with the Rendez-Vous with French Cinema event promoting French films with British distributors, thus creating a one-stop event for French cinema in Britain. Unifrance recognized the potential of the French Film Festival in the promotion and the dissemination of French films in the U.K.: in combining the promotion of upcoming releases with gala screenings – for which the programme promised: 'Actors and directors will be in attendance in packed cinemas, and many top journalists and television crews will talk to them' – as well as the traditional programming of the French Film Festival U.K., the 2006 edition was able to become more media-friendly without losing its appeal for local audiences. The link was abandoned the following year, however, with changes in the French organization, and instead 2007 saw the Unifrance event stand alone in the British capital before disappearing in 2008. Unifrance continues to provide help by organizing the guest appearances of French actors and directors in the French Film

Festival U.K., which now bridges the gap created by the disappearance of the Unifrance events, to some extent at least: as it had done in 2006, the 2008 festival included a preview section within its programme, advertising the upcoming release of seven titles by various British distributors, with special screenings in the presence of actors and directors. It is a promotional exercise very similar to the one undertaken until then by the Unifrance/Renault event.

Programming and Sponsorship

Despite the changes in scheduling as well as structure (which could have had an adverse effect on the festival, destabilizing its already precarious identity still further), the popularity of the French Film Festival U.K. has been growing steadily over the last sixteen years. Audiences have grown from three thousand in 1992 to fifteen thousand in 2008, while the number of venues has risen from two in two cities in 1992 to thirteen spread across ten different cities in 2008. This expansion can perhaps be attributed in part to the fact that the festival does not merely give previews of French films due for release in Britain, as is the case for all the similar endeavours mentioned above. Rather, the French Film Festival U.K. offers a unique opportunity to see films which might never be commercially released in Britain, offering these works a very limited theatrical run within the structure of the festival, mainly for the benefit of local audiences, but also in the hope that their success in that short period of time might grab the attention of distributors and tempt them into buying the film (Renaud 2007). Some of those films may have had additional screenings in Britain within the London Film Festival or the Edinburgh International Film Festival. However, this group represents only 20 per cent of the films shown in the French Film Festival U.K. since 2001. It is in this respect that the French Film Festival U.K. goes beyond the French tours or seasons already organized in Britain to constitute a festival, an event at which audiences can see films which might not otherwise be shown in Britain, let alone receive distribution.

Dinard similarly selects for its competition section films which are likely to have problems finding French distributors. Its highest prize, the *Hitchcock d'or*, offers €3,000 to be spent on French distribution, as well as a free extra print of the winning film, and a personal grant for the director of €1,600.[5] The *Festival du film britannique de Dinard* has always been keen to innovate and show films which might not get distribution even in Britain, although it also includes a showcase selection, premiering films which have already found French distributors, offering a national media platform for their upcoming French release, since the festival is usually covered by the major national newspapers such as *Le Monde* or *Libération* as well as receiving extensive coverage in regional newspapers. This showcasing of major British films does not, however, betray the original aim of the festival. The selection for the competition typically involves six British films, mostly from young directors, with largely unknown casts. The showcase of twenty to thirty bigger productions, bringing more famous directors and actors to Dinard, adds glamour to the festival, thus giving by association more publicity to smaller films in competition.

The Dinard festival has, from its inception, been involved in reinvigorating British production, organizing round tables, discussing the problems faced by the British industry and provoking policy changes, most notably in loosening the conditions of access to French funding for coproductions in terms of shooting language and nationality of technicians (Pham 1991). It aims to broaden the visibility of British cinema in France and the rest of Europe, inviting to the festival – with the help of the U.K. Film Council – distributors from most European countries and other territories. Producer Sally Hibbin reported that *Yasmin* (2004), winner of the Silver Hitchcock in 2004, owes its British distribution, albeit limited to television and DVD, to its performance in the festival (quoted in Jeffries 2005). Despite positive reviews following its Edinburgh screening, the film had indeed failed to secure British theatrical distribution, although it was subsequently picked up for cinema release in numerous European countries including France, Germany, Switzerland and the Netherlands, as well as in Brazil.

A high-profile event such as Dinard requires major funding and stars to help secure sponsors seeking glamour by association. Sponsors of the *Festival du film britannique de Dinard* feature mainly in the glossy programme in the form of adverts, but an important part of its funds are secured from Dinard's Town Council, as well as the *Centre national de la cinématographie* (CNC) and its British equivalent, the U.K. Film Council. The French Film Festival U.K., on the other hand, does not receive as much benefit from the public sector as its French counterpart, and therefore depends to a greater extent on private sponsorship. Even though the sponsors do not play the same eponymous role in the French Film Festival U.K. as in the Martell French Film Tour, for instance, its partners still appear on the brochures, listed on a double page as well as in the adverts. Cognac brands thus seem to have had a strong presence in the dissemination of French cinema in Britain. Martell had its own tour, but the French Film Festival U.K. was in early years sponsored by Hennessy and even incorporated Cognac-tasting sessions and the Hennessy Prize, given by the audience to the best first or second film screened in the festival. While Hennessy is no longer a sponsor, it has been replaced by the wine brand Blason de Bourgogne, including once again free tasting sessions after screenings. Grand Marnier also sponsors both festivals. All in all, most of the sponsors of the French Film Festival U.K. evoke a certain idea of continental luxury (wine and liqueurs obviously, but also Ligne Roset and its designer furniture, and the delicatessen company Tray Gourmet), conforming to a great extent with existing stereotypes of France. It is a somewhat paradoxical strategy, reiterating active perceptions of French cinema as part of an attempt to broaden audiences for it, and it is one which may extend into iterations of the films themselves, with the synopses of the films occasionally appearing to play upon preconceptions of French sensuality and a longstanding reputation for producing risqué cinema (see Mazdon and Wheatley 2008). This is especially true of earlier editions of the programme. For instance, the 1995 programme introduces *A la folie* (1994) as: 'A classic French sexual melodrama', and the 1997 programme presents *La Femme défendue* (1997) as belonging to 'the classic tradition of French cinema, dealing with a married man's covert affair with a younger woman'. Here, it seems the adjective 'classic' is applied less to the films' form, genre or canonical status than to the narrative trope described, the implication being that French film has a long history of sexual provocation.

Far from shying away from stereotypes of French cinema, then, it seems the French Film Festival U.K. even exploits them in the name of attracting audiences. To what extent this has been successful is uncertain, but it is informative in this regard that Hussam Hindi, director of Dinard's *Festival du film britannique* since the mid 1990s, similarly deploys contemporary stereotyped perceptions of French and British cinema in order to advertise the festival. Perceptions of British cinema in France tend to be

Figure 4.1: Publicity material for the eighteenth *Festival du film britannique de Dinard*, 4–7 October 2007.

divided between social realism, partly generating the view sometimes found in the French press of British films as bleak and taxing,[6] and lighthearted comedy, which the *Festival du film britannique* has also highlighted in recent years within its programmes. Hindi is thus repeatedly quoted in the French press underlining the lighter side of British films and presenting British cinema as the alternative to French cinema: 'We like them [British films] because they're youthful, humorous and relevant .... In contrast, French cinema is bourgeois. It turns away from social issues. There's a lot of navel-gazing. Our films have beautiful people doing ordinary things. In Britain, you have ordinary-looking people achieving the extraordinary' (quoted in Gritten 2006).

Hindi also highlights the commonly held belief that British films tend to do better in France than in Britain. One proof often cited in support of this claim is the number of prints of Ken Loach's films that circulate in each country: *Land and Freedom* (1995), for example, was shown in 150 cinemas in France against fifty-three in Britain (Jenkins 2008). Similarly, Mike Leigh's *Secret and Lies* (1996) gathered as much in one weekend in France as it did in the whole of its British theatrical exhibition, according to producer Andrew Eaton (Vezin 1996) – a remarkable statistic given that this was one of Leigh's more successful films in the U.K. Both festivals thus attempt to challenge the traditional image of French and British cinema, in their programming as well as their presentation. Indeed, the French Film Festival U.K. presented, from its first year, both popular genre films and art-house films, featuring in the same year the Josiane Balasko / Daniel Auteuil comedy *Ma Vie est un enfer / My Life is Hell* (1991) on the programme cover, as well as screening Arnaud Desplechin's first film: *La Vie des morts* (1991). The 2007 edition similarly showed the hugely popular *Camping* (2006), as well as presenting on the same page in the brochure *OSS 117: Le Caire, nid d'espions / OSS 117: Cairo, Nest of Spies* (2006) – a James Bond type spoof – and the more challenging 'art-house' film *Le Pont des Arts* (2004).

The programme sections are themselves symptomatic of this attempt to confront the popular equation of French cinema with auteur cinema. The festival programme contains three main sections. The Panorama section features films from established names in French cinema, and although these will often be directors, they will also sometimes be actors. The second main section was entitled New Waves until the name was changed to Discovery in 2006, in what might be considered a move away from the influence of the New Wave on British perceptions of French cinema; it is dedicated to first and second features. Until 2006 and the introduction of the Gala Screenings, subsequently renamed the Preview section, the Retrospective was the only section featuring films which might already have found British distribution. The choices for retrospectives have also tried to move away from a traditional auteurist vision of French cinema. Although its focus on one individual lends itself to the celebration of recognized auteurs such as Agnès Varda and Bertrand Tavernier, less famous directors, such as Christian Vincent, and actors, notably Alain Delon in 2004, have also been included in an attempt at least to broaden the definition of French 'auteurs'. The format of the published programme also attempts to veer away from the auteur tradition. In the very first editions of the French Film Festival U.K., film synopses have featured biographies; while these often focused on the director, they regularly included the main actor, the score composer or the scriptwriter. Dinard's programme information, on the other hand, focuses solely on the director in a more explicitly auteurist fashion. Interestingly, these inserts seem to have disappeared from the programmes of the French Film Festival U.K. after 2004, to be replaced in the latest programmes with easily digestible quotes in English from the International, British and French press (*Variety, Le Monde, Time Out* and *Cahiers du cinéma*, for instance). It is a change which can perhaps be seen as a further attempt to move away from a certain idea of French cinema as 'high brow' and elitist.

It is telling, too, that the linguistic format of the programme has also changed greatly over the years. Originally featuring the titles in French first, followed by the English translation, this format has been reversed since 2004 in an attempt to make the films, as well as their titles, more accessible to non-French speakers. The earlier programmes tended to integrate more French phrases, the cover page always featuring a French slogan: '*Vive le Cinéma*' for the first two editions; '*La Passion du*

Figure 4.2: Publicity material for the 2008 French Film Festival U.K., 7–20 March. Image courtesy of French Film Festival UK / Richard Mowe.

cinéma' in 1995; '*Le Cinéma en fête*' in 1996; '*C'est du cinéma!*' in 1997. The 1998 issue even featured a two-page article on René Clair entirely in French. As well as becoming progressively glossier and sleeker as the numbers of attendees and locations have grown, the French Film Festival U.K. programme has also reduced the amount of French text in an attempt to appeal to non-French speakers and lend greater accessibility to the films. Dinard's festival literature, meanwhile, from the programme to the daily festival newspaper, has adopted a bilingual approach and includes a French as well as an English version of every feature. In ensuring all festival literature appears in both languages, the festival's dual audience is thus catered for: the British film industry and the local filmgoers.

The concern with language does not end here. For the organizers of both festivals, the broadening of the target audience also implies educating viewers, exposing them to foreign-language films, so they become accustomed to subtitles at an early stage. Pre-festival school screenings are organized in Dinard, where every year six thousand seats are filled by French pupils coming to see British films. The French Film Festival U.K. has chosen to take the films to the pupils and at the end of the festival further screenings are organized in Scottish schools, complete with film packages for class discussion set up by the Glasgow office of the *Alliance française*. In 1995 two different versions of *Un Indien dans la ville / Little Indian, Big City* (1994) were presented to a school screening in the Glasgow Film Theatre. The children were shown both the subtitled and the dubbed version and Richard Mowe recounts that they preferred the former, as the American dubbing seemed both out of synch and confusing, since the action was set in Paris (Renaud 2007). Screenings and events are also organized in association with Glasgow and Edinburgh Universities, with some of the guests giving talks and participating in Q&As, for example Bertrand Tavernier's attendance at an event hosted by the University of Glasgow in 2006.

The French Film Festival U.K. works on educating younger generations of British filmgoers, then, and in so doing it aims to expand the potential British audiences for foreign-language films in general. This issue concerns the festival organizers even more since they created Cinéfrance. Established in 2001, this distribution company specialized at first in French films and changed its name to Cinéfile in 2004 after broadening its scope to include other foreign-language cinemas. The festival also provides a test platform for films of interest for Cinéfile distribution, as was for instance the case with *Change of Address / Changement d'adresse* (2006). Similarly, through its support for British cinema during the difficult period of the early 1990s, Dinard has become an essential event in the distribution of British films in France. It has also proven a key moment for film production thanks to the various encounters between filmmakers during the festival, as was the case for *Babymother* (1998) (Malcolm 1998), or more recently the Franco-British coproduction *Sous les bombes / Under The Bombs* (2007) (Jury 2008).

Conclusion

The French Film Festival U.K. and the Dinard *Festival du film britannique* embody two different approaches to a similar goal: to screen and promote a better understanding of the cinematic culture from across the Channel. If the Dinard event has opted for a more concentrated, industry-intensive formula, the French Film Festival U.K. has aimed at spreading itself broadly to reach audiences; yet both have offered programmes extending existing perceptions of French and British cinema. As for the future, the French Film Festival U.K. does not seem threatened in any way, with growing audience figures and ever larger venues. The event broadened its reach in 2008 in a partnership with television exhibition, when the Sky Arts channel programmed a series of French films throughout March to accompany the festival. It does suffer from common festival issues with funding and logistics, but technological developments seem to favour festival logistics as well as foreign-language film exhibition as a whole. The use of digital technology has already been a great help in the promotion of the French Film Festival U.K. Digital trailers for the festival are now screened in the various venues, a promotional strategy which would not have been affordable had this technology not become widespread. Similarly, digital screening of the films themselves, although still subject to problems in some venues and with some directors, should, once standardized, help reduce the cost of subtitled prints, and therefore minimize the risks taken by small distributors of foreign-language films. In terms of festival logistics, they would also allow the French Film Festival U.K. to spread to even more locations and virtually remove their main expenditure and logistical difficulty: print transportation. The future of Dinard's *Festival du film britannique* seems similarly bright despite talks of a future Franco-British film festival in Bergerac (Vezin 2008). Originally a three-day event, the Dinard festival had to be extended over a four-day period to accommodate crowds more numerous every year. In an era marked by the proliferation of festivals, the longevity perhaps of those two events epitomizes the popularity of specialized events in the ever growing international film festival circuit, as well as offering a surprisingly sunny perspective on the current state of Franco-British cinematic relations.

Notes

1. Despite Dinard being in Brittany and Cherbourg in Normandy, the two locations are actually just over seventy-three miles apart on the same coastline.
2. Figures published on the official website of the *Festival du film britannique* under the heading: '*19e Festival: Bilan positif*'. Retrieved 20 February 2009 from http://www.festivaldufilm-dinard.fr/
3. Although De Caunes was scheduled to appear at the Glasgow events of 1998, he did not in fact attend. However, he was present at the Edinburgh events.
4. They later went on to set up the Italian Film Festival which is, at the time of writing, still running – although not on the same kind of scale as the French Film Festival U.K.

5. Those figures are for 2008; for comparison the prize for 1991 was FF30,000.
6. In 2006, a series of articles in the French press had for instance such titles as 'La vie en noir [Life in the dark]' (*Le Figaro*, 09 October 2006) and 'Un cinéma brut de décoffrage [A rough and uninspiring cinema]' (*Ouest-France*, 09 October 2006).

Bibliography

Dobson, P. 1991. 'UK Films Bask in French Glow', *Screen International*, 1 November: 8.

French, P. 1999. 'Brits Take Plaudits by the Seaside', *The Observer*, 10 October: 8.

Gallen, C. 2001. 'Dinard, rendez-vous d'un cinéma britannique dans le creux de la vague', *Agence France Presse*, 6 October.

Gritten, D. 2006. 'Vivent les Rosbifs! A Small Town in France Has Developed a Taste for British Film', *Daily Telegraph*, 14 October: 16.

Harbord, J. 2002. 'Film Festivals: Media Events and Spaces of Flow', in J. Harbord (ed.), *Film Cultures*. London: Sage, pp. 59–75.

Heymann, D. 1992. 'Entente Cordiale pour sa troisième édition, le Festival du film britannique de Dinard a confirmé son utilité et sa cohérence', *Le Monde*, 29 August.

Jeffries, S. 2005. 'Coming to a Small Screen Near You', *The Guardian*, 13 January: 16.

Jenkins, D. 2008. 'Do Britflicks Work Abroad?', *Time Out*, 13 February: 82.

Jury, L. 2008. 'No Script, No Money, Just Two Stars and a War', *Evening Standard*, 27 March: 41.

Malcolm, D. 1998. 'Dinard is Served', *The Guardian*, 8 October: 10.

Mazdon, L. and C. Wheatley. 2008. 'Intimate Connections', *Sight and Sound* 18(5): 38–40.

Pham, A. 1991. 'Dinard, deux fois plus de spectateurs qu'en 1990', *Le Film français*, 11 October: 41.

Renaud, C. 2007. *Interview with Richard Mowe, Director of the French Film Festival UK.* Recording and transcription University of Southampton.

Vezin, A. 1996. 'Les Films britanniques en majesté à Dinard', *Le Monde*, 10 October.

———. 2008. 'Bergerac mérite son festival', *Sud Ouest*, 22 July.

Winn, D. 1993. 'Brit Flicks and Finesse', *The Guardian*, 23 August: 11.

Filmography

A la Folie. 1994, Diane Kurys, France.

Babymother. 1998, Julian Henriques, U.K.

Birds, The. 1963, Alfred Hitchcock, U.S.A.

Bridget Jones's Diary. 2001, Sharon Maguire, U.K.

Camping. 2006, Fabien Onteniente, France.

Change of Address / Changement d'adresse. 2006, Emmanuel Mouret, France.

Femme défendue, La. 1997, Philippe Harel, France.

Femme française, Une / A French Woman. 1995, Régis Wargnier, France.

Indien dans la ville, Un / Little Indian, Big City. 1994, Hervé Palud, France.

Land and Freedom. 1995, Ken Loach, U.K.

Ma Vie est un enfer / My Life is Hell. 1991, Josiane Balasko, France.

OSS 117: Le Caire nid d'espions / OSS 117: Cairo Nest of Spies. 2006, Michel Hazanavicius, France.

Pont des Arts, Le. 2004, Eugène Green, France.

Secrets and Lies. 1996, Mike Leigh, U.K.
Under The Bombs / Sous les bombes. 2007, Philippe Aractingi, France/U.K.
Vie des morts, La. 1991, Arnaud Despleschin, France.
Yasmin. 2004, Kenneth Glenaan, U.K.

CHAPTER 5

The Language of Love? How the French Sold *Lady Chatterley's Lover* (Back) to British Audiences

Catherine Wheatley

In November 1960, while the British courts were still debating the censorship of D.H. Lawrence's infamous 1928 novel, *Lady Chatterley's Lover* had already been available to certain sections of the British public for some four years in the form of Marc Allégret's 1955 film adaptation (released in the U.K. in 1956). Starring Danielle Darrieux in the titular role, Allégret's was the first of three adaptations of Lawrence's novel to be produced with (largely) French funds and helmed by a French director – the other two being Just Jaeckin's 1981 softcore pornographic version featuring *Emmanuelle* star Sylvia Kristel, and, more recently, female director Pascale Ferran's *Lady Chatterley / Lady Chatterley et l'homme des bois*, which was heralded as an art-house hit by British critics and, according to one critic, offered 'proof that French really is the language of love (and sometimes lust)' (Russell 2007).

As Louis K. Greiff points out in his book-length study of Lawrence on film, *Lady Chatterley's Lover* is the most adapted of Lawrence's works (2001: 16). It is also unique within the Lawrentian canon as the only work to have been filmed in a language other than English (in addition to the French adaptations, there are Italian and Japanese versions, and even a Philippine film in existence) (Greiff 2001: 17). One might well ask, then, why it is that arguably the most English of Lawrence's novels – one essentially bound up with questions of class and language – has spawned two foreign-language adaptations, while his other, less nationally specific works, have failed to travel?[1] One obvious explanation for the appeal of Lawrence's novel to foreign filmmakers may of course have to do with its once outrageous sexual content. Yet by contemporary standards the book itself seems rather tame, its scurrilous reputation having been buoyed up by the various screen adaptations which have used the book's provocative history as a launch pad for their own promotional campaigns, thus perpetuating a myth of explicitness which may otherwise have faded with time. As the distributors of these films know only too well, sex sells. And as we shall see, it has played a significant role in selling French versions of *Lady Chatterley's Lover*, shot through as they are with that country's own reputation for sensuality and scandal, back to the British.

If sex is inescapably bound up with the Chatterley myth, however, its links to the cinema may be just as insidious, as Tanya Krzywinska suggests in her introduction to *Sex in the Cinema*: 'whether sold directly as a sex film or couched in the generic trappings of romance, art cinema, comedy, crime, tragedy, high fantasy or melodrama, sex and sexuality have proved a primary means to sell films to potential audiences throughout cinema history' (Krzywinska 2006: 2). Sex in the cinema, Krzywinska goes on to state, is framed and contextualized by a dizzying number of factors, some of which are formal and media-specific and others institutional and conceptual. 'In exploring the factors that shape the cinematic representation of sex and sexuality', she posits, 'it is possible to build a picture of the way that the various facets of such representations are keyed into and fashioned by broader contexts' (Krzywinska 2006: 6). It will be my contention here that the French origins of these three films are just such a factor, and it is therefore precisely such an exploration that will constitute the body of what follows within this essay, which will examine not the representation of sex within the films themselves, but within their marketing campaigns. The frameworks within which it will be considered are both national and historical: what, I shall ask, can the ways in which sex is used to sell these three versions of *Lady Chatterley's Lover*, bound together as they are by nation and inspiration, tell us about the film culture of the periods in question? How are the films' explicit contents married to British national stereotypes of the French and their films in their marketing campaigns? What other preconceptions might be being exploited in promoting French adaptations of Lawrence's novel to British audiences? And what can this begin to tell us about Franco-British cinematic relations over a period of some fifty years?

'They dared to film the book they banned!': Melodrama and the X Certificate

The 1950s was a period of rapid progression in terms of the representation of sex on both sides of the Channel, as well as, of course, across the Atlantic. With television luring audiences away from film theatres, sex started to be strategically deployed in order to mark a distinction between competing media, and the lure of erotic sensationalism – hitherto more commonly used to market exploitation films that were less stringently regulated than mainstream cinema – became a primary selling technique (see Klinger 1994: 37–41). Films such as *Baby Doll* (1956) and *Written on the Wind* (1958) from the U.S.A. (what Barbara Klinger refers to as 'adult melodramas'), and from France, Roger Vadim's *Et Dieu créa la femme / And God Created Woman* (1956) were pitched to U.K. audiences through sensational advertising campaigns which suggested an unprecedented level of sexual content for mainstream films.

In fact, as Krzywinska points out, many films of the era have far less sexual content than their advertising suggests. It is a view anticipated in the comments of Dr H.P. Newsholme, Medical Officer for the City of Birmingham, speaking at a meeting convened by the Birmingham Cinema Enquiry Committee on 7 November 1939, to discuss the cinema and its influence:

> One can say, I think without great hesitation, that [the blemish of sex obsession] is put on to the Cinema Posters, and on their hoardings, but that those posters are actually in many cases an exaggeration of elements in the films themselves, they are an exaggeration which simply is intended to appeal to the appetites or to the itch for sensation ... to just recruit custom for cinemas.[2]

Dr Newsholme may have a valid point. For while regulation of course has had a profound shaping effect on film, it also has a profound shaping effect on audience tastes: by outlawing certain topics and types of films, censorship bodies also consolidate the encoding of them as more intensely transgressive – and this is a factor regularly capitalized upon in the marketing of certain films as what one might term 'forbidden fruit'. So it is that since the introduction of censorship practice exploitation films have traded on 'what the censors didn't want you to see'.

Columbia, the U.K. distributors of Marc Allégret's adaptation of *Lady Chatterley's Lover*, were particularly fortunate in this regard – as they were able were to benefit from a dual censorship context. The first of these contexts is of course the ban placed on the original text (whose lasting fame, as one critic put it, 'is almost entirely due to the fact that literary censorship in England is controlled not by taste but by the Home Secretary and those subtle aesthetes, the Metropolitan police' – *The Daily Mail*, 1956); the second is the film's hard-won X certificate. At the time this was still something of a novelty, the certificate having only been introduced in 1951. Prior to this, only two classification categories existed in Britain – U 'for all ages', and A 'recommended only for those over 16'. The X was introduced by the British Board of Film Classification (BBFC) to allow the censors a 'third way', between passing films as family friendly (a move which regularly entailed severe cuts) or issuing an outright ban. From 1951 onwards, a great number of works that would have otherwise faced such a ban were thus able to be shown in British cinemas, albeit to a restricted audience.

In fact, *L'Amant de Lady Chatterley* was only passed in the U.K. after extensive cuts totalling some fifteen minutes (I.I. 1956: 102); but while the BBFC wrestled with these editorial changes, the press machine was already in motion, with papers speculating as to whether British audiences would ever be allowed to see the screen version of D.H. Lawrence's notorious novel. Coming on the heels of this 'advance hype', the X certificate played a central role in the film's promotional campaign.[3] The U.K. posters for *L'Amant de Lady Chatterley* feature an image of a bare-shouldered Danielle Darrieux lying in a prone position, her eyes gazing dreamily into the middle-distance, with Erno Crisa's (as Mellors) head placed suggestively on her chest, apparently sheltering what would be her otherwise exposed breasts from the viewer's gaze. Across its top, a banner reads, 'They dared to film the book they banned', while an X is displayed prominently after the title. Smaller, 'teaser' advertisements for the film for placement in magazines and newspapers feature only the title, the certificate, and a series of strap lines, bearing legends such as: 'The story they said they could never be filmed'; 'Xactly what every woman wants'; 'There's something Xceptional about Lady Chatterley's Lover'; 'A Challenge to Every Husband... A Charmer for Every Woman' (Columbia Distributors 1956). Meanwhile, advertisements taking the form of short notes were placed in magazines such as *Today's Cinema*, bearing the text: '...and I can't wait, darling, until we meet again at the Curzon. I want you. I want you. I want you. Always.... Lady Chatterley

Figure 5.1: Publicity material for *L'Amant de Lady Chatterley* (1955), featured in *Today's Cinema*. Image courtesy of the BFI stills department.

X' (6 July, 1956). Here the letter X bears a dual significance, functioning both as a symbol – an iconic representation of a kiss – and a sign – a bearer of information about the film's classification and therefore an indication of its explicit content.

In addition to placing these advertisements with the press, the distributors issued an advice leaflet suggesting a numbers of 'stunts' that exhibitors could perform in order to raise the film's profile still further, including the delivery of the placement of personal advertisements in local newspapers reading, 'Who is Lady Chatterley?'/ 'Lady Chatterley can be seen at (Cinema, leave date out)' / 'Don't Miss Lady Chatterley at ... Theatre next week'; the display of a mock dictionary in the cinema foyer, turned to R and with the entry (to be viewed through an attached magnifying glass) stating, 'You'll find Romance here... in *Lady Chatterley's Lover*, next week'; and, most amusingly perhaps, the distribution of hundreds of small envelopes overprinted on the front with the words 'Don't show this to your wife or girl friend' and bearing a card which read, 'Be sure and see me at [Theatre] on [Date] – Lady Chatterley'. A press release, issued to magazines and newspapers, perhaps sums up the saucy tone of the marketing, its closing pun playing on the Mitfordian jargon of the English upper classes, but also making another, sly dig at the censorship system:

> Noblesse très Obiglant! [sic]
> That much-banned, but very widely-read novel, Lady Chatterley's Lover, has now been filmed by Columbia pictures and had rave notices after its British premier engagement in London. Danielle Darrieux and Leo Genn co-star in 'Lady Chatterley's Lover' – which is based on the hotly-controversial D.H. Lawrence story about the marital problems of a titled English couple. It's a story of noblesse obligé to carry on the line, but the husband thinks she's carrying on too far, when the other man in the case is a gamekeeper (played by Italian actor Erno Crisa).
> Definitely non-U, in fact! (Columbia Distributors 1956).

The promotion of *L'Amant de Lady Chatterley* typifies a pattern of exploitation (or we might say, X-ploitation) within the distribution of French and Continental cinema common in Britain during the 1950s. The vast majority of the first films passed under the banner of the X were foreign-language films, a phenomenon which can be attributed to a number of factors. First, many English-language films were made with an eye on the still strictly censored U.S. exhibition context. Second, since British and American films were often (self-)censored at script stage, there were, at the time of the X's introduction, very few products in existence that would 'merit' the higher rating. Third was the fact of an already-existing body of continental film texts which would, on the other hand, fit the criteria for the X certificate with ease: since continental censors were much more permissive about sexual content than their British counterparts (with politics, as Daniel Bil27teryst's chapter in this volume suggests, being the more prominent factor in debates about what could be shown on screen in France, Germany and Italy for example), films with comparatively explicit sexual content were readily available from Europe for import.

Yet if the X ushered in what Tom Dewe Mathews refers to as 'a new golden age of World Cinema' (Dewe Mathews 1994: 126), it was France that was first through the door. In a piece written for *Public Opinion* in 1951, Paul Rotha claims that Nicole Védrès' *La Vie commence demain* (ironically a politically, rather than sexually, contentious work) had the 'doubtful' honour of being the first X certificate in 1951 (Rotha 1951: 164). It was swiftly followed the same year by Claude Autant-Lara's bedroom farce *Occupe-toi d'Amélie / Keep an Eye on Amelia* (1949) and Max Ophüls's *La Ronde* (1950) – both starring Danielle Darrieux. According to an article in *Sight and Sound* in Spring 1954, of the seventy-two films issued an X certificate in the first three years of its existence, more than one-third of these were French (Anon 1954).

Given its figurehead status in the new category of X-certified films in Britain, it is hardly surprising that at this point in history French cinema came to be associated almost inextricably with this rating, and by extension with the more sensationalist fare it denoted. In her detailed overview of the X's impact on the status of French film in 1950s Britain, Lucy Mazdon cites Dilys Powell, who describes the 'slippage' which 'occurs between the X as applied to truly sensational cinema (of which a fair number are French and other foreign sex films of one kind or another)' and the X as 'a valuable minority legislation in an industry that seldom caters for minorities' (Mazdon 2008: 9). Since during this period some newspapers were still refusing to review foreign films, Mazdon notes, 'an X certificate was considered [amongst some distributors] the only way to sell a continental film' (Halliwell 1956: 24). Little wonder that the critic for *The Times* in 1956 was so quick to draw the link between French film and the X rating when he wrote that, 'Since *Lady Chatterley's Lover* is the most scandalous ... of the novels of D.H. Lawrence and automatically qualifies for "X" certificate, popular reasoning will find it suitable that it should be made into a film in French' (Anon 1956a). Hinting at the paradoxical nature of a situation in which a scandalous British novel becomes ideal fodder for a risqué French film which is then sold back to the British public through the added 'scandal' of the X certificate, the quotation reveals the complex nature of the Anglo-French interchange surrounding Allégret's adaptation of Lawrence's novel.

The industrial tendency to exploit the X for commercial gain swiftly led to circumstances in which foreign-language film became economically viable only when branded with the X: so much so that when London's Cameo-Polytechnic refused to show X certificates on moral grounds, 'much of the profitable continental product' thus became unavailable to them, and it found itself at a severe market disadvantage (Mazdon 2008). But while the Cameo-Polytechnic stuck steadfastly to the principles of its board of directors – consequences be damned – the cinema which premiered Allégret's film, the Curzon, was swift to capitalize upon the X's box-office potential. Following its inauguration in 1934, the Curzon carved a niche for itself as an exhibitor of continental films and latterly of provocative works, exhibiting many of the first X-certificated films and continuing to associate itself with 'risqué' foreign-language film up to the 1980s, when its then-director Roger Wingate enforced a turn towards independent British film and high-brow heritage film. Throughout its history of X-ploitation, French cinema has remained a *cause célèbre* for the Curzon:

having exhibited *La Ronde* to great public debate (and interest) in 1951,[4] it caused a scandal in 1967 when it opened *Belle de jour* and in 1973 the cinema was taken to court by Mary Whitehouse for showing *La Grande Bouffe* (Wingate 2009).

It is surely no coincidence that the three films were some of the Curzon's greatest money spinners (Wingate 2009), for it should be clear from the above that a film's X-rated status could play a central role in the image its distributors projected to potential audiences, even when it seems there is little to shock within the work itself, as is arguably the case with Allégret's film. A review in the *Monthly Film Bulletin* describes the film as 'a rather frowsy melodramatic triangle' (I.I. 1956: 102). Likewise, *Today's Cinema* remarks that as a result of cutting 'there remain very few visual X-points', although 'the title should prove a very strong sales asset' (M.M.W. 1956: 8). Certainly, the film looks coy to modern eyes: there is no nudity, save for the odd calf or shoulder, no corset-ripping love scenes, but rather the familiar modest aversion of the gaze whenever the lovers fall into an embrace.[5] Nonetheless, *The Daily Film Renter* rather cynically speculated that the film would do well at 'specialist houses – and wherever "X" is the box-office vote', describing the film as a work that, despite having been directed with 'typical French good taste', was 'bristling with exploitation values', and Marc Allégret as 'a darling of British longhairs' (F.J. 1956: 5). Ultimately *The Daily Film Renter's* critic seems to have been proved right: following its successful run at the Curzon, the film transferred to Leicester Square (a rare event for foreign-language film in the 1950s) before returning to the specialist theatres for a tour of the provinces (Anon 1956a).

In the face of this popular success, it is interesting to note that the film's critical reception was not, however, wholly positive. One of the main criticisms levelled at the film in contemporaneous reviews has to do with its 'Frenchified' version of Lawrence's Sheffield (referred to by one critic as 'Wragley-sur-Loire' – Anon 1956b): the mangled linguistics of the British writer's prose, the disappearing class-politics, and the 'bistro full of berets' described by Dilys Powell (1956). Louis K. Greiff puts it generously when he writes that the film goes 'beyond language and genre to translate *Lady Chatterley's Lover* into French in cultural and historical terms as well' (Greiff 2001: 163); C.A. Lejeune (1956) perhaps comes closer to summing up the feelings of many when she writes that the film is '[n]either French nor English'.

The critical disappointment expressed at the film's 'Frenchness' may seem surprising given that it was filmed in France, by a French director with French stars. What else might the critics have expected? Yet it appears less so in the face of the almost total absence of any emphasis on the film's Gallic origins within the publicity campaign. Such effacement of a film's nationality was common practice for French film in the U.K. during this period; in fact, it points to one more way in which promotion and exhibition of *L'Amant de Lady Chatterley* is in many ways exemplary of the manner in which French film was being sold at the British box office in the mid-1950s. For as Lucy Mazdon has detailed in various articles (See Mazdon 2001; 2008) there was during the 1950s a tendency to downplay the French provenance of certain films in favour of an emphasis on the elements which brought them closer to Hollywood (a key example she draws upon in this context is the *Le Salaire de la peur*

/ *The Wages of Fear* (1953), marketed on the basis of its international cast and use of action/adventure genre conventions).

However, it seems that in the case of *L'Amant de Lady Chatterley*, neither 'French nor English', the strategy of yoking the risqué reputation of a British novel to a film shot through with a distinctly French worldview can only be seen as successful in part. The X-factor may have proved a hit with popular audiences, but to those critics whose knowledge of the book exceeded its scurrilous reception, Allégret's film failed to live up to expectations of both literary adaptation and/or French cinema at large.

'Chocolate box pornography': Softcore in the 1980s

Released by London-Cannon Films in 1981, the second of the three versions of *Lady Chatterley's Lover* under consideration here should have borne the burden of British expectations of French cinema less heavily than its predecessor, since it was nominally a domestic production. Its inclusion within this discussion is indicative, however, of its more complex status: in fact, the film was coproduced with London-Cannon's French partner, Producteurs Associés; cowritten by the English screenwriter Christopher Wickling and its French director, Just Jaeckin; and starred in the lead role a Dutch actress, Sylvia Kristel, familiar to British audiences from her appearance in a French softcore porn film, *Emmanuelle* (1974) – according to Guy Austin the biggest box-office attraction in France of the decade (Austin 2003: 67).

As Tom Dewe Mathews (1994) and Eric Schaefer (1999) have noted, the regulation of sex in mainstream film has tended to promote an excluded niche cinema that actively entices curious audiences with the lure of the outré. Tanya Krzywinska adds that commercial pressures within mainstream cinema can prompt filmmakers and producers to look to excluded cinemas to promote renewed interest in mainstream products (2006: 12). This means that at certain junctures in the history of cinema the lines between the legitimate cinema and the excluded or fringe cinemas become blurred. Such is the case with the adult melodramas of the 1950s, including Allégret's *Chatterley* adaptation, where aspects of exploitation cinema were adopted by a particular type of mainstream film and within certain parameters. A similar exchange occurred, Krzywinska observes, during the 1970s, when elements of softcore sex films were adopted into mainstream works that focused on sexual initiation themes (2006: 16).

According to Krzywinska, prior to this period, sexual initiation films had been the preserve of what she terms the 'European film' and the exploitation film (2006: 72). Yet during this decade, a shift occurred in cultural and institutional registers that enabled the format to enter into the mainstream: the introduction of the sexual self-discovery dimension to the initiation format produced a hybrid between porn and psychological melodrama. Krzywinska offers Jaeckin's *Emmanuelle* as the blueprint for this narrative format, claiming that the film sparked a raft of softcore films designed for mainstream distribution, including Jaeckin's own version of *Lady Chatterley's Lover*, which married 'a risqué ... sexual self discovery theme to a "pretty" art-cinema aesthetic' with the result that the films often proved commercial successes

(Krzywinska 2006: 73). In this film (as in subsequent variants on the theme such as *The Story of O* and *Bilitis*) the central female character embarks on a journey of sexual self-discovery and development, realized through lush art-cinema-style photography and mise en scene; soft-focus lenses, carefully staged sets, dreamy music and glamorous locations each contribute to the melodious aura of idyllic fantasy (ibid.). Sex is 'graceful, often perfectly complementary (even if the participants are not matched conventionally) and visually rich, providing a significant contrast to the raw see-all-the-details glare of low-budget hard-core sex films' (ibid.). The quality production values of these softcore films are designed to reposition sex-based films and broaden their potential market, as the inclusion of such legitimized formal elements made the films more commercially and culturally acceptable (much like the strategy used by the 'adult melodramas' of the 1950s). It is precisely this reassurance that the U.K. distributors for *Emmanuelle* play on when describing it in the U.K. radio campaign as 'The film that makes you feel good without feeling bad'; as John Ellis so pithily puts it, 'Pornography minus Shame equals Eroticism' (Ellis 1982: 79).

The film which made Jaeckin's name in Europe, *Emmanuelle* was a significant factor in determining expectations of 1981's *Lady Chatterley's Lover*, not least due to the repeat appearance of its star, Sylvia Kristel, in the adaptation. If genre is often used to define the target audience for a given film, then more often that not this may involve the use of particular directors or stars. Of course, to some extent, this much is also true of Allégret's adaptation. Danielle Darrieux's prominent status on the poster for Allégret's film is matched by her star billing: her name is placed above the title, before Allégret's, while Lawrence's credit is placed below in much smaller font. And indeed, by the time that *L'Amant* was released in the U.K., Darrieux was an established star on both sides of the Channel who had moved from youthful, romantic roles in the early 1930s to portrayals of strong, highly sophisticated women by the 1950s, thus making her a fitting match for the character. But more significantly she had, as mentioned above, appeared very recently to British audiences in a pair of high-profile X-rated French hits, *La Ronde* and *Occupe-toi d'Amélie*, and was therefore a potential (mis)indicator of the film's more risqué qualities.

It was however, as we have seen, the 1955 film's rating, rather than its star, which served as its major selling point, with, as Joachim Lembach has it, 'the glamour of multinational stardom that only foreign language films could deliver' serving primarily as a complement to their major draw: 'the titillation of the X cert' (Lembach 2003: 35). The marketing of Jaeckin's film on the other hand centres almost exclusively on Kristel, whose image, like that of Darrieux before her, dominates publicity stills and posters. The film's British poster superimposes one still from the film (in silhouette long-shot a clothed Lady Chatterley receives from her would-be lover, Mellors, the key to the hut where she will conduct her trysts) upon another (in close-up a naked Lady Chatterley and Mellors lie in postcoital bliss on a straw-strewn floor – an image which makes explicit what is implicit in the U.K. poster image for Allégret's film); in later VHS and DVD releases the image is replaced with one of Kristel alone, naked, eyes closed and head thrown back in what would appear to be orgasmic bliss. Unlike in the French promotional material,

Figure 5.2: DVD cover for *Lady Chatterley's Lover* (1981), U.K. release.
Image courtesy of the BFI stills department.

Jaeckin's name is effaced from both film poster and home release covers, suggesting that in the U.K., it was the female star indicative of genre, rather than the male director indicative of auteurism, who was the dominant factor in shaping perceptions of the film. And although Columbia's ill-fated Betamax release of 1985 reinstates the director, inserting the subtitle 'A Just Jaeckin Film' and billing the work as a 'high calibre classic' from 'the team who made "Emmanuelle"' it is noteworthy that not only does Kristel retain top billing but the packaging features a proliferation of naked images of the star.[6]

Kristel is moreover employed in a much more 'active' manner as a promotional figure for the film than was her 1950s counterpart, via the numerous interviews to U.K. magazines and newspapers the star gave in the months preceding the film's release. While Darrieux was part of an 'old guard' of movie stars, rarely photographed outside of prearranged shoots, her persona created through films and articles in women's magazines and specialist film publications, Kristel was, quite literally, more exposed – famous not only for her often naked body, but also her much publicized relationships with actors such as Briton Ian McShane (who was, according to a *Photoplay* magazine report of January 1982, originally slated for the part of Mellors: two years before the film was released, *The News of the World* was speculating as to whether the pair would be starring together in the forthcoming 'sex shocker' (Anon 1980b)). She was also a one-trick pony, paradoxically (in the face of such interest in her private life) indistinguishable from her most notorious role. Headlines in the British press such as 'Emmanuelle's action as sizzling Lady C!' conflated actress and role, transposing the Emmanuelle figure to the Chatterley narrative (Waterman 1981), while *The Sunday Mirror* remarks that there can be only one reason for this piece of casting: '[Kristel's] bare body that made her famous in the soft-porn Emmanuelle movies' (Harmsworth 1981).

The article in question is just one of the numerous set-reports commissioned by London-Cannon during the production of Jaeckin's film and featured in the British press alongside a vast range of steamy stills from the ongoing shoot, which offered a deceptive 'sneak-peak' at what audiences could expect. Perhaps appropriately, the majority of prerelease 'hype' surrounding the film appears in more popular and populist publications than is the case for the previous – and, as we shall examine in due course – subsequent adaptation of the novel: including the aforementioned *News of the World* and *The Express* but also *The Daily Mail* and *The Sun*. These publications displayed a horrified delight (or delighted horror) at the imminent prospect of the film, whose publicity materials were appearing with not unremarkable frequency within their own pages. The official studio message issued to these papers about the film meanwhile was something of a mixed one: speaking to *The News of the World*, the film's producer Menahem Golan assured the paper that 'It will be the most erotic film ever made', but that 'anyone who thinks that we're making pornography will be disappointed'. Fans of D.H. Lawrence, he announced somewhat overconfidently, 'will love it' (Anon 1980). Kristel meanwhile played it typically coy: 'Of course there will be nudity', she told *The Express*, 'But this is not exploitation of sex. This is art' (Anon 1980a). The papers, however, reported the star's assurances with a cheeky nudge to their readers, with Sylvia apparently only managing to gasp out such statements after she had 'come up for air' (Anon 1981). A legal tussle with the owners of Wrotham Park, the stately home in which the cast and crew were filming, only added to the sordid intrigue.

Of course, it was to be expected that the redtops would be quick to pigeonhole the film as softcore porn, a view in keeping with the film industry's more general approach to Lawrence's novel during the late 1970s and early 1980s, when a raft of hard and soft porn adaptations that took the Lady's name in vain was spawned, including *The Loves of Lady Chatterley*, *Lady Chatterley in Tokyo*(!) and, perhaps most famously, Alan Roberts's *Young Lady Chatterley*, released in British cinemas in 1977. Yet any prurient hopes about the Chatterley narrative once more go unfulfilled by the film itself – which is not only short on sexual content, but also features some rigorous period recreation; vivid, colour-saturated cinematography; a very unsympathetic portrayal of the British upper classes (much more scathing that Allégret's rather wishy-washy critique); and, again in marked contrast with Allégret's film, a pronounced dedication to capturing the English landscape in detail. The film's adherence to the letter of the novel is also surprising: unlike the pornographic movies mentioned above, Jaeckin's film sticks to just the four sex scenes detailed by Lawrence.

In French reviews of what was promoted as 'Just Jaeckin's *Lady Chatterley's Lover*', these details are much remarked upon: the cult of the auteur held its grip in 1980s France, however tenuous this might have been in relation to this genre of films. In

Britain, however, we can see that the promotion of and response to the 1981 adaptation mirrored that of the 1955 film: sold as a sexy adaptation of a scandalous book (even some twenty years after the ban on Lawrence's novel had been lifted), upon opening at the Leicester Square Theatre in London's West End it was judged on these same terms and for the most part found sadly wanting. Across the range of publications, the film was viewed first and foremost as a pornographic production, albeit one dressed up with high-end production values – 'chocolate box pornography', as *The Sunday Telegraph* dubbed it (Castell 1981). Some took the marketing campaign at face value: *The Observer*'s Philip French counselled his readers that, '[t]his isn't a serious attempt to match Lawrence's impassioned social and psychological analysis; it's just Jaeckin's constant star Sylvia Kristel ... crossing the Channel to inspect her British troops' (French 1981). Broadly speaking, the broadsheets viewed the film with a wry scepticism, with even those reviews which did recognize the film as more seriously intentioned taking an arch tone. Writing in the high-brow arts magazine *The Listener*, Gavin Millar commented on Sylvia Kristel's 'very well-shaped breasts' before going on to reassure readers in his most sarcastic tone that, '[s]ince this is a class piece of very soft porn, based on a real hardcover library book, the bouts are few and far between, and linked by interminable passages in the best possible taste' (Millar 1981). *The Guardian*'s critic Derek Malcolm meanwhile advised that the film 'could quite safely be put before the servants', but that 'it might bore their pants off' (Malcolm 1981).

A cynical marketing campaign on the part of the distribution company thus conspired with British preconceptions of the film's cast and crew to undermine Jaeckin's own vision of his film. Where the French press saw an (admittedly poor) attempt to create art, the Brits heaved a weary sigh at what they considered a badly dubbed and pretentious European variant on the porn industry's seemingly endless slew of Chatterley adaptations. Perhaps the *décalage* between the two national responses is best expressed by Mellors himself, or rather the actor who played him, Nicolas Clay, when he states that 'to the French it may be amour ..., to [the] British it's a bit of How's yer father' (Waterman 1981).

'A classy French movie': Quality and Comfort

If sex was the major selling point for French versions of *Lady Chatterley's Lover* in 1956 and 1981, it was no longer the case by the time Pascale Ferran's adaptation of Lawrence's novel was released in 2007. The marketing summary produced for the U.K. release of Ferran's *Lady Chatterley* by the distributors Artificial Eye leaves little doubt as to what the target demographic for the film was, nor what the angle of approach would be. And as we shall see, it reveals a marked development in attitudes to selling French cinema to the British.

Ferran's *Lady Chatterley* was from the outset pitched to its potential audiences as what one critic later referred to as 'a classy French movie' (Anon 2007). Outside of the usual poster campaigns on London public transport, hoardings and in specialist cinema chains, print advertisements were placed in the national daily broadsheets, Sunday supplements, and specialist film magazines such as *Sight and Sound* and *Empire*. No tabloids were targeted. A thirty-second commercial ran on the specialist, high-brow television channels More4, Film4, TCM, Artsworld Hallmark and Biography, while the radio campaign was exclusive to Classic FM, and featured a tie-in with the film's classical soundtrack (by Béatrice Thiriet, distributed by Warner Classics and Jazz). The station website also featured a dedicated microsite, as did *The Radio Times*, both of which incorporated a downloadable PDF document with chapters on synopsis, cast, the trailer and Lawrence, as well as wallpaper downloads and a link to the distributor's website (Artificial Eye 2007b). A fortnight before the film's release (24 August 2007), a special preview was arranged for members of the Curzon with an introduction by Dr Hugh Stevens, a University College London English lecturer and Lawrence specialist. The Curzon's main competitor meanwhile, the Picturehouse chain, ran a series of London-based and regional previews in conjunction with *The Guardian*, with a promotional voucher offered in the supplements *Film and Music* and *The Guide* for screenings taking place a week prior to release.[7]

As with the campaign for Allégret's and Jaeckin's films, the film's literary origins were emphasized. But while the book (and its ersatzes) figured in the promotion of the earlier films as a symbol of scandal and a pornographic narrative trope respectively, in 2007 it was treated with po-faced gravitas. In place of giant models of 'the book they banned' sported as sandwich boards, was a competition in *The*

Figure 5.3: Marina Hands and Jean-Louis Coulloc'h in a publicity still for Pascale Ferran's 2006 *Lady Chatterley*. The image featured on posters and the cover of a new edition of *The Second Lady Chatterley* published by Oneworld books.
Image courtesy of the BFI stills department.

London Review of Books e-newsletter, and a tie-in with Oneworld Classics, the publishers of a new edition of *John Thomas and Lady Jane* (now released as *The Second Lady Chatterley*) (Lawrence 2007), copies of which were on sale in all cinemas playing the film as well in bookshops, its cover art matching that of the film's posters and emblazoned with a sticker promoting the film. Where copies were sold in bookshops, an A3 mini-poster was distributed with each. In return, the Oneworld Classics logo featured on all the promotional material produced by Artificial Eye. Continuing with the high-end promotional crossovers, CDs of the soundtrack were also sold in all Curzon sites (Artificial Eye 2007b).

On both sides of the marketing process – press communiqués and the articles responding to them – emphasis was placed on the fact that this was the second edition of the novel: one which, according to the Oneworld book jacket, is 'more positive in tone and without the verbosity that occasionally weighs down the novel's standard incarnation', as well displaying 'many key differences in plot and characterisation' (Lawrence 2007). Interestingly, both Louis K. Greiff (2001) and Neil Taylor (1993) suggest that this second draft was most likely also to have been the inspiration for the two earlier adaptations under discussion, and yet no mention of such is made in any of the literature surrounding their U.K. releases. In the case of Ferran's film, the repeated references to the second edition serve a dual purpose, acting as a 'hook' for discussions of the film and source material within literary sections of the broadsheets, in addition to attenuating the Chatterley narrative's vulgar and brutal reputation, situating the film as an unusually explicit love story, rather than an excuse for softcore titillation. The presence of another intertext looms large in this regard: the European exoticism of the two earlier versions may have lent them an erotic allure, but by 2007 it was left to the French to bring some class to the Chatterley myth in the wake of Ken Russell's 1993 bawdy television adaptation. The critic James Mottram, writing for *The Times*, was amongst several to make an explicit comparison between the two most recent adaptations: 'While [Ferran's] film is rated 18 in the UK, it crucially resists turning Lawrence's story into lurid spectacle. Just compare it to Ken Russell's 1993 version, where Sean Bean and Joely Richardson sexed it up as if they were characters in a Danielle Steel novel' (Mottram 2007: 16). Across the board, a contrast is made between British bawdiness and French sensuality: Nicolas Clay might have been ahead of his time when he contrasted British 'how's yer father' with French 'amour'.

In 2007, then, it was the intellectual and aesthetic angle that dominated the promotion of a French Chatterley adaptation. The young, relatively unknown, actress incarnating Lady Chatterley this time around, Marina Hands, was interviewed for a handful of magazines and broadsheets (born in England and raised in France, Hands herself made much of her status as neither French nor English); however, it was the film's two authors – Lawrence and Ferran – on whom the majority of press attention fell, with articles taking the shape of critical reappraisals of the by-now unfashionable Lawrence's works or auteurist examinations of the rather-mysterious Ferran's work to date.[8] Perceptions of the latter as a serious artist were reinforced by the withering attack on the French funding system for film that she gave as part of her César acceptance speech (James 2007). However, while there is the occasional mention of the multiple Césars that the film was awarded in France prior to its U.K. release amongst the British reviews, the awards play a much greater role in the French reception of the film. It is instructive to note here that the Césars are rarely used in U.K. marketing of French films and are little known in the U.K.; tellingly, the pressnotes 'translate' the awards into English, describing them as 'the French equivalent of the Oscars' (Artificial Eye 2007a).

The novel, too, is thought of much more highly amongst French critics. Reviews of Ferran's film on that side of the Channel praise her loyalty to the text; in Britain on the other hand critics lauded the film precisely for taking liberties with it, somewhat ironically given the focus in the marketing of the film on the book and the film's comparative fidelity to the text. With Lawrence fallen out of fashion, the film was apparently all the better for abandoning Sheffield and the novel's class politics. *The Independent's* Antony Quinn judged that 'the French have paid this distinctively English writer a better tribute than one might have thought he deserved' (Quinn 2007). Jenny McCartney, for *The Sunday Telegraph*, stated: 'The screenplay is spoken in French, but set in England, which works rather well: it serves to bypass the class-ridden clash of English accents and allow one to focus on the love-affair' (McCartney 2007: 22). But it is David Sexton, Literary Editor of *The Evening Standard*, who best sums up the common consensus when he writes that: 'The film comes garlanded with froggy prizes ... Some mistake? A cross-cultural misunderstanding surely? For DH Lawrence's *Lady Chatterley's Lover* is, let us admit it, an absolutely ludicrous book' (Sexton 2007: 28). At the end of his review he declares that, 'the entire texture of the film is better for being so thoroughly French' (Sexton 2007: 29).

Conclusion: Sex, Art and Exploitation

What exactly is it that is 'so thoroughly French' about Pascale Ferran's *Lady Chatterley*? For Jessica Winter, 'Ferran's film effortlessly shrugs off its softcore template ... through sheer magnificent execution' (Winter 2007: 79). Kevin Maher's response is less positive: 'Ferran is an academic who lectures in cinema at the French state film school *La Femis* (which explains a lot – only a navel gazing academic could bang on for this long)' (Maher 2007). What unites these two divergent assessments of the film – and indeed, the vast majority of reviews – is the overriding association of French film with a certain level of 'quality': that is, with technical expertise and an unsensationalist, cerebral approach to its material. Where sex is mentioned, it is as a hurdle which Ferran's film must cross, rather than a saucy selling point. Even Jamie Russell's review, in which he offers up the film as 'proof that French really is the language of love ... and sometimes lust', praises Ferran's 'moving' restraint in portraying the sex as 'frank without being sensational' (Russell 2007).

Clearly, a change in attitudes to and expectations of French cinema has occurred in the sixty-one years between the releases of Allégret's film and Ferran's. Admittedly this chapter presents only three films for comparison – albeit three films linked by a common factor – and moreover some attention to the textual nature of the films themselves would be necessary to discern to what extent this determines critical response. Nonetheless, they are three films not only adapted from the same source material, but made by directors who can clearly be considered 'auteurs', with aspirations to artistic seriousness: to some extent this is reflected more acutely in the French reception of the films (particularly Jaeckin's) than in the British reception. It is therefore my contention that surveying the historical promotion of Gallic adaptations of *Lady Chatterley's Lover* allows us to trace the shifting relationship between the twin discourses which have framed French cinema in the U.K.: on the one hand, sensual and sexy, on the other hand, artistic and intellectual. These two discourses have circulated around French films in the U.K. since the advent of sound cinema, and they each play a role within the perception, if not the promotion, of French cinema throughout the timespan under consideration: one need only consider the repeated references to typical French 'taste' that surface in reviews of all three films (see, for example, F.J. 1956; Millar 1981; Quinn 2007). Lawrence's novel has evidently been surrounded by similar discourses – it is for this reason perhaps, that the two make such natural bedfellows. But over the course of time, the balance between Lawrence's novel and its French adaptations has shifted: where Lawrence's novel has lost its power to shock alongside its reputation for literary greatness, French film has seen its artistic standing in Great Britain soar, perhaps even supplanting its risqué reputation.

Which is not to say that French film has not maintained, to some extent at least, its British association with the sexual. The films of what has been dubbed the 'New French Extremism' stand as testament to this (Quandt 2004). Yet as the much commented-upon BBFC report on *Romance* testifies (see Wilson 2001), explicit depictions of sexuality from the French continue to be considered within an intellectual context. For both David Sexton and Jonathan Romney, Ferran's film reverses preconceptions about images of sex on both sides of the Channel, with the latter stating that:

> The flesh has had a rough time in French art cinema lately, with directors tending to show sex as a vicious, violent affair (Gaspar Noé), as brutish rutting with overtones of existential anguish (Bruno Dumont), or as a source of outright gloom to be accompanied by abstruse philosophising (Catherine Breillat). But Ferran reminds us that the French can do good sex too (Romney 2007: 52).

Quite to the contrary of Romney's position, I would venture that Ferran's film only serves to compound the overriding current perception of French cinema as concerned with sex but never gratuitously, its explicit images always deployed in service of a greater purpose. It is symptomatic of a gradual process of establishing French cinema, within Britain, as what Nick James calls 'the gold standard of Art cinema': a safely exotic, unchallenging 'other' aimed at middle-class art house audiences seeking intellectual – rather than sexual – gratification from their French films (James 2005: 15).

This being the case, I believe that exploitation must still be a key term within discourses surrounding the marketing of French film to British audiences in the twenty-first century. Today, cinematic stereotypes are still being peddled by distributors and exhibitors in the U.K.: Artificial Eye in 2007, no less than Columbia in 1956 or London-Cannon in 1981, deliberately manipulated existing audience desires and expectations of French cinema in their marketing campaigns in order to increase the box-office potential of the film that they were promoting, little matter whether those films fulfil this promise (and as the press reception to each of the films under consideration demonstrates, they frequently do not). However, what is being exploited is different. For while the films of the New Extreme have some allegiances to the historical genre of exploitation cinema as Krzywinska or Schaefer, for example, delineate it, this is less true of Ferran's *Lady Chatterley*. Expectations of this film did not centre around the possibility of seeing something sordid on screen, but rather around the framing of the sexual act within a distinctly French tradition of, as one distributor of French-language film in the U.K. puts it, 'intelligent, thought-provoking cinema' (Gant 2007).

If critical reviews mirror our *responses* to the films, marketing campaigns shape, mirror and exaggerate our *expectations* of them. What the history of French adaptations of *Lady Chatterley's Lover* might reveal, then, in a first instance, is that when it comes to selling French cinema, sex is no longer the first point of recourse for distributors, and nor is it necessarily the first thing that crosses the target audience's mind. Of course, its spectre still hovers around the edges of the art-house. But it has perhaps finally been supplanted, or at least, equalled by the impression of quality, class, intelligence and artistic integrity that has likewise circulated around French cinema. That it is this discourse that dominates British impressions of French cinema, even in the case of a film whose key intertexts are overwhelmingly bound up with the sexually explicit, suggests a significant shift in the balance of the twin stereotypes surrounding French cinema over the last half-century.

Notes

The Author would like to thank Zena Howard and Alistair Leach at Artificial Eye for their gracious help supplying information about the marketing of Pascale Ferran's *Lady Chatterley*.

1. Henceforth I shall refer to the films by their original titles, as *L'Amant de Lady Chatterley* (Allégret), *Lady Chatterley's Lover* (Jaeckin) and *Lady Chatterley* (Ferran), in order to avoid confusion between the three.
2. Notes of proceedings at a meeting convened by the Birmingham Cinema Enquiry Committee held at the University of Birmingham in the Medical Theatre, Edmund Street, Birmingham, 7 November 1939, to discuss the cinema and its influence at the time, held in the BFI library special collection pertaining to the BBFC.
3. The information pertaining to the marketing campaign for Allégret's adaptation comes courtesy of a leaflet distributed to exhibitors and made available for consultation at the British Film Institute (BFI) library.

4. When, in 2009, The Curzon Group celebrated its seventy-fifth anniversary, *La Ronde* was indeed one of the four films selected for revival at the Curzon Mayfair (the others being Jean Vigo's 1934 *L'Atalante*; Louis Malle's 1965 *Viva Maria*; and James Ivory's 1985 *A Room with A View*). The programme notes report that *La Ronde* enjoyed a seventeen-month engagement between 1951 and 1952, and 'allegedly created the "X" certificate' (Curzon Cinemas 2009).
5. Despite the general perception that it was a much tamer affair than the marketing campaign made out, controversy continued to surround the film even after its release, with Croydon Town Council refusing to show the 'nasty' film on screen (*The Evening Standard*, 14 August 1956).
6. The 'blurb' for the 1991 VHS edition does make mention of 'the creators of Emmanuelle', who have created 'another high calibre classic with the emphasis on eroticism'; this has, however, disappeared from the 2007 edition.
7. It is interesting to note that in areas where the Picturehouse group was not represented, these screenings instead took place at the more mainstream-oriented Cineworld cinemas; more interesting still that despite this campaign to align the film with the middle-class liberal, arts-oriented newspapers, *The Guardian's* film critic, Peter Bradshaw, was one of the few U.K. critics to give Ferran's film a negative review – and his was indeed negative in the extreme (Bradshaw 2007).
8. Ferran's reputation rests on one feature film and a second made for television. The former, *Petits arrangements avec les morts*, won the *Caméra d'Or* at Cannes in 1994; the second, *L'Âge des possibles* (1995), is a low-budget, critically acclaimed, theatrical ensemble piece.

Bibliography

Anon. 1954. 'Report on the "X"', *Sight and Sound* 23(3): 123–24, 153.

———. 1956a. 'Lady Chatterley on the Screen', *The Times*, 4 July.

———. 1956b. 'L'Amant de Lady Chatterley', *Time and Tide*, 14 July.

———. 1956c. 'L'Amant de Lady Chatterley', *The Daily Mail*, 6 July.

———. 1980a. 'Emmanuelle Plays Lady Chatterley', *The Express* [no date].

———. 1980b. 'Now for the Film Shocker', *The News of the World* [no date].

———. 1981. 'Sylvia Sizzles as Lady C', *The Sun*, 2 June.

———.1982. 'Lady Chatterley's Lover', *Photoplay*, 1 January.

———. 2007. 'Loving Lady Chatterley', *Cinema Business* 34(1 May): 55.

Artificial Eye. 2007a. Marketing Report for U.K. Release of *Lady Chatterley*, August.

———. 2007b. Pressnotes to U.K. Release of *Lady Chatterley*.

Austin, G. 2003. *Stars in Modern French Film*. London: Arnold Press.

Bradshaw, P. 2007. 'Lady Chatterley', *The Guardian*, 24 August.

Castell, D. 1981. 'Lady Chatterley's Lover', *The Sunday Telegraph*, 20 December.

Columbia Distributors. 1956. Pressnotes to U.K. Release of *L'Amant de Lady Chatterley*.

Curzon Cinemas. 2009. Special Commerative Programme, celebrating 75 years of Curzon Cinemas.

Dewe Mathews, T. 1994. *Censored: The History of Film Censorship in Britain*. London: Chatto and Windus.

Ellis, J. 1982. *Visible Fictions: Cinema, Television, Video*. London: Routledge.

F.J. 1956. 'L'Amant de Lady Chatterley', *The Daily Film Renter*, 4 July: 5.

French, P. 1981. 'Lady Chatterley's Lover', *The Observer*, 20 December.

Gant, C. 2007. 'Spreading It Too Thin', *Sight and Sound* November: 9.

Greiff, L.K. 2001. *D.H. Lawrence: Fifty Years on Film*. Carbondale: Southern Illinois University Press.

Halliwell, L. 1956. 'A New Look from the One-and-Nines', *Everybody's*, 11 February: 24, 33.

Harmsworth, M. 1981. 'Lady Chatterley's Lover', *The Sunday Mirror*, 20 December.

I.I. 1956. 'L'Amant de Lady Chatterley', *The Monthly Film Bulletin*, 1 August: 102.

James, N. 2005. 'French Cinema: The Anti-Hollywood', *Sight and Sound* August: 14–15.

———. 2007. 'Seizing the Moment', *Sight and Sound* April: 5.

Klinger, B. 1994. *Melodrama and Meaning: History, Culture and the Films of Douglas Sirk*. Bloomington and Indianapolis: Indiana University Press.

Krzywinska, T. 2006. *Sex and The Cinema*. London: Wallflower.

Lawrence, D.H. 2007. *John Thomas and Lady Jane* (now released as *The Second Lady Chatterley*). London: Oneworld Classics.

Lejeune, C.A. 1956. 'L'Amant de Lady Chatterley', *Observer*, 8 July.

Lembach, J. 2003. *The Standing of the German Cinema in Great Britain After 1945*. Lewiston, N.Y.: Edwin Mellen Press.

Maher, K. 2007. 'Angst in Their Pants', *The Times*, 23 August: 15.

Malcolm, D. 1981. 'Lady Chatterley's Lover', *The Guardian*, 18 December.

Mazdon, L. 2008. 'Vulgar, Nasty and French: Selling French Films to British Audiences in the 1950s', conference paper presented at the University of Stirling November 2008. A version of this paper will be published in *The Journal of British Cinema and Television* in 2010.

———. (ed.). 2001. *France on Film: Reflections on Popular French Cinema*. London: Wallflower Press.

———. and C. Wheatley. 2008. 'Intimate Connections', *Sight and Sound* May: 38–40.

McCartney, J. 2007. 'Lady Chatterley', *The Sunday Telegraph*, 26 August: 22–23.

Millar, G. 1981. 'Plunderers', *The Listener*, December.

M.M.W. 1956. 'L'Amant de Lady Chatterley', *Today's Cinema*, 5 July: 8.

Mottram, J. 2007. 'Lady Chatterley', *The Times*, 16 August: 16.

Powell, D. 1956. 'L'Amant de Lady Chatterley', *The Sunday Times*, 8 July.

Quandt, J. 2004. 'Flesh and Blood: Sex and Violence in Recent French Cinema', *ArtForum* February: 126–32.

Quinn, A. 2007. 'Lady Chatterley', *The Independent Arts and Books Review*, 24 August: 8.

Romney, J. 2007. 'Lady Chatterley', *The Independent on Sunday*, 26 August: 52–53.

Rotha, P. 1951. 'The Writing on the Wall', *Public Opinion*, 19 January. Reprinted [1958] in *Rotha on the Film*, Fair Lawn, N.J.: Essential Books, pp. 164–65.

Russell, J. 2007. 'Lady Chatterley's Lover'. Retrieved 1 April 2009 from http://www.bbc.co.uk/films/2007/08/20/lady_chatterley_2007_review.shtml

Schaefer, E. 1999. *'Bold! Shocking! Daring! True': A History of Exploitation Films 1919–1959*. Durham and London: Duke University Press.

Sexton, D. 2007. 'Lady Chatterley', *The Evening Standard*, 16 August.

Taylor, N. 1993. 'A Woman's Love', in P. Reynolds (ed.), *Novel Images*. London: Routledge, 105–21.

Waterman, I. 1981. 'Emmanuelle's Sizzling Action as Lady C', *News of the World*, 15 March.

Wilson, E. 2001. 'Deforming Femininity: Catherine Breillat's Romance', in L. Mazdon (ed.), *France on Film: Reflections on Popular French Cinema*. London: Wallflower, 145–57.

Wingate, R. 2009. 'A Short History of The Curzon Mayfair'. Retrieved 4 April from www.actproductions.co.uk/iabout_company.asp

Winter, J. 2007. 'Lady Chatterley', *Cinema Scope* 32(Fall): 78–79.

Filmography

L'Atalante. 1934, Jean Vigo, France.

L'Âge des possibles. 1995, Pascale Ferran, France.

L'Amant de Lady Chatterley / Lady Chatterley's Lover. 1955, Marc Allégret, France.

Baby Doll. 1956, Elia Kazan, U.S.A.

Belle de jour. 1967, Luis Buñuel, France/Italy.

Bilitis. 1977, David Hamilton, France/Italy.

Emmanuelle. 1974, Just Jaeckin, France.

Et Dieu créa la femme / And God Created Woman. 1956, Roger Vadim, France.

Grande Bouffe, La. 1973, Marco Ferreri, France/Italy.

Histoire d'O / The Story of O. 1975, Just Jaeckin, France/West Germany.

Lady Chatterley (TV series). 1993, Ken Russell, U.K.

Lady Chatterley / Lady Chatterley et l'homme du bois. 2006, Pascale Ferran, France.

Lady Chatterley's Lover. 1981, Just Jaeckin, France/Britain.

Occupe-toi d'Amélie / Keep an Eye on Amelia. 1949, Claude Autant-Lara, France.

Petits arrangements avec les morts. 1994, Pascale Ferran, France.

Ronde, La. 1950, Max Ophüls, France.

Room with a View, A. 1985, James Ivory, U.K.

Salaire de la peur, Le / The Wages of Fear. 1953, Henri-Georges Clouzot, France.

Storia de Lady Chatterley, La / The Loves of Lady Chatterley. 1989, Lorenzo Onorati, Italy.

Tokyo Chatterley Fujin / Lady Chatterley in Tokyo. 1979, Katsuhiko Fujii, Japan.

Viva Maria. 1965, Louis Malle, France / Italy.

Written on the Wind. 1958, Douglas Sirk, U.S.A.

Young Lady Chatterley. 1977, Alan Roberts, U.S.A.

PART II

Reception and Perceptions

CHAPTER 6

Disciplining the *Nouvelle Vague*: Censoring *A Bout de Souffle* and Other Early French New Wave Films (1956–1962)

Daniel Biltereyst

In *La Nouvelle Vague?*, one of the first books to appear on the French New Wave, the film critic Jacques Siclier (1961) tried to offer a perspective on recent developments in French cinema in terms of scandal, contempt and controversy. Siclier, who made an uncredited appearance in Jean-Luc Godard's *A bout de souffle / Breathless* (Godard, 1959), argued that aesthetics and the notion of authorship might be insufficient to understand the revolution which had taken place. The critic suggested rather that while their work was aesthetically diverse, the new young filmmakers were bound together by a quite similar 'moral conception' of the world. Writing that, 'since the arrival of the new directors, French cinema has become an object of scandal' (Siclier 1961: 94), Siclier devoted a long final chapter to how films like *Et Dieu créa la femme / And God Created Woman* (Vadim, 1956), *Les Amants* (Malle, 1958), *Le Bel âge* (Kast, 1959) and *A bout de souffle* revealed an 'anti-morality' and a 'cinema of contempt', full of crude images of debauchery, adultery, anarchy and nihilism (Siclier 1961: 105). For Siclier, the New Wave, and Godard in particular, propagated a dangerous cinema which 'ignores human beings' and in which 'morality is only aesthetic' (Siclier 1961: 121).

Siclier was not the only one to talk about the French New Wave in this double register (see Sellier 2005: 40–1), indicating aesthetic innovation, modernity and authorship on the one hand, but also underlining the societal and moral provocations on the other. Although the artistic component soon took the lead in debates and scholarship on the New Wave, the historical reception of the new films was strongly marked by public concern about their perceived amorality and sexual explicitness. Traces of a discourse of moral panic can be detected in alarmist press reviews and negative film criticism, in publications by parents' organizations warning against harmful films, in severe morality codes given by the French Catholic film organization, or in social science research dealing with New Wave ethics.[1] These concerns about public morality were also implicit in decisions taken at various state levels, whereby local mayors, department prefects or representatives of the police and the judicial system hindered free circulation and exhibition of particularly controversial films. A key player in critically scrutinizing French New Wave pictures in France was the *Commission de Contrôle des Films Cinématographiques* (Film Control Commission, hereafter the Commission), a state film control board established in July 1945. Acting as a strongly disciplining force within the field of film production, distribution and exhibition, the Commission had the power to impose age restrictions, cut and ban films.

Inspired by a materialist perspective on historical reception analysis (Staiger 1992), this chapter focuses on the various ways controversial pictures from the early French New Wave movement were received and censored in France and subsequently in the U.K. It will concentrate upon the years 1956 to 1962, often regarded as the apex of the movement, starting with the controversy around *Et Dieu... créa la femme* (Esquenazi 2004: 49), and ending with the severe problems around Godard's *Vivre sa Vie* (1962) and François Truffaut's *Jules et Jim / Jules and Jim* (1962). Special attention will be given to *A bout de souffle,* a key picture, which was released at a moment when the New Wave reached its culmination both as an aesthetic film movement (Marie 2007: 6) and a public event with a sharp symbolic economy in terms of social critique and provocation (Esquenazi 2004: 5). Although Godard's first feature film is among the most profoundly analysed pictures of modern cinema, relatively little attention has been given to its censorship and the controversy it provoked.

It is my contention that French New Wave films played an important role in challenging the power of censorship boards at the end of the 1950s and the start of the 1960s in both France and Britain. The two censorship boards reacted differently to this type of material, which was considered to go beyond accepted boundaries in its representation of sexual, political, social and moral issues. The connection between the French New Wave and censorship is interesting, precisely because in this time frame decisive battles were fought in both countries by the New Wave directors – with Godard being a first-class *provocateur* – against the traditional censorial system, which often acted as both a public moral guardian and a powerful arm of the state. However, to claim that the New Wave directors denied, openly refused or continuously fought against the censors in the name of some holy belief in authorship, is, as we will see, a bridge too far.

Relying upon original film censorship files, censors' internal correspondence and classification sources, I will try to illustrate that there was a more complex, sometimes productive interplay between this group of filmmakers and censors on both sides of the channel. This interplay had a solid power centre, of course, with the censor often imposing its will (bans, cuts, age limits and so forth), but in many cases there was room for negotiation. I will argue that in these negotiations French and

British censors were increasingly more receptive to artistic intent, thereby using the double register of morality and art as the criteria for judging films and their acceptability for public viewing. Within the British context, as will be demonstrated, the films' specific 'Frenchness' held a special relation to these criteria.

New Wave, State Censorship and Other Disciplining Forces

In an attempt to support his account of the New Wave as a 'cinema of amorality', Siclier (1961: 120) referred to the ratings given by one of the most powerful pressure groups in French cinema. In France and other European countries with a substantial Catholic population, the Church had given local organizations permission to act upon the cinema from a religious perspective. One of the strategies developed by the French *Central Catholique du Cinéma* (Catholic Film Central, hereafter CCC) was to rate films and use morality codes. Much like the Legion of Decency in the U.S.A., the CCC acted as both a parallel censor and a whip for the official film censorship board. Given the strength of the Catholic educational system and the wide network of local Catholic communities, parents and family organizations, the CCC was able to spread its codes and propagate its moral judgements. These were widely distributed through leaflets and posters, which were nailed up in the more than forty thousand parochial halls and churches, and were also published in Catholic film magazines (e.g. *Télé-ciné, Choisir, Radio-Cinéma-Télévision*) and newspapers (e.g. *La Croix*) (Schlosberg 1955). Trying to (in)form a mass audience, the CCC hoped that negative ratings could have an harmful commercial effect on 'bad movies'.

By 1960, when the movement was at its height as a well publicized critical and public event, the New Wave label was also mobilized by its opponents, but this was often in a hostile and sometimes alarmist sense. While critics from the journal *Positif* questioned the aesthetic and cinematic novelty of the work by the young *cinéastes*, others condemned their pictures on the basis of their morally and socially controversial nature. The resistance was most clearly reflected in CCC morality codes. Looking at an overview of these ratings (Rochereau 1960), it is clear that the new filmmakers were extremely controversial. In May 1960, more than half of the films grouped together under the New Wave umbrella received a negative rating, while only a small proportion of titles were deemed 'acceptable for adults'. In its review of forty-four New Wave films, the CCC indicated thirteen titles with the severe '5' code (i.e. 'to be avoided'), while eleven others received a '4B' code ('not advised') and eleven works got the '4A' code ('with strong reservations'). Seven pictures received the '4' code for 'adults', while only two of the forty-four pictures got a code intended for family viewing. *Et Dieu créa la femme* and *Les Amants* were among the code 5 pictures, the latter coming with the advisory warning that: 'Christian discipline demanded not to go and see this film'.[2] In its moral condemnation of Vadim's picture ('very low morality, completely centred around passion, jealousy and desire'), the CCC referred to earlier cuts in the work and explicitly criticized the moral laxity of the official censors.[3] Among the 'not advised' pictures was Alain Resnais's *Hiroshima mon amour* (1958), described as an 'amoral meditation about love and time'.[4]

Representing an influential pressure group within conservative and Catholic parts of French society, the CCC also tried to propagate its moral authority by organizing boycotts and influencing local mayors, prefects and other political arenas. This '*censure des maires et des préfets*' (mayors' and prefects' censorship) can easily be seen as a second force in disciplining French cinema. In the 1950s the number of local prohibitions strongly increased – the result of boycotts, lobbying and pressure groups, with pictures such as *Avant le Déluge / Before the Deluge* (1954), *Le Diable au corps / Devil in the Flesh* (1947) and *Le Blé en herbe / The Game of Love* (1954) banned in the name of public order. Nonetheless in 1959/60 a second wave of boycotts by municipalities and local administrations emerged. This offensive hit many films and directors, with New Wave filmmakers such as Claude Chabrol, Louis Malle and Roger Vadim as prime targets. A case in point was *Les Liaisons dangereuses / Dangerous Liaisons* (1960), Vadim's picture on infidelity and adultery starring Jeanne Moreau, which was first granted a visa by the official censors for screenings for over-sixteens. Once the film went into circulation it quickly became the target of the CCC and conservative family organizations. The film grew into a public controversy and was confronted by theatre boycotts and a vehement press campaign. *Les Liaisons* was forbidden in more than forty municipalities and cities all over France, while twenty others decided to impose severe age restrictions. In an article entitled 'La Pornographie pratiquée comme un des Beaux-Arts' ('Pornography practised as an art'), published in *Cinéma 60*, a critic called the New Wave label an alibi for 'degradation', 'libertinage' and 'eroticism' (Barkan 1960: 81). The huge controversy only helped the film to become a major box-office hit, but the controversy surrounding *Les Liaisons*, *Les Amants, J'irai cracher sur vos tombes / I Spit on Your Grave* (Gast 1959) and other pictures finally led to tough 1961 censorship reforms (Douin 1998: 194–8).

In contrast to the British Board of Film Censors (BBFC) in the U.K., French state film censorship had the reputation for being relatively tolerant towards violence, sex and other social and moral issues. The exception to this relative leniency was political *censure*, particularly in relation to film export. The Commission had to advise the minister of Cultural Affairs (or Information) on the attribution of a film's visa: recommending cuts and age restrictions not only for domestic but also for foreign markets. Although the film industry had representatives in the Commission, the majority or at least half of the Commission was designated by the different ministries. As a result the Commission was highly susceptible to governmental pressure – a system which was strengthened during the Fifth Republic under Général de Gaulle with more power for the government and representatives of family organizations (Sadoul 1961). In relation to politics, the image of France and French national interests abroad, the Commission could not, then, afford to be generous.

Due to political instability, the process of decolonization and French involvement in the Cold War, the 1950s and 1960s turned out to be periods of tight film censorship (Douin 1998: 194–201; Hayward 2005: 32). Between 1946 and 1951, for instance, sixty-one films were completely forbidden in France, mostly under governmental pressure. In the mid-1950s more films were banned, with fourteen forbidden titles in 1952 alone. In the postwar period the Commission was highly susceptible to Soviet propaganda, but soon other films were forbidden such as Alain Resnais's and Chris Marker's *Les Statues meurent aussi / Statues Also Die* (1953) – apparently because the picture might hurt French colonial policy (de Baroncelli 1955; Hervé 2001: 119–28). Also Resnais's *Guernica* (1950) and *Nuit et brouillard / Night and Fog* (1955) encountered huge problems. A crucial year was 1960, with the Algerian War reaching a critical stage, when ten films were banned and forty-nine titles forbidden for minors under eighteen years (Séry 1971). One of those films was Godard's second, *Le Petit Soldat / The Little Soldier* (1960), to which we shall return, and which was banned because the picture was seen as an open critique of the French army's use of torture.

An extended comparison with the British situation is instructive in this context. In fact, the commonly held idea that French film censorship was more tolerant than the BBFC, often considered to be a bulwark of conservatism, is questionable. The BBFC, which was and continues to be an independent, nongovernmental body financed by the industry, was strict and encountered intensive criticism, but it was less directly under state control. Moreover, the BBFC had decided in 1951 to introduce a new classification, the X certificate: both the French and British national film censor not only encountered politically explicit material, but in the 1950s they were challenged by other more provocative content in terms of sexuality, violence or drugs; the X enabled the censors to circumvent an outright ban of this type of adult material. The category excluded children and young adolescents, but made it possible that adult entertainment would be allowed (Dewe Mathews 1994: 125–6) – indeed, after its inception outright bans became almost obsolete, with the last film to be refused a certificate by the BBFC being American juvenile delinquency movie *The Wild One* (László Benedek, 1953), which was rejected in 1955 and once more in 1959.

In order to avoid the R (or rejection) rating and to gain acceptance into the new X category, more frequent editing and extensive cutting became a standard practice. This often involved a process of negotiation. Rather than the censor simply imposing cuts, the different parties often sought to reach a consensus on morality, mostly when the picture was finished but sometimes before shooting on the basis of a script (although this was more often the case with domestic product than foreign works). John Trevelyan, who took over the daily workings of the BBFC in July 1958, knew that times were changing and wrote in his memoirs that he used 'to enjoy script discussions', adding that he was glad that filmmakers 'regarded [him] more as an adviser or consultant than a censor' (1973: 208–9). This did not mean that the BBFC were consistently concerned with the matter of artistic integrity – on the contrary, the British censors were regularly sterner with their cuts than the French Commission. *Les Liaisons dangereuses*, for instance, received an X certificate in the U.K. only after the BBFC had imposed seven cuts.[5] However, the introduction of the X certificate and the ascendance of Trevelyan to the helm of the BBFC inarguably ushered a new era of relative permissiveness in British censorship.

With this in mind, let us turn our attention back to the New Wave in order to examine how it was treated by both the French and British censors. For although from the mid-1950s onwards controversial material came from various sources, the New Wave authors played a significant part in challenging the censors and caused some of the most heated censorship battles. One of the first was *Et Dieu créa la femme*. In September 1956 the Commission came to the conclusion that the picture could not receive a visa due to 'the high number of risqué scenes'.[6] This rejection was the start of a long and difficult censorship and negotiation process that lasted several months, at the end of which Vadim and his producer and cowriter, Raoul Levy, finally accepted fifteen cuts including the elimination of a shot showing Juliette (Brigitte Bardot) behind a sheet in the opening scene. Following these negotiations the Commission argued that the trailer had to be cut too, while an age restriction of sixteen years was imposed. Furthermore the film was banned from export to Spain, Canada, the Soviet Union and a whole series of other countries. Only in 1983 did the socialist minister of Culture, Jack Lang, decide that the picture could be shown without any restriction. By comparison, the BBFC granted *And God Created Woman* an X upon its initial presentation in March 1957, after a comparatively tough series of ten cuts. (One of these was the removal of the infamous shots showing Juliette sunbathing in the nude in the first reel; also excised was a bed scene, as well as a low-angle shot in which 'we see Juliette dancing between two negroes and only her bare legs are visible').[7]

The French New Wave directors continued to have difficulties with the French Commission, especially after the 1961 reform. Truffaut's *Jules et Jim*, for example, caused another worldwide controversy. In November 1961 the French Commission decided that the picture should be forbidden for youngsters under eighteen.[8] A large majority of the board argued that 'the continuous amorality' was not suitable for minors, while the trailer was passed uncut. It is unsure what happened afterwards, but Truffaut certainly contacted the Commission and there were negotiations over the picture, clearly without results. In any case, three years after *Jules et Jim*'s première, Truffaut wanted to rerelease the picture, and now he wanted to reach a wider audience. In a new letter, dated 23 June 1965, Truffaut referred to earlier discussions and proposed a long series of cuts. In fact, he wrote that he had shortened the film by eight minutes himself, modifying three scenes, completely cutting four others, and eliminating practically one character. Adding that this new version had improved the picture's rhythm, Truffaut also claimed that the film 'did not contain any scene of violence or eroticism any more'.[9] Although Truffaut's request for a more lenient rating was supported by Jean Cocteau and Jean Renoir, the Commission's president could not accept the offer, arguing that the original decision was not inspired by specific scenes, but was based on the overall 'moral climate' of the picture.[10] Nonetheless, Truffaut persisted, and six months later, in December 1965, *Jules et Jim* was introduced before the board again. After two rounds of votes the board now decided to make the picture available to all audiences. In a letter to the minister the board's president argued that the decision was based on the 'change of public morality', the 'quality of the movie', and the author's 'pure intentions' and reputation.[11] Although Truffaut's censorship battle indicated his willingness to comply with the censors in order not to harm the picture's career, the *Jules et Jim* case illustrates the importance of negotiation, self-censorship and the value of artistic criteria and reputation as a gateway for passing films. In the U.K., where Truffaut's earlier feature films *Les Quatre cents coups* (*The 400 Blows*, 1959) and *Tirez sur le pianiste* (*Shoot the Pianist*, 1960) were cut and received a strict age limitation (A), the subtitled version of *Jules et Jim* was granted an X certificate without cuts in April 1962.[12]

On the other hand, the British and French response to Louis Malle's *Les Amants*, one of the key films of the early New Wave, were more closely aligned. In France the picture was restricted to those aged sixteen and above in September 1958, after two long cuts. The age limitation and cuts were due to 'the numerous scenes where the lovers are in bed or in the bathroom'.[13] In the following months the Commission was attacked by various family organizations, condemning the board's lax attitude and leading to local bans and boycotts. In the U.K. the picture was seen in an art-house circuit only after major cuts were made.[14] One notorious elimination was a substantial part of a love scene where we see Jeanne Moreau in close-up and where 'there were clear implications of "cunnilingus"', which the BBFC 'regarded as censorable', as Trevelyan later admitted (1973: 106).

Of all the New Wave directors, however, it was Jean-Luc Godard who faced the most problems with the censors, and whose films can be said to be the most illuminating in a comparison of the key issues in Franco-British censorship debates during the period in question. We will come back to his first feature, *A bout de souffle*, in due course, but in general none of Godard's first films passed in either country without severe age restrictions or cuts. One early example is *Une femme est une femme / A Woman is a Woman* (1961), Godard's brilliant 'musical-comedy-tragedy' about a stripper, which was examined by the French Commission in May 1961. The film 'stayed within the confines of decency', but the Commission nevertheless argued that *Une Femme est une femme* contained 'scabrous scenes and situations which are not suitable for children'.[15] The censors tried to issue an age-eighteen restriction, but this was rejected in a first round of votes (ten against seven votes), finally resulting in the film being restricted to those of thirteen years and above. *Vivre sa vie* (1962), Godard's experimental picture about the life of Nana, a prostitute, was much more controversial, especially when the censorship board forbade both the picture and the trailer, in June 1962, for anyone under eighteen. The censors also asked for cuts to a key scene showing Nana and a client. Godard and his producer, Pierre Braunberger, negotiated the case, leading to (minor) changes in the picture and the trailer.[16] Another, well known example of Godard's censorial problems is *La Femme mariée* (literally: *The Married Woman*), where the board initially voted for a total ban, mainly due to the 'innumerable scenes of nakedness' and the 'salacious illustration of scenes of sexuality'.[17] While the ban was widely picked up on by the press, Godard approached the French Minister of Information and agreed to cut the work and to change its title into the more indefinite, and apparently more appropriate, *Une femme mariée* (*A Married Woman*, 1964). In November 1964, the board finally voted for an eighteen certificate (Bergala 2006: 224).

The most notorious case of Godard's early problems with the censors is *Le Petit Soldat*, his feature about a deserter during the Algerian War. The film, which is often cited as a classic example of political film censorship, faced a complete ban for more than two years in France. It was rejected in a plenary meeting of the board in September 1960, mainly because the act of desertion in the picture was 'justified by a mixture of moral, intellectual and even aesthetic considerations'.[18] Besides this general theme, the board took offence at several more specific scenes, including torture, the representation of FLN (Algerian Liberation Movement) agents, and the idea that French special forces were linked to political terror. In January 1963, *Le Petit Soldat* was released only after Godard had substantially cut the film, mainly in the torture scene. The release was accompanied by more public protests and controversy, with Godard even receiving death threats (Bergala 2006: 72–5; Douin 1998: 216; Sellier 2005: 120–2).

The picture's tumultuous and complex censorship history in France preceded its arrival on British shores: it was a major news item all over the continent and in Britain, where the censors examined the picture in March 1963. Trevelyan found the torture scene to be 'sadistic and somewhat dangerous if shown to an audience which included young hooligans since forms of torture could be imaginative'.[19] Finally agreeing to issue an X without a cut, the BBFC stipulated that the film could only be shown within the circuit of specialized cinemas: were it to pass outside of this, a reappraisal would be necessary.[20] In Britain, all of Godard's first features, from *Breathless,* his short film *Charlotte and Her Boyfriend* (*Charlotte et son Jules*, 1960) and *A Woman is a Woman,* until *The Soldiers* (*Les Carabiniers*, 1963) and *A Married Woman* (1964), all received an X certificate without cuts.

It is interesting to note how the BBFC integrated cultural capital and distinction, as well as artistic merit and the limited distribution to a specialized audience, into its final decision. In a first internal examination of *A Married Woman,* for instance, in March 1965, several cuts were proposed, but in an internal viewing report a BBFC examiner argued that 'I would vote for giving an X certificate without cuts' because 'it is a complex, ... pure and beautiful film which ought not to be suppressed'. In a letter to the U.K. distributor of *A Married Woman* (Kenneth Rive), Trevelyan justified his decision because the picture had 'the artistic quality to justify passing it without cuts for limited distribution to art-theatres', a move typical of U.K. censorship patterns for continental 'art' films across the age of cinema. Indeed, as Melanie Selfe's chapter in this collection demonstrates, 'artistic intention' remains a crucial determining factor in discourses surrounding foreign-language film and the limits of acceptability.[21]

Censoring *A bout de souffle*

The fact that *A bout de souffle* was almost immediately considered by film critics to be artistically innovative and that the picture is now part of a modernist film pantheon should not put into the shade the provocative qualities and the problems the film faced when it came out in 1960. Concentrating upon how these problems were reflected in censorship decisions, it is interesting to look at Godard's film from a 'censorial' point of view. *A bout de souffle* features theft (a car is stolen) and violent crime (the sudden, quite anarchic shooting of the motorcycle-mounted police officer five minutes into the film), and dialogue referring to love-making is rife. The picture also shows a bathroom and contains references to a toilet (forbidden in Production Code Administration (PCA)-controlled films in the U.S.A.), while Godard included three short close-ups of a man and a woman kissing. These possibly controversial items, though, are often short, unexpected and actually not particularly upsetting. Though film censors and conservative critics turned out to worry mostly about the long bedroom scene where we see Michel (Jean-Paul Belmondo) and Patricia (Jean Seberg) on/around the bed talking, *A bout de souffle* is a rather tame picture, at least in terms of graphic content. Contrary to *J'irai cracher...*, *Les Amants* and other early New Wave pictures, Godard did not show female nudity – except in a couple of frames where we see a photograph of two naked women in a book. He is extremely careful, for instance, to confine nudity to a naked back in a scene of Michel's girlfriend undressing that appears around nine minutes into the film. In the later bedroom scene Godard is again cautious: showing Michel's naked torso but avoiding any female nudity while implying that Seberg has undressed off-screen. In the same sequence, the act of love-making is only vaguely suggested, never shown explicitly. In a move perhaps to be expected of a director who has consistently demonstrated a fascination with the game of showing, hiding and veiling reality, it appears that Godard played a game with the censors: the only explicit reference to physical love-making is literally hidden (the scene where we see Patricia and Michel hiding and writhing under a white sheet), and even the lovers' kiss is short, disruptive and lacking sensuality, typical of the distance Godard places between men and women in his first works (Sellier 2005).

Whether or not the evasiveness of these scenes was the result of self-censorship or Godard's (Protestant/anarchic) worldview is not so important. The fact is that Godard and Georges de Beauregard, his producer, heavily promoted the work as a provocative piece of scandal. In France, *A bout de souffle* was first introduced before the Commission in December 1959. After what clearly had been a very difficult meeting, the board decided to give a visa to the film, but only under very precise conditions.[22] The film still had to face the most severe age limitation, eighteen years and above only, even after the board had cut the picture. In general, the Commission was shocked by the 'young man's behaviour', his easy use of violence, his 'growing influence upon the girl', and the 'nature of the dialogue'. The board explicitly asked Godard to cut a scene in which De Gaulle and the U.S. President, Eisenhower, were seen on the Champs-Élysées. Two weeks later, the censors also imposed a cut in the trailer and, quite exceptionally, demanded that the trailer had to inform audiences that the film could not be seen by anyone under eighteen.[23]

In the face of such severity on the Board's part, it comes as something of a surprise to learn that only fifteen years later, in April 1975, they decided that *A bout de souffle* was suitable for children and adolescents. This stringent censorship, with its severe age limitation, cuts and special trailer, raises questions about the target audience and about who finally saw the film. The picture was released in March 1960, after having received the Jean Vigo Prize, and was soon followed by an impressive amount of criticism, mostly welcoming the picture as a great piece of art and lauding its stylistic novelty – in terms of editing, camera movements, characters, dialogues and working methods, *A bout de souffle* was considered to be important, both as a 'pure form of cinema' and as 'witness' of its time (Dubreuilh 1960). Looking at the astonishing number of articles and other press material published at the time of its release, it is clear that the film was quickly seized upon by the media as a launchpad for debates on the representation of young people, crime, love and sexuality. The most negative criticisms were, not surprisingly, printed in conservative and Catholic newspapers and magazines. In these reviews, which followed the negative CCC rating (4b, or 'forbidden'), *A bout de souffle* was taken as an extreme example of the New Wave's amorality. The popular newspaper *Paris Presse*, for instance, criticized the obscenities in the picture, and was particularly disapproving of the fact that the young gangster appeared to have only one thing on his mind: 'trying to get the young woman into bed' (Aubriant 1960). *L'Express* argued that the picture was 'totally corrosive towards all traditional moral and social rules', and that *A bout de souffle* showed the 'misery of a human being without God' (Guyonnet 1960). In an article entitled 'Un Pastiche pour les professionnels' ('A Pastiche for Professionals'), *France Catholique* identified the picture as a typical New Wave 'apology of impertinence', cynicism and 'absurd disorder', full of 'bedroom scenes, promiscuity and coarseness' (Besseges 1960). Despite recognizing its cinematographic qualities, *Témoignage Chrétien* also heavily attacked *A bout de souffle* for its moral confusion, 'fatalism' and 'Nietzschean anarchism' (Carta 1960).

The French media hype around Godard's film was further fuelled by the film's receipt of an award at the Berlin film festival, leading to a quick release in foreign territories including the U.K. *Breathless* was first introduced before the BBFC in its original version in October 1960, when, as I have stated, it received an X certificate without cuts. The picture's release in a subtitled version at the Academy Cinema in July 1961 was accompanied by a large number of reviews. These mostly stressed the New Wave signature of the picture – evident not only in its style, but also in its worldview. For *The Daily Herald* (7 July 1961), *Breathless* signalled that Godard, Truffaut and Chabrol had pooled talents to produce a picture 'which crashes like a seventh wave on the shocked senses'. The newspaper criticized the 'script's frankness', the 'ruder words' and references to sex in dialogues. Recognizing *Breathless* as the 'most original, insolently gifted and shattering work the young French directors have yet produced', the *Observer* called Truffaut's dialogue 'anarchic' and criticized the 'dazzlingly protracted bedroom scene, spiked with private jokes and small narcissistic cruelties' (Gilliatt 1961).

Breathless' distributor in the U.K., David Kingsley, decided to release a dubbed version, which was given for examination to the BBFC in October 1961. This time around the Board objected and asked for some firm cuts. These included references to sleeping together, sentences about having a child, and a shot of Michel stroking Patricia's bottom. Trevelyan added that the BBFC might want some further cuts and that he wanted to have a closer look at the dubbing dialogue sheets, justifying his problems with the argument that 'the trouble about dubbing continental films is that the policy of Anglicization … alters the character of the film'. Trevelyan argued that the 'kind of dialogue to which our Examiners are objecting is pretty direct and not the kind of thing they would allow in a British picture'.[24] The cuts and translations were made, followed by a further examination of the modified picture, resulting in an X rating. In another letter to the distributor in November 1961, the BBFC Secretary complained that two of the cuts were clumsy, and that they were too obvious and should be improved. Trevelyan concluded that 'we do not like bad cuts since they tend to be blamed on the censors, so I hope that you will be able to improve them'.[25] This quote is interesting not only as an illustration of the role of ego and professional pride in discourses relating to British censorship, at least, but it also underlines the censor's willingness to be part of the industry and of the creative process of filmmaking. Although it is beyond the limits of this chapter to analyse it in depth, we might raise the question here, too, of whether British censorship, in comparison with its Gallic counterpart, was a context less dominated by institutions and more by individuals, one in which questions not only of morality and art, but also of personal taste, defined the landscape.

Conclusions

Looking back at the historical reception of *A bout de souffle* and other early New Wave works, it is clear that the pictures grouped together under this umbrella played a key role in challenging the censors, not only in France but also in the U.K. Knowing perfectly well the extent to which scandal and censorship battles could be lucrative, the new French directors were often openly provocative in how they dealt with sexuality and other social and moral issues. And yet the New Wave authors still had to take into account the censors' sensibilities, resulting in diverse strategies of negotiation. In France in particular, the filmmakers concerned had to deal with various kinds of pressure from the multifarious censorship bodies with whom they had contend, all of whom drew on a wide variety of strategies to discipline the new cinema. But in Britain, too, censorship was a complex process of give and take, rather than a unilateral imposition of institutional will.

In both countries, the New Wave authors were part of a wider process of change in the traditional censorship system. I have tried to indicate the extent to which artistic or aesthetic criteria were important in this process of slow relaxation in terms of morality and ethics – facilitating classification and – later – leading to the end of cutting. Besides arguments about artistic value and integrity, I have revealed how the double register used in the censor's discourse (morality and art), took into account the specificities of viewing contexts. 'Art' and the 'art-house' are terms consistently mobilized in the defence of censorial generosity; yet when an art-house picture threatened to traverse these categories, growing into a big audience success and entering into major film theatres, censors turned out to use different criteria of social capital. One has only to witness the BBFC's response to the dubbed version of *A bout de souffle* as evidence of this. What is particularly interesting in this respect is that by dint of their 'Frenchness', the New Wave films benefited from an enhanced veneer of artistic integrity when transported to the U.K.; it is unlikely to be a coincidence that their treatment was generally less severe at the hands of the BBFC than their cross-Channel counterparts. When the film became 'Anglicized', however, its artistic merit was perceived to have been diminished – and with it its capability for intellectual moral comment.

Turning to the public debate on the New Wave, finally, it might be interesting to speculate about the concept of a moral panic, or the situation where public 'moral guardians' express their anxiety about central societal norms and values being in danger, eventually leading to concrete actions of suppression, legal action and even censorship. Although it seems outdated to talk about moral panics today, one can at least observe traces of such a discourse in the case of the New Wave pictures at the end of the 1950s and early 1960s, admittedly more so in France than in Britain. One function of the censors in both countries, though, was to anticipate or try to temper public denouncement. In histories of controversial media on both sides of the Channel, then, it is useful to look at the public debate about the New Wave pictures as a cultural seismograph, an important indicator of social change and the power of those able to define it. By comparing the discourses surrounding the films making up this 'movement' in both Britain and France and, moreover, drawing the links between them, we can move beyond the insights that such analysis can offer into the discreet national cultural contexts of the two countries, throwing crucial light on intercultural relations between France and Britain at the time and on the transition that French cinema of the period undergoes as it crosses the Channel.

Notes

Within the body of this work, all translations from French into English are the author's own, unless otherwise stated.

1. In 1961 the first issue of *Communication* contained a special section on the New Wave, including a long research article with the results of a wide-scale project focusing upon the ethics in New Wave pictures (Bremond, Sullerot and Berton 1961).
2. CCRT (Centrale Catholique du Cinéma, de la Radio et de la Télévision) *Les Amants* file, December 1958, Brussels: DOCIP archive.
3. CCRT *Et Dieu... créa la femme* file, January 1957, Brussels: DOCIP archive.
4. CCRT *Hiroshima, mon amour* file, July 1959, Brussels: DOCIP archive.
5. BBFC Minutes of Exceptions, April 1962, London: BBFC.
6. CNC *Et Dieu... créa la femme* file, Report of the board meeting, 5 September 1956, Paris: CNC.
7. BBFC Minutes of Exceptions, March 1957, London: BBFC.
8. CNC *Jules et Jim* file, Report of the board meeting, 21 November 1961, Paris: CNC.
9. Letter from F. Truffaut to the President of the Commission de Contrôle, 23 June 1965, *Jules et Jim* file, Paris: CNC.
10. Letter from the President of the Commission de Contrôle to F. Truffaut, 2 July 1965, *Jules et Jim* file, Paris: CNC.

11. Letter from the Commission's President to the Minister of Information, 11 December 1965, Paris: CNC.
12. BBFC *Jules et Jim* file, April 1962, London: BBFC.
13. CNC *Les Amants* file, Report of the board meeting, 17 September 1958, Paris: CNC.
14. BBFC Minutes of Exceptions, August 1959, London: BBFC.
15. CNC *Une Femme est une femme* file, Report of the plenary meeting, 31 May 1961, Paris: CNC.
16. CNC *Vivre sa vie* file, June 1962, Paris: CNC.
17. CNC *Une Femme mariée* file, October 1964, Paris: CNC.
18. CNC *Le Petit soldat* file, Report of the plenary meeting, 7 September 1961, Paris: CNC.
19. Letter from J. Trevelyan to G.M. Hoellering, 6 September 1963, *Le Petit soldat* file, London: BBFC.
20. The information on the BBFC website on this picture (www.bbfc.co.uk), indicating that cuts were required, is not completely correct on this point. Retrieved from: http://www.bbfc.org.uk/website/Classified.nsf/0/81ECB7A264721313802566C80051F 039?OpenDocument. Last Accessed 18 January 2010.
21. Letter from J. Trevelyan to K. Rive, 29 March 1965, *Une Femme mariée* file, London: BBFC.
22. CNC *A bout de souffle* file, Report of the board meeting, 2 December 1959, Paris: CNC.
23. CNC *A bout de souffle* file, Report of the board meeting, 23 December 1959, Paris: CNC.
24. Letter from J. Trevelyan to D. Kingsley, 6 October 1961, *Breathless* file, London: BBFC. The information on the BBFC website is not completely correct. Please see: http://www.bbfc.org.uk/website/Classified.nsf/0/617270828E57ACFD802568F8002A5 7AD?OpenDocument. Last accessed 18 January 2010.
25. Letter from J. Trevelyan to D. Kingsley, 14 November 1961, *Breathless* file, London: BBFC.

Bibliography

Aubriant, M. 1960. 'A bout de souffle', *Paris Presse*, 17 March.

Barkan, Raymond. 1960. 'La Pornographie pratiquée comme un des Beaux-Arts', *Cinéma 60*, June : 81.

Bergala, A. 2006. *Godard au travail*. Paris: Cahiers du Cinéma.

Besseges, A. 1960. 'A bout de souffle: Un Pastiche pour les professionnels', *France Catholique*, 25 March.

Bremond, C., E. Sullerot and S. Berton. 1961. 'Les héros des film dits "de la Nouvelle Vague"', *Communications* 1(1): 142–77.

Carta, J. 1960. 'A bout de souffle: Mort d'un enfant', *Témoignage Chrétien*, 8 April: 13.

de Baroncelli, J. 1955. 'Les Censures cinématographiques II', *Le Monde*, 19 August.

Dewe Mathews, T. 1994. *Censored: The Story of Film Censorship in Britain*. London: Chatto Windus.

Douin, J.-L. 1998. *Dictionnaire de la censure au cinéma*. Paris: PUF.

Dubreuilh, S. 1960. 'A bout de souffle', *Libération*, 23 March.

Esquenazi, J.-P. 2004. *Godard et la société française des années 1960*. Paris: Colin.

Gilliatt, P. 1961. 'A bout de souffle', *The Observer*, 9 July.

Guyonnet, R. 1960. 'A bout de souffle', *L'Express*, 17 March.

Hayward, S. 2005. *French National Cinema*. London: Routledge.
Hervé, S. 2001. *La Censure du Cinéma en France à la libération*. Paris: ADHE.
Marie, M. 2007. *La Nouvelle Vague*. Paris: Colin.
Rochereau, H. 1960. 'La Grande pitié du cinéma français', *La Croix*, 21 May.
Sadoul, G. 1961. 'A bas la supercensure', *Lettres Françaises*, 16 March.
Schlosberg, L. 1955. *Les Censures cinématographiques*. Paris: Union Rationaliste.
Sellier, G. 2005. *La Nouvelle Vague: Un Cinéma au masculin singulier*. Paris: CNRS.
Séry, P. 1971. 'La Censure cinématographique en question', *Le Monde*, 9 February.
Siclier, J. 1961. *Nouvelle Vague?* Paris: Ed. du Cerf.
Staiger, J. 1992. *Interpreting Films: Studies in the Historical Reception of American Cinema*, Princeton: Princeton University Press.
Trevelyan, J. 1973. *What the Censors Saw*. London: Michael Joseph.

Filmography

A bout de souffle / Breathless. 1959, Jean-Luc Godard, France.
Amants, Les / The Lovers. 1958, Louis Malle, France.
Avant le déluge / Before the Deluge. 1954, André Cayatte, France.
Bel Âge, Le. 1959, Pierre Kast, France.
Blé en herbe, Le / The Game of Love. 1954, Claude Autant-Lara, France.
Carabiniers, Les / The Soldiers. 1963, Jean-Luc Godard, France.
Charlotte et son Jules / Charlotte and Her Boyfriend. 1960, Jean-Luc Godard, France.
Diable au corps, Le / Devil in the Flesh. 1947, Claude Autant-Lara, France.
Et Dieu... créa la femme / And God Created Woman. 1956, Roger Vadim, France.
Femme est une femme, Une / A Woman is a Woman. 1961, Jean-Luc Godard, France.
Femme mariée, Une / A Married Woman. 1964, Jean-Luc Godard, France.
Guernica. 1950, Alain Resnais, France.
Hiroshima mon amour. 1958, Alain Resnais, France.
J'irai cracher sur vos tombes / I Spit on Your Grave. 1959, Michel Gast, France.
Jules et Jim / Jules and Jim. 1962, François Truffaut, France.
Liaisons dangereuses, Les / Dangerous Liaisons. 1960, Roger Vadim, France.
Nuit et brouillard / Night and Fog. 1955, Alain Resnais, France.
Petit Soldat, Le / The Little Soldier. 1960, Jean-Luc Godard, France.
Quatre cents coups, Les / The 400 Blows. 1959, François Truffaut, France.
Statues meurent aussi, Les / Statues Also Die. 1953, Alain Resnais and Chris Marker, France.
Tirez sur le pianiste / Shoot the Pianist. 1960, François Truffaut, France.
Vivre sa vie. 1962, Jean-Luc Godard, France.
Wild One, The. 1953, László Benedek, U.S.A.

CHAPTER 7

The Reception of the *Nouvelle Vague* in Britain

Geoffrey Nowell-Smith

The French New Wave, or *Nouvelle Vague*, was a major event in French cinema. But it also had major international ramifications. It – or simply the fact that it existed – inspired dramatic new developments in the cinema across the world, from Britain to eastern Europe to Japan to Brazil. And its own life was prolonged by its international success, since export sales of *Nouvelle Vague* films helped finance continuing production even when a film had flopped in its home market.

This chapter will look at two aspects of the early reception of the *Nouvelle Vague* in Britain: the critical and the commercial. The two tended to proceed in tandem. Sometimes criticism followed commerce, in that a film would be written about by reviewers at the time of, or shortly after, its release in Britain. But sometimes unreleased films would be written about in the specialist press and picked up for distribution on the basis of the reputation thus acquired. My principal sources on the critical side are the magazines *Sight and Sound* and *Films and Filming*, both of which had a U.K. circulation of around ten thousand copies, but I shall also make reference to *Oxford Opinion*, a student magazine with a tiny circulation but huge critical resonance. The commercial data are for distribution and exhibition in the London area, which is easiest to trace. Exhibition in major provincial cities tended to follow the pattern set in the metropolis. In the case of two films – Jean-Luc Godard's first feature, *A bout de souffle / Breathless* (1960), and François Truffaut's second, *Tirez sur le pianiste* (1960: Hereinafter referred to under its U.K. release title *Shoot the Pianist*) – this chapter will also look at critical reaction in the mainstream press. I have done no work on audience reaction (apart from a bit of introspection) so the responses to New Wave films I can report on are either critical (what did the critics say?) or commercial (what did distributors and exhibitors think worth putting before the public?) – bearing in mind that the distributors and exhibitors were not calculating machines; they were people with tastes of their own and often a strong commitment to what they considered good cinema.

As to what the *Nouvelle Vague* was, I shall be calling *Nouvelle Vague* what was called *Nouvelle Vague* at the time, the period in question being between 1958 and 1961. The starting date is provided by an article by Pierre Billard, published in the French cine-club magazine *Cinéma 58* in February 1958, which is generally cited as containing the first recorded example of the phrase being used about film.[1] Actually Billard's remarks are not particularly positive about the wave patterns he saw developing in the French cinema at the time. He first asks who are the new generation ('*nouvelle vague*') of French filmmakers, notes that there are not very many, and then declares that there was not much of a wave happening at all but rather a trough ('*un creux*') between two waves. Looking forward to the next wave, if and when it were to materialize, he identifies a small number of filmmakers likely to compose it: Alexandre Astruc, Roger Vadim, Alex Joffé, Louis Malle (all to some degree established), and Edouard Molinaro, Jacques Rivette, François Truffaut and Claude Chabrol (very much at the beginning of their careers). Also mentioned are Pierre Kast and Agnès Varda. Astruc, Vadim, Kast and Varda are further commended, presciently, for the freedom, sincerity and modernity of their portrayal of relations between men and women. As for an end date, I have set it in 1961 because that was when after the heady atmosphere of 1959 and 1960 a reflux set in. The public success of *Les Cousins / Cousins* (1959), *Les Quatre cents coups*[2] and *A bout de souffle* was not repeated. The next films by Chabrol, Truffaut and Godard all did badly at the French and British box offices and in the spring of that year the critic Jacques Siclier brought out a book entitled *Nouvelle Vague?* (Siclier 1961) which declared the wave to be already over and done with.[3] During this period Jacques Rivette, Eric Rohmer, Jacques Demy and Agnès Varda all completed their first features. Alain Resnais made two, Truffaut and Godard three each, and Claude Chabrol no fewer than six. Also within the period falls Marcel Camus's *Orfeu negro / Black Orpheus* (1959) which shared the limelight at Cannes 1959 with *Les Quatre cents coups* and *Hiroshima mon amour* (1959).

That is the French time frame. The British time frame lags slightly in relation to it. The films tended to come to Britain, if at all, with a six- to eighteen-month delay while distributors mulled things over, haggled over the price, or waited for a slot at one of the three or four art-house cinemas at which a foreign film could be successfully launched. But during the period of time lag, films which were not yet released could nevertheless be talked about. Magazines had their Paris correspondents, critics could go to Cannes and other festivals, and even without Eurostar or Easyjet British cinephiles could go to Paris and catch up with films they were unsure of being able to see at home. The discourse of the *Nouvelle Vague* ran ahead of the general audience experience – so much so that when Siclier wrote in *Sight and Sound* in Summer 1961 about the *Nouvelle Vague* being over, readers, particularly in the provinces, were entitled to ask: 'Well, what was that when it happened, because it hasn't come here yet?' Even so the sense of the wave as a wave – as opposed to the continuing work of filmmakers whom the wave had thrown up – had evaporated almost as quickly in Britain as it did in France itself. For this reason, I shall more or less finish the story, as far as British reception is concerned, at the end of 1961, by which time any of the distinctive early *Nouvelle Vague* films which were going to get distribution in Britain had either got it or were a lost cause.

The first hint for English audiences of something new happening in France came when David Robinson saw two films which were shown at Cannes in May 1958 out of competition: Truffaut's short *Les Mistons* (1957) and Chabrol's recently completed first feature, *Le Beau Serge* (1958). Robinson was so struck by both films that he arranged for them to be shown at the National Film Theatre (NFT) in London in early September under the Free Cinema banner. Neither director was in attendance and the films do not seem to have caused a particular stir. It is, however, worth noting that this was better than what happened in Cannes itself, where *Le Beau Serge* had been pulled from competition by the French authorities and where Truffaut had been refused accreditation to the festival because of his attacks on it the previous year. The NFT event may have been low key, but at least it was positive.[4] At the London Film Festival that autumn, the French films chosen by the festival director, Richard Roud, were Jacques Baratier's *Goha* (1958), which died without trace, and Louis Malle's *Les Amants* (1958), which went on to have a widespread commercial release in Britain, aided by its notorious sex scene, which despite censor's cuts was remarkably explicit for the period.[5]

The screening of *Le Beau Serge* and *Les Mistons* was followed up in the Winter 1958/59 issue of *Sight and Sound*. This issue contained a tribute to André Bazin, who had died in November, by Louis Marcorelles, and an interview by Bazin with Jean Renoir and Roberto Rossellini. Separately, Marcorelles reported from Paris on the making of Jacques Rivette's *Paris nous appartient*, on the fact that Chabrol had made *Le Beau Serge*, that Truffaut was shooting *Les Quatre cents coups*, and that Resnais was in Japan shooting *Hiroshima mon amour*. Marcorelles concluded with a quote from Truffaut about how the future belonged to him, Malle, Chabrol, Baratier, Resnais and Varda. Marcorelles wrote occasionally for *Sight and Sound* but was also a regular contributor to *Cahiers du cinéma*, sharing many of *Cahiers*'s cinematic tastes but taking a distance from what he saw as the infantile rightism of some of the *Cahiers* in-group, Truffaut and Godard in particular. Neither in the quote from Truffaut nor elsewhere in his report does Marcorelles use the phrase *Nouvelle Vague*.

There followed a period of silence. *Le Beau Serge* and *Les Cousins* were released in Paris more or less simultaneously, in February and March 1959 respectively. But *Les Quatre cents coups* and *Hiroshima* were kept under wraps on completion, to be premiered at the Cannes Festival in May. The general buzz of excitement created by their showing at the festival was echoed in the British press. *Sight and Sound* again took the lead. In its Summer/Autumn 1959 issue, the Cannes report from John Gillett said relatively little about the trio of French films which had won prizes at the Festival, but only because pride of place in the issue was given to a long article by Georges Sadoul celebrating the emergence of an entire new generation in French cinema. But there was already, even before the first *Nouvelle Vague* film had been shown in Britain, a slight sniffiness emerging in *Sight and Sound*'s response. Since this was a double issue, it also contained a Venice report from Penelope Houston, the editor of the magazine, in which she remarked about Chabrol's fourth film, *A double tour*. 'It is not particularly encouraging that he [Chabrol] has been quoted as finding this the most satisfying of his pictures'.

Meanwhile the more downscale monthly *Films and Filming* also had its reports from France, generally written by Ginette Billard, the wife of the same Pierre Billard who had asked the question about when the new wave was going to happen. Ginette was not over-impressed by novelty. She went to the short film festival in Tours in 1958 and noted the success there of Agnès Varda's *Du côté de la côte* (1958) while deploring the tendency of Varda's friends Marker and Resnais to clutter up their films with commentary (Billard 1959a). Cannes was covered for the magazine by Peter Baker (1959), who enthused about *Les Quatre cents coups*, enjoyed *Orfeu negro* while finding it lightweight, thought *Les Cousins* a better 'youth' film than veteran Marcel Carné's *Les Tricheurs / Youthful Sinners* (1958), regarded *Hiroshima mon amour* as an interesting failure, and concluded that Malle, Truffaut, Chabrol and Resnais were the most exciting newcomers in French cinema. He did not at this point refer to them as constituting a wave.

In October, however, the magazine featured for the first time something called '*La Nouvelle Vague*'. Alongside some soundbites from Camus, Robert Hossein, Malle, Edouard Molinaro, Jean-Daniel Pollet, François Reichenbach, Truffaut and Baratier, Ginette Billard gave thumbnail sketches of Resnais, Truffaut, Kast, Pollet, Chabrol (*Les Cousins* a 'deception' [sic]: presumably what the translator should have said was 'disappointment'), Varda, Marker, Jacques Doniol-Valcroze and Reichenbach (1959b). She noted that the eroticism in their (or some of their) films was not new for French cinema but that there was a certain freedom in the films which came not from their defying the censor but from their refusal to be self-censoring.

The year 1959 closed, as far as the New Wave and *Films and Filming* were concerned, with a Venice round-up in November in which John Francis Lane (1959) deplored Chabrol's *A double tour* (1959) as garish exploitation and concluded with a quote from René Clair, chairman of the Venice jury, who, when asked if the New Wave was really new, apparently replied, 'Look at the sea, my friend: all waves are new, are they not?'

Meanwhile the first *Nouvelle Vague* film to be released in Britain, *Les Cousins*, opened at the Curzon Cinema on 25 September 1959 with an X certificate and ran for two months. The London Film Festival showed *Les Quatre cents coups* and *Orfeu negro* but not *Hiroshima*, which was withheld by its distributor, Gala, so as not to spoil its planned release in the New Year. This took place on 8 January 1960 and, to celebrate the event, Gala renamed one of their cinemas, previously the Roxy Westbourne Grove, the International Film Theatre.

This was a significant event because up to then Gala could not really count as a prestigious distributor/exhibitor. The company owned six cinemas in London showing mainly continental films, but 'continental' in this context meant exploitation, since most of the films shown were softcore films which the British censor had allowed in with an X certificate but had more sex content than was allowed in British or American films. Besides Gala, other independent distributor/exhibitors were the Classic chain (eight cinemas in central London and the suburbs), which did not do new releases; the two Cameos (the Cameo Royal in Charing Cross Road and the Cameo Poly in Regent Street on the site of the London Polytechnic where the first Lumière shows took place in Britain in 1896) which were also on the art/sex boundary; and the three prestige outlets, the Academy in Oxford Street, the Paris Pullman in Chelsea and the Curzon in Mayfair. Outside the West End and a small arc of west and northwest London, there were also a number of independently owned cinemas such as the State Leytonstone or the Globe Putney, which had access to the films distributed by Gala and other art/exploitation film distributors, but only after they had had a first run in the West End. Most of the serious business in the field was done by a small handful of firms, and for a film to do well a first run at the Academy, Paris Pullman or Curzon was generally judged essential. Gala's premiere of *Hiroshima mon amour* at the pretentiously renamed International Film Theatre was not only the occasion of the arrival of the *Nouvelle Vague* on British commercial screens but an inaugural moment for the 1960s art-film culture as a whole.

The market which *Hiroshima mon amour* entered, followed in March by *Les Quatre cents coups* at the Curzon, was dominated at the arty end by Ingmar Bergman and at the less arty end by films with titles like *Dolls of Vice* (*Les Clandestines*, 1955), with some art films disguised as sex films – e.g. *Swamp of Lust* a.k.a. *Republic of Sin* (Buñuel's *La Fièvre monte à El Pao*, 1959) – or vice versa. As mentioned earlier, Malle's *Les Amants* did good business all over London, and was followed by Chabrol's *Les Cousins*, which popped up in a number of suburban cinemas after its first run at the Curzon. *Hiroshima mon amour* by contrast, after a phenomenal first run at the International Film Theatre, hardly reappeared at all. In this it was not helped by a review by Josh Billings in *Kine Weekly* which on the one hand described it as a romantic melodrama and on the other hand as having as its main plus factor 'terrific snob values' (1960a).[6] This was not likely to inspire a cinema manager in Tooting or Barking to want to book it. The most widely shown of French films in 1959 and 1960 in fact were Jacques Tati's *Mon Oncle* (1958) and Claude Autant-Lara's *La Jument verte / The Green Mare's Nest* (1959), and not *Nouvelle Vague* films at all.

In fact, although *Nouvelle Vague* films started appearing in the cinemas, there was little sense of their distinctiveness except that they might be arty, like *Hiroshima*, or sexy, like *Les Cousins*. It was not until the rather belated appearance of Godard's *A bout de souffle* in June 1961, nearly eighteen months after its first release in Paris, that the sense emerges that this was really a new cinema, not just a new batch of French films. Alongside Truffaut's *Shoot the Pianist*, which had been released in January, there now seemed to be what we might describe as 'a certain tendency in French cinema', a strange mixture of French existentialism and the American B-picture, equally threatening to the mainstream values of either the Academy Award type of Hollywood picture or the classic art film.

The most interesting responses to this novelty were contained in a long article by Gabriel Pearson and Eric Rhode in *Sight and Sound* (Pearson and Rhode 1961) and in the quality press reviews of *A bout de souffle*. *Sight and Sound* at the time was embroiled in a spat with the *Cahiers du cinéma*-inspired Young Turks of *Oxford Opinion* in which it generally came off worse. But on the matter of the equally *Cahiers*-inspired *Nouvelle Vague* the roles were reversed and it was the old guard of *Sight and Sound* who proved, after a shaky start, to be in the avant garde. *Oxford Opinion* ran a very thoughtful review article by Paul Mayersberg on *Shoot the Pianist* and *Les Cousins*, and Ian Cameron contributed a cheery review of Doniol-Valcroze's *L'Eau à la bouche* (1960), whose evident sensuality clearly delighted him (Cameron 1960; Mayersberg 1961). When the *Oxford Opinion* authors regrouped as *Movie* a year or more later they continued to take notice of the *Nouvelle Vague* but their focus was much more on mainstream U.S. cinema and they tended to be cautious about films which deviated too far from the classical aesthetic that they mostly endorsed. (A good example of this is V.F. Perkins's article on Godard's 1962 *Vivre sa vie* in *Movie*, January 1963). Further confusion was added by the fact that the Young Turks liked Franju's *Les Yeux sans visage / Eyes Without a Face* (1959), although Franju was up to then admired more by the left-of-centre art film crowd.

Pearson's and Rhode's article was entitled 'Cinema of Appearance' and appeared in *Sight and Sound's* Autumn 1961 issue. It caused a bit of a stir when it first came out, but its argument went somewhat against the intellectual grain of the time and it has now been largely forgotten. Several spins of the critical wheel later, when one of its central pillars – Melanie Klein's view of the construction of the human psyche – is once again on the agenda, it is worth returning to it, both for its argument in itself and for what it says about the reception of the *Nouvelle Vague*.

The article is in three parts. The first, entitled 'The Humanist's Approach', summarizes the classic view of what constitutes great art – basically its ability to give a sense of the coherence and continuity of the outer and inner worlds, or, in other terms, of reality and the consciousness that we, as artists or as readers/viewers, have of it. The second, entitled 'The Artist's Approach', looks at the way some recent films, major and minor, appear to challenge the assumptions of the humanist approach. The films chosen to illustrate this thesis (both of them in the authors' opinion 'relatively slight', but representative of a wider trend in the cinema of the period and modernist art more generally) are *A bout de souffle* and *Shoot the Pianist*. In these films, the classic assumptions about human nature and art's ability to represent it coherently are overthrown. *A bout de souffle* in particular offers up a picture of a world which is discontinuous, both physically (jump-cuts) and mentally (Michel's 'existentialist' immoralism and recourse to the *acte gratuit*). *A bout de souffle* (and to a lesser extent *Shoot the Pianist*), the authors argue, shows a world of pure appearance which makes no attempt to match this appearance with any form of underlying reality.

In the third part, entitled 'The Humanist Position Reconsidered', Pearson and Rhode pull the Kleinian rabbit out of the hat, declaring *A bout de souffle* and its hero to exemplify an extreme form of manic defence against the external world, victims of a process of splitting which makes impossible any form of (re)construction of the world and the ego's relationship to it on a coherent basis. *Shoot the Pianist* is to some extent exempted from this indictment because its hero, Charlie, is shown as able to reconnect with the world and himself through his love for Lena (even if Truffaut spares the audience the embarrassment of a blatantly false 'happy end' by cruelly having her die in her attempt to rescue the child Fédo). For all their occasional brilliance and their ability to catch something of the dazzling surface of modernity, the article concludes, *A bout de souffle* and *Shoot the Pianist* are examples of a form of art that does not do justice to human potential. On the other hand there is nothing new in works of art which show the world and the human subject in this way: the surprising thing, in fact, is that it has taken the cinema so long to create works of this kind.[7]

This is a massively heavy argument to hang on the fragile peg of two newly released films whose long-term critical status was at best unproven. What is interesting about it is firstly the attempt to rescue a humanist aesthetic which was increasingly under attack as wishy-washy ideology by grounding it in a theory of human nature, and secondly, and perhaps more pertinent here, the sense it gives of the profound tremors that *A bout de souffle* in particular had generated in intellectual circles.

Meanwhile, shortly before 'Cinema of Appearance' came out, the *Observer* changed its film critic. Out went veteran C.A. Lejeune, who had struggled with *Shoot the Pianist*, and in came Penelope Gilliatt, who knew nothing about cinema but was intelligent and eclectic and who responded to the originality of *A bout de souffle* in her own original way. Quoting Mary McCarthy's observation that 'sensibility and sensation were 20th century twins which, in the novel, [had combined to] abolish the social and a sense of character', Gilliatt placed *A bout de souffle* along with Shirley Clarke's *The Connection* (1962) on the 'masculine' side of sensation, and Antonioni's *L'avventura*, Peter Brook's *Moderato cantabile* (both 1960) and *Les Amants* on the 'feminine' side of sensibility.[8] She then summed up *A bout de souffle* as 'the most original, insolently gifted and shattering work the young French directors have yet produced' (Gilliatt 1961).

These responses to *A bout de souffle* mark the imminent opening up of a divide in the reception of European cinema in Britain and to some extent in the United States as well. There continued to be a public for the sort of films which were commercial successes in their home country before becoming 'art cinema' on crossing the Channel (or Atlantic) – Federico Fellini's *La Dolce vita* (1960), for example, or Vadim's *Les Liaisons dangereuses* (1959). But there was also a new public emerging which vigorously sought out experiment, novelty and (increasingly) political radicalism. French and Italian producers were quick to cotton on to the financial value of this new Anglo-American public and were soon followed by the Hollywood studio companies in their guise as worldwide distributors of films of whatever origin. A Godard film like *Les Carabiniers* (1963), which bombed in Paris on first release, could nevertheless be a viable investment for its producers – in this case Carlo Ponti and Georges de Beauregard – on the basis of export box office and presales. By mid-decade, new waves were springing up all over – most notably in eastern Europe, Brazil and Japan. For the producers of the films of Miloš Forman, Dušan Makavejev, Glauber Rocha or Nagisa Oshima, export into the markets which had taken to the work of Antonioni, Godard and Rivette was a godsend. As well as supporting Godard and Antonioni, Ponti also invested in Forman's *Firemen's Ball* (1967) and, a bit later in 1976, Anatole Dauman famously rescued Oshima's *Empire of the Senses*, which he had coproduced, when Oshima's own company was told by the Japanese government to hand over the negative and prints. By this time, however, the art-film culture had changed entirely. If there is any single point where the change can be said to have begun it is with *A bout de souffle* and the at first puzzled and then enthusiastic reception it received in France, Britain and elsewhere.

Notes

1. The phrase *Nouvelle Vague* itself originated with a series of articles by Françoise Giroud in the weekly *L'Express* in 1957, which, however had nothing to say about film.
2. Truffaut's film has two English titles: one, literal but meaningless in English, is *The Four Hundred Blows*; the other, which unfortunately did not catch on, was *Wild Oats*.
3. The date of printing of this book is given as 20 February 1961, so presumably it came out round about April. The dismal box-office figures for Truffaut's *Shoot the Pianist* (1960), Chabrol's *A double tour* (1960) and Godard's *Une femme est une femme* (1961) are to be found in Marie (2003: 66–7). Godard's second feature, *Le Petit Soldat* (1960), was not released at all, having been banned by the state censorship.
4. Thanks to Christophe Dupin for pointing this out.
5. Ninety seconds of cuts by the British censor ensured that the cunnilingus in the love scene towards the end was not visible or even fully deducible. This did not prevent spectators from being aware that something was going on altogether more daring than was usual in films at the time.
6. Josh Billings, who did the weekly round-up for the paper, tended to call all films which were not clearly members of other genres 'melodramas'. *Shoot the Pianist*, however, stumped him, and he described it (1960b) as an 'off-beat gangster comedy melodrama'. Genre theorists take note.
7. Rhode, who went on to become a distinguished Kleinian psychoanalyst, was probably the main author for this third part of the article. Pearson, a literary critic and founder with Stuart Hall of *The Universities and Left Review*, would have been mainly responsible for the first part, while the second part, at a guess, would have been shared.
8. McCarthy's precise words were: 'Sensation and sensibility are the poles of each other, and both have the effect of abolishing the social. Sensibility, like violent action, annihilates the sense of character' (McCarthy 1961: 276). McCarthy was much more categorical in her gender divide than Gilliatt: all the writers she placed on the side of sensation were men, while those on the side of sensibility were almost all women (plus E.M. Forster).

Bibliography

Bazin, A. 1958/59. 'Cinema and Television; Jean Renoir and Roberto Rossellini', *Sight and Sound* 28/1: 26–30.

Billard, P. 1958. *Cinéma 58*, February 1958: 31–4.

Billard, G. 1959a. 'France', *Films and Filming*, February 1959: 33.

———. 1959b. 'La Nouvelle Vague', *Films and Filming*, October 1959: 7–8.

Billings, J. 1960a. *Kine Weekly*, 14 January: 10 and 28.

———. 1960b. *Kine Weekly*, 22 December.

Baker, P. 1959. 'Cannes 1959: A Festival Review', *Films and Filming*, July 1959: 11, 30–31, 33.

Cameron, I. 1960. 'L'Eau à la bouche', *Oxford Opinion* 42: 37–8.

Gillett, J. 1959. 'The Festivals: Cannes', *Sight and Sound* 28/3–4: 138, 140–41.

Gilliatt, P. 1961. *The Observer*, 9 July.

Houston, P. 1959. 'The Festivals: Venice', *Sight and Sound* 28/3–4: 142–43.

Lane, J.F. 1959. 'Festival in Venice', *Films and Filming*, November 1959: 11, 30–31 .

Marcorelles, L. 1958/59a. 'Paris Nous Appartient', *Sight and Sound* 28/1: 34.

———. 1958/59b. 'André Bazin', *Sight and Sound* 28/1: 30.

Marie, M. 2003. *The French New Wave: An Artistic School*. Oxford: Blackwell.

Mayersberg, P. 1961. 'Fairy Tales of Paris', *Oxford Opinion* 47: 31–2.

McCarthy, M. 1961. *On the Contrary*. New York: Farrar, Straus.

Pearson, G. and E. Rhode. 1961. 'Cinema of Appearance', *Sight and Sound* 30/4: 160-168.

Perkins, V.F. 1963. 'Vivre sa vie', *Movie* 6: 26–27.

Sadoul, G. 1959. 'Notes on a New Generation', *Sight and Sound* 28/3–4: 111–117.

Siclier, J. 1961a. *Nouvelle Vague?* Paris: Editions du Cerf.

———. 1961b. 'New Wave and French Cinema', *Sight and Sound* 30/3: 116–120.

Filmography

A bout de souffle / *Breathless*. 1960, Jean-Luc Godard, France.

A double tour. 1959, Claude Chabrol, France/Italy.

Ai no corrida / *Empire of the Senses*. 1976, Nagisa Oshima, Japan/France.

Amants, Les / *The Lovers*. 1958, Louis Malle, France.

Avventura, L' . 1960, Michelangelo Antonioni, Italy/France.

Beau Serge, Le. 1958, Claude Chabrol, France.

Carabiniers, Les. 1963, Jean-Luc Godard, France/Italy.

Clandestines, Les / *Dolls of Vice*. 1955, Raoul André, France.

Connection, The. 1962, Shirley Clarke, U.S.A.

Cousins, Les / *The Cousins*. 1959, Claude Chabrol, France.

Dolce vita, La. 1960, Federico Fellini, Italy/France.

Du côté de la côte. 1958, Agnès Varda, France.

Eau à la bouche, L'. 1960, Jacques Doniol-Valcroze, France.

Femme est une femme, Une. 1961, Jean-Luc Godard, France.

Fièvre monte à El Pao, La / *Swamp of Lust* a.k.a. *Republic of Sin*. 1959, Luis Buñuel, France.

Goha. 1958, Jacques Baratier, France/Tunisia.

Hiroshima mon amour. 1959, Alain Resnais, France/Japan.

Hori, ma panenko / *The Firemen's Ball*. 1967, Miloš Forman, Czechoslovakia.

Jument verte, La / *The Green Mare's Nest*. 1959, Claude Autant-Lara, France/Italy.

Liaisons dangereuses, Les. 1959, Roger Vadim, France.

Mistons, Les. 1957, François Truffaut, France.

Moderato cantabile. 1960, Peter Brook, France/Italy.

Mon oncle. 1958, Jacques Tati, France/Italy.

Orfeu negro / *Black Orpheus*. 1958, Marcel Camus, France/Italy/Brazil.

Paris nous appartient. 1958 (released 1961), Jacques Rivette, France.

Petit Soldat, Le. 1960, Jean-Luc Godard, France.
Quatre cents coups, Les / *The Four Hundred Blows*. 1959, François Truffaut, France.
Tirez sur le pianiste / *Shoot the Pianist*. 1960, François Truffaut, France.
Tricheurs, Les. 1958, Marcel Carné, France/Italy.
Vivre sa vie. 1962, Jean-Luc Godard, France.
Yeux sans visage, Les / *Eyes Without a Face*. 1959, Georges Franju, France/Italy.

CHAPTER 8

'New Waves, New Publics?': The *Nouvelle Vague*, French Stars and British Cinema

Sarah Street

When critics heralded the French *Nouvelle Vague* at the end of the 1950s the term 'New Wave' was soon attached to British films produced by independents, many of which were adaptations from novels and plays written by the so-called 'Angry Young Man' generation. Because of their nomenclature, one would assume the New Wave British films resembled or aspired to being similar to the *Nouvelle Vague*. Immediately, however, critics keen to herald experimentation in French films tended to see British films as not pushing at formal boundaries in quite the same way. Penelope Houston compared *The Loneliness of the Long Distance Runner* (1962) unfavourably to *Les Quatre cents coups / The 400 Blows* (1959): 'Where Truffaut's style grew out of his theme, Richardson's looks like the result of a deliberate act of will so that the bits and pieces remain unassimilated' (Houston 1963: 121). Victor Perkins confirmed this negative judgement in an article in *Movie* written in 1962 that dismissed British films as being inferior to other European styles: 'The British cinema is as dead as before .... We are still unable to find evidence of artistic sensibilities in working order' (Perkins 1972: 7). The *Nouvelle Vague*'s perceived innovatory status overshadowed cinematic developments in Britain, while in France, despite some critical acclaim for the New Wave British films and their social commitment, *Cahiers du cinema* critics and others were dismissive of recent trends (Wimmer 2009: 132–3).

Yet one must go beyond these damning critical judgements to analyse what was emerging, what kinds of transnational exchanges were actually evident at the level of formal experimentation, popular stardom and reception, often involving films not conventionally considered to belong to the 'New Wave'. In this chapter I suggest that in many ways the critical reception in Britain of the *Nouvelle Vague* created difficulties for British cinema, introducing a standard of comparison which led to a misunderstanding of key aspects of the British New Wave and other contemporary films. I argue that instead of using the *Nouvelle Vague* as a primary frame of reference there is another, French-associated, transnational movement that is perhaps more applicable to much of British cinema in this period, namely, poetic realism. While the connection has been made between British films (particularly the Free Cinema documentaries of the 1950s) and 'the poetic realism of the everyday', there is a case to be made for looking at this more closely, rather than simply using it as a convenient, older contextual milieu for Franco-British stylistic affinities. In addition, the contribution of French actresses to British films during this period provides a further, comparative frame of reference.

Poetic Realism and British Cinema

Classic poetic realism has been primarily associated with French cinema of the 1930s to mid 1940s (Andrew 1995). The style typically included working-class settings, exhibiting expressions of urban pessimism and 'a duality between the everyday and the lyrical/emotional, the poetry arising precisely *from* the everyday' (Vincendeau 1995: 336). Yet it was also a transnational development affecting the film industries of Europe more generally, particularly in the field of set design (Bergfelder, Harris and Street 2007). While the significance of French films deploying poetic realism is not to be underestimated, rather than limit its influence to one particular country and decade, it is possible to cite instances of its recurrence in other national cinemas and in this respect British films are no exception. B.F. Taylor (2006) has also questioned the usefulness of locating British films of the late 1950s and early 1960s solely in relation to the *Nouvelle Vague*. Of particular note is his rereading of scenes and shots from British films of the New Wave period that were dismissed by *Movie* and *Sight and Sound* critics as 'unassimilated' and superfluous to the narrative. I want to take this approach further by arguing that, with their precise locations, such scenes and shots resemble the logic of poetic realism – a fact often ignored by those analyses which concentrated on the *Nouvelle Vague* as a frame of comparison. Moreover, critics' preoccupation with an overly auteurist conception of film style tended to neglect the significance of broader considerations of space and place, mise en scene, stars, gender and audiences.

Previous analyses of the British New Wave films concentrated on their social commentary, so much so that elements which do not appear to support this narrative logic are dismissed as an 'aestheticism of urban squalor' (Lay 2002: 63), or more positively, as Higson argues, as poetic spaces for characters' reflection (1996: 150–1). Yet in spite of this influential observation the French roots of this approach have not been made explicit or subject to sustained consideration. In *A Taste of Honey* (1961), for example, Richardson uses location very well, insofar as his 'efforts here successfully incorporate internal and external spaces into a compelling and well-realised depiction of a young girl's struggle to find a position for herself within her world' (Taylor 2006: 65). A core tenet of poetic realism was that locations were a reflection of the internal emotions of the characters, enabling an intensification of emotional development. This is a little different from Higson's view of such scenes as distancing, interiorized and reflective spaces that relate primarily to aestheticization. While he acknowledges poetic realist affinities, he also observes that as far as 'That Long Shot of Our Town from That Hill' is concerned, there is a tension between 'moral commitment' and 'authorial mastery of aesthetics'. For Higson, 'poetic realism as a loosely articulated discourse can only struggle to hold the two ends together' (Higson 1996: 151). However, it is productive to conceive of the poetic realist influence as more than a 'loosely articulated discourse', especially with reference to interior sets. For in poetic realist analysis décor in particular is more akin to a character, representing the symbolic element inherent in the everyday, which was a key register in the British New Wave films. This shifts the analysis of space and place from exteriors to interiors, and what is striking is how, when linked to deep emotional journeys and acute sensibilities, décor transcends a purely realist function.

Simone Signoret as Poetic Realist Star

The following analysis, which foregrounds a poetic realist framework for British films of this period, will be supported by case studies of two key performances in British films by the French actress Simone Signoret: in *Room at the Top* (1959) and *Term of Trial* (1962). Signoret is particularly interesting in this regard since as a star she is associated with poetic realism, particularly as concerns her roles in French cinema during the first ten years of her career and later in the phase in which she starred in genre films that Hayward (2004) has described as *réalisme noir*. Signoret's association with the style made her uninteresting to directors of *Nouvelle Vague* films who considered her films to be old-fashioned and retro. But at the same time, she was courted by British directors who wanted to inject a bit of exoticism and sexuality into their films, particularly when censorship was enabling certain films to be marketed as 'X' products. Alexander Walker points to some critics' negative reaction to the casting of Signoret as indicative of a cynical pursuit of the international box-office (1986: 47): this despite the fact that in the U.S. she had found it difficult to get roles in the aftermath of Senator McCarthy's witch hunts against left-wing sympathizers in the film industry, of whom she was one (Signoret 1979: 244). But James Woolf, financier of *Room at the Top*, had experience of working in Hollywood and very much had an eye to the international market. The casting of Signoret as Alice had been suggested to him by Peter Grenville, who had been involved in the project at an early stage but did not end up directing *Room at the Top*. The final choice of director, Jack Clayton, also approved of Signoret's casting. The decision to cast the French star created a significant departure from John Braine's source novel, which depicted Alice as an English woman (Murphy 1992: 304, n12). It paid off, however: the film was successful at the U.K. and U.S. box offices, having been sold largely on the risqué qualities evident in its trailer. This short piece of marketing cues viewers to understand the film entirely in these terms, beginning with the commentary: 'Because all trailers must carry a "U" certificate, we are unable to show you scenes the censor has passed for adult audiences only'. John Braine's novel is described as 'Scorching' and Signoret as 'one of Europe's greatest stars' in the part of Alice, who is 'French and All Woman, ten years older than Joe, ten years more experienced...'. The shots used in the trailer show Signoret on a bed in sensuous pose, and the sultry background music invests the film with a seedy, sexualized and sensationalized impression that, as we shall see, gives a misleading impression of the overall poetic realist tenor of the scene.

But there was more than sexual titillation to this particular representation of a French woman living in the north of England. As Christine Geraghty (2000: 93–111) has pointed out, European women in British films during the postwar period often reflected Britain's ambivalence about closer political ties with Europe. The sexuality of French characters such as Alice in *Room at the Top* was both presented and received as different from that of British women, as representative of the erotic other who was not rewarded with lasting love and affection, which could be reflective of Britain seeking to maintain a distance from Europe. However, as Geraghty also points out, *Room at the Top* is set in the immediate postwar period, despite being released at the end of the 1950s. While being associated with a loosening of sexual norms that found fuller expression in the 1960s, it also presents Alice as a tragic figure who is the moral force of the film. This is key since:

> The character of Alice is based on past memories of women characters whose sexual availability is beyond criticism because it is so strongly associated with the sense of fate engendered by European experiences of the war. In narrative terms, Alice could have been a banal character who over-invests in a love affair and worries about growing old. But as a European woman, played by Signoret, her mature sexuality still has a tragic dimension even though the political explanation for that dimension has slipped away (Geraghty 2000: 111).

Britain had not joined the Common Market (established in 1958) at this point, and subsequent attempts to do so were thwarted by France in the 1960s, suggesting an interesting perspective on broader Franco-British political relations during this period which were, on different occasions, characterized by ambivalence on both sides.

With this in mind, it is clear how in *Room at the Top* Signoret as Alice is presented as an outsider who constantly has to compete with the British institutions of class, hypocritical moral standards and outdated social conventions, losing out to all of these at the film's tragic closure. In true poetic realist fashion, the film uses Alice's observations about and experience of living in the industrial north of England as a form of critique which lays bare the human consequences of capitalist development. Her alien, French 'eye' accentuates the film's poetic realist style, since many such moments are associated with her viewpoint both literally and symbolically. To emphasize this function, she is distinguished from other characters in significant ways that enhance her role as poetic observer. As a French woman trapped in an unhappy marriage, she is marked as different from our first introduction to her. This coincides with the central character Joe Lampton's (Laurence Harvey) first sight of her at an amateur dramatics meeting soon after he has moved to Warnley for a new job. Instead of seeing her, we *hear* her saying a line from the play, a strategy which emphasizes the incongruity of linguistic difference. Joe sits in the audience and asks his workmate, 'Who is she?' We cannot see Signoret yet, only Susan (Heather Sears), a young, gauche English woman who is also on the stage. Despite this point of view – of being denied the visual origin of the French voice – Joe's friend starts talking about Alice, assuming that Joe must be asking about her. We then understand that in keeping with the cinematographic structure which has hitherto excluded Alice, the object of Joe's gaze has instead been Susan. This creates an interesting play on point-of-view since audiences, as we have seen from the trailer, would have been anticipating the appearance of Signoret. Although the scene keeps us waiting because of Joe's point of view, which is fixated on Susan, Signoret nevertheless remains the main focus of interest, all the more so because of her literal absence at first from our sight.

This early scene is telling in terms of the subsequent narrative in which Joe is clearly more interested in Susan, her father's connections and money, than in a French woman living in Warnley. In this introductory scene we see him persist in his pursuit of Susan, while we can see Alice notice Joe as he is leaving in a shot that emphasizes her looking at him, while he does not return her gaze. This is a prelude to their affair, which allows Joe a 'poetic' space outside the social competitiveness in which he has caught himself with his wanton ambition to have the money, power and social status his background has hitherto prevented. This takes expression in his simultaneous pursuit of Susan as a sort of game to prove that he can rise to the top despite his social disadvantages. The affair with Alice continues in a set of spaces and places which are indeed invested with all the attributes of poetic realism. These include night scenes, in which Signoret is again associated with otherness and in keeping with her *réalisme noir* persona; Sparrow Hill, the open space where lovers meet; the flat of Alice's friend Elspeth (Hermione Baddeley) who, as a drama teacher from the south, is also associated with cultural difference and freer sexual morality,

Figure 8.1: *Room at the Top* (1959): Alice notices Joe as he is leaving in a shot that emphasises her looking at him, while he does not return her gaze. Image courtesy of ITV Global Entertainment.

Figure 8.2: *Room at the Top* (1959): Elspeth's flat, designed by Ralph Brinton. Image courtesy of ITV Global Entertainment.

and a cottage where Joe and Alice enjoy a brief holiday towards the end of their affair. When Joe rejects Alice in favour of marrying Susan, a position which will grant him the social and financial position he craves, Alice is devastated and dies in a road accident (ironically and tragically at Sparrow Hill), with the implication that this might have been suicide.

Alice's outsider status and her extramarital affair with Joe render transgressive the physical spaces they occupy. While Elspeth's flat (designed by Ralph Brinton, Figure 9.2) is in many ways ordinary, its location as the major interior set for their affair is rendered exotic and different (poetry arising precisely *from* the everyday), particularly in the love-making scenes that – encouraged by the risqué tone of the trailer – so shocked the public when the film was first released. The lighting is particularly remarkable for showcasing both the stars and the realist set, a technique for which Brinton was noted, hence his speciality of designing several New Wave British films. While the trailer used the set of the flat as indicative of one of many sexual encounters between Joe and Alice, when such scenes are viewed within the poetic realist context of the film they are far less fixated on these aspects, again illustrating a gap between the film's reputation as sexual titillation and what it actually does offer in terms of investigating an Anglo-French relationship. While Elspeth's flat and the holiday cottage are associated with happy moments shared by the couple, they are also inflected with a foreboding sense of the transient nature of their happiness. In this sense Alice's anxiety about the future, voiced towards the end of their stay in the cottage, melds with the environment in classic poetic realist fashion, as they inhabit an idyllic space that can only ever be short-term, just as Elspeth's flat can never be their own private space. As Alice's friend, Elspeth's sympathy and caring attitude towards Alice marks her as different from most of the other English characters. In this sense she is an ally of Alice, perhaps made possible by her difference as a southerner. Ultimately, however, Alice's Frenchness and all that it represents (outsider status; culture; moral force) cannot compete with the dominance of class, money and privilege which thwart her affair with Joe and their chance of happiness.

This representation is one that in many ways frustrates Anglo-French congeniality, since Alice's time in England has obviously been marked by difficulty.

We learn that she came to England as a French-language teacher, met her husband George and married. When Joe asks Alice if it is 'funny' being French in Warnley, she replies that 'it's not funny'. By this she does not mean that it is not strange but that she is unhappy. In this way she dodges the question of what it really feels like to be French in the north of England. From what we see of her life in the film it is miserable, since she is labelled a whore and has few friends. Even though George does not love her he forbids a divorce, trapping her in an environment which, apart from the spaces she temporarily enjoys with Joe, is depicted as narrow, tough and unyielding; France and England are incompatible. Alice's Frenchness is used to expose the hypocrisy of the British, hence it serves as a self-reflexive device rather than as a serious exploration of transnational exchange. The experience of French women coming to live in England therefore receives a poignant analysis in the film. This is cast in a somewhat ironic light considering that although economic prosperity was increasing in France in the 1950s and early 1960s there was still a very repressive and paternalistic social regime, with no contraception or abortion sanctioned and divorce being very difficult to obtain. The married life Alice may have thought would be easier in England therefore was not necessarily the case, since the film depicts her as being subject to conservative attitudes which in many respects mirror those still pertaining to the U.K.

In 1962 Signoret starred again in a British social realist film called *Term of Trial* (directed by Peter Grenville, who had suggested her for the role of Alice in *Room at the Top*) as Anna Weir, another unhappy French woman living in the north of England. This film has not received much critical attention in comparison with other British social realist films, receiving a curt dismissal from Alexander Walker as an overblown drama that 'has the feeling of bits broken off from earlier, better British films' (1986: 160). It starred Laurence Olivier as Anna's husband, Graham, a schoolmaster teaching in a tough Secondary Modern school who becomes the object of infatuation for Shirley (Sarah Miles), a fifteen-year-old pupil. The situation escalates on a school trip to Paris. He is clearly fond of her and is flattered by her attentions, but when she declares her love for him he gently refuses her advances. Angry at being rejected, on their return from the trip Shirley reports to her mother that she was assaulted, a charge that results in a trial. After an impassioned speech by Graham in court about the innocence of their relationship and the hypocrisy of those determined to find him guilty, Shirley admits that she lied and Graham is acquitted. Back at school, however, this does not protect him from rumour, insinuation and continued suspicion from staff and pupils. In all of this his wife, Anna, stands by him, since they clearly love each other, although she suspects he should have been alerted to the possible dangers of Shirley's dependence, which had developed when Graham gave her private coaching.

The end of the film is strange since Anna accuses him of weakness, of not being a man, and tells him that she will leave him. This continues a strand in the film that relates to him having been a pacifist in the Second World War, to his being unable to see the danger of Shirley's attraction to him, and to his not being capable of doing anything dramatic, whether that be to kill himself or even to have taken advantage of

Shirley. In order to keep Anna he lies at the end of the film, saying that after all he did assault Shirley, to which Anna replies that he is 'less of a mouse' than she thought. This remark perhaps makes sense when related to Geraghty's stress on the visibility of the Second World War in films which involve French characters even as late as *Term of Trial.* In this reading Anna encourages Graham to abandon his pacifism according to principles which she has made clear are more important – in certain circumstances one must take risks and be decisive, as in the War, in order to survive.

Despite location shooting in Paris, *Term of Trial*'s engagement with France and Frenchness goes little beyond the implied stereotypes of *Room at the Top* about culture, exoticism and otherness. The films share a similar device of having the French woman living as if she were in exile, unhappy with her bleak, northern surroundings. Like Alice, Anna is an outsider, a casualty of a cross-cultural marriage whose very at-odds presence serves as a commentary on English society. Crucially, she is not able to influence her husband when she can very clearly see that the situation with Shirley risks getting out of control. We do not see her work; she waits for him at home each day and cooks dinner after he returns from school. The house where they live (the film's production designer was Wilfred Shingleton) is claustrophobic, dark and marked with a Victorianism that at that time was unpopular, with one striking shot showing Anna as literally trapped in the house,

Figure 8.3: Laurence Olivier stands in the dock in *Term of Trial* (1962).
Image courtesy of the BFI stills department.

looking out from behind the glass of the front door. The décor is symbolic of her trapped state, revealing an oppressive side to the 'poetry' of the everyday, and is akin to the *réalisme noir* associated with Signoret's previous roles. Additionally, Anna feels a failure since she is not able to have children, which is suggested as the explanation for Graham's involved and protective attitude towards his pupils. Despite being French Anna is not allowed to accompany him on the fateful school trip to Paris, which features an interesting use of location to replicate the transient, tourist experience of place. Along with the customary sightseeing of monumental landmarks such as the Louvre, we see the schoolteachers misbehaving as one of Graham's colleagues goes off with a prostitute he meets in a bar. Paris is also the location for Graham's extended time with Shirley, as he accompanies her for much of the day after she fabricates a reason to break away with him from the rest of the group. This is when her attraction for Graham escalates, resulting in the declaration of love in a London hotel when travel problems force the group to stop off for the night on the return leg of their journey. As in *Room at the Top* the character played by Signoret in *Term of Trial* uses her outsider perspective and Frenchness to offer sagacious comments that indicate emotional maturity and locate her as possessing the moral insight associated with many poetic realist protagonists. These representations may have to do with Signoret's casting, combined with a shorthand, cinematic 'Frenchness' on screen which was evident in other British films starring French actresses that did not belong to the New Wave social realist genre.

Other French Stars in British Cinema

To place Signoret's performances in a broader context and to extend this analysis beyond the group of films conventionally classified as New Wave, I will now turn to *The Greengage Summer* (1961), a film directed by Lewis Gilbert, produced by Victor Saville and based on the novel by Rumer Godden. Unlike *Room at the Top* and *Term of Trial* the film takes place entirely in France; it is a 'coming of age' story about Joss (Susannah York), a young woman on holiday with her younger brothers and sisters in France. Their mother is taken ill and while she is recovering in hospital the children are looked after by Eliot (Kenneth More), a kind but secretive English man who has a semipermanent residence in the hotel where they are staying. The hotel is owned by Zizi (Danielle Darrieux) and managed by Madame Corbet (Claude Nollier). Eliot is having an affair with Zizi which causes anxiety on her behalf when he pays attention to the attractive, fifteen and a half-year old Joss. Joss is similarly drawn to Eliot who turns out to be a criminal hiding from the police.

The Greengage Summer is a world away from the social realist films that are usually taken to typify British cinema in the early 1960s. Shot in colour and set in a stunning chateau in northern France, the film celebrates France as a rural paradise for the children who are used to an unspectacular life in Bexhill-on-Sea. The freedom provided by the absence of their mother and the attention they receive from Eliot mark their time in France as special, particularly for Joss who falls in love with Eliot and learns how she can manipulate men with her attractiveness. City referents are absent, except for mention of Eliot's mysterious trips to Paris where we eventually discover he is part of a jewellery theft operation and that he is a former war hero who failed to adjust to peacetime life.

Danielle Darrieux's performance as Zizi portrays her as a somewhat pathetic figure who is terrified of losing Eliot to Joss. By the late 1950s Darrieux had established a reputation as a distinguished French actress who had appeared in many notable films since the 1930s. Like the characters played by Signoret, Zizi is concerned about her age, about losing her attractiveness, and tries whatever she can to keep Eliot away from the children. Unlike Anna in *Term of Trial*, however, she has no confidence that she can compete with the young, beautiful English girl. None of the main French characters in the film are sympathetic: Zizi is a desperate woman whose obsession with Eliot prevents her from being kind to the children of whom she is jealous; Madame Corbet is also pathetic since she is jealous of Eliot's hold over Zizi, the implication being that she is in love with Zizi, and the hotel employee, Paul, is depicted as a simple young man whose infatuation with Joss leads him to drink and eventually to his accidental death. At the same time, Kenneth More as Eliot overcomes his casting as a secretive thief since his persona as the benevolent and dependable Englishman dominates the film, so much so that he retains the moral upper hand through his kindness to the children even though his life as a criminal has been exposed.

The beauty of France is conveyed throughout the film, heritage-style, with many lingering shots of the countryside, the rivers, a nearby church and the spacious interiors of the chateau that is the hotel (the art director here being John Stall). While it has none of the associations with industry or urban identity evident in poetic realist films, the concentration on 'heritage' aesthetics nevertheless invests it with a poetry of natural realism which has a specific moral dimension, since we learn that the children's mother wanted to bring them to France to visit the war cemeteries, to gain a sense of the past and knowledge about wartime sacrifices and heroism. This film therefore shares with *Room at the Top* and *Term of Trial* reference to fairly recent history but unlike them it does not place the burden of moral responsibility for this with the lead female character. In all of these films the leading men are marked by their wartime experiences: Joe as the soldier who survived being a prisoner of war and is desperate to find 'room at the top' of the social ladder; Graham in *Term of Trial*, whose pacifism prevented him from getting a better job in peacetime and who has been marked as a coward; and finally Eliot, a distinguished war hero who has been unable to adjust to peacetime and lives a dangerous life of crime in France. The films can therefore be seen as exemplary of British cinema's preoccupation in this period with male problems, masculinity and recovery from the War.

Concentration on the representation of French characters and the depiction of France in the films does, however, enable us to depart from simply linking them with British cinema's common themes of male angst in the late 1950s and early 1960s. Dominant critical appraisal of the British New Wave tended to ignore appreciation or understanding of poetic, 'feminine' sensibilities (readdressed to some extent by

Lovell's (1996) influential essay on *A Taste of Honey*) in favour of discussions which cited examples of innovative film form allied to the genius of the male *auteur* director, or to an aestheticization of place which was seen to work against the expression of a coherent poetic realist discourse (Higson 1996: 151). As we have seen with Signoret's performances in particular, there is a fascination with her voice and body which is striking since, as Susan Hayward points out with reference to *Room at the Top*, in this film the majority of the close-ups are devoted to Laurence Harvey (Hayward 2004: 89–91). Her French accent had an important function in that it enabled her to be perceived as being outside conventional English class structures in spite of being associated with education, culture and art (Walker 1974; 1986: 47). The casting of French actresses moreover reflects a greater internationalization of British cinema which was deemed necessary as part of financial arrangements with U.S. companies who frequently cofinanced and distributed the films. Indeed, these casting decisions were influential for the films: Alice in John Braine's source novel for *Room at the Top* is not French, nor is the schoolmaster's wife in the novel by James Barlow (1961), on which *Term of Trial* was based. Darrieux had previously starred in French and Hollywood films; *The Greengage Summer* was her first and only British film. Claude Nollier had been in *Moulin Rouge* (1952), registered as a British film and directed by John Huston. Signoret had previously appeared in British films *Against the Wind* (1947) and *Four Days' Leave* (1948). Both *Term of Trial* and *The Greengage Summer* had U.S. involvement via, respectively, Warner Brothers and Columbia, at a time when Hollywood investment in British cinema was increasing. This created pressures to increase the number of French actors appearing in British films, as promoted by Harry Saltzman, the American financial 'angel' who was responsible for cofunding *Saturday Night and Sunday Morning* (1960). In the wake of the box-office success in Britain and in the U.S.A. of *Room at the Top* Saltzman wanted to cast Signoret and Leslie Caron as the mother and daughter in *A Taste of Honey*, a suggestion rejected by director Tony Richardson (Walker 1974; 1986: 91).

In conclusion, the negative assessment of British films in comparison with those produced by the *Nouvelle Vague* during this period has obscured more positive and enduring features that have to do with the films' connections with France. In addition, a refusal to see beyond the qualities of auteurism or of formal experimentation has deflected attention away from the range of representations in British cinema, and from correspondences with styles such as poetic realism within fiction films. As we have seen, the casting of French actresses reinforced this theme in particular ways, and opened up the films to internationally comparative frameworks. It strikes me that the obsession within film criticism with the *Nouvelle Vague* was at this particular time unhelpful for a British cinema that showed signs of increased international collaboration, albeit tied, as we have seen, to a rather limited range of representational tropes about France and Frenchness that tend to serve as devices to comment on the films' preoccupation with British identities and themes.

What they do highlight, however, is something of the difficult experiences of some French women living in the U.K. in a context of greater geographical mobility in the 1950s and 1960s. This also can be related to the film industry since it is significant that French stars had been attracted to British projects, even if it was partly a response to their own career objectives rather than a positive affirmation for what British cinema could offer. While Frenchness in British cinema opened the films to the international arena of film festivals and Signoret's celebrated success with an Academy Award for her performance in *Room at the Top*, the films were not particularly popular in France. This indicates perhaps that the chance to appear in a British film was only attractive to stars who were not in acute demand in France, as in Signoret's case. Darrieux, in the later stages of her film career, was exploring the possibilities offered by roles outside France; this only came to be seen as a more positive option when directors such as Polanski made films in Britain, and the 1960s developed into a decade when European directors and stars found work in the U.K.

As regards Franco-British cinematic relations in this pivotal earlier period, then, there seem to be similarities with the general expressions of ambivalence about closer political ties. Much as Signoret's characters in *Room at the Top* and *Term of Trial* experienced, France was represented as being very different from Britain, much as Alice and Anna were from their British neighbours; from the opposite perspective, Joss in *The Greengage Summer* is briefly touched by France as an agent of her sexual awakening but then returns to mundane life in Bexhill-on-Sea. Characters like Alice, Anna and Eliot, who remove themselves from their country for long periods of time, are marked as unhappy, as blighted by their dislocation to another country. This uncertainty perhaps explains the persistence of references to the War, to a time when the Allies' common cause forged allegiances that persisted in memory. In the postwar world these correspondences were maintained with ambivalent feelings on both sides as New Waves had to woo new publics in perhaps more ways than cinema at that time was able to offer.

Bibliography

Andrew, D. 1995. *Mists of Regret: Culture and Sensibility in Classic French Film*. Princeton, N.J.: Princeton University Press.

Barlow, J. 1961. *Term of Trial*. London: Hamish Hamilton.

Bergfelder, T., S. Harris and S. Street. 2007. *Film Architecture and the Transnational Imagination: Set Design in 1930s European Cinema*. Amsterdam: Amsterdam University Press.

Geraghty, C. 2000. *British Cinema in the Fifties: Gender, Genre and the 'New Look'*. London: Routledge.

Hayward, S. 2004. *Simone Signoret: The Star as Cultural Sign*. New York: Continuum Press.

Higson, A. 1996. 'Space, Place, Spectacle: Landscape and Townscape in the "Kitchen Sink" Film', in A. Higson (ed.), *Dissolving Views: Key Writings on British Cinema*. London: Cassell, pp. 133–56.

―――. 1963. *The Contemporary Cinema*. London, Harmondsworth: Penguin Books.

Lay, S. 2002. *British Social Realism*. London: Wallflower.

Lovell, T. 1996. 'Landscapes and Stories in 1960s British Realism', in A. Higson (ed.), *Dissolving Views: Key Writings on British Cinema*. London: Cassell, pp. 157–77.

Murphy, R. 1992. *Sixties British Cinema*. London: BFI.

Perkins, V. 1972. 'The British Cinema', in I. Cameron (ed.), *Movie Reader*. London: November Books, pp. 7–11.

Signoret, S. 1979. *Nostalgia Isn't What It Used to Be*. London: Grafton Books.

Taylor, B.F. 2006. *The British New Wave*. Manchester: Manchester University Press.

Vincendeau, G. 1995. 'Poetic Realism', in G. Vincendeau (ed.), *Encyclopedia of European Cinema*. London: British Film Institute/Cassell, p. 336.

Walker, A. 1986. *Hollywood, England: The British Film Industry in the Sixties*, 2nd edn. London: Harrap.

Wimmer, L. 2009. *Cross-Channel Perspectives: The French Reception of British Cinema*. Bern: Peter Lang.

Filmography

Against the Wind. 1947, Charles Crichton, U.K.

Four Days' Leave. 1948, Leopold Lindtberg, Switzerland/U.S.

Greengage Summer, The. 1961, Lewis Gilbert, U.K.

Loneliness of the Long Distance Runner, The. 1962, Tony Richardson, U.K.

Moulin Rouge. 1952, John Huston, U.K.

Quatre cents coups, Les / The 400 Blows. 1959, François Truffaut, France.

Room at the Top. 1959, Jack Clayton, U.K.

Saturday Night and Sunday Morning. 1960, Karel Reisz, U.K.

Taste of Honey, A. 1961, Tony Richardson, U.K.

Term of Trial. 1962, Peter Grenville, U.K.

CHAPTER 9

Mirror Image: French Reflections of British Cinema

Ian Christie

'The English did what they always do in cinema: nothing.'
– Jean-Luc Godard, 1999.

Consider a typical French collection of critical writings on cinema.[1] Jérôme Prieur was a rising young critic in 1980 when he published *Nuits blanches: Essai sur le cinéma*, based on over sixty reviews of films ranging across six decades. In nearly four hundred pages, no British film or filmmaker is mentioned, apart from Chaplin and Hitchcock. Nor is Prieur an exception: the same absence would be found in most French publications on cinema, other than reference works. Like the notorious surrealist map of the world, in which both Britain and the U.S.A. were suppressed in favour of exotic alternatives such as Mexico and Easter Island, British cinema remains largely invisible on most French cinematic maps.[2] Unless it is the explicit focus of an article or book, there is rarely any need to acknowledge it among the sources of important or innovative films.

Why should this matter? After all, French taste and prejudice would dismiss many aspects of *la culture anglaise* as self-evidently insular, and often inferior to their French counterparts. But in the case of cinema, French judgement has combined with native insecurity to produce a distinctive *schadenfreude*. 'Bollocks to Truffaut', declared Stephen Frears in his 1996 documentary *Typically British*, recalling the famous remark by François Truffaut about 'a certain incompatibility between the terms "cinema" and "Britain"'.[3] Truffaut's observation that Hitchcock had found greater creative scope in Hollywood than in London was by no means a uniquely French judgement – Robin Wood had implied much the same two years earlier (Wood 1965: 29) – but it touched a raw nerve among an emerging generation of English critics and filmmakers, as if to confirm their negative judgement of domestic production. And to prove that the nerve remains raw, a recent French listing of the contents of a '*cinémathèque idéal*' which included no British works (Anon 2008) was reported in the U.K. with indignation (Berlins 2008).

French blindness to British film and a generally unreciprocated British admiration for French taste have become familiar tropes since the 1960s. However, the origins of British anxiety about its filmic abilities lie much further back, when the first canonization of cinema as a 'seventh art' was largely accomplished in France in the decade following 1918, notwithstanding important contributions from Germany, Soviet Russia and the U.S.A. This marked cinema's entry into what could be termed the '*beaux arts*' system, when it began to seek, and acquire, status among the 'other' arts; when the verdict of the pre-First World War period – that it would never be an art in its own right – was reversed; and French writers such as Leon Moussinac articulated the idea of cinema as the literature of the future and the quintessential art of the twentieth century.[4] Moussinac's views proved highly influential. His books and articles circulated widely, just as the international journal *Close Up* was being launched, and they certainly helped shape the first generation of cinema's historian-critics.[5] The most important of these, at least in the English-speaking world, was Paul Rotha, whose confident survey *The Film Till Now* appeared in 1930 and remained in print, in various versions, for the best part of forty years (Rotha 1930).

The Film Till Now was structured in two parts, 'The Actual' and 'The Theoretical', with the first offering a typology of genres followed by a series of chapters surveying the achievements of various national cinemas. Three of these deal with U.S. cinema, while Soviet, German, French and British film are covered in a series of successively shorter chapters. In many respects, the last two form a pair. 'The British film is established on a hollow foundation', Rotha begins in solemn and slightly Shakespearean tones (Rotha 1930: 226). Beneath the 'flatulent flapdoodle' of journalistic promotion and self-congratulation – epitomized by the profusion of 'national film weeks' and similar schemes – he diagnosed a fundamental fault: 'the British film has not yet discovered its nationality'. He quotes Moussinac: 'England has not yet made an English film' (Moussinac 1929), and goes on to castigate British producers who 'imitate without understanding' (1930: 226).

Among Rotha's complaints were the pursuit of a specious modernism rather than true avant-garde experiment; the neglect of places and themes beyond London, and of the rich potential offered by the Empire; and more generally the apeing of all things American, with Elstree Studio being touted as the 'new Hollywood'. Against these endemic shortcomings, Rotha lists a modest number of items which 'demand some notice': Grierson and the example of *Drifters* (which he detects as having 'something that was lacking' in Eisenstein's *Potemkin*!);[6] the promise of Asquith and Hitchcock; the output of British International Pictures, with its star visiting director, E.A. Dupont; Ivor Montagu's comedies based on scripts by H.G. Wells; and 'numerous nature films', hailed as the 'sheet-anchor of the British Film Industry' in what might be considered either a dismissive or a prescient verdict by the future documentary filmmaker (1930: 220–1).

Interestingly, Rotha's view of French cinema was almost as critical. He accused French *cinéastes* of 'denying the existence of the French film despite ever-constant proof to the contrary' (Rotha 1930: 209). They are obsessed, he believes, with everyone else's cinema except their own – formerly German and Swedish, now Soviet and especially American. Rotha clearly considered this enthusiasm for American cinema misguided, complaining at the French neglect of their own avant garde, as the best training for a filmmaker. Why, he wondered, do they not value what they do best, making small-scale 'artistic' films, such as those by Louis Delluc, Germaine Dulac, Jean Epstein and Marcel L'Herbier, or even Abel Gance, considered after *Napoléon* 'the *grand maître* of the French cinema, theoretically the apotheosis of great directors, but in practice always out of date with ideas'? Rotha reserved his highest praise for René Clair, Jacques Feyder and Carl Dreyer (considered French on the strength of *La Passion de Jeanne d'Arc*). But in spite of journalistic jousting, what also emerges is his clear understanding of the central role of France in taste-making, or canonization. What would count as great cinema was already decided in and by France – and France was fascinated by Hollywood, seeing it from quite a different angle than Britain did.

It was from France that the next influential history of cinema would emerge, with Maurice Bardèche and Robert Brasillach's *Histoire du cinéma* (Bardèche and Brasillach 1935), which retained and amplified Rotha's national cinema structure. But here Britain was simply omitted from all but the first kindergarten years of moving picture development. Even when Bardèche and Brasillach was translated by the English-born Iris Barry in 1937/8, with a critical postscript, Barry added only a passing mention of Hitchcock, included in a list of mainly Hollywood directors (Bardèche and Brasillach 1935 [1938 U.K. edn]: 386).

After the Second World War, the diagnosis of Britain as a country without a cinematic identity began to acquire empirical foundations as film history became more ambitious, still largely under French leadership. In his monumental *Histoire générale du cinéma*, Georges Sadoul entitled the chapter dealing with British cinema before the First World War 'Stagnation Britannique' (Sadoul 1951: 257). British production, he noted, had been in the forefront of world output in 1900, but after 1906, when the cinema started to industrialize, production in Britain remained the business of small-scale artisans, lacking capital, apart from the efforts of Charles Urban, an enterprising American who worked in Britain from 1898 to 1916. Their main export market had been the United States, since France and much of continental Europe were served by French companies, so the formation of the Edison's Motion Pictures Patent Company in 1908 struck a grave blow, with only Urban being accepted into this cartel. British producers tried to fight back by forming the International Projecting and Producing Company in 1909, but this proved ineffective and, although an 'open door' policy returned in the U.S. by 1913, as the English historian Rachael Low observed, 'the damage was done' (Low 1948: 137).[7]

Meanwhile, British producers' share of their own market declined dramatically, from 15 per cent in 1909 to around 2 per cent in 1914. At the same time, exhibition grew in the U.K. in almost inverse proportion, from some 2,500 cinemas in 1911 to some 4,000 by 1914, reaching a pro rata level that put the British ahead of all other European countries as consumers of film, albeit mostly imported. As the Marxist

Sadoul observed (1962), this was undoubtedly connected with the high level of industrialization in the U.K., where only 20 per cent of the population lived in the countryside, compared with 50 per cent in France. In fact British production had rallied in 1912–1913, with a burst of literary adaptations and commemorative films – forerunners of a later so-called 'heritage cinema' – and also with some notable realist and topical productions, already regarded as Britain's special contribution to cinema and foreshadowing the official documentary movement of the 1930s. But these could hardly compete with the achievements of Griffith at Biograph and his progression to *Birth of a Nation* and *Intolerance*, or with the Danish psychological film, the Italian spectacle, the French adventure serial or the Swedish costume drama; nor did the increasingly monopolistic tendency of global film distribution after the First World War favour small producers, effectively denying British films an export market (Thompson 1985; Low 1971). So Britain largely vanished from the international scene, and henceforth its domestic production had to compete against the pressure and popularity of U.S. imports, with only documentary film achieving a beleaguered cultural recognition at home and abroad.

Ironically, Sadoul had made his diagnosis of Britain's historic problem during the very period when a combination of wartime factors had enabled British production to flourish as never before, in genres ranging from the realist to the melodramatic, including literary adaptation and poetic allegory. Much of this output also achieved international distribution in the immediate postwar period, giving rise to an unusually wide spectrum of critical comment. By the end of the decade, however, Ealing Studios' output had become the quasi-official British export cinema, no doubt in part because it confirmed an international image of 'Britishness'. In this climate, Sadoul would identify Alexander Mackendrick as 'without doubt the best of the English directors who made their debut in the Forties', in his influential *Dictionnaire des cinéastes* (Sadoul 1962: 161). Significantly, Mackendrick's pedigree is given there in terms that link him with the filmmakers 'shaped by documentarism'; and among new talents, Karel Reisz is characterized as 'very brilliant' on the strength of his documentary background (1962: 228). But what of those from different backgrounds, or in revolt against the documentary tradition?

Michael Powell and Emeric Pressburger offer a prime example of this category, owing their initial partnership to Korda and its subsequent consolidation to Rank's early 1940s Independent Producers consortium, together with the unusual challenges of wartime production. Their pivotal essay in fantasy-propaganda, *A Matter of Life and Death*, was widely shown abroad in 1946/7 as a film intended to promote international understanding, and the French reviews offer an intriguing range of responses. According to the London-based surrealist Jacques Brunius: ' It is pretentious when it has nothing to say, and sleep-inducing when it aims at gravity' (Borel 1946).

A year later, when the film had been released in France, André Bazin, the future father figure of the *Nouvelle Vague*, expressed qualified admiration:

The two planes of action, in heaven and on earth, work well dramatically
...[and] the whole film makes the journey of life as exciting as a police story

…. However[,] some serious weaknesses prevent this film, for all its richness, achieving the level of a masterpiece (Bazin 1947).

The most controversial aspects of the film – apart from Marius Goring's caricatured French aristocrat as the Conductor – appeared to be the irreverence of its décor and celestial conceit, compared unfavourably by more than one French critic with Marcel Carné's more solemn wartime allegory *Les Visiteurs du soir* (1942).[8]

Several other 1940s films by Powell and Pressburger would be distributed in France and receive reviews ranging from the polite to the puzzled, with *The Red Shoes* (1948) both praised *and* condemned for its 'bad taste' in different works by Sadoul (Sadoul 1962; 1964).[9] So for the postwar generation in France, British cinema could safely be ignored as a landscape undistinguished by any significant landmarks. A poignant confirmation of this perception can be found in a speech by Michael Powell to the Foreign Press Association of London in 1957.[10] On this occasion Powell took as his text a recent article by Louis Marcorelles (1957: 5), published in *The Observer*, in which the rising young French critic took Powell and Pressburger's *Battle of the River Plate* as an excuse to castigate British cinema at large for its bland conformism, preferring 'the Victorian clichés so dear to the English theatre … to the melancholy contradictions of the "jet age"'. Marcorelles doubted that British cinema could offer 'any real "authors of films," total creators capable of moulding a subject after their own personal vision', worthy to set alongside Renoir, Clair, Ford, Welles or Eisenstein. Instead, he noted, such 'revelations' as Robert Hamer and Mackendrick had either been silenced or driven into exile 'by the hostility of the British film industry to all individuality' and by 'its unwillingness to think except in clichés about national grandeur'. The only signs of renewal that Marcorelles detected were in such modest independent productions as *Together* and *Sunday By the Sea*, which alone had saved 'English honour' at recent festivals.[11]

Such a diagnosis of British cinema's state was not, of course, uncommon in the late 1950s. It had been urged by the *Sequence* group of young English critics for nearly a decade, and would soon be taken up by the critics-hoping-to-turn-filmmakers of *Movie*.[12] Nor did Powell entirely reject it, despite an entertaining display of indignation. We know now, although he did not reveal it at the time, that his partnership with Pressburger was foundering in the barren climate that Marcorelles had identified; and that his own attempt to make a more personal and contemporary film with *Peeping Tom* (1960) would provoke outrage from those who were themselves critical of British cinema's stagnation. Powell did not defend his own films on this occasion, but he criticized obliquely all those who were smothering 'the craftsman and the artist' and losing sight of the 'Love and Daring' without which 'no good film has ever been made'. Powell ended his speech with a poignant plea: 'perhaps out of all this gentle muddle we shall make English films as true and successful as English novels and English poetry, as inspiring to millions of people of all colours as English dreams, English ideals'.

When Britain's 'New Wave' broke in 1960, heralded by Karel Reisz's *Saturday Night and Sunday Morning*, it was welcomed by Marcorelles (now an editor of *Cahiers du cinéma*):

It demystifies, in the best sense of the term, the capitalist system, and above all it is one of the few films made west of the Elbe which has an authentic worker as hero. Particularly interesting because it breaks with the Victorian conformism of the normal British Rank film.[13]

Sadoul added to his dictionary entry on *Saturday Night and Sunday Morning* a remark by André S. Labarthe which sums up the prevailing French standpoint: 'British cinema is paralysed: we should remember that Reisz helped it take its first steps' (1983: 279).

First steps, however, would not convince either French cinephiles or their British followers that a major change had taken place. The new social realist cinema typified by Woodfall Films was as suspect to many as its predecessors, seen as still deeply literary in its aims and methods – as if Dickens and Shakespeare adaptations had merely been replaced by those of Osborne and Sillitoe. Meanwhile, the generation of critics now turned filmmakers associated mainly with *Cahiers du cinéma* had lent prestige to what amounted to a *second* canonization of cinema. According to this view, buttressed by the '*politique des auteurs*', many of the greatest achievements of sound-era cinema were by Hollywood filmmakers who had managed to put their personal stamp on otherwise industrial projects (*Cahiers du cinéma* 1972). A select number of French, Italian and Japanese filmmakers were included in this new canon, or would be added to it as their work began to circulate through the 'art cinema' networks of the 1960s. But the effect of the *politique*, especially as it was taken up by American and British critics during the 1960s and 1970s, was to validate directors who were seen as having escaped or transcended the Hollywood system, often favouring those who worked in genre cinema rather than on projects deemed 'literary' or prestigious.

The effect of this second canonization, based on the ranking of *auteurs* and on a connoisseurship of 'style', was to condemn almost all British filmmakers to a low status. In the notorious table comparing British and U.S. directors published by the young critics of *Movie* in 1962, and strongly influenced by the aesthetics of *Cahiers*, only Howard Hawks and Hitchcock (now deemed wholly American) were considered 'great', and only Joseph Losey (considered 'British', since fleeing HUAC persecution in the mid-1950s) was considered 'brilliant' among British directors, compared with eleven Americans (Anon 1962). The table continued in similar vein, with only the Argentinian-born Hugo Fregonese considered British and 'very talented', and only Robert Hamer, and the newcomers Seth Holt and Karel Reisz, ranked as 'talented' among British directors. All other British directors were relegated to 'competent or ambitious' and 'the rest'. A similar *Cahiers*-influenced exercise ranking U.S. filmmakers was produced by Andrew Sarris later in the decade (Sarris 1968), further reinforcing the perception of older British directors, such as Lean and Reed, as being overrated ('less than meets the eye' was Sarris' dismissive category for these), and leaving others who had not worked in Hollywood in a kind of critical limbo.

During this period, which was crucial to the formation of critical and soon academic opinion in Britain, French criticism would, however, play an important role in defending the fantastic, the perverse and the unfashionable (often on grounds of 'taste' in terms of genre material) against a widespread English embrace of the naturalistic and the merely fashionable. At the same time as Chabrol, Rohmer and Truffaut were laying the foundations for future Hitchcock scholarship, French critics were already alert to the implications of *Peeping Tom* as a key to reconceiving Powell's career and indeed 'Englishness' in rather different terms from those of Sadoul (Török 1960; 1972).

It would be wrong to claim that *Positif* and *Midi-Minuit Fantastique* alone 'discovered' Powell as a neglected English auteur. Raymond Durgnat and Ian Johnson had already begun this process with pioneering articles in the new British film press (Johnson 1963; Durgnat 1965). But there can be little doubt – and here I speak from my own experience of encountering Powell and Pressburger piecemeal during the 1960s – that the writings of Török, Tavernier, Lefevre and Lacourbe were influential in conferring authority on what was still a sporadic process of personal discovery. The French critics associated with *Positif* who had also contributed to the French-led revolution in the critical mapping of cinema were now admitting Powell (largely ignoring Pressburger at this time) to the canon, and forging powerful links with figures respected elsewhere. When, for instance, Tavernier revealed that the director Jean-Pierre Melville, one of the father figures of the *Nouvelle Vague*, admired Powell and particularly *The Life and Death of Colonel Blimp*, this and many other Powell and Pressburger films still could not be seen except in corrupted versions, and such endorsements provided an incentive in Britain.[14] Later, in the early 1980s, when Powell-Pressburger retrospectives became frequent, and the films began to be restored, *Positif*'s rival *Cahiers du cinéma* developed its own distinctive position on Powell, seeing him as the last of the masters of studio spectacle, following in the tradition of Méliès (Assayas 1981).

Powell (still usually without Pressburger in French criticism, reflecting an entrenched directorial bias) is a prime, although not an isolated case of French validation. This has tended to seize upon filmmakers who can be cast as outsiders in relation to the tradition of academicism or '*qualité anglaise*', considered the British equivalent of the French '*tradition de qualité*' attacked by Truffaut. Terence Fisher was an early beneficiary, with his Dracula trilogy and other lurid Hammer horror films satisfying a distinctively French appetite for the Gothic. Later, Joseph Losey and Stanley Kubrick – both reversing Hitchcock's trajectory to leave America for permanent residence in England – would become subjects of French veneration, along with such emergent figures of the 1960s as John Boorman, Ken Loach and Peter Watkins, none of whom have received equivalent sustained attention in their native Britain. Of the filmmakers who emerged, or continued, in the 1970s, Stephen Frears, Mike Leigh, Peter Greenaway, Alan Clarke and Peter Chelsom would benefit particularly from recognition by French critics and festivals, giving them a status which they had hardly achieved at home.

Amongst these, the case of Loach is perhaps exceptional. While his often embattled political commitment has tended to marginalize him within Britain, his reputation as an 'engaged' filmmaker has remained high in France, with his films regularly selected for Cannes, and widely shown and admired throughout Europe, while often failing to receive any significant theatrical release in Britain. What has been most striking in French critical writing about Loach is a willingness to see his career as an evolving whole, giving equal weight to the films of different periods. Philippe Pilard, for instance, writing in 1996, singled out *Looks and Smiles* (1981) – a film barely released in Britain and little praised – as one of Loach's most trenchant, and also one of the most effective anti-Thatcher films, while relating it to thematic constants from the 1960s to the 1990s (Pilard 1996: 102–104). Equally, French critics have tended to see Loach's work in wider and more comparative terms than their British counterparts, who have long type-cast him as a dour polemicist. In an anthology on 'documentary images', a French writer compares Loach's use of nonprofessionals to that of Georges Rouquier or Robert Bresson, while another discusses his portrayal of women under duress in terms of the recurrent frontal images of them weeping, suggesting that this 'immodest display of emotion is startling, indecent and yet invigorating' (Blangonnet 1997: 10).

These are unlike the perspectives normally brought to bear on Loach in Britain; and what they convey is a sense of Loach as filmmaker, rather than as merely a social critic or propagandist – roles which are seen in Britain as in some way precluding the aesthetic. No doubt there are reasons for the continuing French interest in Loach, and in Mike Leigh, which may point to perceived absences in French cinema that have begun to be addressed post–2000. But the fact remains that these are the latest in a long series of British filmmakers treated as significant artists in a way that they are not domestically. The major retrospective of British cinema held at the Centre Pompidou in 2000 provided an occasion to stake claims for even more British filmmakers whose careers have been largely ignored at home – especially when their work has been largely commissioned by television, as in the cases of Alan Clarke and latterly Antonia Bird – and also to take issue with earlier French judgements. Godard's dismissal of British wartime cinema as 'doing nothing' was challenged by Laurent Roth in his essay on 'the greatness of Humphrey Jennings', where he noted that Godard would simply not have seen Jennings' work, which his mentor Henri Langlois 'venerated' (Pilard and Binh 2000: 120). And the case of Powell has advanced considerably, with a substantial essay (Cerisuelo 2000) in the edited collection *Typiquement British* (Pilard and Bihn 2000), a major conference devoted to him in Paris in 2005, followed by other essays by French scholars on his work (Leutrat 2000; Thiéry 2009).[15]

Behind a critical stance that continues to regard great cinema from Britain as an exception to the rule of conservatism and academicism (and latterly sheer commercialism, in what are essentially U.S. studio films produced in Britain, such as the Harry Potter series), there are indeed many gaps in awareness of British cinema history, as well as an ambient suspicion of English culture's innate conservatism. Roger Boussinot suggests, in the entry for '*Grande Bretagne*' in his influential encyclopaedia, that the reasons for so relatively few works of the highest quality emerging from a cinema that is so well equipped technically may be 'bourgeois businessmen, indifferent intellectuals and technicians without imagination' (Boussinot 1995: 890).

Even if France's high level of interest in non-French and non-Hollywood cinema can be partly explained by means of a cultural tradition committed to plurality and internationalism, combined with very high levels of subsidy for domestic *cinema d'art et essai*, the result is still an instructive counterbalance to the near-invisibility of much British filmmaking on its own territory – which in turn explains why French opinion on British cinema continues to matter to British critics. Like Lacan's famous account of how the child's (mis)recognition of itself as another in a mirror plays an important part in forming its subjectivity, so the reflected image of 'British cinema', however distorted or partial, played a vital part in creating an identity for British cinema at a time when little in British culture offered any such basis. Arguably, cinema itself still lacks a secure place within the hierarchy of British culture, which explains why confident – if still often erratic – French canonization continues to exercise its fascination, even if the study and curatorial care of British filmmaking now has other points of reference, and other terms of validation, upon which to draw.

Notes

1. An earlier version of this chapter was published in 1999 (Christie 1999).
2. The *Surrealist Map of the World* appeared in a special issue of *Variétés*, entitled 'Le Surréalisme', published in Brussels in 1929 and since widely anthologized.
3. Truffaut's remark originally appeared in the context of his book-length interview with Hitchcock (1967), contributing to the *politique* of detaching Hitchcock from 'British cinema'. British cinema was not the only object of Truffaut's deliberately polemical style, but the slur gained particular currency in Britain, where it has been frequently quoted.
4. Early commentators in most countries denied that cinema could be an 'art', but many leading writers, playwrights, poets and painters would change their minds around 1913–15. In Britain, these included George Bernard Shaw, J.M. Barrie and Sir Hubert von Herkomer. In France, a generation of would-be artists turned to cinema at the end of the First World War. Leon Moussinac's writings appeared in several collections, including *Naissance du cinéma* (1925) and *Panoramique du cinéma* (1929).
5. *Close Up*, published in Switzerland in a mixture of English and French, was launched in 1927.
6. *The Battleship Potemkin* had received its belated British premiere at the London Film Society in November 1929, in a programme that included *Drifters*.
7. Low is cited by Sadoul as his source for the information about early British cinema, and both his *Histoire générale* (1951) and Low's (1948; 1971) contemporary multivolume history of British cinema seem to have drawn inspiration from the other.
8. See, for example, 'Jacques Borel' [Brunius] and André Bazin, in Roland La-courbe, ed., *Question de Vie ou Mort, L' avant-scène du cinéma,* no. 258, Dec 1980, pp. 45–6.
9. In Sadoul's *Dictionnaire des films* (1964), *The Red Shoes* is praised for it originality, but in the *Dictionnaire des cineastes* (1962/84), Powell is accused of bad taste, said to predominate in *The Tales of Hoffmann*, and of subsequently producing only 'mediocrities', apart from *Peeping Tom* (1960), which was already a celebrated *film maudit* among French critics.
10. 'Speech given by Mr Michael Powell at the Foreign Press Association Dinner, 19 March 1957'. Typescript in the Powell Papers (Thelma Schoonmaker-Powell / British Film

Institute). Attached is Marcorelles's article, 'Hollywood's Baby Brother?' (1957). (Marcorelles also claimed that Britain remained 'content with the role of submissive junior to Hollywood's Big Brother', which was acknowledged as well as challenged by Powell.)

11. *Together* (Lorena Mazzetti, 1956), supported by the British Film Institute's Experimental Film Fund, and *Sunday by the Sea* (Anthony Simmons, 1951), were both realist films (although the former is a drama), anticipating the *cinéma-vérité* idiom that Marcorelles would chronicle in his book *Living Cinema* (1973).

12. *Sequence* was launched in Oxford in 1947; *Movie* started in 1962.

13. Quoted in Sadoul (1964: 279). Karel Reisz was born in Czechoslovakia.

14. Bertrand Tavernier, interviewing Powell with Jacques Prayer (1968), told him that Melville 'considers *Colonel Blimp* one of the best films in the world', to which Powell replied, 'That's someone I'd really like to meet'; and there is a photograph of the two together. The restoration of *Colonel Blimp* was not completed until 1985.

15. The conference was organized by Natacha Thiéry at Paris V, in association with *Positif*, in 2005.

Bibliography

Anon. 1962. 'The Talent Histogram', *Movie* June: 8–9.

———. 2008. 'Une Cinémathèque idéale', *Cahiers du cinéma*, November. Retrieved from http://www.cahiersducinema.com/imprime.php3?id_article1337. Last accessed 18 January 2010.

Assayas, O. 1981. 'Redécouvrir Michael Powell', *Cahiers du cinéma* 321(March): 10–19.

Bardèche, M. and R. Brasillach. 1935. *Histoire du cinéma*. Paris: Denoël et Steele. Trans. and ed. I. Barry (1938) as *History of the Film*. London: George Allen & Unwin.

Bazin, A. 1947. *L'Ecran français* 116(September).

Berlins, M. 2008. 'A List of the Best 100 Films, Without a Single British Movie – Is There an Anglophobic Conspiracy?', *The Guardian*, 26 November.

Blangonnet, C. 1997. 'Introduction', *Images documentaires* 26/27.

Borel, J. [better known by his pen-name Jacques Brunius]. 1946. *L'Ecran français* 72(November).

Boussinot, R. 1995. *Encyclopédie du cinéma*. Paris: Bordas.

Cerisuelo, M. 2000. 'Michael Powell', in P. Pilard and N.T. Binh (eds), *Typiquement British: Le Cinéma Britannique*. Paris: Editions Pompidou, pp. 101–104.

Christie, I. 1999. 'Mirror Images: French Reflections of British Cinema', *La Lettre de la Maison Française d'Oxford* 11(Trinity-Michaelmas): 82–92.

Durgnat, R. [writing as 'O. O. Green']. 1965. 'Michael Powell', *Movie* 14.

Godard, J.-L. 1999. *Histoires du cinéma*. Paris: Gallimard, vol. 3a.

Johnson, I. 1963. 'A Pin to See the Peepshow', *Motion* 3. Retrieved 10 May 2009 from http://www.powell-pressburger.org/Reviews/60_PT/Motion.html

Lacourbe, R. ed., 1980. *Question de Vie ou Mort, L' avant-scène du cinéma*, no. 258, Dec: 45–6.

Leutrat, J.-L. 2005. in I. Christie and A. Moor (eds), *The Cinema of Michael Powell: International Perspectives on an English Film-maker*. London: BFI, pp. 132–42.

Low, R. 1948. *The History of the British Film*, vol. 2, 1906–14. London: George Allen & Unwin.

———. 1971. *The History of the British Film*, vol 4, 1918–29 London: Allen & Unwin.

Marcorelles, L. 1957. 'Hollywood's Baby Brother?', *The Observer*, 3 February.

Moussinac, L. 1925, Paris: Editions J. Povolozky et Cie.

_____. 1929, *Panoramique du cinéma*. Paris: Le Sans Pareil.

Peigne-Giuly, A. 'La Femme, figure de compassion chez Loach', *Images documentaires* 26/27.

Pilard, P. 1996. *Histoire du cinéma britannique*. Paris: Nathan.

———. and N.T. Bihn (eds). 2000. *Typiquement British: Le Cinéma britannique*. Paris: Editions du Centre Pompidou.

Prieur, J. 1980. *Nuits blanches: Essai sur le cinéma*. Paris: Gallimard.

Rotha, P. 1930. *The Film Till Now*. London: Jonathan Cape.

Sadoul, G. 1951. *Histoire générale du cinéma: Le Cinéma devient un art, 1909–1920. Vol. 1: L'Avant-guerre*. Paris: Denoël.

———. 1962/84. *Dictionnaire des cinéastes*. Paris: Editions du Seuil. After Sadoul's death in 1967, this was regularly updated, while retaining most of his own contributions.

———. 1964. *Dictionnaire des films*. Paris: Seuil. Also updated after Sadoul's death.

Sarris, A. 1968. *The American Cinema: Directors and Directions 1929–1968*. New York: E.P. Dutton.

Tavernier, B. and J. Prayer. 1968. [Interview with Michael Powell], *Midi-Minuit Fantastique* 20: 8–9.

Thiéry, N. 2005. 'That Obscure Object of Desire: Powell's Women, 1945–50', in I. Christie and A. Moor (eds), *The Cinema of Michael Powell: International Perspectives on an English Film-maker*. London: BFI, pp. 224–38.

———. 2009. *Photogénie du désir. Michael Powell et Emeric Pressburger 1945–1950*. Remmes: Presses Universitaires de Rennes.

Thompson, K. 1985. *Exporting Entertainment: America in the World Film Market 1907–1934*. London: British Film Institute.

Török, J.P. 1960. 'Regardez la mer: *Peeping Tom*', *Positif* 36.

———. 1972. 'The Hazards of Insularity', *Monogram* 3: 11–14 [translated from *Positif*, June 1971].

Truffaut, F. 1967. *Hitchcock*. New York: Simon & Schuster. Rev. edn 1985.

Wood, R. 1965. *Hitchcock's Films*. London: Zwemmer / New York: A.S. Barnes.

Filmography

Battle of the River Plate, The. 1956, Michael Powell and Emeric Pressberger, U.K.
Battleship Potemkin. 1925, Sergei Eisenstein, USSR.
Birth of a Nation. 1915, D.W. Griffith, U.S.A.
Drifters. 1929, John Grierson, U.K.
Intolerance. 1916, D.W. Griffith, U.S.A.
Life and Death of Colonel Blimp, The. 1943, Michael Powell and Emeric Pressburger, U.K.
Looks and Smiles. 1981, Ken Loach, U.K.
Matter of Life and Death, A. 1946, Michael Powell and Emeric Pressburger, U.K.
Napoléon. 1927, Abel Gance, France.
Passion de Jeanne d'Arc, La. 1928, Carl Dreyer, France.
Peeping Tom. 1960, Michael Powell, U.K.
Saturday Night and Sunday Morning. 1960, Karel Reisz, U.K.
Sunday By the Sea. 1951, Anthony Simmons, U.K.
Together. 1956, Lorena Mazzetti, U.K.
Typically British. 1996, Stephen Frears, U.K.
Visiteurs du soir, Les. 1942, Marcel Carné, France.

CHAPTER 10

'Incredibly French'?: Nation as an Interpretative Context for Extreme Cinema

Melanie Selfe

The depiction of sexual violence has long been one of the most problematic areas in which the British Board of Film Classification (BBFC) is expected to exercise its judgement. This chapter draws on an independent academic study commissioned by the BBFC in 2006. The research team was led by Professor Martin Barker and the author worked as research assistant on the project. When the BBFC asked Professor Barker to conduct a study into audience responses to a selection of films that they had recently struggled to classify, it was notable that all five of the titles they chose were non-Hollywood imports: *A ma soeur!* (Breillat, France, 2001), *Baise-moi* (Despentes and Trinh Thi, France, 2000), *House on the Edge of the Park / La Casa Sperduta nel Parco* (Deodato, Italy, 1980), *Ichi the Killer / Koroshiya 1* (Miike, Japan, 2001) and *Irreversible* (Noé, France, 2002). Of these, three were examples of what journalists had begun to term the New French Extremity (Quandt 2004; Romney 2004).[1]

By the time the study was conducted in 2006 the 'new French extreme' was a well established concept in professional and amateur film writing. However, in the various phases of our research into the English-language reception of the French films, the emerging subgenre was only one element among the layered expectations created by existing perceptions of European cinema, art-cinema, horror, exploitation and, of course, French film. In this chapter I will revisit the materials we generated, exploring how viewers mobilized generic and national classifications in relation to the different films. In particular, I will focus on the specific ways in which notions of 'real' and mediated 'Frenchness' functioned for our U.K.-based respondents, and consider the impact of perceptions of the place and meaning of French film on viewers' abilities to engage with the difficult depictions of human sexuality presented on screen.

The Study

In the course of our study, we used three methods to gather the views of audiences who had seen the films, in any version or format, as part of their normal viewing activity. In order to build a picture of the expectations, experiences and meanings associated with each film, it was important to locate its existing audiences rather than construct experimental ones.[2] As it is not possible to define the entire population that has watched any film of its own volition, creating statistically representative samples of these viewers was never an option. However, through the first stage of the research – a survey of the naturally occurring online debates about the films – we aimed to identify a range of audiences, discussion spaces and discourses associated with each title. This enabled us to target and include different kinds of viewers in the later research phases.

Phase one revealed that all five of the titles were visible to varying degrees across overlapping art-house, cult, horror and exploitation film cultures. At one end sat *A ma soeur!*, predominantly discussed in art-house terms. The old 'video nasty', *House on the Edge of the Park*, provided its mirror image, circulating almost exclusively within the realm of cult and exploitation.[3] The remaining three titles, however, had strong presence across the spectrum, with many viewers making readings that contested the BBFC's generic categorizations.

While the BBFC had evaluated *House on the Edge of the Park* and *Ichi the Killer* as 'horror' and 'fantasy' respectively, the three French titles were evaluated as 'dramas' (in *Baise-moi*'s case 'adult drama'). Although operating at the very limits of acceptability (and in one or two places, beyond them), the French films were judged to be serious in purpose. And while *House on the Edge of the Park* and *Ichi the Killer* received extensive cuts, perceived authorial intentions (and the implied likelihood that the target audience would be seeking them) appear to have been a recurring factor in the BBFC's justification of a light touch on the French titles.[4] Online, however, the arty 'drama' *Irreversible* was often tackled seriously in horror spaces, and attracted both earnest and flippantly 'gross' interpretations on the more mainstream Internet Movie Database (IMDB) discussion boards. *Baise-moi* had both feminist and exploitation fan-bases, and even *A ma soeur!* appeared in horror and extreme cinema forums.

The first phase of our study had covered reviews and message board posts originating from anywhere in the world (as long as they were in English), and in these, assertions of national meaning were often a feature of collisions between writers from different countries. Viewers declaring themselves as British were well represented in the online spaces we explored, and for our second phase, an online questionnaire, more than two-thirds of the 900-plus responses we gathered came from within the U.K.: a fact which can be attributed, at least in part, to targeted promotion of the questionnaire, but also to the British censorship context of the research, which probably attracted a disproportionate number of U.K. responses from international forums. The third phase, a series of twenty discussion groups (four per film), focused entirely on British responses. These groups were often explicitly designed to explore facets of the particular viewing dispositions (art house, horror, exploitation) that had been identified in the earlier stages of the research. This allowed us to consider the nature of sustained engagements with the films in more detail. Although the observations in this chapter are informed by the research as a whole, the examples analysed in depth will be drawn from these live U.K.-based discussions.

As prior research commissioned by the BBFC had indicated, how acceptable and responsible viewers judge depictions of sexual violence to be is heavily dependent on notions of 'context' (Cumberbatch 2002: 54). Moreover, as our own research went on to explore in detail (Barker et al. 2007), what constitutes an appropriate context is by no means universally agreed.[5] Opinions on specific sequences and films varied greatly, according to the way each viewer interpreted a number of interlinked textual and extratextual factors.

In order to get to grips with this, we identified five 'fields of context' that we considered to have distinct (if interconnected) interpretative roles within viewer responses.[6] 'Impact on self' covered accounts of physical, emotional and cognitive responses. 'Intratextuality' concerned the relationship between the different narrative, character and aesthetic elements: namely the ways in which the key sequence was perceived to contribute to or disrupt the internal integrity of the film. 'Intertextuality' encompassed the relationship to other films and media forms, including generic and national cinema categorizations, and assertions of authorial forces. 'Relations to reality' covered a variety of 'real world' comparisons and assertions of more abstract 'truths'. Lastly, 'relations to "other" audiences' was unsurprisingly a key factor in judgements about the social acceptability of the sexual violence, as it related to the ways in which viewers imagined the responses of other kinds of viewers. Considered in these terms, 'national cinema' is not a single contextual factor but, as the examples will show, a feature of all five context fields.

International Relations

Considering national cinemas from the perspective of audiences, rather than industries, legislators or conventional academic categorizations, follows Andrew Higson's 1989 call for a shift in the focus of their study away from the point of production and towards the point of consumption, specifically, 'to an analysis of how actual audiences construct their cultural identity in relation to the various products of the national and international film and television industries, and the conditions under which this is achieved' (Higson 1989, reprinted in Fowler 2002: 141). Although, two decades on, a radical recentring of the subject around historically, geographically and culturally specific, and therefore inherently *sub*national, audiences is little closer, in the intervening years numerous scholars (including Higson himself, for example, in 2000) have turned their attention to the complex international relationships involved in the production and circulation of cinema. Similarly, complex conceptual international relationships are involved in the ordinary interpretative use of national cinemas, and in approaching these, Doreen Massey's arguments about 'relational geography' are useful.

Like most contemporary spatial theorists, Massey eschews the idea of trying to excavate the 'true' indigenous identities of places. But in arguing for an understanding of place as a continuous process of competing claims she emphasizes the way in which perceived relationships to other places are central to each definition (1994: 5). If one 'understands both space and place as constituted out of spatialized social relations – and narratives about them' (Allen, Massey and Cochrane 1998: 1), then nations, as imagined through their national cinemas (among other means), become points in a network of constantly evolving, interlinked conceptual spaces, defined and contested in relation to each other.

For the viewers who took part in our discussion groups, France and its cinema could be approached and 'known' in a number of ways. Ken, taking part in a North West group discussing *Ichi the Killer*, spontaneously used one of his favourite films, *Hidden / Caché* (Haneke, France, 2005), to explain what he found so difficult about comprehending *Ichi*:

> [I]t's a Japanese film so there's part of that culture that is extremely opaque. But another film that I watched this year which has the ultimate tricky ending is *Hidden*, but *Hidden* is European ... [and] part of it is about the way the Algerians have been treated in France. I know about that, so I can bring the knowledge to bear on the film. I know the guy who's made it is Austrian, I've been to Austria, I looked at their inability to look at their own history. So that comes when I watch the film. So although the film has a tricky ending, I have more [pause] *resources* to figure it out with a European film than I do with a Japanese film.

In the following quote Mike (a fan of a wide range of 'intelligent' films, in his 60s, taking part in a predominantly horror/exploitation-orientated discussion of *Baise-moi* in London) explores the way that, for him, the opposition between French cinema and Hollywood form one side of a triangular relationship:

> I've always liked French cinema, um, it's always err, I've been impressed with it, the fact what I do like about it is, is it's not Hollywood, if anything it cocks a snook at Hollywood, and it does it very successfully, I only wish we, here, could do a bit better than what we do. I mean, you know, the trouble is, you know, it's either a Blockbuster type thing or a *Carry On* type thing and ninety-nine times out of a hundred it doesn't work, whereas with the, for the French it does work.

Here, French cinema is somewhat idealized: held up as the model of a more successful national cinema, competing with Hollywood through attitude rather than scale. Although, in his questionnaire, Mike cites the big Anglo-American blockbuster, *Lawrence of Arabia*, as one of his all-time favourite films, in this more abstract account, he presents Hollywood as a negative and monolithic entity. Hollywood needs to be challenged, and not only is British cinema not up to the task, it is somewhat frivolous or derivative when compared to its Gallic counterpart.

Of the titles we explored, *A ma soeur!*, Catherine Breillat's film about two sisters' troubling first sexual experiences on a family holiday, was perceived to be the most characteristically French. Indeed as Clare, discussing the film in the North East, suggested, 'how *incredibly* French'. The all-female group responded with much laughter and agreement and, when asked, took turns to explain why. Mary, a Canadian, long resident in the U.K., went first. Her overall response was the most ambivalent in the group; she appreciated the film as a character study but strongly disliked the sudden, violent ending. Here, she begins to define Frenchness as a particular kind of interaction between the characters:

> Whenever I see a French movie, and I see looaads of French movies, I'm always astonished at how [pause] uh, eh, how blunt and how rude people are, and how mean people are! I think, is this country really like this?! Do people really speak this way to other people?! The parents are so mean in that movie, and, um, err, just the way the children talk to their parents, not just in this movie, but in other French films ... that's what always strikes me about French films.

Lucy then echoes this observation, asserting it as representative of genuine national characteristics:

> I've been to France so many times I recognize the behaviours and, from lots of other foreign films. I've seen lots of Japanese films and lots of Spanish films, I don't recognize the behaviour as such but with French films I think [pause] 'oh, yeah', French people are actually like that! [Laughter]. It's just a completely different culture, but it's recognizable [pause] so when you see the film you just look at people talk to each other and it's quite [pause] blunt.

While Ken's consideration of *Hidden* had drawn on national and political knowledges, Lucy invokes the evidence of more intimate and obviously subjective judgements. In her account, France is still presented as quite separate – 'a completely different culture' – but Nat, a relative newcomer to art-house viewing, then proceeds to blur this boundary, as she explores in more detail the nature of the recurrent onscreen qualities:

> I've probably seen more French films than I have, say, Japanese or German, but, I always notice the focus on, on relationships when they love conversation, whereas a lot of films are all action. They really go deeply into the way people think and everyday life .... [*A ma soeur!*] was in the middle, quite slow, not in a boring way though, but it just had this real, real life feeling as it was just moving the way time should be really.

As she considers the pace and verbosity of French depiction, Nat starts to break down the residual distance between France and the U.K., talking in terms of a more universal realism which ultimately will allow her to connect to the characters. The issues of transposability and uniqueness are then taken up by Clare, an enthusiastic advocate of the film, who expands:

> I agree with all those things, but, there seems to be something about the *colour* as well, there's something about it that's very misty, [a] thing that she does. Y'know, it's um, it's a bit like Sunday afternoons used to be in Britain, but, y'know, it's very difficult to explain that kind of [pause] that sense of truly *boring*, um, y'know, and the fact that they're on this holiday which they're dragged along on and can't even stand to stay on holiday, that is incredibly French it seems to me, ...[. I]f it was an American film you'd have much more kind of bright colours [pause] we're on holiday, it's got be bright sky and bright sunshine and things but actually it's quite misty when they drive back home, it's raining and things like that [pause] so, it's that kind of very everydayness and sort of boringness of the French [general laughter].

This begins to combine a sense of a distinct French aesthetic with a sense of national character. The mundanity of the experience is equally British, but the sustained insight into it is peculiarly French: 'they're the only people who would make a whole film about it'. The imagined American version, in contrast, would have much less resonance with the British experience.

Generic Expectation and National Specificity

In terms of its perceived status as a French film, *Baise-moi* was by far the most problematic of the three titles. It contained and promoted many recognisably French elements: it was in the French language, made by French writer/directors and lead actors, and featured depictions of the kind of deprived suburbs and specifically French racial issues that had previously been explored to great critical acclaim in *La Haine* (Kassovitz, France, 1995). However, it also had many elements that made viewers think of U.S. cinematic forms. Moreover, aspects of the film's marketing, such as the poster/cover image of an underwear-clad woman pointing a gun at the camera and the frequent 'bargain-bin' discounting of the video, were seen as making low-brow appeals that cut against the film's subtitled status and presumed address to a 'serious' audience.

Crucially, and equally problematically, the film also contained an excess of an element that British viewers widely regarded as integral to French cinema. While comparatively graphic and challenging representations of sexual activity have long been an expected and appropriate subject for European art-cinema in general, and French films in particular, this film had crossed a boundary by including unsimulated sex.

The film follows two women: Nadine, a prostitute, and Manu, an unemployed North African woman. Each suffers a traumatic event (Nadine's junkie best friend is killed; Manu and another woman are gang raped), and each kills someone in an argument related to the event (Nadine assaults her flatmate; Manu shoots her brother). They then meet by chance and go on the run together, killing many more people and picking up men for casual sex. The BBFC had required the removal of a penetration close-up from the gang rape scene plus a matching cut to a shot of the insertion of a gun into a man's anus in a later scene where the two protagonists kill the patrons of a sex club; however, much explicit footage remained. Moreover, the 'real' status of the sex was prominent in the press coverage and both the writer/directors and the lead actresses had well publicized previous careers in the sex and porn industries. The combination of onscreen depictions and extratextual information stimulated debates about whether the film *was* porn (in this context, an almost exclusively negative judgement) or a film about porn, made by women with a unique critical perspective.

This prompted viewers not only to consider the film in terms of their own conceptual relationships to the value of French and U.S. cinema but also to imagine the ways in which others might approach it. In the Scottish *Baise-moi* discussion, Brian explained that while he thought that the BBFC were responding to the film primarily as a feminist work and as part of a 'greater French tradition of maybe intellectual porn', his own critical response to the film had been coloured by the circumstances in which he had acquired a copy; it was concealed in his new flat, in a room that he knew had previously belonged to a teenage boy. He speculated that it had been used as porn and that this was the way in which much of the audience would be approaching it, suggesting 'the BBFC have only passed it because they've been confused by it. If that had been by a Californian guy there is absolutely no way [pause] they would have passed it. But because it's French people will [pause] treat it a bit more seriously'.

This common and perhaps not entirely unjustified impression of a BBFC bias towards French films was echoed strongly and even more critically in the South East *House on the Edge of the Park* group. As long-time fans and collectors of European exploitation cinema, this group acknowledged the popular conflation of French film and art cinema, but refuted it, enthusiastically claiming *Baise-moi* as part of the exploitation canon. Although they disagreed over whether or not it was also a feminist film, there was a consensus that it had missed its true audience and a suggestion that language might have played a part. After Cliff described his amusement at seeing hundreds of copies reduced to £2.99 in the sales:

Ant: Cos no-one wants to buy a cut exploitation movie.
Cliff: No [laughs]. In French.
Ant: In French.

Here it is important to note that much of the exploitation canon originates from Italy, where dubbing has historically been a routine and unproblematic industrial practice, facilitating the use of international casts. By comparison, a subtitled French exploitation film could appear linguistically precious.

Following the early, gritty *banlieue* scenes, *Baise-moi* changes pace and style, and viewers frequently related it to generic traditions commonly perceived as American:

Figure 10.1: Karen Bach in *Baise-moi* (2000).
Image courtesy of the BFI stills department.

the action movie, the road movie, the crime spree and the rape/revenge film. *Baise-moi*'s generic evolution was sometimes interpreted as an intelligent French critique of Hollywood norms via borrowings from the international exploitation tradition, but more often, it was seen as a fault: an inept apeing of U.S. mainstream and low-brow forms and a dilution of the film's Frenchness.

This was an issue for Stephen in the predominantly art-house orientated Yorkshire *Baise-moi* discussion group. Like many other critical viewers of the film, his expectation of French cinema was firmly nested within a sense of European art-cinema and constructed in opposition to both mainstream Hollywood and lower-budget U.S. film forms. Moreover, unlike some of the more positive *Baise-moi* respondents, the specifically European elements of exploitation did not appear to be significant to his frame of reference. In his questionnaire, Stephen had described 'films with psychological realism!' as his preferred kind of viewing, citing *The Dreamlife of Angels / La Vie rêvée des anges* (Zonka, France, 1998) as a favourite. The following exchange with the interviewer (myself), begins to explore the mismatch between Stephen's expectations of *Baise-moi* and the stylistic and narrative elements he perceives in the film:

St: I don't think it has a lot to offer really er, it seems to copy like a Quentin Tarantino-esque type of thing about it, a *Thelma and Louise* type thing about it as well um, but with graphic sex in it which is really pushing the boundaries of what has been er shown before.

Mel: What, what does that mixture of styles mean for you in terms of how you can respond to it?

St: I think it does sort of put you off what its really about when you see the violence and the sex in it, it's, you distance yourself from what it's really trying to say, so I think in that respect it's less important than say *Irreversible* [pause]

Mel: ok

St: [pause] or kind of films that deal with er with rape like er *The Accused*, films like that, and that's strange because *The Accused* is like a Hollywood film you know and er, it's [*Baise-moi* is] supposed to be like an art-house film, it's supposed to be have something to say really, or so you think.

Although Stephen does not explicitly refer to 'French cinema', the examples he uses to explain what he had wished for in the film are telling. As a film about rape, *Baise-moi* falls far short of *Irreversible*, and later in the discussion it becomes clear that, as a film about the underbelly of French society, it is less successful than *La Haine*.

For Stephen, the rape scene is the most memorable and powerful aspect of *Baise-moi* – 'it hits you full on' – setting up a clear expectation of a serious treatment of the subject: 'you know from the very beginning what kind of film it's going to be.' However, the introduction of a pop soundtrack in the next (sex) scene is judged to take the film from 'the real world' to the 'non-real kind of hip world' and the rest of the film becomes a betrayal of the earlier scene's impact on him.

Through his extremely positive questionnaire response to *Irreversible* – a film that left him 'mentally shattered' – it becomes clear that it is not graphic and brutal sex and violence *per se* that are the problem, but the nature of their expression. Both films are judged to have some 'B movie' qualities, but where for *Baise-moi* he felt that layers of poor special effects, a low-budget look and unconvincing character motivation robbed the film of its realism, in contrast, his narrative of *Irreversible* is one where ultraconvincing effects and a bold, unflinching visual direction and soundscape produce something as 'realistic as a film can get'. For Stephen, realism is an essential precondition for meaning. It can be stylized, as long as this is perceived as authored rather than generic. *Baise-moi* becomes generic and thus loses its ability to speak seriously and its right to be so disturbing; however, Noé's 'distinctive style' becomes the successful, if brutal, conduit for *Irreversible*'s message.

As Mark Betz has noted, in the Anglo-American circulation of European art-cinema, 'original' language and directorial authorship are understood as congruent and mutually reinforcing markers of artistic status (2001: 16–17). In his study, he observes a U.S. cinephile preference for versions of international 'auteur'-led coproductions subtitled in the language of the director, even if the cast was international and the original release was dubbed. Conversely, in Stephen's response to *Baise-moi*, the absence of either an established auteur presence mobilized outside the text or a nascent one announcing itself within the text, via the tropes of an assured and recognisably European visual style, means that the French-subtitled status of the film acts as a false signal of artistic authenticity.

Another frustration for Stephen was a sense of geographic dislocation. The film did not convey that the crimes were taking place within *French* society, and the women's physical journey was unclear: 'you don't really know where they are, where it's based'. This became causally related to the failed depiction of a more metaphorical journey: 'so it's not too surprising what happens really ... characters don't really go anywhere really do they, they don't really develop as, as characters'.

In contrast, the London group were much more successful in constructing a sense of place for the women's transformation. Where Breillat's middle-class minutiae had seemed quite recognizable to the North East *A ma soeur!* group, the world presented by *Baise-moi* was more of a challenge. As a result, the London group grounded their collective understanding of the film's France in first-hand experience of the country, but drew on knowledge absorbed from reports about the film's production and French economic and social conditions to bridge the gaps between the tourist's view and the film's presentation of 'an underground part of France that you don't imagine' (Mike).

Rob anchored the film in a newsworthy 'real' France by using French terminology that had begun to appear in articles about the culture of '*tournantes*, the gang rapes that happen in the *banlieue*'.[7] This consolidated an earlier exchange, in which Rachel noted that she thought the early scenes had been filmed in Marseille, where she had spent some time, and Mike followed this with an account of getting lost in the towns on the outskirts of Paris: 'they're absolutely *awful*. You know, you go in there, and you drive down, and it's so bleak there, you know, there was nothing there at all'. Rachel returned the conversation to the specifics of Marseille, tentatively bolstering her personal observations of the postindustrial decay of the city through reference to external data on city populations. She finished by widening out the applicability of the socioeconomic deprivation: 'there are probably a million places like that in France, in England, and in anywhere in the world'. This echoed the sense of others in the group that although the situation was specifically French, it was valuable partly because it depicted the lives of a more widespread underclass.

For this group – equally comfortable with the tropes of conventional art-cinema and those more common within a range of exploitation and horror films – the consensus seemed to be that while French cinema in general was more real than Hollywood, through its raw exploitation elements, *Baise-moi* was also more real than many French films. By using a filming style that had what Rob, a fan of Asian extreme cinemas, referred to as an 'almost "dog meat" quality', the film was seen as being 'honest' in its form of expression. This enabled Rob to overcome his 'mixed feelings' about how 'introspective' a lot of French films were.

French Cinema and Cinematic Trust

As noted already, audiences critical of the BBFC often accused it of a superficial and snobbish bias towards French cinema. However, for some of the viewers who engaged positively with the more conventionally 'French' titles, I would argue that the films' French status offered more than the reassurance of respectably risqué viewing. Rather, it could function in a way that was personally significant, facilitating a deeper engagement with the films.

Here, Ken (once again, making international comparisons in the *Ichi* group) discusses feeling able to view *Irreversible* and endure its 'almost unwatchable' uncut rape 'centrepiece':

> Had it been an American film I don't think I'd have watched it. Erm, I think there's a certain bias in favour of French films, you know, they can do stuff that other, other film cultures can't do or I wouldn't watch. But it's, it's, it's incredibly horrible.

In this account the sense of agency is multilayered and ambiguous. Ken acknowledges both an official cultural sanction and the way in which this contributes to his personal willingness to remain emotionally open and to trust French cinema to take him to really difficult places. His assertion of what 'they' (French filmmakers) 'can do' is as much about what he will permit them to do *to him* as it is about what they are allowed to get away with by the censors and society at large.

French cinema's place as both a serious and an erotic cinematic space is well established in U.K. (and U.S.) film culture. As a result, this notion of cinematic trust was particularly relevant for responses to challenging depictions of sexuality. For Kerry (a young woman, taking part in the South East *A ma soeur!* group), this familiarity enabled her response to a long seduction scene, in which a fifteen-year-old girl is coerced by her older boyfriend into painful anal sex:

> to start off with I s'pose I was responding to it in the way that you respond to lots of films and just getting a you know vicarious thrill, voyeuristic almost of you know watching it, watching a beautiful girl and a beautiful guy getting it on, umm in quite a sensual way which isn't you know, necessarily something that you see outside of French cinema.

Here, her degree of comfort with French cinema as inherently erotic and potentially *personally* arousing is central to the film's ability to provoke an integrated intellectual and emotional response to the scene, resulting in a deeply felt consideration of the complex nature of power and consent:

> umm, and then as it carried on then it became more a much more personal and much more umm about relationships and umm, manipulation and umm what it is to say yes and no and that sort of thing, so it was really quite powerful, to start off by feeling, you know that it was a, a quite an arousing scene to then it being turned on its head, umm, in a really subtle way I thought.

For some British viewers, the historical legacy of French cinema as both erotic and artistic can enable it to function as a space from which to rethink the more difficult aspects of gender and sexual relations in an emotionally engaged way. Particularly when this starts to approach 'thinking the unthinkable', the conceptual proximity of France is important. While responses to *Ichi the Killer* tended to present both Japan and the film's aesthetics as too culturally alien for the film to have anything relevant to 'say' about the nature of gender relationships and sexual violence in the U.K., France was recognisably close enough – but not too close. At different moments in the discussions, and according to interpretative need, it could be linguistically pulled towards or held away from viewers' personal and social experience.

Conclusion

Across the many interpretations we encountered in the study, mobilizations of 'French', 'European', 'Hollywood' and 'American' qualities were a recurrent and interrelated feature of the way viewers negotiated positive and negative meanings for the three French films. Moreover, British viewers frequently positioned themselves *as* British viewers, explicitly situating their understanding of French cinema as one site of potential meaning within a complex international network.

In measuring the different films against external reality, viewers were prompted by the texts and their extratexts to mobilize different versions of the 'real' France, and in the discussions groups, personal accounts, factual assertions and cultural impressions combined to produce collective pictures of place and national meaning.

For viewers who successfully engaged with one or more of the French films, a preexisting sense of French cinema was frequently a core element of building 'intertextual' frameworks, and consequently of defining the terms on which the fine grain of 'intratextual' coherence (and the acceptability of controversial scenes) could be judged. For those positively disposed towards French films, a title which did not jar with their aesthetic expectation of Frenchness could potentially be trusted to deliver significant meaning through challenging content. However, strong generic national expectations could also work against a film; some viewers lacked the means to reconcile the more extreme elements to their personal understanding of the French cinematic tradition.[8] Conversely, precisely because *Baise-moi* did not sit comfortably within the 'French film as art film' stereotype, it could work well for viewers who were frustrated by more conventionally 'French' fare.

Notes

Due to the British reception focus of this chapter, U.K.-release titles are preferred throughout, with original-language titles – if different – given the first time each film is mentioned. Other English-release titles in common circulation via online debates are noted in the filmography.

1. Although the films were often being reviewed with reference to each other before this, Quandt is usually credited with naming the extreme 'genre', in an article highly critical of the trend (2004).
2. One special uncut screening was held for *House on the Edge of the Park*, in order to ensure enough female responses for analysis. However, responses from this event received a separate identifier, enabling us to account for the rather different spectrum of motivations (including curiosity, civic duty and a sense of moral witness) and expectations involved in taking part in a research screening of a 'banned' film.
3. This had recently been reconsidered for DVD release and had the most complex international identity. It was an Italian-made exploitation thriller, with an American star, narrative setting and dubbed dialogue, and a U.K. reception context dominated by its censorship history and cult status as a banned film on the DPP list of 'video nasties'.
4. In difficult classification cases, multiple BBFC examiners view the film and meet to discuss their evaluations. The Board supplied the research team with summary decision notes that drew on these meetings, enabling us to gain some insight into the core arguments surrounding the decision on each film.
5. See Barker (2005) for a response to the Cumberbatch report and an early exploration of viewers' use of context in relation to sexual violence. See Selfe (2008) for an account of the commissioning of the study.
6. For an account of the other structures we used for analysing the ways people remembered films, 'embracer' and 'refuser' position taking, and levels of investment, please see Barker et al. (2007: 8–21).
7. *Tournante* or 'pass round' rape culture is a term that seems to have entered the British discussion of the film via an influential 2003 article about the phenomenon by the journalist Rose George.
8. Various writers have observed the way in which the art/trash binary has become porous within both academic and cult film cultures (see for example, Sconce 1995; Hawkins

2000). However, confident dismissal of taste distinctions is often dependent on a mastery of these discourses. In the Yorkshire and London *Baise-moi* groups, the most complex positive readings of the film came from women who shared an appreciation for a 'punk' aesthetic and a knowledge of academic as well as vernacular feminism.

Bibliography

Allen, J., D. Massey and A. Cochrane. 1998. *Rethinking the Region*. London: Routledge.

Barker, M. 2005. 'Loving and Hating Straw Dogs: The Meanings of Audience Responses to a Controversial Film', *Participations* 2(2). Retrieved 10 March 2009 from http://www.participations.org/volume%202/issue%202/2_02_barker.htm

———. et al. 2007. 'Audiences and Reception of Sexual Violence in Contemporary Cinema', Report to the British Board of Film Classification upon completion of the research project, Aberystwyth: University of Wales, Aberystwyth. Retrieved 11 December 2008 from BBFC, Policy and Research http://www.bbfc.co.uk/downloads/index.php

Betz, M. 2001. 'The Name Above the (Sub)Title: Internationalism, Coproduction, and Polyglot European Art Cinema', *Camera Obscura* 16(1): 1–44.

Cumberbatch, G. 2002. 'Where Do You Draw the Line? Attitudes and Reactions of Video Renters to Sexual Violence in Film', Report prepared for the British Board of Film Classification, Birmingham: Communications Research Group. Retrieved 11 December 2008 from BBFC, Policy and Research http://www.bbfc.co.uk/downloads/index.php

George, R. 2003. 'Revolt Against the Rapists', *Guardian*, 5 April. Retrieved 11 December 2008 from http://www.guardian.co.uk/world/2003/apr/05/france.gender

Hawkins, J. 2000. *Cutting Edge: Art-horror and the Horrific Avant-garde*. Minneapolis: University of Minnesota Press.

Higson, A. 1989. 'The Concept of National Cinema', *Screen* 30(4), reprinted in C. Fowler (ed.), 2002. *The European Cinema Reader*. London: Routledge, pp. 132–42.

———. 2000. 'National Cinema(s), International Markets and Cross-cultural Identities', in I. Bondebjerg (ed.), *Moving Images, Culture and the Mind*. Luton: University of Luton Press, pp. 205–14.

Massey, D. 1994. *Space, Place and Gender*. Cambridge: Polity Press.

Quandt, J. 2004.'Flesh & Blood: Sex and Violence in Recent French Cinema', *Artforum* February: 126–32.

Romney, J. 2004. 'Le Sex and Violence', *The Independent on Sunday*, 12 September 2004. Retrieved 11 December 2008 from http://www.independent.co.uk/arts-entertainment/films/features/le-sex-and-violence-546083.html

Sconce, J. 1995. '"Trashing" the Academy: Taste, Excess and an Emerging Politics of Cinematic Style', *Screen* 36(4): 371–93.

Selfe, M. 2008. 'Inflected Accounts and *Irreversible* Journeys', *Participations* 5: 1. Retrieved 11 December 2008 from http://www.participations.org/Volume%205/Issue %201%20-%20special/5_01_selfe.htm

Filmography

A ma soeur! / *Fat Girl* (U.S. title) / *For My Sister* (Aus. title). 2001, Catherine Breillat, France.

The Accused. 1988, Jonathan Kaplan, U.S.A.

Baise-moi / *Rape me* (U.S. title). 2000, Virginie Despentes and Coralie Trinh Thi, France.

Dreamlife of Angels / *La vie rêvée des anges.* 1998, Eric Zonka, France.

Haine, La / *Hate* (U.S. title). 1995, Matthieu Kassovitz, France.

Hidden / *Caché.* 2005, Michael Haneke, France.

House on the Edge of the Park / *La Casa sperduta nel parco.* 1980, Ruggero Deodato, Italy.

Ichi the Killer / *Koroshiya 1.* 2001, Takashi Miike, Japan.

Irreversible / *Irréversible.* 2002, Gaspar Noé, France.

Thelma and Louise. 1991, Ridley Scott, U.S.A.

CHAPTER 11

British Audiences and 1990s French New Realism: *La Vie Rêvée des Anges* as Cinematic Slum Tourism

Ingrid Stigsdotter

At the time of its French release, a *Cahiers du cinéma* critic described Erick Zonca's first feature film, *La Vie rêvée des anges / The Dreamlife of Angels* (1998), as fitting very neatly into international expectations of French cinema from the 1990s, and corresponding particularly well to the idea of French contemporary cinema promoted at the Cannes film festival (Burdeau 1998: 71). Elodie Bouchez and Natacha Régnier received a shared Best Actress award at the 1998 festival for their performances as Isa (Bouchez) and Marie (Régnier), two young women with very different personalities who share a flat together in the city of Lille in northern France. The buzz around the Cannes festival helped generate audience interest in France, where the film became a minor box office hit, one of the few examples of this type of auteur cinema from the 1990s that proved popular with French audiences (Vanderschelden 2007: 15). The Cannes award was also important in securing the sales of *La Vie rêvée des anges* to many territories outside of France, including Britain, where Zonca's film managed to attract audience figures of around fifty-seven thousand, making it one of the most successful French films at the British box office in 1998. The film has also been shown on television and been released on VHS and subsequently DVD formats in Britain.[1]

Both French and British critics compared Zonca's film to the work of the British directors Mike Leigh and Ken Loach, as well as earlier traditions of 'kitchen-sink' drama in British film culture. There have also been debates regarding the status of the film's realist strategies in relation to the notion of political cinema. It is therefore interesting to consider to what extent audiences in Britain connected *La Vie rêvée des anges* to British realist filmmaking and to investigate whether audiences appeared to perceive the film as political. This chapter is based on empirical audience data from

Figure 11.1: Natacha Régnier in *La Vie rêvée des anges* (1998). Image courtesy of the BFI stills department.

my doctoral research on responses to recent French and Swedish cinema and film audiences in Britain (Stigsdotter 2008), the questionnaire responses analysed here having been collected at two screenings of *The Dreamlife of Angels* at the University of Southampton's Avenue campus and the New Park Cinema in Chichester in 2005.

Le Jeune Cinéma Français and the Politics of New Realism

In research on recent French cinema, *La Vie rêvée des anges* has often been labelled as an example of *le jeune cinéma français* or 'new realism', two concepts that partly overlap in terms of the films that they attempt to designate. The term *jeune cinéma* features in the titles of three French publications concerned with 1990s French cinema (Trémois 1997; Marie 1998; Prédal 2002) and has also appeared in the British broadsheet press (Romney 1999). The label has been applied to filmmakers who were either relatively young or attracting attention in the mid-to-late 1990s but who otherwise are a fairly diverse bunch, including Robert Guédiguian (*Marius et Jeannette / Marius and Jeannette*, 1997), Sandrine Veysset (*Y aura-t-il de la neige à Noël? / Will it Snow for Christmas?*, 1996), Claire Denis (*J'ai pas sommeil / I Can't Sleep*, 1994), Manuel Poirier (*Western*, 1997) and Bruno Dumont (*La Vie de Jésus / Life of Jesus*, 1997). Will Higbee has criticized the concept, suggesting that the notion of 'youth' is confusing because it fails to address the emergence of films addressing themes around race, ethnicity and cultural identity in contemporary French society in this period and he therefore prefers to discuss the films under the label of 'new realism' (Higbee 2005: 310, 316–7).

With narratives focussing on questions like 'immigration, racism, unemployment, exclusion and social fracture' (Higbee 2005: 308), many French films made in the late 1990s could be described as examples of 'social realism'. As Julia Hallam and Margaret Marshment explain, this critical term has been applied to 'films that aim to show the effects of environmental factors on the development of character through depictions that emphasize the relationship between location and identity' (Hallam and Marshment 2000: 184). Like many of the other films labelled as *jeune cinéma* or 'new realism', *La Vie rêvée des anges* combines low-budget production values with a setting in a contemporary provincial reality and a focus on people in the social margins. Historically, cinematic social realism has been linked to 'gritty' and 'raw' depictions of urban life, often using an 'observational' style and 'episodic' narrative. In contemporary cinema, however, the stylistic and narrative features of social realism have become increasingly eclectic, incorporating influences from both the modernist avant garde and popular melodrama among its aesthetic strategies (Hallam and Marshment 2000: 184, 192).

The narrative of *La Vie rêvée des anges* centres on the overlapping lives of the two protagonists as they eke out dead-end existences on the cusp of poverty. The women's attitudes to life determine their fate: while the melancholy and volatile Marie finally finds life so unbearable she commits suicide, Isa, a more upbeat character, ends intact, with the possibility of a better future dangled tenuously before her. To describe the film as an example of 'new realism' rather than 'social realism', however, is to suggest that Zonca approaches the sociopolitical dimensions of everyday life in a different way to previous generations of filmmakers (Higbee 2005: 310). Martin O'Shaughnessy defines new realism stylistically, in terms of 'an unpolished, naturalistic image' and seemingly loosely structured 'episodic plots'; and thematically, as films that deal with 'contemporary socio-political issues and debates, such as unemployment, the *banlieue* or the world of work' (O'Shaughnessy 2007: 135). In combination with the use of nonprofessional actors such characteristics fit into historical traditions of social realism on screen, but O'Shaughnessy argues that the films also feature 'melodramatic qualities' such as 'the production of moments of confrontation and collision; the corporeal and the gestural; the restoration of ethical transparency to a world that has become opaque; the emotive focus on individuals and families rather than abstract forces' (O'Shaughnessy 2007: 136).

This emphasis on the individual as opposed to the collective, together with the filmmakers' limited connection to traditional leftist party politics is what seems to differentiate French filmmakers in the 1990s from historical precedents of realism in French cinema (Powrie 1999: 12–15; Cf. Higbee 2005: 307–8). In France, some critics described new realism as pseudopolitical because of the films' inability to offer solutions to the social problems they depicted. By contrast, O'Shaughnessy argues that the 1990s saw a genuine and potentially fruitful return to political cinema in France (O'Shaughnessy 2007: 21–35). The research presented in this chapter partly challenges this claim, arguing that audience interpretation should be taken into account into any discussion of whether political cinema can be deemed successful, in the sense of actually provoking political awareness or action. O'Shaughnessy discusses the French sociopolitical context and critical debates surrounding the films, but his approach to their political dimension is based on textual analysis and does not address the issue of how audiences in France or elsewhere might react to the films. It will therefore be particularly interesting to consider the findings from my audience study in relation to O'Shaughnessy's work. Because the research audience included some French film viewers, I will also be able to explore differences between French and British responses to the depiction of social reality in Zonca's film.

The Research Audience and Emotional Engagement

The average age of research participants attending screenings of *La Vie rêvée des anges* was thirty-nine years old and the film attracted an equal share of male and female respondents. The audience was predominantly middle class, and a significant number of them had a taste for films beyond mainstream popular cinema.[2] Almost 40 per cent of the audience members were nonnative English-speakers, and the share of participants who stated that they had intermediate to fluent command of three or more languages was almost as large.[3]

My research suggests that for audiences participating in this project, emotional reactions were intrinsic to the film-viewing process. It is beyond the scope of this chapter to provide a full account for the diverse and complex ways in which audiences viewing *La Vie rêvée des anges* engaged emotionally with the film, but by highlighting a few examples of responses to the film's protagonists it is possible to gain a sense of the importance played by sentiment in audience reactions.

Research participants who disliked the film invariably reported having difficulties relating emotionally to the main character, but most viewers were able to empathize with the character of Isa.[4] She was generally perceived as a sympathetic character, associated with compassion, care, openness, gentleness, truthfulness and a courageous approach to life. Marie, on the other hand, alienated many respondents by her self-destructive and aggressive behaviour. The person with the most positive attitude towards Marie was one of the youngest participants in this case study, a nineteen-year-old student, who wrote that 'Marie was passionate, desperately unhappy. Very much in need as though she was being strangled, slowly. I think everyone can relate to that, every once in a while. I could'. The way in which this research participant stressed the potentially universal aspect of her own experience fits with a common tendency among respondents to either categorize their own experience as 'natural' or 'universal', or to emphasize how specialist knowledge or sensitivity allowed them to appreciate aspects of a film that other viewers might not understand. This viewer, who represented the former category, explained that, 'Marie's violent outbursts to Isabelle and Chris were things I could relate to, if not in that extreme'. Her willingness to relate directly to the more destructive elements of the protagonists' personalities was fairly unrepresentative of the audience as a whole, but several respondents compared the main characters to friends or relatives; in particular Isa seemed to remind several viewers of a friend or someone they had known in the past. This recalls O'Shaughnessy's observation that 'new realist' films have an 'emotive focus on individuals and families rather than abstract forces' (O'Shaughnessy 2007: 136) and suggests that *La Vie rêvée des anges* managed to touch a chord with viewers by appealing to a personal rather than a sociopolitical experience of reality.

Research participants' comments about emotional engagement could be placed across a spectrum ranging from complete rejection to close identification, with pity, critical sympathy and warm empathy in between. One young man wrote that he felt sympathy for the characters, but at the same time, he was critical of their behaviour, stating that: 'you tend to think harshly about their lack of enterprising initiatives. They just survive, they are so disillusioned. They should be more active in finding a job.' Some film viewers appeared able to find ways of connecting imaginatively to fictional characters despite not feeling in any way similar to them, while other respondents looked for character traits that they could identify with in order to engage with the film. Furthermore, for some research participants it was not sufficient to recognize themselves in the characters; they wanted to find a positive recognition of sympathetic character traits in the film. For these viewers, the fact that the protagonists sometimes behaved in ways that were not logically motivated, and that there were negative sides to their personalities – which other viewers by contrast considered human or realistic – made it impossible to like them or to be interested in what happened to them.

Realism at Home and Abroad

Participants with a negative response to the film often articulated their dislike in terms of not being able to care about the characters, as in the case of one man in his late fifties who compared the film to Ken Loach's work and 'kitchen sink' realist films, but deemed *La Vie rêvée des anges* less emotionally effective because 'most of the characters had no connection other than they just met'. His references to specific examples of British cinema place *La Vie rêvée des anges* within a realist cinematic tradition and are consistent with critical writing about Zonca's film in Britain, where Loach and Mike Leigh often featured. It is worth noting that this British viewer compared a French realist film negatively with a well known tradition in British cinema. It is therefore possible that he felt more at ease with realism in films associated with his own culture, whereas he expected French cinema to offer a form of cinematic tourism with a more appealing depiction of reality. Giuliana Bruno has written suggestively about the parallels between cinema, travel and tourism, describing tourism and film viewing as popular leisure activities associated with the pleasurable consumption of images and spectacle and experiences confined to a specific duration (Bruno 2002: 79–82), and Mazdon and Wheatley have made specific connections between the tourist gaze, British audiences and contemporary French cinema (Mazdon and Wheatley 2008: 39).

Alternatively, Loach could be seen to represent a more traditional approach to social realism, in which case it would be new realism's alleged departure from established models that annoyed this respondent. Whatever the reason for his rejection of the film's realism, his criticism focused on the fact that he was unable to relate to the protagonists because they and their relationships were in his view 'shallow'.

Closure and Interpretation

At the end of the film, Marie takes her own life. One respondent described Marie's suicide as the film's 'last scene'. For this woman, the sudden death of Marie followed by the sound of 'children playing in the background', showing 'life continuing without Marie', appears to have had an overwhelming impact; she did not seem to remember that the scene she described is followed by a sequence showing Isa seated at a workstation among other women in a large electronics factory, about to start a new job.

The final shot of Isa at work was commented on by other respondents. A research student in his mid-twenties who was a frequent cinemagoer wrote:

I thought that the ending was particularly significant – she has to put the right wires in the right holes, and this means knowing which colours 'communicate' (does the supervisor use this word?). The supervisor then says "You must have been doing this all your life"! It has a sort of double meaning; putting the right things together / making the right decisions. I thought it was very good.

For another viewer, like the previous respondent a frequent cinemagoer in his mid-twenties, the same sequence was disappointing; he thought that 'for a film that had lingered on its main characters for so long, to suggest that each of these women lived the same way [...] in such an obvious way struck me as cheap'. The first of these two respondents adopted an original and multilayered interpretative strategy that allowed him to see the final scene as a celebration of the qualities that he appreciated in the character of Isa. The second viewer's way of reading the final sequence was more conventional, in the sense that many British film critics also interpreted this scene as establishing a link between Isa as an individual and the female factory workers as a collective (Johnston 1998: 6; Smith 1998: 64). Unlike these reviewers, however, this respondent was not comfortable seeing the narrative's central protagonist reduced to part of a collective.

Film Taste, Class and Politics

It is interesting to consider how a research audience consisting primarily of film viewers from the middle to upper socioeconomic categories approached the fact that the protagonists of *La Vie rêvée des anges* live on the margins of society, in a reality removed from the British audience context not just geographically, but also in terms of social stratum. Most respondents were of the opinion that *La Vie rêvée des anges* would attract an audience with a particular high cultural sensibility. They described the film's intended audience as 'cinema enthusiasts', or viewers with a taste for 'ambitious' or 'serious' films, who did not go to the cinema just 'for amusement', but 'sensitive' and 'intelligent' viewers 'willing to learn something'. In some responses the target audience was defined negatively as 'not the "standard Hollywood" audience', and one student wrote that the mainstream audience would have disliked a long take showing Isa crying in a church after a row with Marie. This allowed him to distance himself from the average cinemagoer, emphasizing his own cultural distinction by asserting that he found that particular scene beautiful. A teacher in his early fifties specified that '[t]he French and English audiences would be different. In France, I think mainly younger people (student age to under fifties) who like regular cinema'. Although this viewer did not specify in what way the British audience for *La Vie rêvée des anges* would differ from the French audience, he seemed to imply that in Britain the film would attract older viewers with a film consumption profile veering towards art cinema rather than the larger film releases dominating the British cinema market.

As some of the comments cited above suggest, many members of the research audience consciously or unconsciously perceived themselves as different from mainstream popular cinema audiences in Britain. However, if it was common for viewers to identify with film tastes that could be described as elite and thus implicitly associated with a higher social stratum, most respondents stayed away from addressing the issue of class directly in their comments. This is particularly interesting considering that critical and scholarly debates surrounding *La Vie rêvée des anges* both in Britain and France, albeit in slightly different ways, have tended to focus on sociopolitical questions and the representation of work, unemployment and class (O'Shaughnessy 2007: 88, 100–101) and it raises questions about how film audiences relate to the notion of political cinema.

Realism, Melodrama, Morals and Emotion

As Torben Grodal observes, realism is more commonly associated with downbeat than upbeat representations of the world, and he notes that we base our understanding of concepts such as 'realism' and 'reality' on 'normative evaluations of what is typical of real life' (Grodal 2002: 70). He suggests that the tendency in realist representations to focus on misery rather than the bright side of life can be understood not simply in terms of a 'a political wish for advocating empathy, but also a feeling that pain and deprivation are more real than pleasure' (Grodal 2002: 87).[5] Similarly, films about ordinary people tend to be perceived as more realist than depictions of celebrities; a film about a family on a council estate is more likely to be considered as realist than a portrayal of the royal family, regardless of the fact that technically, both films can base their representations on real-life models and use formal strategies associated with realism.

Among audience members whose film consumption was dominated by English-language film there was a tendency to summarize the film's overall meaning in slightly moralistic terms that emphasized the responsibility of the individual. One young female student wrote that '[l]ife continues – only you can change it to make it better. We're all responsible for our own lives'. For another young woman, the film showed that there were 'two kinds/categories of people, those who despite hardships of life ... succeed at the end, and by contrast ... people who do not want to try'.[6] These interpretations of *La Vie rêvée des anges* are constructed in moral terms that seem to correspond to the respondents' preexisting ideas about how life should be lived. In this context, it is interesting to return to O'Shaughnessy's claim that new realism incorporates melodramatic elements such as the 'restoration of ethical transparency to a world that has become opaque' (O'Shaughnessy 2007: 136). Historically, melodrama has been associated with popular cinema and with a female audience. Furthermore, melodramatic qualities are seen to elicit emotional viewer responses, whereas it has generally been accepted as a given in debates around art cinema and realism that formal innovation cues viewers to interpret films intellectually rather than emotionally (Hallam and Marshment 2000: xiv).

Realism and melodrama are often defined as binary opposites; while realism is associated with 'authenticity and truth', melodrama stands for 'exaggeration, sensationalism and sentimentality' (Hallam and Marshment 2000: 19). O'Shaughnessy summarizes conventional perceptions of the relationship: 'Associated to a high degree with a flat, dedramatized and documentary-like recording of the world, realism would seem irreconcilable, on the surface at least, with the heightened and contrived effects of melodrama as well as with the declamatory and apparently artificial nature of the theatrical' (O'Shaughnessy 2007: 131). However, drawing on Peter Brooks' *The Melodramatic Imagination* (1976), he argues that 'realist and melodramatic drives can exist in complex and productive tension' (O'Shaughnessy 2007: 131). With specific reference to realism in recent French cinema, he describes films such as *La Vie rêvée des anges* as melodramatic and theatrical; thematically, by 'drawing on highly charged stories of individuals ... as a way to dramatize contemporary systemic violences' and formally, by 'restoring eloquence to a real that no longer speaks to us adequately' (O'Shaughnessy 2007: 131). O'Shaughnessy's discussion of melodramatic characteristics such as 'climactic moments when characters confront one another with full expressivity to fix the meaning of relationships', using 'accentuated gestures and statements' (O'Shaughnessy 2007: 132) provides a perceptive description of Zonca's film, and may provide a textual clue to the keen interest in the relationship between characters that could be observed across responses in this study. Furthermore, the film's emotional impact appeared to be a highly significant aspect of the viewing experience for this audience. By acknowledging the coexistence of melodramatic and realist elements in *La Vie rêvée des anges* and the importance of viewers' emotional responses to the film, the findings challenge traditional distinctions between art and popular cinema and raise questions about how we define the formal characteristics associated with these labels in relation to the ways in which audiences approach and interpret the films.

Visions from Two Sides of the Channel

Many of the participants in this study connected Zonca's film to their own perceptions of French national culture. The findings must be approached carefully because the film viewers knew that they were taking part in a study of audiences for European and French cinema in Britain and the questions that they were asked within this context did of course also influence the type of responses obtained. However, the comments made by a forty-year-old man, who expected French films to involve 'liberated sex scenes!' and described 'the casualness of the sex scenes' as a culturally specific characteristic in Zonca's film, are noteworthy because they fit into a perceived historical tradition of 'sexy and sordid' representations of France (Mazdon and Wheatley 2008: 39). Sensationalist French films imported to Britain in the 1950s and 1960s have contributed to British expectations of French cinema offering a kind of risqué realism associated with sexual explicitness (Mazdon and Wheatley 2008: 39. See also Elsaesser 2005: 146). As Joel Black argues, with reference to the increased use of graphic material in contemporary films, physicality and explicit sex on film can be seen as creating a reality effect through viewers' heightened awareness of the use of film as 'photographic evidence' and surveillance in relation to crime (Black 2002: 8). However, in the research audience for *La Vie rêvée des anges*, the association between sex and French cinema did not seem linked to realism. One young woman described French films as 'funny, erotic, bright, good music, good food shown', and went on to cite scenes showing 'sex' and 'cooking' as examples of what made Zonca's film seem French to her. Her comments do not conjure up an image of graphic realism, but rather a feel-good film, fulfilling an appetite for food and sex whilst entertaining through humour and music.

None of the French audience members thought that nudity or sex scenes were a particularly French characteristic; they were more likely to associate French films with good storytelling and acting or simply with the French language. The French respondents cited the film's realism, reliance on acting performances, setting and rough cinematographic style as examples of the film's French identity. This suggests that auteur cinema rather than popular genre films defined French national cinema for these viewers. One of the French respondents also provided a specific suggestion about how firsthand experience of French culture might affect interpretations of the film, pointing out that the 'job market for instance is seen very differently in France and England, because of a higher unemployment rate (which was already true at the time)'. The same viewer, a man in his mid-twenties, also described 'women rebelling' as a French theme. This idea has some similarities with the comments made by a female French respondent of a similar age, who thought that French cinema was characterized by 'characters with a lot of personality', and singled out 'the attitudes of the girls (strong personality)', as an aspect of *La Vie rêvée des anges* that she saw as specifically French.

It is interesting to contrast these ideas about strong French women on the screen with the views of a British woman in her late twenties, whose expectations of French film were summarized as 'odd, very inward-looking, possibly a bit full of itself .... Oh, and nudity'. For her, the most culturally specific thing about *La Vie rêvée des anges* was the 'club owner with his multiple lovers and the women accepting this'. A comparison of these seemingly incompatible interpretations – on the one hand, a representation of French women as strong, feisty and rebellious, and on the other what appears to be a criticism of women putting up with men behaving in unacceptable ways – makes it clear that respondents tend to look for evidence that support their own predetermined views on French culture. Whether or not the protagonists of Zonca's film do or do not correspond to the notion of strong female characters is irrelevant; the interesting point is that viewers interpreted the female roles in a manner that confirmed their preexisting ideas about women's position in French society. The interpretation thus says more about the opinions of the respondents themselves than about the content of the film, highlighting the importance of context in relation to film interpretation. With regards to the British woman cited above it is important to keep in mind that one statement taken out of context cannot explain the often complex set of emotions and thoughts that a film can provoke. The nuances articulated through the contradictions between the detailed comments on the film supplied by this viewer are very interesting. For instance, she associated Isa with 'unassailable optimism', yet the film gave her 'the sense that there's no escape', and when asked how she would categorize the film she wrote that 'it was a fairly serious film although it didn't always feel like it'. While the French respondents who referred to strong female personalities in French culture clearly saw this as a national character trait evident in *La Vie rêvée des anges*, it is important to acknowledge that appreciation of one's 'national heritage' can arguably be reinforced in a different cultural context, whether through nostalgia or simply through pleasure in being reminded of little details such as the sound of the language or the look of everyday objects.

I have dwelt upon the difference between responses from French research participants and other audience members not in order to suggest that British viewers have an erroneous idea about French film or culture, or that the views of these particular French viewers should in any way be seen as representative of French audiences more generally. However, the findings suggest that British audiences approach French cinema with an interpretative framework based on the selection of French film available in Britain together with a discourse surrounding French cinema that stems not only from film journalism, but also relates to broader ideas about French culture. This interpretative framework contrasts sharply with the expectations French viewers bring to French films.

New Realism, Neorealism and Cinematic Slum Tourism

This chapter has discussed how a largely middle-class group of film viewers in Britain engaged with a French film portraying working-class protagonists on the verge of homelessness. Their reluctance to discuss class-related issues suggests that their external, privileged perspective on representations of social marginalization has become naturalized; the question of class fades into invisibility in a process similar to that described by Richard Dyer (1997) in relation to whiteness and race.

The notion of elite audiences consuming films about the lower classes, and specifically the lower classes in other countries, in what could be termed a form of cinematic slumming has a long history within the context of art cinema. The neorealist movement in Italy in the early postwar period is an emblematic example of this. Popular audiences in postwar Italy preferred the commercial cinema that neorealism reacted against, so it is largely because of the favourable reactions from critics and art-cinema audiences abroad that neorealism has become canonized as a significant milestone in the history of both cinematic realism and European cinema (Hallam and Marshment 2000: 6, 17, 41).

In his discussion of 1990s French cinema, O'Shaughnessy points to formal similarities between new realism and Italian neorealism, arguing that both film movements relied on a combination of melodrama and realism (O'Shaughnessy 2007: 179–80). However, his focus on the French context means that O'Shaughnessy neglects parallels in terms of export and international critical attention.[7] When considered in relation to issues concerning audiences, reception and cultural transfer, his argument about the use of melodrama in new realist films could be seen as having implications that contradict his definition of recent French cinema as politically committed. The tension between melodrama and realism that O'Shaughnessy identifies in films like *La Vie rêvée des anges* seems in fact to allow audiences to engage with the film in an apolitical way. The research audience in this study focused on the emotional turmoil of the protagonists rather than on the representation of material poverty and social insecurity, enjoying the emotional intensity of the relationships between characters without necessarily engaging with their social situation. This arguably undermines O'Shaughnessy's claim about the political potency of new realism. Furthermore, as the differences between responses from French and British respondents in this case study indicate, the political dimension of a film is likely to be construed differently when the film is viewed by an audience approaching the topic from a different cultural perspective.

I have argued elsewhere that Jean-Pierre Jeunet's international hit *Le Fabuleux destin d'Amélie Poulain / Amélie* (2001) has come to dominate the public conception of contemporary French cinema in Britain to the extent that it is the benchmark against which all other contemporary French films are measured (Stigsdotter 2008: 121–5).[8] Mazdon and Wheatley have linked *Amélie*'s popularity in Britain to the appeal of the 'safely exotic' (Mazdon and Wheatley 2008: 39). It may be easier to connect *Amélie*'s postcard representation of Paris to the notion of cinematic tourism than the realist images of less picturesque locations in northern France in *La Vie rêvée des anges*. However, a recurring theme in my audience research was viewers' interest in exploring another culture on the screen. Even the markedly nontouristic imagery in *La Vie rêvée des anges* may create a sensation of imaginary travel for British viewers, allowing them to experience '[c]ultural and emotional (dis)placements, as well as journeys between the familiar and the unfamiliar, the ordinary and the extraordinary' (Bruno 2002: 83). Indeed, it might not be too far-fetched to see *La Vie rêvée des anges* as a cinematic equivalent to the concept of slum tourism (see Gentleman 2006). Like many of the other French new realist films, it provides British audiences with an intense, emotional visit to a social reality that they are unlikely ever to participate in, inevitably followed by a presumably reassuring return to their own world.

Notes

1. At the time of the research screening the film had only been released on VHS in Britain; a Region 2 DVD is now available.
2. All of the audience data cited below can be consulted in the appendices of my thesis which also incorporates contextual statistical material about audiences for specialized cinema in the UK (Stigsdotter 2008: 271–488).
3. This chapter is thus about audience responses in Britain (or more specifically, southern England) rather than about the responses of viewers with British nationality. The linguistic and cultural diversity can be partly explained by the fact that the film screening at the University of Southampton attracted a significant number of international students as well as British students of Modern Languages. However, also at the New Park Cinema in Chichester about one-quarter of the participants were nonnative English speakers. Most viewers with a non-English mother tongue had a European cultural background, with German and French respondents being the two largest groups among the nonnative English speakers. It is worth keeping in mind that the cultural diversity expanded the audiences' frame of reference for situating *La Vie rêvée des anges* in relation to other non-Hollywood films from France, Europe and the rest of the world.
4. Around 80 per cent of those who attended the screenings of *La Vie rêvée des anges* explicitly described their experience of the film as positive. Among the remaining 20 per cent, about half actively disliked the film while the other half were unsure, or had an ambivalent response to the film.
5. As Grodal points out, Freud labelled psychological mechanisms linked to pain the 'reality principle' (2002: 87).
6. Cf. the following statement from a research associate in her late twenties: 'you get from life what you put in – two people can be in the same social/economic situation, but if their outlooks are different then what they experience will also be different. It's about engaging with life'.
7. For more on the significance of neorealism's international reputation see Hallam and Marshment (2000: 41).
8. An early report based on my research into the reception of *Amélie* in Britain has been published (Stigsdotter 2007) but these preliminary findings concentrate largely on critical reactions, whereas my thesis (Stigsdotter 2008) provides a more detailed and nuanced analysis of empirical audience data.

Bibliography

Black, J. 2002. *The Reality Effect: Film Culture and the Graphic Imperative*. New York: Routledge.
Brooks, P. 1976. *The Melodramatic Imagination: Balzac, Henry James, Melodrama, and the Mode of Excess*. New Haven: Yale University Press.
Bruno, G. 2002. *Atlas of Emotion: Journeys in Art, Architecture, and Film*. New York: Verso.
Burdeau, E. 1998. 'L'Etincelle et la cendre', *Cahiers du cinéma* 527: 71, 73.
Dyer, R. 1997. *White*. London: Routledge.
Elsaesser, T. 2005. *European Cinema: Face to Face with Hollywood*. Amsterdam: Amsterdam University Press.

Gentleman, A. 2006. 'Slum Tours: A Day Trip Too Far?' *The Observer*, 7 May, Travel Section. Retrieved 15 August 2008 from http://www.guardian.co.uk/travel/2006/may/07/delhi.india.ethicalliving

Grodal, T. 2002. 'The Experience of Realism in Audiovisual Representation', in A. Jerslev (ed.), *Realism and 'Reality' in Film and Media*. Copenhagen: Museum Tusculanum Press, pp. 67–91.

Hallam, J. and M. Marshment. 2000. *Realism and Popular Cinema*. Manchester: Manchester University Press.

Higbee, W. 2005. 'Towards a Multiplicity of Voices: French Cinema's Age of the Postmodern: Part II – 1992–2004', in S. Hayward (ed.), *French National Cinema*, 2nd Edition. London: Routledge, pp. 293–327.

Johnston, T. 1998. 'Party Girls', *The Scotsman*, 29 August: 6. Retrieved 20 December 2005 from Lexis-Nexis database.

Marie, M. (ed.) 1998. *Le Jeune cinéma français*. Paris: Nathan.

Mazdon, L. and C. Wheatley. 2008. 'Intimate Connections', *Sight and Sound* 18(5): 38–40.

O'Shaughnessy, M. 2007. *The New Face of Political Cinema: Commitment in French Film Since 1995*. New York: Berghahn Books.

Powrie, P. 1999. 'Heritage, History and "New Realism": French Cinema in the 1990s', in P. Powrie (ed.), *French Cinema in the 1990s: Continuity and Difference*. Oxford: Oxford University Press, pp. 1–21.

Prédal, R. 2002. *Le Jeune cinéma français*. Paris: Nathan.

Romney, J. 1999. 'J'aime l'amour', *The Guardian*, 22 January: 19. Retrieved 20 December 2005 from Lexis-Nexis database.

Smith, G. 1998. 'La Vie rêvée des anges', *Sight and Sound* 8(11): 64.

Stigsdotter, I. 2007. '"Very funny if you can keep up with the subtitles": The British Reception of *Le Fabuleux destin d'Amélie Poulain*', in I. Vanderschelden and D. Waldron (eds), *France at the Flicks: Trends in Contemporary French Popular Cinema*. Basingstoke: Cambridge Scholars, pp. 198–211.

———. 2008. 'British Audiences and Approaches to European Cinema: Four Case Studies of Responses to French and Swedish Film in the UK Today'. Unpublished Ph.D. thesis, University of Southampton.

Trémois, C-M. 1997. *Les Enfants de la liberté: Le Jeune cinéma français des années 90*. Paris: Éditions du Seuil.

Vanderschelden, I. 2007. *Amélie*. London: I.B. Tauris.

Filmography

Fabuleux destin d'Amélie Poulain, Le / Amélie. 2001, Jean-Pierre Jeunet, France/Germany.
J'ai pas sommeil / I Can't Sleep. 1994, Claire Denis, France.
Marius et Jeannette / Marius and Jeannette. 1997, Robert Guédiguian, France.
Vie de Jésus, La / Life of Jesus. 1997, Bruno Dumont, France.
Vie rêvée des anges, La / The Dreamlife of Angels. 1998, Erick Zonca, France.
Y aura-t-il de la neige à Noël? / Will it Snow for Christmas? 1996, Sandrine Veysset, France.
Western. 1997, Manuel Poirier, France.

PART III

Personnel and Performance

CHAPTER 12

'The Meaning of That French Word *Chic*': Annabella's Franco-British Stardom

Jonathan Driskell

Despite being among the most popular French female film stars of the early 1930s, Annabella has become one of cinema's forgotten figures; indeed aside from work by Alastair Phillips (2006), she has largely been ignored by both popular and academic histories of film. This neglect is reflected in the inscription on a plaque that stands outside the Hôtel du Nord on the banks of the Canal Saint-Martin in Paris. Outlining the building's history, it mentions the novel that was set there, *L'Hôtel du Nord* by Eugène Dabit, as well as Marcel Carné's filmic adaptation of this work: 'Released in 1938, it is today better known than the book, due to the work of the director, the dialogue by Henri Jeanson, the sets by Trauner, and the performances of the actors, Louis Jouvet and Arletty.' However, it fails to mention Annabella, the *real* star of *Hôtel du Nord* (1938) – she received highest billing in the credits and on posters, and was given the glamorous marketing treatment characteristic of the period's Hollywood stardom. While it was a 'big break' for Arletty, who is nowadays the film's most famous performer, it was the culmination of Annabella's prewar work, a period in which she became one of French cinema's most popular stars and appeared in some of its most canonical films: *Napoléon vu par Abel Gance / Abel Gance's Napoleon* (Abel Gance, 1927), *Le Million / The Million* (René Clair, 1931), *Quatorze juillet / Bastille Day* (René Clair, 1932), *La Bandera / Escape From Yesterday* (Julien Duvivier, 1935) and, of course, *Hôtel du Nord*. But her status is also evident from the fact that she embarked upon an international career towards the end of the 1930s, which ended with her Hollywood work from 1938 onwards, with her making such films as *The Baroness and the Butler* (Walter Lang, 1938) and *Suez* (Allan Dwan, 1938).

However, before her move to Hollywood Annabella also appeared in three British films, all produced by New World Pictures, a subsidiary of Twentieth Century Fox:

Wings of the Morning (Harold D. Schuster, 1937), which was Britain's first Technicolor film, *Under the Red Robe* (Victor Sjöstrom, 1937) and *Dinner at the Ritz* (Harold D. Schuster, 1937). There were other examples of French film stars in British Cinema, such as Pierre Fresnay (Alfred Hitchcock's 1934 *The Man Who Knew Too Much*), Renée Saint-Cyr (*Strange Boarders*, Herbert Mason, 1938), and Maurice Chevalier (*The Beloved Vagabond*, Curtis Bernhardt, 1936 and *Break the News*, René Clair, 1938), but Annabella's centrality to her films – in each case she was promoted as the leading star – and the significance with which she was discussed in the film press may have made her the most important instance of French stardom in 1930s British cinema.

This chapter is therefore concerned with the significance of the meeting between one of France's most popular female stars and three high-profile British films. In order to examine this meeting and its importance for understanding Franco-British cinematic relations, I shall focus on the transformations in Annabella's persona from her French to her British film work, and consider what such transformations reveal about British notions of French femininity. In order to explore these questions I would first of all like to outline in more detail the nature of her phenomenally successful French stardom of the early 1930s, before moving on to a consideration of her persona in her British film career, which commenced in 1937.

The Glamorous Midinette

Annabella's importance to the French cinema of the 1930s stemmed in large part from her being a new type of star. The majority of performers at this time began their careers in the theatre and progressed to cinema, when the coming of sound meant that films needed performers talented in the use of their voice. Key female instances of this type include the aforementioned Arletty, as well as Orane Demazis, Gaby Morlay and Jacqueline Delubac, all of whom appeared in the decade's 'filmed theatre' – film versions of boulevard plays. In contrast to this were a number of stars who entered the cinema directly, bypassing the stage. Today, the most famous examples of this latter group are Danielle Darrieux, Michèle Morgan, Simone Simon and of course, the pioneering example of this type of stardom, Annabella herself.

While the nature of her entry into the cinema may seem like a minor issue, it had a profound affect on Annabella's star status and the hugely popular persona that she developed. As would be expected, one of the main ways in which Annabella differed from the stars who had begun their careers in theatre was through the nature of her performance style. In contrast to the 'theatrical' performances exhibited by highly 'gestural' and verbose performers like Arletty, whose strong Parisian accent 'crackles, granulates, grates, and cuts' (Simon cited in Turk 1989: 143), Annabella's acting was more naturalistic, nuanced and low key, her accent more 'neutral' – thus designed to suit 'cinematic' approaches to filmmaking, such as that of René Clair, with whom Annabella made several films. Such acting also placed greater emphasis on her stunning, photogenic appearance: she was youthful, and possessed well proportioned features, almond-shaped eyes, a straight nose, a small mouth and well styled blond hair. It was no coincidence that Annabella was so camera-friendly; as a star who had entered cinema directly, she had been cast precisely on the basis of her physical features. Indeed, because she was discovered by Abel Gance, we can understand more fully the importance of her appearance – he was a member of the French Impressionist film movement, whose theory of *photogénie* centred on the essential beauty and, as Robert B. Ray (2001) has argued, *glamour* of the moving image.

Because of these qualities, Annabella, like the other stars who entered the cinema directly, represented a French version of Hollywood stardom: whereas the theatrical stars' accents, overtly expressive performance styles and appearances in film versions of boulevard plays gave them strong regional identities, Annabella, with her youthful beauty and glamour, seemed timeless and universal – qualities associated with Hollywood stardom. The emergence of such 'cinematic' stars in the French context can partly be explained by the aesthetic needs of the directors who frequently used them, such as René Clair, Julien Duvivier, Marcel Carné and Jean Renoir, all of whom opposed the decade's filmed theatre. This stardom was also created in order to help the French film industry compete with domestic stage entertainment, such as boulevard theatre and cabaret, and with Hollywood cinema. While providing audiences with the 'aura' and 'elevation' of Hollywood stardom, these stars, as *French* women, also offered the possibility of a more nuanced form of identification for their native fans. Moreover, Annabella's glamour meant that she was, like many Hollywood stars, an example of 'the modern woman', a new and emancipated form of femininity that became globally popular in the interwar period.

At the same time, however, her modernity conflicted with another, more central aspect of her persona during the early 1930s, namely her embodiment of the *midinette*. This form of femininity, which had its roots in the period before the First World War, initially referred to women who worked until midday (hence the prefix *midi*). These working-class women performed artisanal, nonindustrial jobs, making them belong very much to a premodern world. In culture, *midinettes* were celebrated nostalgically as a romantic and idealized populist type, elements that are captured in Tino Rossi's song, '*Midinette* de Paris': '*Midinette* of Paris, / when you sing everyone smiles. / In your eyes full of sky / it's eternal April. / Beautiful rose of springtime, / Love is on the look-out for twenty-year-olds. / The whole world repeats / this lovely refrain, / *Midinette* of Paris' [my translation]. The *midinette* continued to be popular into the 1930s, and during this decade there was even a women's magazine called *Midinette*, which celebrated this version of femininity, its pages featuring pictures of delicate and pretty things that *midinettes* were supposed to like (and *be like*), such as butterflies and flowers. It also placed a huge emphasis on romantic love, with poems and stories all centring on this topic. Moreover, its letters page highlights the fact that the *midinette* was a type that many women could identify with – readers were addressed, 'Dear *Midinettes*'.

Annabella was a clear embodiment of this type. Her delicacy was represented through her youthfulness, her petite frame and her self-effacing, nuanced acting style (particularly when she was placed alongside theatrically trained performers). This is especially evident in a recurring pose, suggesting shyness, which she strikes in many of her films: she plays nervously with her hands in front of her, her head tilted slightly to one side, with a downcast, submissive gaze. Her characters would also tend to be passive in their relationships with men. In *Le Million*, when she catches her boyfriend kissing another woman she tears up a picture of him. But this limited display of empowerment is short lived; minutes later she tapes it back together again. Such humility is also conveyed by the working-class status of the characters she embodied. In *Le Quatorze juillet* she is a flower seller, and then a waitress, and she lives in an old-fashioned *quartier* of Paris. The film's sets, designed by Lazare Meerson, romanticize Paris's rickety rooftops, winding staircases, courtyards and cobbled streets. Likewise, Annabella is also romanticized to a significant degree. In part this is because she portrays sweet, innocent and wistful young women; it is also because of her glamour, which idealizes the humble *midinettes* that she plays. Although she lives in rundown *quartiers*, her appearance is always impeccable: her clothes are neat, her complexion is clear, her hair is flawless.

Annabella's success in French cinema came from this combination of her glamour and her personification of the humble, old-fashioned *midinette*. The importance of this can be explained through reference to general notions of film stardom discussed by Richard Dyer in *Stars*. Dyer highlights the fact that stardom is based upon a simultaneous expression of ordinariness and extraordinariness (1998: 22). On the one hand, stars are *different to us* – they are extraordinary individuals, distant from everyday life, often due to their beauty, glamour and/or charisma. At the same time, stars are appealing because they are also *like us* – they are in many ways presented as ordinary individuals with whom we can identify. In France Annabella's success was dependent upon her successful embodiment of this tension. Her glamour and beauty made her extraordinary; her status as a humble *midinette* made her a figure for identification. Moreover, as a star who had had been 'discovered' and had become famous without theatrical training, her identity as an ordinary girl was stressed further. In an autobiographical feature that appeared in *Pour Vous* she stated: 'This is the life of a little girl from La Varenne, who has become happy and who has had the chance to realize her life's dream' (Annabella 1933: 11). As we shall see, the manifestation of this dichotomy between ordinariness and extraordinariness was different in her British film work, which reveals assumptions relating to British notions of French femininity. The following section, after providing a brief overview of Annabella's three British films, will consider two aspects of her persona that place emphasis on her extraordinariness and difference: her exoticism and her embodiment of French *chic*. I will then consider the ways in which she is simultaneously presented as more attainable, as a figure of identification.

Exotic and Chic

In her first British film, *Wings of the Morning*, Annabella took two roles: in the prologue, set in 1889, she plays a 'gypsy' princess called Marie who marries an Irish nobleman, Lord Clontarf (Leslie Banks); then, in the present, she plays Marie's great-granddaughter, Maria, a Spanish duchess who travels to Ireland to escape the civil war in Spain. Taking place in the United Kingdom, Spain, and, for the majority of the film, Ireland, *Wings of the Morning* includes many stunning Technicolor shots of the countryside and features cameos from the celebrated Irish tenor, John McCormack, and leading jockey, Steve Donoghue. Annabella's next film, *Under the Red Robe*, was a love story involving Gil de Berault (Conrad Veidt) and Lady Marguerite of Foix (Annabella), set in seventeenth century France against the backdrop of Cardinal Richelieu's (Raymond Massey) war on the Huguenots. The film is also notable for being the final directorial effort of the Swedish film director

Figure 12.1: Henry Fonda and Annabella in *Wings of the Morning* (1937). Image courtesy of the BFI stills department.

Victor Sjöstrom, who would later star in Ingmar Berman's *Smultronstället / Wild Strawberries* (1957). In Annabella's final British film, *Dinner at the Ritz*, she plays a modern-day Parisian – the daughter of a murdered banker. This 'whodunnit', which takes place in Paris, Monte Carlo and the United Kingdom, centres upon her efforts, assisted by Paul de Brack (David Niven), to find her father's murderers.

Within this body of work, Annabella's U.K. persona is, to a large extent, based upon her distance and difference from the British. At one extreme she is an exotic figure, which places her in a broader tradition at this time, discussed by Sue Harper (2000: 138), who sees 'exotics' as one of the main 'clusters' of female type present in 1930s British cinema. In addition to Annabella, she refers to Renée Saint-Cyr, Yvonne Arnaud, Anna May Wong, Marlene Dietrich and Merle Oberon, as key instances of this type. Such exoticism, embodied by Annabella, is stressed in press notes for *Wings of the Morning*, which refer to her as 'an exciting new star, as alluringly *different* as her unusual name! [my emphasis]' (Twentieth Century Fox 1937). Her one-word name was indeed commented upon by numerous writers and taken as an index of her essential cultural difference (her real name, Suzanne Charpentier, is rarely mentioned). Of course, her accent was also an important aspect of her exoticism, particularly as its 'foreignness' was used in her British films to signify a range of nationalities: in *Wings of the Morning* she is a 'gypsy' and a Spanish woman; in the other two films she is French. In *Wings of the Morning* her exoticism is also facilitated by the film's use of Technicolor, a feature that brings out the brightness of her many costumes and which highlights the different make-up treatments that she receives – her skin and hair are darkened when she plays the 'gypsy', Marie, at the beginning of the film, but they are lighter as the Spanish woman, Maria. One of the film's posters makes clear a connection between the brightness of the Technicolor and the exoticism of its star, by stating: 'A picture as colourful and exciting as its new and unusual star!' This association with the exotic was continued in *Dinner at the Ritz*, in which her character, Ranie, disguises herself first as a Spanish woman, and later as an Indian woman. Importantly, then, Annabella's Frenchness facilitates her portrayal of exotic characters.

In addition to this general exoticism (in which her Frenchness can easily be used to help her portray a range of nationalities), Annabella's status as, more specifically, a Frenchwoman is, as would be expected, central to her identity in British film culture at this time. Her nationality is constantly returned to in the film press, and, as mentioned, in two of her films she plays French characters. In these, there are many well known French motifs and icons: in *Dinner at the Ritz*, following a brief establishing image of the Eiffel Tower, we see her being driven through the Place de la Concorde, and later in the film, at a fancy dress party, she appears to be dressed as Marie Antoinette. Her Frenchness was presented as a deep-rooted and fundamental part of her identity. This is implicitly conveyed by one magazine article, which refers to the (true) fact that she was born on the fourteenth of July, Bastille Day, which suggests a timeless connection with her nation's history. The same article stresses, more explicitly, that her Frenchness gives her particular *innate* qualities: 'She is intelligent, travelled, a "woman of the world" and possesses, in addition, the gift of *chic*, that divine birthright of French women' (Miller 1937: 93).

Indeed, the defining feature of Annabella's Frenchness in the British context is her *chic*, a dominant notion of French femininity, which presents French women as sophisticated, elegant and fashionable. It was certainly a prominent French female type in Britain in the 1930s. It is evident, for example, in adverts for Bourjois cosmetic products, which appeared in a number of British magazines in 1937. In a version of the advert printed in the April issue of *The Modern Woman* there is an image of a woman who is clearly a *chic Parisienne* – evident from her long black dress, her neatly coiffured hair, and her pose, which combines control with nonchalance: her hips are casually and elegantly to one side, her arms are lifted to shoulder height as she leans backwards, her right hand faces downwards, her left is held up; her head is tilted towards a man who is stood behind her, but her eyes are closed, her face looking away from him. It is unclear whether she is rejecting or inviting the man's advances, whether her left hand is held up as if to say 'stop', or is purposefully placed beyond his head, thus allowing him to come closer. Either way, she appears in control of the situation, which conflates her sophistication with a show of empowerment – another key facet of the *Parisienne*. Interestingly, the advert also states that '"Evening in Paris" powder gives your skin an exquisitely flattering "soft focus" finish', a claim that associates French glamour with the cinematic, and, by extension, with film stardom.

Consequently, Annabella, as a top French female star, was ideally suited to the embodiment of such notions: as already highlighted, her *chic* is referred to as a 'birthright'; another article, appearing in *Film Pictorial* in 1937, entitled 'Annabella Personifies the Meaning of That French Word Chic', stressed this point further. With images of her in a range of outfits, these articles, which are almost entirely devoted to her beauty and clothing, discuss the fact that Annabella was recently voted 'the world's best dressed woman' by a number of top Parisian couturiers. Inevitably, this *chic* was brought to the fore in her film roles. To some extent this comes about through her 'star treatment': she appears in many close-ups that celebrate and accentuate her beauty, with soft, glamorous lighting. Here her cinematic treatment in British works is comparable to that which she receives in her French films. Indeed, because she was a star who was defined by her glamour, appearing in a Hollywood-funded Technicolor star vehicle was a logical progression. Each of her three British films also accentuates her *chic* through her clothing, designed by René Hubert, who also designed the costumes for some of her most famous French films, such as *Quatorze juillet*.

Like the *Parisienne* in the Bourjois advert, Annabella's U.K. persona involves a strong sense of empowerment and independence. This contrasts with her French identity, which as we have seen was based largely upon a delicate and passive form of femininity. Indeed, the posture of the confident woman in the Bourjois advert is in stark contrast to Annabella's recurring pose as a *midinette*, which stresses her shyness and self-effacement. As already mentioned, the fan magazines commented upon her being a 'woman of the world' (as she was an international star, this is unsurprising), a quality that takes her beyond the confines of the working-class Parisian *quartier*. Moreover, *Film Pictorial* reported on Annabella's confident, rebellious and outgoing behaviour, which again conflicted with the humility of the *midinette*.

She is a thorough person, definite in her ideas, and strong-willed beneath her captivating manner.

While she was making *Wings of the Morning*, she took a house at Bray, not very far from Denham, entertained many English guests, and occasionally sent the studio transport department into hysterics because, if her own car wasn't handy, she drove off in the first one she saw (The Nomad 1937: 3).

This dimension of her U.K. persona was also expressed in her films. In *Wings of the Morning* there is a lengthy sequence in which she is dressed as a boy, initially as a disguise to help her character escape from the Spanish Civil War. However, once in Ireland this outfit also tricks other characters, such as Kerry Gilfallen (Henry Fonda), into thinking that she is male. She clearly enjoys the experience and the increased agency the clothing affords her, entering into heated arguments with Kerry, negotiating the exchange of her great-grandmother's horse (the 'Wings of the Morning' of the title) for six of his, and engaging in other 'male' activities, such as smoking a cigar (though she does this badly). In *Under the Red Robe*, in the absence of her brother, Annabella's character takes charge of the Foix household, helping to coordinate its operations in its war against Cardinal Richelieu. And, in *Dinner at the Ritz*, her character is the main agent of the narrative, taking it upon herself to pursue those who murdered her father – De Brack (Niven) struggles to keep up with her as

Figure 12.2: David Niven and Annabella in a publicity still for *Dinner at the Ritz* (1937). Image courtesy of the BFI stills department.

she moves from place to place. As a foreign woman, then, Annabella (in various guises) is allowed more agency than in her French films, which adds to her 'extraordinariness' – she has power that many ordinary British women would not have had available to them.

Because these elements – exoticism and *chic* – form Annabella's extraordinariness, her 'escapist' qualities, we can see that through her star persona Frenchness becomes a highly marketable commodity. But while these elements make her attractive and exciting, they present her as far removed from the British audiences to which she was being sold. To counter such distance, stars, as discussed, should also be presented as ordinary. Yet while the *midinette* made her easy to identify with in France, could British women fantasize about being *like* Annabella, a star whose persona stressed her Frenchness and her difference?

Identification

While Annabella's difference as a French woman was central to her U.K. persona, she was simultaneously shown, in her films and the publicity surrounding them, to be a potential figure of identification. Simply by living and working in Britain, and by appearing in British films, she was shown to some extent to be close to the audience and to have a degree of investment in the nation's film industry – in a way that a star whose films were imported, but who remained in another country, would not.

The main features of Annabella's 'cinematic' stardom also facilitated this identification. As stated, in her French films she would appear in many close-ups, would perform with a naturalistic style of acting, and would often be shown alone in private (by contrast, theatrical stars, such as Arletty, commonly portrayed women who performed role-play in public contexts). These elements of Annabella's stardom carried over into her British work, which facilitated an intimate engagement between star and audience. This is evident in a sequence from *Wings of the Morning*, occurring shortly after it is revealed to Kerry that Maria is a woman. In a montage we are shown their courtship; they row a boat together and walk in the Irish countryside. To some extent the sequence emphasizes the extraordinary and distant qualities of Annabella's British stardom – while she portrays a Spanish woman at this point in the film, the scene is clearly evoking her intertextual *chic* persona. With a number of wide shots, the sequence functions as a fashion show. Indeed, one article encouraged this type of engagement with the film:

> Annabella's wardrobe is worthy of your special attention next week when you see her in *Wings Of The Morning*. You can learn so much from watching a girl who knows good clothes – and, more important – how to wear them. If you would really like to earn the term *chic* for yourself, this is your opportunity. You will be able to study the different types of clothes – and how they should be worn – easily, from the film (Peta 1937: 26).

At the same time, the sequence contains elements that foster a degree of closeness with the audience. For one thing, while the invocation of French *chic* may imply notions such as sophistication and refinement, the scene also stresses naturalness. In part this is conveyed by the natural settings. Whereas the *chic Parisienne* would traditionally be shown in public, walking on Paris's *grands boulevards*, here she is shown in the Irish countryside, complete with waterfalls, woodland and wild horses. Annabella's naturalistic performance style also reduces the extent to which her refinement may appear artificial, particularly when she laughs in a spontaneous-looking way as she rows the boat with Kerry. Here, then, Annabella's natural quality presents her as more than just a glamorous *Parisienne* (the type embodied by the woman in the Bourjois advertisement); there is the implication that the scene's intimacy and naturalness reveals to us a deeper, more private aspect of Annabella's personality.

Another way in which Annabella was made more 'attainable' was through the injection of elements of passivity into her persona, which appeared simultaneously and functioned in tension with the empowerment and independence already discussed. While her emancipation – a product of her Frenchness as transported to Britain – made her extraordinary, the more passive aspects of her persona made her more readily identifiable as an ordinary woman. To some extent Annabella was very well equipped to portray such femininity – as discussed, her identity as a *midinette* relied on these very notions. Some aspects of this identity were used in the British context. For instance, we can see her humility in images of her in *The Modern Woman* (Miller 1937: 66–7). In contrast to the confident and seductive *Parisienne* in the Bourjois cosmetics advertisement, Annabella combines her sophistication (in each she is modelling a fashionable outfit) with a degree of vulnerability: in one she stands, smiling, with her arms folded across her chest (a pose that suggests insecurity); in another she is stood side-on, looking coyly over her shoulder, making her large innocent eyes the main focus of the image.

More importantly still, there are a number of explicit attempts in promotional materials to present her as someone with whom British women could identify. This involves efforts to make her French *chic* more accessible, with one article including the following exchange: 'I asked if she considered it impossible for an Englishwoman to achieve a French air of *chic*. "But, no," she replied quickly. "In many ways your Englishwomen are really *très chic*! They can compete very well with our Frenchwomen!"' (Miller 1937: 93). She also gives down-to-earth, pragmatic fashion advice, designed to be useful to ordinary women:

> When a woman plans her new season's outfit it is silly to think first of all: 'What is the mode?' Better, far better, to ask herself what she requires for her own daily life, whether at work or in society – and then to consider carefully whether the new fashion can be made to adjust itself to these things (Miller 1937: 93).

Attempts to encourage British women to see themselves in terms of French *chic* are supported by the article's reference to a feature published in the previous edition of

The Modern Woman, entitled 'Straight From Paris' (Troy 1937: 61), which offered readers advice on how they too could attain the Parisian 'look', like the big French star of the moment, Annabella.

Conclusion

Annabella's spell in British cinema was a successful period in her career. She was given a contract in Hollywood on the strength of these films, and received high praise in numerous reviews and fan-magazine articles. A number of pieces discussed with regret her move to Hollywood: 'We did, to a certain extent, seize our opportunity so far as the delightful Annabella is concerned, it is true, but even then we allowed Hollywood to snatch her away from us' (M. Phillips 1937: 22). In France, too, her appearances in British films were celebrated as a triumph. In *Cinémonde* a weekly feature entitled '300 jours au studio: Annabella', which ran from 25 March to 22 April 1937, reported keenly on her activities in Britain. This would be one of the last high points in her career; she was not a success in Hollywood and her popularity soon began to decline. But beyond what this period meant for her career, her British work highlights the role stardom can play in constructing Franco-British cinematic relations.

Despite the geographical closeness of France and Britain, historically the relationship between the two nations has fluctuated between friendship and rivalry, cooperation and hostility, closeness and distance. This has been explored in Robert and Isabelle Tombs's book on the relationship between the two nations: *That Sweet Enemy: Britain and France: The History of a Love–Hate Relationship* (2006). In this work they discuss the interwar period's various shifts – from wartime solidarity, to postwar disagreements about how to deal with the defeated Germany, to a renewed friendship in the late 1930s in anticipation of the next war. They also highlight that these political changes also impacted upon relations in the cultural sphere, with various links being forged between the two nations in the late 1930s, the time when Annabella was working in Britain: 'In the late 1930s, when cordiality became frighteningly urgent, efforts were made in both countries to bring public feeling into line with strategic necessity. Artistic events were organized' (Tombs and Tombs 2006: 526). To some extent, in her British film work Annabella's stardom stresses the distance that existed between the two nations. In part this is an intentional aspect of her persona; because her Frenchness is central to her stardom in the British context, her extraordinariness becomes about asserting and celebrating her cultural difference. Distance is also highlighted inadvertently – the reduction of her *midinette* persona to the stereotype of the *chic Parisienne* exposes a clear cultural gap between the two nations. But at the same time, her U.K. persona not only presents her as different, but also as a figure of potential identification. And as a star who attained prominence on both sides of the Channel and was discussed favourably by each nation's film press, she was something that each country could agree on. Consequently, her British stardom speaks not only of distance, but also, in this moment of political and cultural cooperation, of the closeness between the two nations and their cinemas.

Bibliography

Annabella. 1933. 'Des souvenirs par Annabella (7)', *Pour Vous* 236(25 May): 11.

Anon. 1937. '300 jours au studio: Annabella', *Cinémonde*, weekly from 25 March to 22 April.

Dyer, R. 1998. *Stars*, new edn. London: British Film Institute.

Harper, S. 2000. 'From Wholesome Girls to Difficult Dowagers: Actresses in 1930s British Cinema', in J. Ashby and A. Higson (eds), *British Cinema, Past and Present*. London/New York: Routledge, pp. 137–51.

Miller, M.M. 1937. 'Annabella: "World's Best Dressed Woman"', *The Modern Woman* 17(150, November): 66–67, 93.

The Nomad. 1937. 'Unknown Girl Makes Hit In First British Colour Film', *Film Pictorial* 10(258, 30 January): 3–4.

Peta. 1937. 'Annabella Personifies the Meaning of that French Word Chic', *Film Pictorial* 11(286, 14 August): 26–27.

Phillips, A. 2006. 'Changing Bodies, Changing Voices: French Success and Failure in 1930s Hollywood', in A. Phillips and G. Vincendeau (eds), *Journeys of Desire: European Actors in Hollywood, A Critical Companion*. London: British Film Institute, pp. 187–200.

Phillips, M. 1937. 'Continental Sex Appeal Comes Back', *Picturegoer* 7(326, 21 August): 22.

Ray, R.B. 2001. *How a Film Theory Got Lost and Other Mysteries in Cultural Studies*. Bloomington: Indiana University Press.

Tombs, R. and I. Tombs. 2006. *That Sweet Enemy: Britain and France: The History of a Love-Hate Relationship*. London: William Heinemann.

Troy, E. 1937. 'Straight From Paris', *The Modern Woman* 17(149, October): 61.

Turk, E.B. 1989. *Child of Paradise: Marcel Carné and the Golden Age of French Cinema*. Cambridge, MA & London: Harvard University Press.

Twentieth Century Fox. 1937. Press notes to *Wings of the Morning*. Available at the British Film Institute library.

Filmography

Bandera, La / Escape From Yesterday. 1935, Julien Duvivier, France.

Baroness and the Butler, The. 1938, Walter Lang, U.S.A.

Beloved Vagabond, The. 1936, Curtis Bernhardt, U.K.

Break the News. 1938, René Clair, U.K.

Dinner at the Ritz. 1937, Harold D. Schuster, U.K.

Hôtel du Nord. 1938, Marcel Carné, France.

Man Who Knew Too Much, The. 1934, Alfred Hitchcock, U.K.

Million, Le / The Million. 1931, René Clair, France.

Napoléon vu par Abel Gance / Abel Gance's Napoleon. 1927, Abel Gance, France.

Quatorze juillet, Le / Bastille Day. 1932, René Clair, France.

Smultronstället / Wild Strawberries. 1957, Ingmar Bergman, Sweden.

Strange Boarders. 1938, Herbert Mason, U.K.

Suez. 1938, Allan Dwan, U.S.A.

Under the Red Robe. 1937, Victor Sjöström, U.K.

Wings of the Morning. 1937, Harold D. Schuster, U.K.

CHAPTER 13

'Those Frenchies Seek Him Everywhere': David Niven in Franco-British Cinematic Relations

Cristina Johnston

In the decades following the end of the Second World War, a complex framework of Franco-British cinematic and cultural exchanges was shaped by the tensions implicit in the interface between 'new representations of the nation' and those 'already in circulation' (Higson 1995: 6). Both France and the United Kingdom were coming to terms with the legacy of the war and its impact on national and gender identities, whilst simultaneously adapting to the dismantling of their respective colonial empires. Against this backdrop, Franco-British cinematic relations offered an outlet for 'a paradoxical desire for both stability and change' (Plain 2006: 140), a means of negotiating a path between prewar attitudes and values and those of a society in evolution. Coupled with a parallel expression of nostalgia and anxiety, this 'paradoxical desire' is perhaps nowhere more evident than in the postwar filmography of British-born actor David Niven.

This chapter will focus on Niven's onscreen persona in a number of works released between 1950 and the mid-1960s. However, it is important to note from the outset that the anchoring of his persona on both sides of the Channel was furthered, throughout his career, as much by his filmography as through aspects of his offscreen existence. Although born and raised in Britain, Niven described his mother as French (Niven 1994 [1971]: 13);[1] he wrote and spoke frequently of time spent in the resorts and villas of the French Riviera, whether filming there or for pleasure, and spent a substantial portion of his adult life in Francophone Switzerland where he died in 1983. On screen, we can find a constant Francophone spine to his filmography, from his first starring role as Paul de Brack in *Dinner at the Ritz* (Schuster, 1937) via a rather bizarre transposition of the British gent to the Louisiana bayou in *The Toast of New Orleans* (Taurog, 1950) to his appearance in the British horror film *Eye of the*

Devil (Thompson, 1966) as French aristocrat Philippe de Montfaucon. He even crops up as Col. Carol Matthews in Gérard Oury's 1969 comedy *Le Cerveau*, alongside Jean-Paul Belmondo and Bourvil. Niven's roles are significant in terms of what they reveal about the bilateral, cross-Channel relationship in the postwar decades: none of the films analysed here is 'straightforwardly' either a 'French' or 'British' production,[2] and yet, through the combination of his iconic Britishness and its transposition to French cultural landscapes, its anchoring in relation to French cultural markers, Niven negotiates a dialogue between past and modernity.

The roles discussed here are also significant, because they remind us, through the spectre of Hollywood, of the intimate triangulation of postwar relations between the U.K., France and the U.S. The primary focus here will be on the Franco-British dimension of this relationship. However, through analysis of a quintessentially British actor's roles in both U.K. and Hollywood productions, the emergence of Americanization as 'a source of both pleasure and anxiety' (Handyside 2002: 175) on both sides of the Channel will also be foregrounded. The U.K.–France–U.S. triangulation serves not merely as a reminder of the cinematic economy of the immediate postwar years, but also to bring to our attention the somewhat perplexing deployment, on the part of Hollywood studios and directors, of Niven's 'debonair gentleman' figure as an embodiment of the negotiation between past and modernity specifically through the prism of French culture.

We can find reasons behind this perplexing choice. The first lies in the status of the 1950s in French film history: as Phil Powrie has noted, 'a fallow period' thanks to what he terms 'the double whammy' of the loss of film personnel during the Occupation and 'a play-safe strategy with the literary cinema of the 1950s' (2006: 5). In other words, for much of the discussion here, Niven's onscreen presence exists against the backdrop not of the explosive New Wave years, but of the much tamer literary adaptations and *tradition de qualité* against which Truffaut and company would soon rail. However, this recourse to a British star embedded in onscreen French culture can also be understood specifically as a response to a 'crisis of masculinity in France that had been exacerbated by defeat and occupation' (Capdevila 2001: 444). On screen Niven frequently played military men,[3] and off screen much was made of his decision, at the outbreak of the Second World War, to join the British Army despite his growing film-star status. Both sides of the Channel were coming to terms with the legacy of the conflict, but their experiences of the war years had differed greatly, and I would argue that Niven's identifiable, recognizable Britishness serves different purposes depending on the context in which it is mobilized. On the one hand, and particularly in Hollywood coproductions, it can stand in for 'the continental' more generally, evidence of Hollywood's persistent trend – with some notable exceptions – for a simplification of the European, a reliance on Niven as provider of what we might term 'a familiar otherness'. However, on the other hand, when the Franco-British side of this triangulation is focused on, and we recall that the films discussed here are released, not only on U.S., but also on European screens, we can begin to see the ways in which Niven's persona negotiates a balance between stability and change. In a sense, Niven takes the pressure off post-

Occupation French masculinity, allowing it to begin its 'quest for masculine identity in a nation fragmented by defeat' (Capdevila 2001: 435).

The exchange between Niven's quintessential Britishness and onscreen representations of an array of aspects of France and French national identity can thus serve as a prism through which to read not only postwar transformations within France, but also public perceptions of these changes beyond the confines of the Hexagon, at both the European and the global level. After all, as Andrew Higson has argued, 'cinema ... helps to reaffirm the boundaries of the national community' (Higson 1995: 8), and yet for Kristin Ross, 'the maintenance of national boundaries is ... increasingly at odds with the potential of the mass media to cross national boundaries and create new, multinational, even global, imaginative territories and cultural spaces' (Ross 1996: 8). The dialogue between Higson's view of cinema's role in both sustaining and producing national identity, and Kristin Ross's seminal study of the evolution of French society over the decade from the mid-1950s, offers an understanding of the ways in which Niven can be read as an embodiment of the tensions arising from the clash between pre– and post–war:

The speed with which French society was transformed after the war from a rural, empire-oriented, Catholic country into a fully industrialised, decolonised, and urban one meant that the things modernization needed ... burst onto a society that still cherished pre-war outlooks with all of the force, excitement, disruption, and horror of the genuinely new (Ross, 1996: 4).

No other British actor of Niven's generation evolves astride the Channel in the same way, striking a delicate balance between stability and change, nostalgia and anxiety, through his depiction of, and indeed reliance upon, the 'hegemonic form of the debonair gentleman' (Spicer 2003: 7), as Sir Percy Blakeney in *The Elusive Pimpernel* (Powell and Pressburger, 1950) and Sir Charles Lytton in the *Pink Panther* series (Edwards, 1963–83), alongside Peter Sellers' bumbling Inspector Clouseau. Alongside analysis of these works, attention will also be paid in this chapter to two films which see Niven taking on a central role in adaptations of French literary texts, first as Raymond in *Bonjour Tristesse* (Preminger, 1958) and second as Phileas Fogg in *Around the World in 80 Days* (Anderson, 1956). These roles see Niven embodying 'the perfect gentleman, the male ideal of the British ruling classes' (Spicer 2003: 8), yet transposed to the French Riviera or to the *châteaux* of the Loire Valley. His roles in the two literary adaptations further illustrate the extent to which his star persona is embedded within a complex network of Franco-British cinematic exchanges. What this chapter seeks to explore are the Franco-British 'imaginative territories' mapped out through David Niven's roles in the 1950s and 1960s, and the tensions and paradoxes that emerge through Niven's embodiment of encounters between 'prewar outlooks' and 'the genuinely new'. Specifically, it will be the contention of this chapter that the cross-Channel displacement of Niven's Britishness allows for the development of a cinematic negotiation of Franco-British 'post-war male restlessness' (Francis 2007: 164) in the context of the trauma of decolonization. Ultimately, it will be argued that, as we follow Niven from his 1950 role as Sir Percy Blakeney into the 1960s, we chart a cinematic 'process of [national] becoming' (Higson 1995: 4) that recognizes the need to reconcile pre- and postwar outlooks, but that leaves us to conclude that a dogged resistance to the consequences of such reconciliation represents a threat to cohesion, whether social or cinematic, on both sides of the Channel.

Heading for Change

Taking *The Elusive Pimpernel* as a starting point, we have perhaps the clearest representation of the tensions and paradoxes of a period of revolutionary change, albeit one which is depicted on a 'schoolboyish' level (British Film Institute 1950). Niven plays Sir Percy Blakeney, the 'Pimpernel' of the title, based on the character created by Baroness Orczy, 'the stupid, indolent dandy in London, [who] is also leader of a league of young men whose purpose is to rescue the French aristocrats from the Terror' (BFI 1950). Here, then, we do not only see Niven as the lone survivor of a different era; we also see him actively engaged in salvaging the values of such times by rescuing aristocrats from the guillotine. Although the film could be read as a parable about the dangers of tyranny the world over, the opening sequences use the backdrop of France and the Terror that followed the 1789 Revolution as a paradigm for the risks represented by unchecked revolutionary change. As the screen fills with furls of red smoke, the date '1792' appears onscreen as though written in dripping red paint and the audience reads: 'All revolutions are started by idealists. Some of them end in –'. Instead of a word to complete the sentence, we see the blade of a guillotine slicing down, following by the looting of a *château* to a brief extract from the *Marseillaise* on the soundtrack. It is only Niven's Sir Percy who can bring any hope to those described in the opening sequences as 'innocent people' by offering them escape from France and the security of their lives and their titles in England. He seems to be saving them as much from the guillotine's blade as from the amputation of their titles.

Released in 1950, *The Elusive Pimpernel* and Niven's Sir Percy begin an engagement with the period that will be further developed through his roles in *Bonjour Tristesse* and *Around the World in 80 Days*. Sir Percy is well and truly a product of a bygone age, of pre-Revolutionary times, and of a fervent desire to see the values of that age preserved, and yet we also learn that his true happiness will only be achieved once he has been reconciled with his wife, with whom he declares himself to be deeply in love. This reconciliation does come – he had thought his wife guilty of having denounced a particular French family, but he discovers that she was not, in fact, responsible – and the film ends with the couple sailing back from France to England and happily ever after. It is through the delicate balance struck between these two strands that we can read Niven as a means of negotiating cultural and societal changes in the postwar era. On the one hand, Sir Percy is the embodiment of conservativism, tradition, and a staunch belief in the values of a national past. However, on the other hand, his own, individual fulfilment comes through a reconciliation with the wife he thought had betrayed his own values during the Revolution and the possibility, thanks to this reconciliation, of a return to domestic bliss. In other words, Sir Percy warns against the dangers of unfettered change while acknowledging the need, certainly in terms of gender relations, for a rethinking of the couple and the family in the light of actions carried out – or feared to have been carried out – in times of great strain. If we consider how Powell and Pressburger's 'schoolboyish' take on post-Revolutionary France can be read as a metaphor for postwar France, the implications of this would appear to be directed, firstly, towards what Ross terms the 'disruption, and horror of the genuinely new', but also towards 'the idealization of the couple' and an ultimate valediction of the home and the domestic sphere (1996: 107).

In order to develop the analysis of this negotiation of cultural and societal change, it is useful to examine two of Niven's roles from the late 1950s, *Bonjour Tristesse* and *Around the World in 80 Days*, the former based on Françoise Sagan's 1954 novel and the latter on Jules Verne's classic adventure story of 1873. At first glance, it may appear that neither the novels nor the characters played by Niven have anything in common. In *Bonjour Tristesse*, he plays Raymond, father to the central character, Cécile (Jean Seberg), a widower with a string of younger girlfriends and a taste for the high life, flitting between dinner parties, casinos and Riviera villas. In *Around the World in 80 Days*, Niven is Phileas Fogg, Verne's Victorian English gentleman who embarks on 'a hair-raising journey carried out as a wager ... [and] who succeeds in circling the globe within eighty days' (Cardinal 1994: ix). On the one hand, a middle-aged 1950s playboy and, on the other, a stuffy Victorian gent who is a stickler for punctuality, the former dashing around the Côte d'Azur in an open-top sports car, the latter travelling the world by means of 'liners, railways, carriages, yachts, trading vessels, sledges, elephants' (Verne 1994 [1873]: 161). However, if we see these films as an example of the construction of a Franco-British 'imaginative territory' within which conceptions of the tensions and paradoxes of postwar Frenchness emerge, connections and parallel readings become apparent.

Looking Backwards, Looking Forwards

Fiona Handyside has analysed the ways in which the star persona of Jean Seberg can be understood to be located 'on the cusp of the censorious 1950s and the liberal 1960s, unable fully to embrace either position' (2002: 168). I would argue that David Niven, appearing alongside Seberg in *Bonjour Tristesse* but also across many of his roles from these two decades, similarly finds himself 'on the cusp'. However, in his case, the balance being struck is not between two decades, but rather between two worlds, a world of 'pre-war outlooks' in collision with the world of 'the genuinely new' – a clash occurring on the Riviera coast but embodied with more than a nod towards what Andrew Spicer (2003: 8) has described as 'the perfect gentleman, the male ideal of the British ruling classes, ... the product of a nineteenth-century synthesis of aristocratic style and bourgeois values'. Niven's Raymond encapsulates

Figure 13.1: Jean Seberg and David Niven in *Bonjour tristesse* (1957).
Image courtesy of the BFI stills department.

the strands that make up Spicer's summary of this particular vision of the male ideal, namely, 'gentlemanliness combined with an idealized medieval chivalry, the delicacy and sensitivity of the cultivated Man of Feeling, the athletic, vigorous manliness of "muscular Christianity" and the Protestant success drive' (2003: 8). Niven's Raymond is the consummate dinner guest and host with impeccable manners and an engaging conversational style; he even goes so far as to buy flowers to decorate Anne Larsen's room for her arrival, arranging the bouquets himself. His vanity and focus on physical appearance are demonstrated, for instance, in an early sequence when we see him checking the size of his stomach in the mirror, commenting on how his abdominal muscles compare to those of his daughter, and then exercising in the sunshine. He and his daughter are wealthy and privileged, living a life of luxury in the perma-sunshine of the Côte d'Azur. Idealized chivalry, delicacy and sensitivity, athletic manliness, and success: Raymond has them all, albeit not necessarily always all at the same time. It is also worth noting that the Riviera as setting also harks back to this notion of aristocratic style and bourgeois values, acting, as it does, as a playground for generations of high flyers, including royalty, literary figures and stars of stage and screen.

While Seberg's star persona 'on the cusp' represents a performance of the 'tensions of Americanization in France as a source of both pleasure and anxiety' (Handyside 2002: 175), Niven's onscreen counterpart in *Bonjour Tristesse* goes further than to engage merely with a contemporary fear of Americanization. Raymond is embedded in future-oriented trends, particularly insofar as he is clearly constructed as a fan of fast living and of fast cars, with discourse around the latter, both onscreen and in literature, having been identified by Ross (1996: 27) as 'futuristic' insofar as it 'to a large extent *precedes* the car's becoming commonplace in French life'. However, his character is simultaneously an outlet for the anxiety this 'futuristic' desire for mobility – whether social or literal – gives rise to and, in order to foreground this anxiety, we see a character looking not forwards, but backwards, from the late 1950s as far back as the ideals of late nineteenth-century Britain. Indeed, Niven's offscreen persona adds to this 'double vision' as even the most cursory of readings of his autobiography *The Moon's a Balloon* makes clear, filled, as it is, with an odd mixture of references to prewar British values and traditions and to mid-twentieth century Hollywood glamour.

This use of 'looking backwards' as a means of exploring the tensions arising in response to an emergent 'futuristic' discourse of mobility and modernity is also emphasized in Niven's role as Phileas Fogg in the big-budget star vehicle *Around the World in 80 Days*. With 730,000 spectators in Paris and the seven major French provincial towns, *Around the World* was one of the '56 most successful films screened in France between 1950 and 1959' (Sims 2004: 165), as well as being a huge hit on international screens and winning five Oscars, including Best Picture. Released in France the year before *Bonjour Tristesse*, the film's engagement with the notions of modernity and mobility is twofold. Firstly, the narrative is explicitly centred on a quest for speed, and specifically an attempt to travel around the globe within the eighty days of the title. Naturally, as they take place in 1872, Fogg's attempts to win the bet cannot be helped by the convenience of car travel. However, Anderson's film opens with an extended travelling sequence following Passepartout around the streets of London riding a penny farthing, a type of bicycle invented by British engineer James Starley in 1871 (Bellis 2008), and thus the height of mobile modernity in the 1870s. From this opening, the narrative follows Fogg as he travels by all manner of modes of transport, through Europe, Asia and America, allowing for the ultimate embodiment of Wolfgang Schivelbusch's notion of 'panoramic perception' developed by Kristin Ross, namely 'the kind of perception that prevails when the viewer sees objects and landscapes through the apparatus that moves him or her through the world. Panoramic perception occurs when the viewer no longer belongs to the same space as the perceived object' (Ross 1996: 38).

Ross's use of the notion of 'panoramic perception' in relation to 1950s France is not limited to the impact of new horizons of travel. Rather, she argues that 'the intensification of [the] two burgeoning technologies' that are the car and cinema 'would produce a qualitative acceleration in panoramic perception; for both cars and movies create perception-in-movement' (1996: 39). It is here that we find a second manifestation of *Around the World*'s engagement with parallel notions of modernity and mobility, namely through the cinematic extravaganza of the film itself. Shot in Technicolor, the film boasted a vast array of high-profile cameos ranging from Noël Coward to Frank Sinatra via Marlene Dietrich, Charles Boyer and Buster Keaton, and a similarly impressive range of locations, some recreated in a studio, others 'the real thing'. The voiceover to the original cinematic release clearly sets the film up as what we might term a superlative piece of entertainment: 'the greatest show now on earth', 'Jules Verne's masterpiece', 'the world's most famous flamenco dancer', 'David Niven – hero of heroes', and so on. The late-1950s audience is transported to a world of exotic locations and high excitement, cinema as a way 'to go some place else', to quote Seberg's Cécile.

However, this deluge of all things modern, this idealization of technology as a means of moving forwards and beyond, is underpinned by something of a paradox. In the year of the nationalization of the Suez Canal and the ensuing crisis, the Hungarian Revolution and the arrival of Soviet tanks in the streets of Budapest, and of declarations of independence on the part of both Tunisia and Morocco, here we have David Niven, as in *Bonjour Tristesse*, playing the role of 'a thorough gentleman' (Verne 1994 [1873]: 3), who harks back to a vision of masculinity firmly anchored in imperial ideals. As the pace of decolonization was quickening, in respect of both the ex-British and the ex-French Empires, and alongside the superlatives outlined above, here we have a film whose trailer makes reference to 'the beautiful Indian princess' being rescued from 'the barbaric Indian Suttee rites' and to a 'battle with the savage Sioux'. It is difficult to reconcile such descriptions, or Fogg/Niven's resolute 'gentlemanliness', with a cinematic culture that is wholly interested in looking forwards to a postcolonial existence. Rather it seems, once again, as though Niven is offering a means of exploring the possibilities of future-oriented goals and technologies, while at the same time according value to foundations firmly laid in a prewar context. In relation to a Franco-British 'imaginative territory', the landscape Niven/Fogg is mapping out here is one in which the desire to move beyond is tempered by the pull of the 'glories' of Empire. And this tension is played out, simultaneously, on both sides of the Channel – thanks to the film's huge popular success both in France and the U.K., but also due, once more, to Niven finding his Victorian gentleman embedded in a desire for modernity and mobility that will not subside.

Sex, Tigers and the 'debonair gentleman'

Niven's '1950s Victorian' shows us a reticence towards past values and beliefs, while showing audiences a means of opening up towards the future in all its 'excitement, disruption, and horror'. His 1960s gentleman, on the other hand, begins to point towards the ways in which a dogged adherence to these past values and a refusal to ever embrace 'the genuinely new' can combine to represent a new threat. In other words, from Sir Percy's warnings in 1950 that heady revolution, unchecked, leads to bloodshed, through the anxieties between modernity and tradition negotiated in *Bonjour Tristesse* and *Around the World in 80 Days*, what we reach with Sir Charles Lytton in *The Pink Panther* is a realization that the disparate strands need to be reconciled in order to avoid stasis. Despite the fact that the first of Blake Edwards's *Pink Panther* films was released in 1964, and is thus the first 1960s film dealt with

Figure 13.2: David Niven and Claudia Cardinale in *The Pink Panther* (1963).
Image courtesy of the BFI stills department.

here, Niven as Sir Charles is cut from the same cloth as Sir Percy, Phileas Fogg and
Raymond. Suave, imperturbable, charming – once again, Niven embodies Victorian
ideals of gentlemanliness, this time transposed to the backdrop of the Alpine resort
of Cortina d'Ampezzo. What is different here is that a head-to-head duel emerges
between 'Frenchness' and 'Britishness' in a way that we have not seen in the roles
previously discussed as Sir Charles and the Inspector battle it out – admittedly
unwittingly on the part of the latter – both in their roles as thief and investigator,

and in their affections for Simone Clouseau (Capucine). There is no denying that Inspector Clouseau is a figure of fun and that the vision of 1960s French masculinity he embodies is constantly undermined. Yet it would be too simplistic to suggest that the flipside of this is the victory of Niven's 'debonair gentleman'. Symbolically, in terms of a projected social order, the coupling of Sir Charles and Simone represents a threat, as the thieves attempt to outwit the authorities, and succeed in so doing. However, as the adulterous couple, the threat they represent is also played out in the interlocking realms of gender and sexuality.

As an image of masculinity, Sir Charles emerges no better than the hapless Inspector. To illustrate this, we can contrast, for instance, a series of scenes in which Monsieur and Madame Clouseau are in bed together, as the former tries, increasingly desperately, to seduce his wife, with the sequence in which Sir Charles, who plans to steal a diamond in the possession of Princess Dala, gets the latter drunk on champagne in his bedroom. It is perhaps unsurprising that Inspector Clouseau's attempts at seduction are thwarted at every turn as Simone uses every excuse imaginable to keep him out of bed, asking for extra blankets, for windows to be closed, and for her husband to run down to the hotel kitchen to get her a glass of milk. The ultimate result of all this is the none-too-subtle image of a bottle of champagne popping its cork in the bed between the couple as the Inspector finally manages to kiss his wife, with the contents of the bottle spilling uncontrollably.

It is, however, more surprising that, as a counter-balance to this, we do not see Sir Charles as a wholly successful seducer; indeed, we see direct mocking of the image of imperial masculinity unprecedented in the earlier works under discussion. Princess Dala throws a small dinner party to which Sir Charles is invited. Conversation turns to gentle teasing of Sir Charles by the other guests and Princess Dala, invited to give her impressions of him, first describes him as 'sort of a contemporary Don Juan'. She is asked to expand upon this comment by her fellow diners and does so as follows:

> It seems to me that any middle-aged bachelor who has never desired the basic rewards of wife and family, and finds it necessary to occupy the major portion of his life making conquest after conquest is trying to prove something that he can never possibly prove... that he's a man.

This seems to suggest the ways in which we can understand Niven's 'debonair gentleman' to be in the process of passing his sell-by date. Dala makes explicit reference to his age, before going on to scold men who shun the pleasures of domesticity in favour of adolescent sexual adventures, and ultimately dismissing Sir Charles's *raison d'être*. If we are to understand Niven's place in postwar Franco-British cinematic relations as a means of negotiating 'postwar male restlessness', surely Dala's remarks here point towards the arrival of a time in which this negotiation is replaced by an acceptance of the realities of contemporary gender relations. This slap in the face to the ideals of imperial gentlemanliness is further compounded when Dala agrees to visit Sir Charles in his room later the same evening, ostensibly in order to apologize for her behaviour. Sir Charles offers her champagne, she accepts, and the action jumps forward to a drunken Princess Dala, lying on a tiger-skin run in front of Sir Charles's fireplace. The pair flirt, but when Sir Charles kisses her, Princess Dala lifts the ear of the tiger towards her mouth and says: 'You make one move on me and I'll set him on you. ... You're outnumbered, two against one.'

It is not insignificant that the climax to the evening's activities comes on a tiger-skin rug, since 'tiger hunting was an important symbol in the construction of British imperial and masculine identities during the nineteenth century' (Sramek 2006: 659). Sramek's analysis of the role played by tiger hunting in nineteenth-century constructions of British masculinity highlights the 'supposed need for British hunters to protect Indian men, women, and children from the savage creature' (2006: 667). As well as reminding us of the call for the 'beautiful Indian princess' to be saved from the 'barbaric Indian rites' by Niven's Phileas Fogg in the trailer for *Around the World in 80 Days*, we can also see here, in *The Pink Panther*, how the embodiment of gentlemanly masculinity offered by Niven has become outmoded. Princess Dala is neither in need of protection, nor at risk, from Sir Charles. She claims her lips have been numbed by the champagne, so – although she agrees to allow Sir Charles to kiss her – she does so jokingly, claiming that she cannot feel a thing, only to then use the tiger-skin that, in the imagery of imperial masculinity, signals 'a struggle with fearsome nature that needed to be resolutely faced "like a Briton"' (Sramek 2006: 659) to ward off her would-be seducer. We can consider this sequence in light of Ross's description (1996: 77) of the manner in which, from the 1950s into the 1960s, 'the colonies are in some sense "replaced", and the effort that once went into maintaining and disciplining a colonial people and situation becomes instead concentrated on a particular "level" of metropolitan existence: everyday life'. What the colonies are 'replaced' by, in Ross's view, is women 'as the subjects of everydayness and as those most subjected to it'. Yet here the 'replacement' fails as Sir Charles is mocked, first directly and then indirectly, for his inevitable failure 'to be a man': the interaction between Sir Charles, the Princess and the dead tiger can be understood as an illustration of 'the powerful intersection of gender and nationality in determining identity' (Handyside 2002: 166).

It is in these domains that we begin to see the ways in which, by the mid-1960s, Niven's playing and replaying of a character straddling pre- and postwar worlds can begin to be read as a threat in its own right. The 'paradoxical desire for stability and change' for which Raymond, Phileas Fogg and Sir Percy all, in their own ways, offered a cinematic outlet, would, it seems, require resolution. Sir Charles, in many ways, recalls the characters discussed from Niven's 1950s films. He is impeccably well dressed and well mannered at all times, whether racing down the slopes after Princess Dala in a natty headband and brightly coloured pullover or falling from a balcony into a snow drift, only to emerge, apparently unruffled by the experience, and to calmly walk back towards his hotel, with a polite 'Good evening' for the unsuspecting bystanders who watch him emerge from the snow. He is fit and agile, as demonstrated by his skiing prowess but also as we see him climb out of a building having just stolen jewels from a safe. He is rich, successful and, as ever, a charming and sought-after dinner guest. In short, just like Sir Percy, Raymond and Phileas

Fogg before him, Sir Charles encapsulates Spicer's vision of 'gentlemanliness', but now it seems to be reaching increasingly into the domain of parody.

Conclusion

By charting David Niven's onscreen encounters with aspects of French national identity in this way, we can see how, from the beginning of the 1950s and Sir Percy Blakeney's warnings about the perils of too quick a march towards unfettered change, we reach a point at which, into the late 1960s, a clear indication is given through the character of Sir Charles Lytton that the time has come to look forward. The implication of the shift would appear to be that the 'debonair gentleman', combining a pull back towards prewar ideals, themselves rooted in a bygone century, with a nascent attraction for futurity, can no longer be understood as representing the way forward into a resolutely postwar world. Rather, doggedly clinging to the characteristics of 'the perfect gentleman, the male ideal of the British ruling classes' (Spicer 2003: 8), Niven's refusal to reconcile these disparate strands leads audiences are led to conclude that his persona has, in itself, come to pose a threat to social cohesion. Through the roles examined here, from Sir Percy to Phileas Fogg, from Fogg to Raymond, and ultimately leading us to Sir Charles, we can read Niven's onscreen persona in much the same way as Ross suggests we understand the role Balzac's influence played in facilitating an expression of the 'hopes, anxieties, fears, and aspirations' of the 1950s and 1960s (1996: 2).

In other words, as the ghost of Hollywood and Americanization looms large, for Franco-British cinematic relations Niven represents 'a recurrent figure in an allegory by way of which the present appears as both a repetition and a difference, a means of continuity and a mark of rupture' (Ross 1996: 2). Niven's 1950 Pimpernel offers post-Revolutionary France as a cautionary tale for postwar France, depicting the beginnings of a need to renegotiate a vision of masculinity at once wedded to prewar ideals but at least forced to acknowledge a shift in the balance of gender relations. Sir Percy points audiences towards the domains in which the tensions and paradoxes of postwar Frenchness will be played out. We have seen how this role places Niven 'on the cusp' between two worlds, between 'pre-war outlooks' and the world of 'the genuinely new'. In his roles as Raymond in *Bonjour Tristesse* and Phileas Fogg in *Around the World in 80 Days*, we understand the ways in which 'looking backwards' towards prewar ideals is used as a means of exploring emergent, future-oriented tensions against the backdrop of the late 1950s, the Suez Crisis and declarations of independence (from France) by Tunisia and Morocco, and (from Britain) by Sudan, with Somalia, the Gold Coast and Nigeria to follow suit soon after. As we reach the 1960s and *Pink Panther* series, Sir Charles Lytton strikes us as a parody of the suave sophistication of Niven's earlier roles. While he may still succeed in seducing the elegant Mme Clouseau, their adulterous couple ultimately represents a threat to social cohesion, and his attempts to seduce Princess Dala are mocked mercilessly through an explicit questioning of his masculinity. We understand that while this 'recurrent figure' has been keeping one foot well and truly entrenched in an imperial past, refusing to fully embrace 'the genuinely new' and to set himself free in the postwar, postcolonial world of shifting gender relations, those around the 'ageing roué' (McFarlane 2003–8) have been preparing for the 'imaginative territory' that lies in 1968 and beyond.

Notes

The quotation in the title of this chapter is taken from Powell and Pressburger's film *The Elusive Pimpernel* in which Niven plays Sir Percy Blakeney, who writes and recites the following rhyme about his alter ego, the Pimpernel: 'They seek him here. They seek him there. Those Frenchies seek him everywhere. Is he in Heaven? Is he in Hell? That damned elusive Pimpernel.' The author would like to thank Andrew Ginger, Kerri Woods and the editors of this volume for their helpful feedback and suggestions for this chapter. Thanks also to the Carnegie Trust for the Universities of Scotland whose generous funding made research for parts of this chapter possible.

1. She was, in fact, Franco-British and born in Wales.
2. *Around the World in 80 Days* is a big-budget Hollywood spectacular; *Bonjour Tristesse* is U.S.-made, financed by Warner and Columbia; *The Elusive Pimpernel* was 'conceived as a co-production between Alexander Korda's London Films and Samuel Goldwyn' (BFI 1950) and resulted in a lawsuit over production costs; and the *Pink Panther* series are all either U.K. or U.K.-U.S. productions but directed by an American.
3. To give but a small selection of such roles: Capt. James Randall in *The Charge of the Light Brigade* (Curtiz, 1936), Lieut. Jim Perry in *The Way Ahead* (Reed, 1944), Major Valentine Moreland in *Appointment with Venus* (Thomas, 1951) and Cmdr. John Finchhaven in *The Extraordinary Seaman* (Frankenheimer, 1969).

References

Bellis, M. 2008. 'Bicycle History'. Retrieved 20 November 2008 from http://inventors.about.com/library/inventors/blbicycle.htm

British Film Institute. 1950. 'The Elusive Pimpernel', *The Monthly Film Bulletin* 17(203): 184. Retrieved 8 December 2008 from www.screenonline.org.uk/media/mfb/1007168/index.html

Capdevila, L. 2001. 'The Quest for Masculinity in a Defeated France, 1940–1945', *Contemporary European History* 10(3): 423–45.

Cardinal, R. 1994. 'Introduction', in J. Verne, *Around the World in 80 Days* and *Five Weeks in a Balloon*. London: Wordsworth Classics, pp. v–vx.

Francis, M. 2007. 'A Flight From Commitment? Domesticity, Adventure and the Masculine Imaginary in Britain After the Second World War', *Gender & History* 19(1): 163–85.

Handyside, F. 2002. 'Stardom and Nationality: The Strange Case of Jean Seberg', *Studies in French Cinema* 3(2): 165–76.

Higson, A. 1995. *Waving the Flag: Constructing a National Cinema in Britain*. Oxford: Clarendon Press.

McFarlane, B. 2003–8. 'Niven, David (1910–1983)', in *Encyclopaedia of British Cinema*. Retrieved 20 November 2008 from http://www.screenonline.org.uk/people/id/458293/

Niven, D. 1994 [1971]. *The Moon's a Balloon*. London: Penguin Books.

Plain, G. 2006. *John Mills and British Cinema: Masculinity, Identity and Nation*. Edinburgh: Edinburgh University Press.

Powrie, P. 2006. 'Introduction', in P. Powrie (ed.), *The Cinema of France*. London: Wallflower, pp. 1–9.

Ross, K. 1996. *Fast Cars, Clean Bodies: Decolonization and the Reordering of French Culture*. Cambridge, MA and London: MIT Press.

Sims, G. 2004. 'Spectators: The Golden Age of Spectatorship', in M. Temple and M. Witt (eds), *The French Cinema Book*. London: BFI, pp. 162–71.

Spicer, A. 2003. *Typical Men: The Representation of Masculinity in Popular British Cinema*. London: IB Tauris.

Sramek, J. 2006. '"Face Him Like a Briton": Tiger Hunting, Imperialism, and British Masculinity in Colonial India, 1800–1875', *Victorian Studies* 48(4): 659–80.

Verne, J. 1994 [1873]. *Around the World in 80 Days*. London: Wordsworth Classics.

Filmography

Appointment with Venus. 1951, Ralph Thomas, U.K.

Around the World in 80 Days. 1956, Michael Anderson, U.S.A.

Bonjour Tristesse. 1958, Otto Preminger, U.S.A.

Cerveau, Le. 1969, Gérard Oury, France/Italy.

Charge of the Light Brigade, The. 1936, Michael Curtiz, U.S.A.

Curse of the Pink Panther. 1983, Blake Edwards, U.K./U.S.A.

Dinner at the Ritz. 1937, Harold D. Schuster, U.K.

Elusive Pimpernel, The. 1950, Michael Powell and Emeric Pressburger, U.K.

Extraordinary Seaman, The. 1969, John Frankenheimer, U.S.A.

Eye of the Devil. 1966, J. Lee Thompson, U.K.

Pink Panther, The. 1963, Blake Edwards, U.K./U.S.A.

Toast of New Orleans, The. 1950, Norman Taurog, U.S.A.

Trail of the Pink Panther. 1982, Blake Edwards, U.K./U.S.A.

Way Ahead, The. 1944, Carol Reed, U.K.

CHAPTER 14

Truffaut in London

Robert Murphy

> He was more afraid of death than of anything else. And he died as he
> thought he would, while the first snows of winter fell.
> *Fahrenheit 451*, François Truffaut, 1966,
> misquoted from Robert Louis Stevenson's *The Weir of Hermiston*

François Truffaut's suggestion, during his interviews with Alfred Hitchcock, that there might be something incompatible between Britain and cinema has had an extraordinarily wide circulation. Charles Barr argues against it in his essay 'Amnesia and Schizophrenia' (Barr 1986); it resonates through Stephen Frears's documentary *Typically British* (broadcast on Channel 4 in 1995), which ends with Frears declaring 'Bollocks to Truffaut!'; and seems to resurface whenever anyone wants to argue that British cinema is not as boring as people might think. What Truffaut actually says is:

> isn't there a certain incompatibility between the terms 'cinema' and 'Britain'?
> This might sound far-fetched, but I get the feeling that there are national
> characteristics – among them, the English countryside, the subdued way of
> life, the stolid routine – that are anti-dramatic in a sense. The weather itself
> is anti-cinematic. Even British humour – that very understatement on which
> so many of the good crime comedies are hinged – is somehow a deterrent to
> strong emotion (Truffaut 1978: 140).

This encounter took place in August 1962, when Hitchcock was still regarded as a slightly unsavoury showman rather than a great auteur by most British and American critics. Hitchcock's response (bearing in mind his under-appreciation in Britain) is restrained. He ignores Truffaut's proposal that there is something in the national character incompatible with cinema and homes in on class, complaining about British intellectuals spurning their own cinema in favour of the European avant garde. The comment comes after 140 pages dealing with Hitchcock's career in Britain and neither Truffaut nor Hitchcock is dismissive of the twenty-three films he made before leaving for Hollywood. Truffaut's suspicion about the merits of British cinema did not extend into Anglophobia, indeed he betrayed a fascination with British culture (or at least with British women) in *Les Deux anglaises et le continent / Anne and Muriel* (1971). But as he told an interviewer in 1968, 'I don't have an international frame of mind. I am terribly French. Abnormally, unhealthily French. Parisian' (Truffaut 1987: 38). When he came to London in January 1966 to make *Fahrenheit 451* at Pinewood Studios, it was inevitably going to be something of a challenge.

Fahrenheit 451 Is My Fifth Film

At the time of his interviews with Hitchcock, Truffaut was working on a script for *Fahrenheit 451*. Ray Bradbury had declined the offer to adapt his novel himself, having struggled with a theatrical dramatization for Charles Laughton that never reached the stage, but he was happy for Truffaut to have a go. Truffaut was well respected for *Les Quatre cents coups / The Four Hundred Blows* (1959) and *Jules et Jim / Jules and Jim* (1962), but a big-budget science fiction film was a risky prospect for French producers, and United Artists, after flirting with the idea, chose instead to back Philippe de Broca's Tintin-inspired *L'Homme de Rio / That Man from Rio* (1964). Unable to get the film off the ground, Truffaut turned to a smaller-scale project, *La Peau Douce* (1964).

Truffaut had been approached by Lewis Allen, a young American producer who specialized in semi-experimental projects such as Shirley Clarke's *The Connection* (1962) and Peter Brook's *Lord of the Flies* (1963), to make a film about the Texas outlaws Bonnie Parker and Clyde Barrow. Truffaut was enthusiastic about the script and had almost overcome his doubts about making a film in America when Warren Beatty bought the rights to the screenplay and arranged to produce and star in the film himself (*Bonnie and Clyde*, Penn, 1967). Previously Truffaut had rejected the idea of casting Beatty as Clyde Barrow, asserting that: 'As far as I am concerned, he and Marlon Brando, and several others, are on a little list I've classified in my head as "Better not to make films at all than make films with these people"' (de Baecque and Toubiana 1999: 212). Fortunately Allen was equally interested in *Fahrenheit 451* and proposed making the film in the U.S. with Paul Newman as Montag, the Fireman who falls in love with the books he is supposed to burn, Jean Seberg as Linda, his zombified wife, and Jane Fonda as Clarisse, the young woman who tempts him into book-reading. But before financial backing for the film had been secured, Newman, who wanted to stress the political and sociological elements of the story (anathema to Truffaut) changed his mind, and Terence Stamp was asked to replace him.

Stamp was keen to work with an art film director like Truffaut (he would later play the mysterious stranger in Pasolini's *Teorema / Theorem*, 1968), but things started to become complicated when Jean Seberg dropped out and Julie Christie, who had an on-off relationship with Stamp, was recruited to play Linda. Christie had become world famous for her performances in *Dr Zhivago* (1965) and *Darling* (1965) and Stamp was chary of her fame overshadowing his. But what really threw the spanner in the works was the idea (proposed by Allen but enthusiastically taken up by Truffaut) to get Christie to play Clarisse as well as Linda. Jane Fonda was ditched and Stamp turned his back on the project, convinced that Christie would become the main focus of the film. Oskar Werner, who had already accepted the role of the playfully evil Fire Chief, reluctantly agreed to switch to the bigger and more demanding role of Montag.

Whatever the consequences for the film, these casting changes made it easier to raise finance. Ironically, Truffaut, who loathed the star system and was dubious about Britain as a place to make films, had secured the services of two Oscar-nominated actors (Christie for *Darling*, Werner for *Ship of Fools*: Christie would win best actress, Werner lose to Lee Marvin in *Cat Ballou*, but they would not find this out until a few days after the end of shooting *Fahrenheit 451*) and London, rather than America, became the obvious place to make the film. The popularity of British cinema, with films as varied as *Tom Jones* (1963), *From Russia With Love* (1963) and *A Hard Day's Night* (1964) enjoying international box-office success, had made London a fashionable place to make films, encouraging the Hollywood majors to set up production bases there. Lewis Allen was able to persuade MCA/Universal that *Fahrenheit 451* should be the first to go into production of an interesting (though

Figure 14.1: Oskar Werner, with shorn hair, and Julie Christie in a publicity still from *Fahrenheit 451*.
Image courtesy of the BFI stills department.

commercially disastrous) programme of films that included Charlie Chaplin's *A Countess from Hong Kong* (1967), Peter Watkins' *Privilege* (1967), Albert Finney's *Charlie Bubbles* (1967) and Karel Reisz's *Isadora* (1967).

Christie had no desire to rush off to Hollywood and was thrilled to be working with Truffaut (especially as he flattered her by casting her in two roles). The fly in the ointment proved to be Werner, who felt he had outgrown European cinema and relished the prospect of becoming an international star. According to the film's cinematographer, Nicolas Roeg: 'Oskar thought this was a film he was doing for François, because he owed him something or he liked him. But at that stage of his career he just wanted to get it over with' (Roeg 1984/5: 44). Werner resented his suggestions about how Montag should be played being ignored or countermanded by Truffaut – who in turn was annoyed by Werner's unwillingness to do as he was told. By the end of the shooting schedule the two men were not on speaking terms. On 15 April Truffaut confided: 'And that's the end of my collaboration with Oskar Werner, whom I shall not see again before his departure for Hollywood tomorrow, nor, I hope, thereafter' (Truffaut 1967: 11).

Everybody Makes Me Feel That I'm Really Being Rather Eccentric

This is all recounted in an amazingly frank way in the diary Truffaut was asked to keep by the editors of *Cahiers du Cinéma*, the first part of which was also published in English before the film was released. He could hardly speak English and although he was pleased and relieved that at last – after a very long gestation – *Fahrenheit 451* was finally going into production, he saw London as a place of exile and wrote the diary as a way of keeping in touch with his friends in France and with Ray Bradbury (who remained a loyal supporter of Truffaut's adaptation to the end) in America.

Truffaut found Pinewood a comfortable and well equipped studio and thought restrictive union rules were balanced out by the efficiency and professionalism of the technicians, who were only too pleased to work overtime (for which they would have been paid at the 'time and a half' rate). He welcomed the fact that British studios only exceptionally worked on Saturdays and Sundays, as it gave him a breathing space to make script changes and revise the shooting schedule with his trusted collaborators Suzanne Schiffman and Helen Scott. He is contrite about his less than complimentary comments about British cinema and impressed by his British film crew:

> I have nothing disparaging to say of the British whose national cinema I dragged through the mud so often when I was a journalist. I have never had so loyal a crew, showing me such kindness and so eager to please me as I have here at Pinewood. Everyone wants to help 'The French Guv'nor' to come out of it as well as possible (Truffaut 1966a: 15).

He becomes more critical later on, taking against his costume designer, Tony Walton (who also designed the set for Montag's apartment), to the extent that he wanted to exclude him from the credits. He also expresses some reservations about the need for a huge crew when on his French films he managed well enough with far fewer people. But what he objects to is big-budget studio production rather than anything specifically British.

Truffaut later confessed that if the 'swinging' London of the mid-1960s was an exhilarating and dynamic place to be, he hardly noticed:

> In London, for *Fahrenheit 451*, I was like under punishment. I lived six months in the Hilton without having a meal outside my room. A car used to come to take me to the studio. When I got back to Paris, everyone said 'So London, a lot happening, eh?' I didn't dare say, 'I've only been in the Hilton.' Six months...' (Truffaut 1987: 40)

He exaggerates slightly. In February and March there was a season of Renoir films at the National Film Theatre in London, which sustained and inspired him. He also managed to find *Citizen Kane* playing at one of the cinemas of the Classic circuit (a valuable feature of the London cinema scene in the 1960s and 1970s) and tracked down *The Magnificent Ambersons* in Chelsea (presumably at the Classic or the Essoldo). But he was homesick for France and overjoyed to return to shoot the monorail sequences at Châteauneuf-sur-Loire, outside Orléans, at the end of March. In Paris he had 'a strong desire not to return to London and the gloomy feeling of going back to school' (Truffaut 1966b: 21). Nonetheless he returned for the final two weeks' shooting and a further three months of postproduction.

Oskar Runs Like a Girl

Truffaut had worked productively with Oskar Werner on *Jules et Jim* and his subtle performance as Jules had revived his film career and led to prestigious roles in *The Spy Who Came In from the Cold* (1965) and *Ship of Fools*. In retrospect Truffaut's earlier choices for the role, Jean-Paul Belmondo and Paul Newman, would have brought more dynamism and charisma, and Terence Stamp's ability to combine innocence with unexpected violence (which he was shortly to display in William Wyler's *The Collector*) made him ideal for Montag. But initially Truffaut was enthusiastic, writing on 27 January that 'I watch Oskar Werner each day literally breathing life into this film' (Truffaut 1966a: 17). The honeymoon was short lived. A few days later he recorded: 'This is the second time since the start of shooting that we've clashed and I realize that it is not possible to tell everything in this diary which is slated to be published before the film is completed' (Truffaut 1966a: 17). Things improved for a short while and on 10 February Truffaut took Werner to see Renoir's *La Règle du Jeu / The Rules of the Game* at the National Film Theatre. But a week later they had a row over Werner's reluctance to use the flamethrower (which he considered dangerous) and Truffaut turned to his stand-in ('a delightful Englishman called John Ketteringham'), whom he found so enjoyable to work with that he resolved to use him whenever possible.

Something of a pugilist despite his dapper appearance, Truffaut made little effort to ameliorate the situation and the diplomatic silence did not last long. He gleefully recounts various small victories over Werner and looks forward to manipulating his performance in the cutting room. Werner had a strong sense of his own importance (he had made his mark as a notable Shakespearean actor in Germany as well as pursuing a career in films) but he was introverted and isolated and must have found the situation far more painful than Truffaut did. Sadly, Werner was to appear in only three more films: *Interlude* (1968), *The Shoes of the Fisherman* (1968) and *Voyage of the Damned* (1976) before he died in October 1984, two days after the death of Truffaut. His powerlessness manifested itself in the reckless act of having his hair cropped with two weeks of shooting still to go, creating serious continuity problems. On 1 April a bemused Truffaut wrote:

Oskar arrives with his hair cut very short, almost shorn, and explains that he went into a barber's shop, fell asleep and too late became aware of the damage .... It all seems very mysterious and I doubt whether we shall ever know the truth about this hair-splitting affair. Some people think it's probably a rebellious gesture against me or the film – it's possible, but it would be the first time that our 'male star', as they say in Hollywood, did something primarily against his own interest (Truffaut 1966b: 21).

Beyond Werner's nervousness with flamethrowers and Truffaut's catty remarks, there was a fundamental conflict over how Montag should be played, particularly in his relationship with Linda and Clarisse. Truffaut wanted Montag to act in an equally dispassionate way with both women; Werner thought he should be impatiently dismissive with Linda and increasingly affectionate towards Clarisse. Truffaut complained that 'Oskar's performance isn't as "cool" as I would like. Clearly he doesn't want to appear less intelligent than Clarisse, although that is the situation. He always manages to sneak in a couple of unnecessary smiles' (Truffaut 1966b: 20). In support of Werner, Christie's Clarisse bears little resemblance to the wise child of the book, and it is hard to imagine Newman, Belmondo or Stamp acting in a more 'cool' way towards her gauche friendliness. The diary gives a one-sided picture but there is at least the possibility that Werner was right and the film would have benefited from Montag being a more human, more emotional character. The real problem, however, is Clarisse.

One can understand Truffaut's decision to cast Christie as both Linda and Clarisse – separately they are unsatisfactory parts, together they might seem to make a whole, though this takes them far from the characters Bradbury created for the book. Christie's Linda, lost in a world of happy pills and afternoon television, shocked and frightened by Montag's sudden interest in books, is surprisingly sympathetic (unlike Mildred, her literary counterpart). Clarisse is less successful. Truffaut was determined to follow Bradbury's interdiction on not allowing the film to become a romance. But in the novel this is much easier: Clarisse is barely seventeen and having disrupted Montag's complacent conformity she disappears, presumed dead. In the film she is twenty-two and as she seems like a livelier version of his wife, romance is obviously a possibility – despite Truffaut's attempts to stamp on any sparks generated between his two stars in favour of Montag's growing love for books.

On 1 March he wrote:

> I have de-sexed Clarisse so as to get neither her nor Montag mixed up in an adulterous situation which has no place in science fiction. Not mistress, Girl Scout nor 'girl friend'. Clarisse is just a young woman, thinking, questioning, who happens to cross Montag's path and who makes him stray from it (Truffaut 1966b: 10).

With Jane Fonda, a tough cookie who could cloak her sexuality in the guise of a tomboy, or Rita Tushingham, who has much more of the otherworldly quality of Bradbury's Clarisse, this might have worked. But desexing Christie was a different matter. Her Clarisse is rather nondescript and gawky – a trainee junior school teacher who is pathetically upset when little boys run away from her – but this makes her lovably vulnerable, inevitably breaking down Montag's dispassionate reserve by arousing his protective instincts. And once Clarisse escapes the dismal, conformist Big Brother society, she turns into the sort of impulsive free spirit Christie had appeared as in earlier roles.

Truffaut tried to impose a steely asceticism on Montag, stressing a monk-like obsession with books that would exclude any sexual interest in women (there is a discreet cut when Linda, revitalized by a blood transfusion, seduces him). But Werner manages to make his detached attitude to Clarisse look more like gentlemanly restraint than lack of interest. Thus when they finally meet again among the book people – Montag looking boyishly invigorated with his cropped hair – romance looks set to blossom and the film ends in optimism rather than despair.

We Must Burn the Books, Montag, *All* the Books

Réné Clement, one of the old guard directors Truffaut and his friends despised, had claimed that 'One by one M. Truffaut's films diminish in quality' (Truffaut 1967: 12). Truffaut concedes that: 'It's possible that I choose them badly and I ought to have accepted *Is Paris Burning?* which Paul Graetz offered me before entrusting it to Rene Clement.' But he has no regrets:

> Truth to tell, I didn't much fancy filming the adventures of Captain Alain Delon telephoning to General Belmondo to ask him to contact Sergeant Orson Welles to get him to obtain from Admiral Mastroianni forged ration cards for Leslie Caron who is in the Resistance and the cousin of Gert Froebe, a colonel in the Free French Forces under the orders of Yves Montand, head of the Gestapo (Truffaut 1967: 12).

Fahrenheit 451 was no multinational epic, but it was a relatively big-budget film with two major stars based on a popular science-fiction novel. It was an important film for Truffaut – his first, and as it turned out his only, film in English – and it might have determined whether his career was to flounder or flourish. Had it been a big box-office success it may have led him to work in Hollywood at a time when Arthur Penn, Mike Nichols, Dennis Hopper, Woody Allen, Francis Ford Coppola, Steven Spielberg, Martin Scorsese and Brian de Palma were attempting to create the sort of auteurist cinema espoused by Truffaut and the other *Cahiers du cinéma* writers. Truffaut despised big-budget star vehicles but he wanted to make films that people liked and was disappointed by the predominantly hostile critical reaction to the film and its indifferent box-office success. But *Fahrenheit 451* confirms that even with an ostensibly commercial genre film, he was prepared to sacrifice conventional solutions and seek what George Bluestone calls 'that beat of sympathetic sadness' which he takes to be Truffaut's most persistent quality (Bluestone 1967: 3).

French critics were lukewarm about Truffaut's excursion into English-language cinema. Some British critics were more generous. Alexander Walker (*The Evening Standard*, 17 November 1966) found it 'absolutely mesmerising'; John Coleman (*The New Statesman*, 25 November 1966) thought it 'typical of the remarkable genius of M Truffaut'; David Robinson (*The Times*, 18 November 1966) declared it 'one of the rare cases where the adaptation improves upon the original'. There was a deep reservoir of affection and respect for Truffaut's work in Britain but the predominant tone was one of disappointment. Ian Wright in the *The Guardian* (17 November 1966), for example, liked the film's 'lyrical movement' but would have preferred a version by Godard or Hitchcock, who would have 'transmitted a sense of evil which the subject needs and which is not in Truffaut's vocabulary'. Ray Bradbury declared that 'Truffaut has given me back a gift of my own book done in a new medium by preserving the soul of the original' (de Baecque and Toubiana 1999: 220). But most U.S. critics were sceptical about the value of Truffaut's reworking of this very American story. *Time* magazine's critic was politely dismissive, concluding that 'The real problem with the picture is that Truffaut might better have made another' (Anon 1966). Pauline Kael pointed out that Truffaut had made the sort of loose-ended film which virtually invited the viewer to improve upon it, observing that '*Fahrenheit 451* is more interesting in the talking-over afterwards than in the seeing' (Kael 1968: 146).

In the first protracted analysis of the film, George Bluestone asked the question: 'Given the subject, his cast, his working conditions, are we forced to conclude that Truffaut, his first time out in color and English, was doomed to fail?' (Bluestone 1967: 3). He concludes that he was, that the film is a 'flawed vision', and sides with Werner over the interpretation of Montag:

> Truffaut wanted Clarisse to be Ariel, leading Montag to renounce the destructive fire and so bring him to redemption. Werner wanted his Juliet. Truffaut wanted a symbol. Werner wanted a woman. We can never know for certain if Werner was right. What we do know is that Truffaut was not. (Bluestone 1967: 7).

Don Allen in *Finally Truffaut*, the first book on Truffaut in English, is judicious and perceptive, but he too regards *Fahrenheit 451* as fundamentally flawed:

> The film does suffer, however, from being made in the English language by a man who did not speak that language. Every other film by Truffaut is enhanced by his ear for the cadences of language, reflected either in the dialogue or the commentary. Every other film allows him scope for a certain amount of improvisation and flexibility with the spoken word, during the shooting and sometimes even at the post-synchronization stage.

He concludes that 'A film whose theme of linguistic deprivation is already difficult enough to portray is seriously impaired by the linguistic deprivation of its director' (Allen 1974: 117).

However, Universal's release of a high-quality DVD of *Fahrenheit 451*, with an entertaining commentary and informative extras, attracted enthusiastic reviews; in 2007 Tom Whalen attempted a positive reassessment of the film, dismissing claims that it was humourless, lacking in courage, politically muddled, and stuffed with stiff, lifeless characters. He vindicates Christie's performance as the 'puppy-brained' Linda, points out the sophistication of Truffaut's mise en scene and offers a detailed analysis of the key sequence when Montag reads *David Copperfield* by the light of the television screen. Surprisingly, he concludes that that it is a cold film, 'spare and dead': 'the final image – a freeze frame on the lake in winter (the screen now emptied of the book-people walking back and forth in front of the camera), a single rower in a boat on the water – tells us all we need to know about how cold *Fahrenheit 451* really is' (Whalen 2007: 189). But his attitude towards the film remains overwhelmingly sympathetic.

The Countryside, the Subdued Way of Life, the Weather ...

Truffaut started *Fahrenheit 451* in a mood of optimism. He was fortunate that Julie Christie and Nicolas Roeg, his cinematographer, could speak fluent French and he was pleasantly surprised by the eagerness and friendliness of his Pinewood technicians. Conflict with Oskar Werner soured the atmosphere but on 20 April, after the editor Thom Noble had cut together the first six reels of the film, Truffaut declared himself satisfied: 'It will surely be an off-beat film, especially for an English-language production, but within its strangeness it seems to me coherent' (Truffaut 1967: 12). Critical and box-office reaction shook his confidence, and he later told Nicolas Roeg that it must have been a bad film because nobody went to see it (Roeg 1984–5: 44). But flawed though the film might be it has stood the test of time and, as the DVD release and Whalen's reassessment of the film suggest, it is now better regarded than when it was first released.

In the first few days of shooting Truffaut expressed his ambivalence about making a film in England:

I am making a British film. I have tried as much as possible to avoid national characteristics of which the English are themselves unaware. 'Above all', I asked, 'no red brick.' So they gave me yellow brick. I've tried to cast actors who have an American look, with symmetrical faces and regular features. In spite of that, now and again Great Britain gets in on the act, via some small-part player whom I have not chosen myself or who is replacing one that I did choose who at the last moment isn't available (Truffaut, 1966a: 14).

He was right to be suspicious but his vigilance proved insufficient to hold back an insidious intrusion of Britishness. The firemen, with the exception of Montag and his nemesis Fabian, played by cold blue-eyed Anton Diffring, and Cyril Cusack's craggy-faced Captain, with his Jesuitical conviction in his own moral certitude, are a blandly forgettable lot. So too are the narcissistically obsessed monorail passengers and Linda's empty-headed friends. The editor, Thom Noble, was impressed by Ann Bell's performance as the woman who is reduced to tears when Montag reads from *David Copperfield*, but he had to cut it back and what remains is not enough to show the tragedy behind her superficiality (*Fahrenheit 451* 2003 [DVD commentary]). But the rebels (the apple eater, the man whose son is tempted to pick up a book at one of the book-burning ceremonies, the little round martyr who goes up in flames with her books) all have faces which are far from regular and symmetrical, and their way of behaving – their subdued way of life, their stolid routine a mask for impulsive and unobtrusively defiant behaviour – is distinctively British.

Truffaut dispensed with Bradbury's lethal Mechanical Hound and nuclear Armageddon and constantly stressed that he wanted the film to be light and playful, declaring: 'Let us make a film about life as children see it – the firemen are lead soldiers, the firehouse a super toy' (Truffaut 1966a: 22). The toy-like red fire engine (a converted Mole-Richardson camera crane) is second cousin to the Titfield Thunderbolt in quaintness, and Bernard Hermann's lively, lyrical score helps create a very different mood from the bleak apocalyptic modernism of Bradbury's story. The hand of oppression is much lighter here, in what could almost be an Ealing Studios version of Bradbury's dystopia.

The book people in the final part of the film seem to belong more to the absurd world of *Alice in Wonderland* than to any realistically conceived resistance movement. Despite Truffaut's attempt to internationalize the situation with a cacophony of voices speaking in various languages, they look the sort of quaint collection of eccentrics one might expect to find at a 1960s Wigmore Hall recital or gathered together in a parish meeting to protest about the opening of a supermarket or the closing of a post office. Even Michael Balfour, a reliable character actor who specialized in ruffians and boxers, adopts a refined accent to apologize for his tramp-like appearance, wryly observing (he is Machiavelli's *The Prince*) that 'you can't judge a book by its cover'. They reminded Dilys Powell (*The Sunday Times*, 20 November 1966) 'of some hideous get-together party game into which one was trapped before one had learned to take a stand against togetherness', and communist critic Nina Hibbin (*The Morning Star*, 14 November 1966) condemned them as 'a fey and Hampsteady lot'. But this only conforms that they are endearingly (or embarrassingly) British.

The book people inhabit Black Park, a sparse Buckinghamshire wood with a river running through it, which for generations (from *Treasure Island* to *Harry Potter and the Goblet of Fire*) has provided a convenient outdoor setting for British films being made at nearby Pinewood. Shooting in early April, production was hampered by heavy rain, and on 14 April (Christie's birthday and the last day of shooting) it snowed. Truffaut's *Tirez sur le pianiste* had gained in pathos from a shoot-out in the snow, and rather than abandoning production, he took full advantage of the weather to create an enchanted world, where the book people's antics take on a tragic dignity.

In perverse defiance of his earlier intentions, Truffaut had encouraged characteristic British humour among the book people (which the American Bluestone found 'all too sad') – rather silly puns and literary jokes – which conspire with the voices, the landscape and the weather to sneak an overwhelmingly British ethos into Truffaut's futuristic fantasy. The reception of *Fahrenheit 451* would have confirmed Truffaut's fears of an incompatibility between cinema and Britain, but if he had been blessed with the longevity of his fellow *Nouvelle Vague* directors Chabrol, Rohmer, Godard and Rivette and been able to look at the film forty years later, he might have been persuaded to change his mind.

Bibliography

Allen, D. 1974. *Finally Truffaut*. London: Secker & Warburg.

Anon. 1966. 'Fahrenheit 451', *Time*, 18 November.

Barr, C. 1986. 'Amnesia and Schizophrenia', in C. Barr (ed.), *All Our Yesterdays*. London: BFI Publishing, pp. 1–26.

Bluestone, G. 1967. 'The Fire and the Future', *Film Quarterly* Summer: 3–10.

Coleman, J. 1966. 'Fahrenheit 451', *The New Statesman*, 25 November.

de Baecque, A. and S. Toubiana. 1999. *Truffaut: A Biography*. New York: Knopf.

Hibbin, N. 1966. 'Fahrenheit 451', *The Morning Star*, 14 November.

Kael, P. 1968. *Kiss Kiss Bang Bang*. Boston/Toronto: Little, Brown.

Powell, D. 1966. 'Fahrenheit 451', *The Sunday Times*, 20 November.

Robinson, D. 1966. 'Fahrenheit 451', *The Times*, 18 November.

Roeg, N. 1984/5. 'Looking at the Rubber Duck: Nicolas Roeg Talks to Richard Combs About Working on François Truffaut's Fahrenheit 451', *Sight and Sound* Winter: 43–44.

Truffaut, F. 1966a. 'Journal of "Fahrenheit 451"', Part One, trans. K. Mander and R.K Neilson Baxter, *Cahiers du Cinéma in English* 5: 11–23.

———. 1966b. 'Journal of "Fahrenheit 451"', Part Two, trans. K. Mander and R.K Neilson Baxter, *Cahiers du Cinéma in English* 6: 11–23.

———. 1967. 'Journal of "Fahrenheit 451"', Part Three, trans. K. Mander and R.K Neilson Baxter, *Cahiers du Cinéma in English* 7: 7–19.

———. 1978. *Hitchcock*. London: Paladin.

———. 1987. *Truffaut by Truffaut*, trans. R.E. Wolf. New York: Harry N. Abrams.

Walker, A. 1966. 'Fahrenheit 451', *The Evening Standard*, 17 November.

Whalen, T. 2007. 'The Consequences of Passivity: Re-evaluating Truffaut's *Fahrenheit 451*', *Literature Film Quarterly* July: 181–90.

Wright, I. 1966. 'Fahrenheit 451', *The Guardian*, 17 November.

Filmography

Bonnie and Clyde. 1967, Arthur Penn, U.S.A.

Cat Ballou. 1965, Elliot Silverstein, U.S.A.

Charlie Bubbles. 1967, Albert Finney, U.K.

Citizen Kane. 1941, Orson Welles, U.S.A.

Connection, The. 1962, Shirley Clarke, U.S.A.

Collector, The. 1965, William Wyler, U.K. / U.S.A.

Countess from Hong Kong, A. 1967, Charlie Chaplin, U.K. / U.S.A.

Darling. 1965, John Schlesinger, U.K.

Deux anglaises et le continent, Les / Anne and Muriel. 1971, François Truffaut, France.

Dr Zhivago. 1965, David Lean, U.K. / U.S.A.

Fahrenheit 451. 1966, François Truffaut, U.K.

Fahrenheit 451. 2003 [1966], François Truffaut, U.K., DVD release. Commentaries by Julie Christie, Thom Noble, Lewis Allen, Steven C. Smith and Annette Insdorf; short documentaries about the making of the film, the music of Bernard Hermann, and an interview with Ray Bradbury.

From Russia With Love. 1963, Terence Young, U.K.

Hard Day's Night, A. 1964, Richard Lester, U.K.

Harry Potter and the Goblet of Fire. 2005, Mike Newell, U.K. / U.S.A.

Homme de Rio, L' / That Man from Rio. 1964, Philippe de Broca, France.

Interlude. 1968, Kevin Billington, U.K.

Isadora. 1967, Karel Reisz, U.K. / France.

Jules et Jim / Jules and Jim. 1962, François Truffaut, France.

Lord of the Flies. 1963, Peter Brook, U.K.

Magnificent Ambersons, The. 1942, Orson Welles, U.S.A.

Peau douce, La. 1964, François Truffaut, France.

Privilege. 1967, Peter Watkins, U.K.

Quatre cents coups, Les / The Four Hundred Blows. 1959, François Truffaut, France.

Règle du Jeu, La / The Rules of the Game. 1939, Jean Renoir, France.

Ship of Fools. 1965, Stanley Kramer, U.S.A.

Shoes of the Fisherman. 1968, Michael Anderson, U.S.A.

Spy Who Came In from the Cold, The. 1965, Martin Ritt, U.K.

Teorema / Theorem. 1968, Pier Paolo Pasolini, Italy.

Tom Jones. 1963, Tony Richardson, U.K.

Tirez sur le pianiste / Shoot the Pianist. 1960, François Truffaut, France.

Treasure Island. 1950, Byron Haskin, U.K.

Typically British! 1995, Stephen Frears, U.K.

Voyage of the Damned. 1976, Stuart Rosenbaum, U.K.

CHAPTER 15

Jane Birkin: From English Rose to French Icon

Leila Wimmer

The figure of Jane Birkin offers an illuminating perspective on Franco-British cultural relations. Making her move before those other well known Channel-hoppers, Charlotte Rampling and Kristin Scott-Thomas, Birkin (born Jane Mallory Birkin in London in 1946) moved to Paris in 1968, and has lived there ever since. This move to France made her an international sex symbol when she recorded 'Je t'aime, moi non plus' with Serge Gainsbourg in 1969, a sexually explicit duet that is arguably one of the most famous Anglo-French cultural products of the last century. Since then, she has led a successful career as a recording artist, playwright, film and theatre actress, and, most recently, as director, with *Les Boîtes / Boxes* (2007). In Britain, her association with Serge Gainsbourg has worked to mask her creative accomplishments, notably in the field of cinema and, on both sides of the Channel, her work as an actress has been symptomatically neglected by film historians. This despite the fact that she has inarguably made her mark on French cinema, having appeared in over seventy films, both mainstream and auteur, and in many ways has become a national institution in the French cultural landscape. She is a media celebrity who seems to have made her life into a performance, whether as a 1960s icon or a 1980s personality (Flitterman-Lewis 1996: 348). The discussion that follows takes as its focus her cinematic career and the nature of her articulation of Franco-British interaction. It will argue that Birkin embodies a form of bicultural hybridity by means of which the particularity of cross-Channel cinematic encounters can be usefully examined. To do so, this study focuses on Birkin's films of the 1960s and 1970s, asking how they illuminate a recasting of French imaginings of Britishness at that particular historical conjuncture, and how they participate in a media-constructed myth of 1960s London associated with youth-orientated consumer culture figured through new figures of British womanhood.

Britain in the 1960s: the French View

As a product of 'Swinging' London, the articulation of Birkin's image needs to be seen within the wider context of the recasting of French images of the British in the 1960s. This was a period when the French stereotype of an outdated, conservative and insular Britain, with its Royal Family and stiff Victorian moral values, was replaced by another set of stereotypical images. Although the French mass media were originally reluctant to engage with British popular culture, from the mid-1960s onwards London was reimagined as a much more dynamic city than Paris. The notion of a vibrant British youth consumer culture, its popular music, fashion, theatre and, to a certain extent, cinema, led to a French vision of a modern and permissive country. The plays of the 'angry young men' were staged; Shakespeare was rediscovered, and British cinema, especially the James Bond series and the films of David Lean, was extremely successful with French audiences and mainstream film critics, if not with a certain faction of French cinephiles who looked down on commercially successful British directors such as Lean and Carol Reed (Wimmer 2009: 75–148). However, it was first and foremost through media constructions of British femininity that the French imagining of Britain came to be reconfigured, especially in cinema, the 'site where issues of femininity, sexuality and nation are vividly dramatized' (Gledhill and Swanson 1996: 6).

In contrast with France, where Gaullist grandeur meant that state power in the media and patronage in the arts culminated in a 'culture state' that combined conformity, bureaucratic control and a touch of nepotism (Tachin 2006), the new image of London of the 1960s appeared to many in France as increasingly libertine and emancipated (Lemonnier 2004: 207). This perception was split along generational lines. As Agnès Tachin has noted, the French perception of Britain at this historical juncture was marked by De Gaulle's 1963 and 1967 vetoes against the entry of Britain into the Common Market, and Britain was generally considered by the older generation as a conservative, declining country turned towards the United States. However, this image was blurred by British popular culture, which was deeply influential with the new generation of French baby-boomers. For French youth, London became a fashionable destination associated with cultural revolution, sexual permissiveness, high fashion (epitomized by Mary Quandt and the mini skirt) and a lively, popular arts scene, especially in terms of music. The increasing vogue for linguistic exchanges, the London of the Beatles, Carnaby Street and the mini skirt gave birth to the new myth of the '*petites anglaises*', which would later be illustrated in *A nous les petites anglaises / Let's Get Those English Girls* (1975), a popular film that tells the story of two middle-class French boys sent to Ramsgate in order to improve their English and gathered 5.7 millions of spectators upon its release. In the rather conservative 1960s French cultural climate of traditional family values, young English women acquired a reputation for being anything but shy in sexual matters, a misogynistic masculine fantasy which would soon fill the minds of French adolescents (Lemonnier 2004: 215).

With the advent of the new stereotype of Swinging London, Britain was thus gradually transformed into a model of sexual liberation and fantasy, and a supposed permissiveness came to be associated with its young women. While British women had previously been seen as asexual creatures with large feet and long teeth, a cliché that had been revived in the mid-1950s with Pierre Daninos's novel *Les Carnets du Major Thompson* (1954), this perception would undergo a change during the 1960s with the new stereotype of the sexually available English girl. These old stereotypes thus gave place to the new icons that were spread in the fashion and youth press, personified by the models Twiggy and Jean Shrimpton, and the middle-class actresses Julie Christie, Charlotte Rampling, Vanessa Redgrave, Susannah York and, of course, Birkin herself. In France, the young London girl became established as an ultrafashionable icon of modernity and an exotic fantasy object of desire: 'the culture of fun cohered in the single icon of the dolly-bird. She symbolized everything that was new, liberated, daring, sexually abandoned, independent and free' (Linda Grant in Green 1999: 76).

Femininity in the 1960s

Before coming to Paris in 1968, Birkin had appeared in seminal Swinging London films *The Knack* (1965) and *Blow Up* (1967), in which she starred as one of the nude models who play around with the trendy photographer played by David Hemmings. Both winners of a *Palme d'or* at Cannes, these two films firmly established her image as a wild child. She had also appeared in another Swinging London film, *Wonderwall* (1968). With a psychedelic soundtrack written by The Beatles' Georges Harrison, the film's narrative revolves around a lonely older professor becoming infatuated and spying upon *Vogue* cover girl Penny Lane (Jane Birkin) through a wall. Much was made of the nudity in *Blow Up* in 1967 and the sexual connotations of Birkin's new breed of woman as it was presented in these three films. The 'Single Girl' was a focal point, London having created the available, seemingly naïve 'dolly bird':

> a utopian fantasy of a woman free from the social and sexual constraints that appeared to limit her mother. Her girlishness also responds to and contains the anxieties that a woman no longer under the yoke of patriarchy (if still subjected to the whims of capital) might evoke. She is a girl, in a state of permanent immaturity. She ultimately cannot challenge an order grounded in the primacy of masculinity (Radner 1999: 10).

Upon her arrival in France, Birkin was thus already established as an emblem of young London, a witness to the values and lifestyle of a new England in the eyes of the French. As she herself states: 'I was an exotic English character – I had the long teeth, the allure and the accent and I had the uniform; the mini-skirt and the little wicker basket. In the Swinging London of the time, there were millions of girls like that; in Paris, I was the only one' (Rioux 1988: 23).

Birkin's first lead role was in *Slogan* (Pierre Grimblat, 1968) and the character she portrayed introduced this new image of British femininity into French cinema. Here, she plays Evelyne, an up-to-the-minute modern girl, the incarnation of a new kind of beauty: young, slim, with long straight hair and long legs, wearing a mini skirt, and indeed carrying a wicket basket. Following her appearance in this film, Birkin's status in France as a sexualized fantasy of a new kind of British femininity was cemented. Several of her early roles play on this image of the fragile, provocative and rebellious adolescent, such as *La Piscine / The Sinners* (1969) and *Les Chemins de Katmandou / The Road to Katmandu* (1969) or, in several films structured around her figure and her accent, on the idea of the foxy but scatterbrained young English girl, as for instance in *Trop jolies pour être honnêtes / Too pretty to be honest* (1972), *Le Mouton enragé / Love at the Top* (1974) and *Comment réussir... quand on est con et pleurnichard / How to Make Good When You're a Jerk and a Crybaby* (1974).

Birkin's representation of the new English woman offers a sexualized image that speaks of masculine projections of desire and anxieties about masculine identity in the 1960s and 1970s. Several of her films see her playing on her relaxed attitude to sexuality and a lack of inhibition equated with innocence; like Monroe, she 'appears natural in her sexiness' (Dyer 1987: 33), seemingly resolving a set of contradictions between uninhibited sexuality and inexperience: 'She can appear nude on the screen in all impunity. Her heart is pure, so we can laugh with her' (Thomann 1979: 85).

For example, then, in *Cannabis / French Intrigue* (1970), she plays Jane, the daughter of a diplomat who falls for a drug trafficker (played by Serge Gainsbourg). A mixture of fragility and innocence, offset by her sexual abandon and submissiveness, defines her character. 'I don't know much about life', she tells Gainsbourg's character when he approaches her early on in course of the narrative: the naïve English girl in Paris, she projects an image of sweetness and vulnerability combined with a soft and passive sexuality. In *Le Mouton enragé* meanwhile she plays a kindly prostitute who redeems the cynical main character played by Jean-Louis Trintignant. She is a loose but clever young woman in *Catherine et Cie / Catherine and Co* (1975), a strip girl in *Comment réussir... quand on est con et pleurnichard*, and, in *Positif* film critic Robert Beyanoun's *Sérieux comme le plaisir / Serious as Pleasure* (1975), she stars as Ariane, a young woman happily living with two men and sleeping with them both. Throughout this body of work, she represents a contemporary ingénue, whose slim and androgynous body, verging on the masculine, is both sexual and asexual, underlying the ambivalence of contemporary attitudes towards femininity and supposed sexual liberation.

Birkin in the 1960s: Object and Star

For some French critics, Birkin heralded 'a new type of perverse ingénue with a foreign accent, long blond hair and a lanky walk' (Garson 1969). In contrast, for critic Marcel Martin, she offered 'with enigmatic grace, a seductive image of the adolescent girl in thrall to the intoxicating effects of perversion' (Martin 1969). The divergent responses were united by their vision of Birkin as the manifestation of the contemporary English woman: spontaneous, vulnerable but sexually willing,

Figure 15.1: Birkin, basket and Gainsbourg at the 1974 Cannes Film Festival.
Copyright Mirkine / Sygma / Corbis.

androgynous, cute and sexy, scandalous but innocent, with a 'funny British accent' (Lenne 1996: 17).

Like her compatriots Charlotte Rampling and Kristin Scott-Thomas, Birkin's exotic eroticism, her accented middle-class Britishness, was crucial to her image. However, in contrast to her fellow female British actors, who often play inscrutable icons of feminine ambiguity, aristocratic English roses who eventually reveal passionate sides to their chilly and haughty personalities, Birkin also made herself a name in the French comic tradition, cultivating the double image of the tomboy and nymphet, a provocative, yet gawky young gamine famous for her humorous qualities. In the comedy *Trop jolies pour être honnêtes*, the story of four young women who try to steal a criminal gang's loot, she provides levity as a counterpoint to the other girls. In one scene in particular, set in a nightclub, as the girls are chatting and dancing with the criminals, bespectacled Birkin is shown grooving to the music on her own, playing the clown by making funny faces while her legs are moving frenetically to the music.

In the mid-1960s, according to Marianne Thesander, the cult of youth brought a change of fashion ideal, moving from the very curvaceous feminine ideal of the 1950s (c. 1947–1964), to the physically desexualized, pubescent body (c. 1965–1978): 'the new fashion ideal was a thin, little-girl type without any obvious female characteristics' (Thesander 1997: 189). For Dominique Veillon, the aesthetic models of femininity offered in French women's magazines in 1974 'oscillate between Catherine Deneuve (who is never copied but always admired), Jane Birkin, a few models and numerous anonymous women who are photographed in the street and project an image of the free woman' (Veillon 2000: 176). Deneuve's star image of the 1960s and 1970s epitomized the chic and glacial French *bourgeoise*, an intimidating, cool beauty with an ice maiden image (Vincendeau 2000: 196–214). In contrast with this dominant model of femininity, in most of her films throughout the 1970s, Birkin's image is that of an uninhibited and tomboyish young woman: childishly comfortable with her body. Her almost immature persona, shy, awkward and slightly dumb, at times projecting a hint of perversity, is unthreatening to the male gaze.

Even today, Birkin's stardom is still predicated to a large degree on an image of her perennial adolescence through her association with 1960s Swinging London, her image resting on the paradoxical initial combination of innocence and sexiness, on the opposition between the ingénue and the libertine. Although, in the 1980s, she would move 'from ingénue to fatal beauty' (Frois 1986) with her new career in auteur cinema, these elements are profoundly interwoven in all of her films of the 1960s and 1970s and have been the structuring principles of her subsequent stardom, within an intertextual interplay between the images projected by her work and her very public off-screen life. Indeed, the condensation of contradictory desires and anxieties inscribed on her body is perhaps summarized by Gabrielle Crawford's description of Birkin as '*a sexual icon without anything sexual*' (Crawford 2004: 5, emphasis in text). The sexualized woman-child has long been a fixture in patriarchal fantasy, embodying the desired yet contradictory identities of virginal innocence and adult sexuality. Simone de Beauvoir, writing about Brigitte Bardot, has noted what she called 'the Lolita syndrome', the sexualization of young women in post-war French culture, and linked it to the context of women beginning to enter the male world. The Lolita syndrome, she argues, was a way of reaffirming the myth of femininity as dangerous and enigmatic: 'The adult woman now inhabits the same world as the man, but the child-woman moves in a universe which he cannot enter. The age difference re-establishes between them the distance that seems necessary to desire' (de Beauvoir 1960: 10).

Birkin's embodiment of this particular form of femininity is highlighted in Roger Vadim's *Don Juan 73*, in which she is cast against Brigitte Bardot. Here, she is braless and wears unisex jeans, projecting an unthreatening image of femininity as opposed to Bardot's experienced, confident and desiring persona. Bardot's pronounced bust and hips, overtly sexual mouth and eyes and accentuated make-up signify an explicit sexuality quite at odds with Birkin's slenderness and the lack of curves that had become a new body type and a reconfiguration of the feminine ideal, and watching the contrast between the two women, one can understand Ginette Vincendeau's claim that Bardot lost her appeal in this permissive age (2000: 92). The high premium placed on the vulnerability of Birkin's persona shows how this value functions at a time of theoretical but not actual equality between men and women. Her androgynous physical allure and foreign accent that gave all of her sentences the awkwardness of a child learning to speak and a resulting sense of fragility were accentuated in most of her films and records of the 1960s and 1970s, with the films playing on her marked English accent as source of comedy. In this dialectical tension between old and new models of femininity, her cultural Otherness is contained and neutralized into a submissive and thus unthreatening exotic glamour.

Birkin was, of course, famously involved with Serge Gainsbourg, with whom she formed *the* French couple of the time. The Birkin-Gainsbourg axis was part of the configuration of her legend, a public image defined by its fashionable eroticism through its notorious duet 'Je t'aime, moi non plus'. This massive international commercial success caused a scandal when it was released, was banned in many countries and thus benefited from a huge amount of publicity. The pair became France's most scandalous couple of the late 1960s and 1970s and their relationship the subject of intense media scrutiny. They appeared constantly on television shows, in the popular press and in illustrated gossip magazines such as *Jour de France* or *Paris-Match*. They were the subject of innumerable articles and interviews, thus multiplying the opportunities for the mediation of Birkin's image. The off-screen couple became a sociocultural phenomenon emblematic of the sexual revolution at a time when cinema as well as culture was becoming much more sexually explicit and tinged with eroticism. As the singer Petula Clark remarked, Serge Gainsbourg 'used Jane's accent much more cleverly than mine … using this accent within an erotic context whereas before English had been associated with good taste, old ladies who drink tea' (Lenne 1996: 33). Their soft-porn duet and the subsequent release of the single '*69 année érotique / 69 Erotic Year*', tapped into the zeitgeist, turning Birkin into an international sex symbol while at the same time consolidating her paradoxical image as a wild but fragile young woman who is totally devoted to one man, thus offering a reassuring image of monogamous female sexuality: a wife, mother and homemaker. This paradox can be linked to stardom's perceived negotiation of a culture's contradictions within the context of the transformation of the family in the 1970s and, with the various crises that hit its institution through divorce, abortion, women's rights and the increasing availability of contraception and so on, to a reaffirmation of its importance to the nation and its history (Mazdon 2001).

It is hard not to use the Pygmalion and muse metaphor when writing of Birkin and Gainsbourg, a metaphor that Gainsbourg widely publicized in the deliberate making of a mythical identity (Birkin in Simmons 2002: 87). But as Marie-Dominique Lelièvre has noted, 'for Gainsbourg, who perpetually needed to renew himself, women are his liaison officers, his data bank and his style bureau' (Lelièvre 2008: 103). The middle-aged Frenchman's association with a young British woman, the epitome of fashionable modernity, thus also enabled his persona to effect a transition and to remain in tune with the most up-to-date youth culture. In the late 1960s and 1970s, eroticism was an essential component of their public image, playing on the juxtaposition of their ages and nationalities: 'On television, they came to represent a hedonistic conception of the family, founded on equality between partners and the search for pleasure' (Lelièvre 2008: 128).

So the sexuality of this young British woman is contained through her association with an older French man and Birkin is just as *les petites anglaises* should be: cherubic with a hint of perversity. In her introduction to this collection Lucy Mazdon cites Robert and Isabelle Tombs's claim that, 'for the French, the British are not much good at straight sex, kinkiness is their forte' (Tombs and Tombs 2006: 642). The combination of the subversive values of both Birkin's films and songs and the paradoxical ultrarespectability of her monogamous lifestyle with Gainsbourg seems to have mesmerized the public. There was also a certain amount of fascination with the fact that this sexual icon for a new generation had emerged from long-standing perceptions of ultrarespectable and repressed Albion. According to François Crouzet, because of the special relationship which has existed between France and England, 'each country has occupied a special place in the consciousness of the other, serving to represent the quintessential foreigner, in relation to which one's identity could be defined' (Crouzet 1990: 465). French images of the British, according to Crouzet, 'have often been characterized by a Manichean vision, hence the binary nature of stereotypes and the notion of an "English mystery", which tended to disconcert the French, in general unable to attribute to their neighbours a dominant quality which would resolve these contradictions' (Crouzet 1990: 479).

Hence despite its seeming sexual liberation, the Birkin–Gainsbourg couple appeared as a model of traditional gender roles, expressing the double bind facing women within the confines of French society: on the one hand, their supposed accession to sexual autonomy and pleasure and on the other, their continuing definition through acceptable cultural models. Christine Bard has suggested that sexual liberalism did not necessarily lead to emancipation and that as sexuality was being redefined within an emerging discourse positing sexual fulfilment as key to psychological well being, many men saw a sexually liberated woman as a woman sexually available to them. Indeed, in many of her films, Birkin seems to embody the idea that 'a liberated woman is a woman who is sexually available' (Bard 1999: 310). In the 1970s, Birkin's sexy image was reinforced when she was photographed nude (often by Gainsbourg) for the cover of *Lui* and *Playboy* magazine, forging an often sadomasochistic image in line with French stereotypes of the British as peculiar about sex (in a feature entitled 'Birkin in bondage', she is handcuffed, gagged, and apparently whipped and beaten). Birkin thus does not escape the status of object: vulnerable and exposed, her disempowered state makes her more attractive 'in a cultural environment attached to a libertine tradition spontaneously thought of as egalitarian and refusing to establish any link between sexual violence enacted on the bodies of women and that, from eroticism to pornography, takes pleasure in imagining sadism as masculine and masochism as feminine' (Bard 1999: 310). As an exotic sexual icon linked to sweetness and innocence, Birkin's model of femininity is a highly paradoxical construct that is inseparable from the gender politics of a time when traditional ideals of femininity are being questioned and masculinity is in a state of anxiety.

Birkin's iconic association with Gainsbourg can also be seen in the light of the representation of paternal seduction resonant in French culture at large (in Doillon's 1981 *La Fille prodigue / The Prodigal Daughter* and Marion Hänsel's 1985 *Dust*, she plays a daughter in love with her father), a master-narrative going back to the eighteenth-century fairy tale *La Belle et la bête* (Vincendeau 1992: 14–17). Although she would never become his muse, Brigitte Bardot had also had a relationship with Gainsbourg; in a renewal of the pairing of beauty and the beast, they recorded several duets together. This dynamic was repeated with Birkin. Inspired by surrealism (especially Salvador Dali), hence his Anglophilia and his preoccupation with the notion of Eros and Thanatos, the figure of the Lolita was one of Gainsbourg's main obsessions. Birkin is the perfect expression of his fascination with the surrealist's flower-woman, playing on their twenty-year age difference and on the master-slave narrative. On the cover of *Histoire de Melody Nelson*, Gainsbourg's concept album of 1971 about the love affair between a middle-aged Frenchman and an under-age English girl, Birkin is an object of sexual innocence, a waif-like girl clutching a rag doll to her naked breast. On record, her breathy, whispery, child-like voice is linked to a body whose androgynous appearance is associated with adolescent femininity rather than womanhood, a child-woman who, in true Surrealist fashion, is perverted by an older master before coming to her death. This configuration would also be the main motif of Gainsbourg's first film as a director, *Je t'aime, moi non plus / I Love You, I Don't* (1975), with Birkin in the role of Johnny Jane, the androgynous young girl who is victim of her infatuation with a gay man played by Joe Dalessendro.

Yet despite the grim sexual politics of what Ginette Vincendeau has described as an 'all too French' master-narrative (Vincendeau 1992), Birkin nevertheless emerged as an immensely popular actress. Thus, while she was Gainsbourg's muse and he her Pygmalion, Birkin was forging herself a successful career as a film actress, especially, as stated, in comedy: one of the most popular French cinematic genres, yet one that has been an almost exclusively a male preserve. Though male rather than female stars tend to work consistently within comedy, Birkin's work in the genre made her popular with a family audience. Comedy is also a male domain in terms of stars and actors; women in comedy are often physically grotesque, ridiculous and generally made ugly. So arguably, as Lucien Rioux has noted, during the first phase of her French cinematic career, Birkin breaks the mould (Rioux 1988: 81).

Birkin's career eventually seems to have eclipsed Gainsbourg's. She often featured on the cover of magazines, even when appearing in what mainstream film critics deemed forgettable films, while her performance was often noted in the films she appeared in and critics praised her comedic skills. This is especially true with regards to the comedies in which she was typecast at the cute, kooky girl with the funny English accent, films that were often a big hit with French audiences.

As we have seen, in the late 1960s and 1970s, Birkin's image perpetually oscillated between vulnerability and fragility, ingenuity and eroticism. But the ultimate dimension that made her image exceptional were the funny connotations of her English accent and her specific use of the French language, what Gérard Lenne has called '*le birkinien*', a language where 'slang, highly literary expressions and Anglo-French neologisms are mixed in all innocence' (Lenne 1996: 7). French directors have long been keen on the marked accented language of beautiful foreign actors and actresses such as Victoria Abril, Anna Karina, Jean Seberg, Romy Schneider and Sergi Lopez, to name but a few. This is perhaps, as Michel Chion has argued, a way to offset the general scarcity of regional and local accents in French cinema (Chion 2008: 17), that often connote the popular and perhaps by extension a kind of vulgarity which is the Other of 'classical' French language.

The singularity of Birkin's persona, then, was constituted in no small manner by her British accent. Thus, unlike Rampling and Scott-Thomas, her kind of enunciation mixed with humour connoted a slightly different kind of Britishness, one that is accessible, in contrast to one that is cold, distant and intimidating. For instance, in the self-reflexive popular success *La Moutarde me monte au nez / Lucky Pierre* (1974), she plays a glamorous film star, yet she is also candid and funny and thus attainable for Pierre Richard's character who, in counterpoint to Birkin's star persona of the story, plays a clumsy and distracted maths teacher.

After the success of *La Moutarde me monte au nez* Birkin increasingly moved away from her provocative roles of the 1970s to work in more family-friendly comedies. Indeed, many critics complained about Gainsbourg's presence in films billed primarily as vehicles for Birkin, such as *Les Chemins de Katmandou, Cannabis, Trop jolies pour être honnêtes, Le Voleur de chevaux / Romance of a Horsethief* (1971) and *Sérieux comme le plaisir*. As one critic put it: 'It is impossible to see Jane on the screen without having to suffer Serge Gainsbourg and his music' (Duran 1969). Alternating work in comedies and small auteur films, throughout the 1970s and 1980s, Birkin was extremely in demand as an actress. She also appeared in both European and international coproductions, for instance, Italian Gothic horror movies such as *La Morte negli occhi del gatto / Seven Deaths for the Cat's Eye / Les Diablesses* (1973), *Death on The Nile* (1978) and *Evil Under the Sun* (1982).

Gradually freeing herself from the constraints imposed by the stereotype of the ethereal, young English girl with a funny accent, the mid-1980s marked a turning point in Birkin's career. Her image shifted with her acclaimed performances in the auteur cinema of Jacques Doillon, Bertrand Tavernier, Jacques Rivette, Agnès Varda and others, whilst continuing to appear in light comedies such as Patrice Leconte's *Circulez y'a rien à voir* (1983) or *Le Garde du corps* (François Leterrier, 1984), pursuing her 'parallel' career as a singer (and winning the prestigious Grand Prix de l'Académie Charles-Cros award with the title track of her 1984 album *Baby Alone in Babylone*), and making her first foray onto the French stage with Patrice Chéreau's version of Marivaux's classical play *La Fausse suivante* in 1985, which she followed with Josiane Balasko's *L'Ex femme de ma vie*, which ran at the *Théâtre du Spendid* during 1989. In 1992, Birkin also wrote and directed a full-length feature film for television, *Oh pardon tu dormais!* As a result of her extensive work in auteur cinema, Birkin acquired a certain cultural legitimacy, moving from the status of popular *vedette* to that of 'serious' actress, becoming, as *Cahiers du cinéma* put it, 'one of the rare French actresses capable of carrying a film' (Philippon 1984: 16). More recently, films by women such as *Reines d'un jour / A Hell of a Day* (2001), *Mariées mais pas trop / The Very Merry Widows* (2003), where she is reunited with Pierre Richard, and *La Tête de maman / In Mom's Head* (2007), where she appears as herself, have enlarged her range of feminine roles within a cinema that traditionally favours young actresses. In the comedy *Mariées mais pas trop*, for instance, she plays a deadly femme fatale, a serial widow and a grandmother.

Conclusion

Though still often described as an eternal adolescent despite the inevitable change that ageing brings, in 2006 the twenty-eighth Créteil International Women's Film Festival honoured Birkin's cinematic career with a special retrospective. In 2007, *Boxes*, her first film for cinema, was released, a largely autobiographical text exploring the mother–daughter relationship and the nature of memory. Jane Birkin remains a popular recording star and has just released a new album, *Enfants d'hivers*, her debut as a songwriter. While working again with Claude Zidi and Jacques Rivette, she also appears in Agnès Varda's latest film, *Les Plages d'Agnès / The Beaches of Agnès* (2008). Through her film work, but also her range of other activities and her upholding of the legacy of Gainsbourg, Birkin has remained in the public eye. Although her stardom was predicated to a large degree on her embodying and her performing of Britishness, providing an anchor point for the construction of national identity, she has graduated from exotic element to the status of French cultural institution. Birkin's image thus brings out the heterogeneous and hybrid nature of 'Frenchness', a signalling of 'overlay, difference, of new formations of the national ... pointing out to the masquerade of nationness' (Perriam 2005: 40, 43). She may thus be seen as an iconic example of the fabricated, performative nature of gender and the national, of the diversity of French identity and of a new negotiation of the nation. Migrants, 'wandering people who will not be contained with the *heim* of the national culture and its unisonant discourse', as Homi Bhabha has observed, are 'the marks of a shifting boundary that alienates the frontiers of the modern nation'. They become a 'mobile army of metaphors, metonyms and anthropomorphisms', Bhabha contends, as 'they articulate the death-in-life of the idea of the imagined community of the nation' (Bhabha 1990: 314–5, emphasis in text). Birkin's persona can be seen, then, to function as a hybrid that 'challenges the separatedness of cultures' (Marks 2000: xii), a connective conduit of Anglo-French intermingling, undercutting notions of cultural origins.

Birkin's immutable accent, the myths and types attached to her voice, her looks and gestures on screen, as well as her signature style of men's slacks and blue jeans, ample cashmere jumpers, oversized jackets and trainers, have also created an iconic and fashionable image of femininity. This figure speaks of a kind of chic and bohemian effortless elegance, for whom the fashion house Hermès created a much coveted luxury handbag. Her gamine and tomboyish fashion style still appeals, especially in France where ultrafemininity is often required of women. She thus seems to provide a model of androgyny 'with which women, often uncomfortable with their own bodies, may identify, and thus imaginatively escape the myriad images of ultra femininity constantly held up to them by our culture' (Modleski 1991: 102).

Jane Birkin's cross-national trajectory and the practice of cultural blending to which it attests, as this discussion has endeavoured to illustrate, offers compelling historical articulations of Franco-British cinematic relations and of the inherent tensions and contradictions of cross-cultural encounters. No discussion of Franco-British intercultural contact would be complete without reference to her: the embodiment of a form of border crossing that offers up a paradigm of transcultural conjunction and hybridity.

Notes

I would like to acknowledge the assistance of the London Metropolitan HALE Research Fund for generously providing funding to support the research for this chapter. All translations from the French are mine.

Bibliography

Bard, C. (ed.). 1999. *Un Siècle d'antiféminisme*. Paris: Fayard.
Bhabha, H. 1990. *Nation and Narration*. London and New York: Routledge.
Chion, M. 2008. *Le Complexe de Cyrano: La Langue parlée dans les films français*. Paris: Editions Cahiers du cinéma.
Crawford, G. 2004. *Jane Birkin*. Paris: Flammarion.
Crouzet, F. 1990. *Britain Ascendant: Comparative Studies in Franco-British Economic History*. Cambridge: Cambridge University Press.
Daninos, P. 1954. *Les Carnets du Major Thompson*. Paris: Hachette.
de Beauvoir, S. 1960. *Brigitte Bardot and the Lolita Syndrome*. New York: Reynal & Company Inc.
Duran, M. 1969. '*Les Chemins de Katmandou*', *Le Canard enchaîné*, 1 October 1969.
Dyer, R. 1987. *Heavenly Bodies: Film Stars and Society*. London: Macmillan Education.
Flitterman-Lewis, S. 1996. *To Desire Differently: Feminism and the French Cinema*. New York: Columbia University Press.
Frois, E. 1986. 'Jane Birkin: De l'ingénue à la beauté fatale', *Le Figaro*, 8 October 1986.
Garson, C. '*La Piscine*', *L'Aurore*, 28 January 1969.
Gledhill, C. and G. Swanson (eds). 1996. *Nationalising Femininity: Culture, Sexuality and British Cinema in the Second World War*. Manchester: Manchester University Press.
Green, J. 1999. *All Dressed Up: The Sixties and the Counterculture*. London: Pimlico.
Lelièvre, M-D. 2008. *Gainsbourg sans filtre*. Paris: Flammarion.
Lemonnier, B. 2004. 'La Culture pop britannique dans la France des années 60, entre rejet et fascination', in L. Bonnaud (ed.), *France-Angleterre: un siècle d'entente cordiale*. Paris: Harmattan, pp. 195–216.

Lenne, G. 1996. *Jane Birkin: La Ballade de Jane B.* Paris: Hors Collection.

Marks, L.U. 2000. *The Skin of the Film: Intercultural Cinema, Embodiment and the Senses.* Durham and London: Duke University Press.

Martin, M. '*La Piscine* de Jacques Deray', *Les Lettres françaises*, 5 January 1969.

Mazdon, L. 2001. 'Contemporary French Television, the Nation and the Family: Continuity and Change', *Television & New Media* 2(4): 335–49.

Modleski, T. 1991. *Feminism Without Women: Culture and Feminism in a Post-Feminist Age.* London: Routledge.

Perriam, C. 2005. 'Two Transnational Spanish Stars: Antonio Banderas and Penélope Cruz', *Studies in Hispanic Cinema* 2(1): 29–45.

Philippon, A. 1984. 'Allers et retours d'une enfant prodigue', *Cahiers du cinéma* 359: 15–17.

Radner, H. 1999. 'Introduction: Queering the Girl', in H. Radner and M. Luckett (eds), *Swinging Single: Representing Sexuality in the 1960s.* Minneapolis and London: University of Minnesota Press, pp. 1–35.

Rioux, L. 1988. *Jane Birkin.* Paris: Seghers.

Simmons, S. 2002. *Serge Gainsbourg: A Fistful of Gitanes.* London: Helter Skelter Publishing.

Tachin, A. 2006. 'La Grande-Bretagne dans l'imaginaire français à l'époque gaullienne', *Revue historique* 638(2): 335–54.

Thesander, M. 1997. *The Feminine Ideal.* London: Reaktion Books.

Thomann, J.P. 1979. *Jane Birkin.* Paris: Pac.

Tombs, I. and R. Tombs 2006. *That Sweet Enemy: The French and the British from the Sun King to the Present.* London: William Heinemann.

Veillon, D. 2000. 'Corps, beauté, mode et modes de vie: du « plaire au plaisir » à travers les magazines féminins (1958–1975)', in G. Dreyfus-Armand, R. Frank, M. Lévy and M. Zancarini-Fournel (eds), *Les Années 68: Le Temps de la contestation.* Paris: Editions Complexes, pp. 161–77.

Vincendeau, G. 1992. 'Family Plots: The Fathers and Daughters of French Cinema', *Sight and Sound* 11(1): 14–17.

———. 2000. *Stars and Stardom in French Cinema.* London and New York: Continuum.

Wimmer, L. 2009. *Cross-Channel Perspectives: The French Reception of British Cinema.* Oxford: Peter Lang.

Filmography

A nous les petites anglaises / *Let's Get Those English Girls.* 1975, Michel Lang, France.

Blow Up. 1967, Michelangelo Antonioni, U.K.

Boîtes, Les / *Boxes.* 2007, Jane Birkin, France.

Cannabis / *French Intrigue.* 1970, Pierre Koralnik, France/West Germany/Italy.

Catherine et Cie / *Catherine and Co.* 1975, Michel Boisrond, France/Italy.

Chemins de Katmandou, Les / *The Road to Katmandou.* 1969, André Cayatte, France.

Circulez y'a rien à voir. 1983, Patrice Leconte, France.

Comment réussir… quand on est con et pleurnichard / *How to Make Good When You're a Jerk and a Crybaby.* 1974, Michel Audiard, France.

Death on the Nile. 1978, John Guillermin, U.K.

Don Juan 73. 1973, Roger Vadim, France/Italy.

Dust. 1985, Marion Hänsel, Belgium/France.

Evil Under the Sun. 1982, Guy Hamilton, U.K.

Fille Prodigue, La / *The Prodigal Daughter.* 1981, Jacques Doillon, France.

Garde du Corps, Le. 1984, François Leterrier, France.

Je t'aime, moi non plus / *I Love You, I Don't.* 1975, Serge Gainsbourg, France.

Knack, The. 1965, Richard Lester, U.K.

Mariées mais pas trop / *The Very Merry Widows.* 2003, Catherine Corsini, France/Belgium.

Morte negli occhi del gatto, La / *Seven Deaths in the Cat's Eye* / *Les Diablesses.* 1973, Antonio Margheriti, France/Italy/West Germany.

Moutarde me monte au nez, La / *Lucky Pierre.* 1974, Claude Zidi, France.

Mouton enragé, Le / *Love at the Top.* 1974, Michel Deville, France/Italy.

Piscine, La / *Sinners.* 1969, Jacques Deray, France/Italy.

Plages d'Agnès, Les / *The Beaches of Agnès.* 2008, Agnès Varda, France.

Oh pardon tu dormais!. 1992, Jane Birkin, France / Switzerland.

Reines d'un jour / *A Hell of a Day.* 2001, Marion Vernoux, France.

Sérieux comme le plaisir / *Serious as Pleasure.* 1975, Robert Benayoun, France.

Slogan. 1968, Pierre Grimblat, France.

Tête de maman, La / *In Mom's Head.* 2007, Carine Tardieu, France.

Trop jolies pour être honnêtes / *Too Pretty to be Honest.* 1972, Richard Balducci, France/Italy.

Voleur de chevaux, Le / *Romance of a Horsethief.* 1971, Abraham Polonsky, Yugoslavia/France/U.S.A.

Wonderwall. 1968, Joe Massot, U.K.

CHAPTER 16

The French Resistance Through British Eyes: From *'Allo 'Allo!* to *Charlotte Gray*

Ginette Vincendeau

Few historical events have connected France and Great Britain so intimately but also so vexedly as the Second World War and the Resistance, both in real life and in the cinema. While the two countries went their radically different ways – Britain heroically resisting, France crushingly defeated and occupied – during this period myriad events brought the two countries closer to each other than at any other time. General de Gaulle's Free French Government set up in London generated a steady stream of French visitors to England and in return prompted Resistance activities on French soil; RAF planes flew back and forth dropping people and equipment over French territory and ferrying Resistants back to England; the coded messages of the BBC's '*Radio Londres*' became the ubiquitous soundtrack of the Resistance; the different sections of the military and intelligence services (the Special Operations Executive (SOE) in the U.K., the BCRA in France)[1] were involved in a dense network of secret missions. These Franco-British activities were a boost to victory, but also the source of rivalry and suspicion. As historians have shown, on the one hand French Resistance activities were eyed – at best – with weariness in Britain, and on the other hand British support was always seen to be wanting from the French point of view, while allied bombings in France caused damage and resentment.

These Channel criss-crossings naturally made their way into film. During the war in Britain and after the Liberation in France, the Resistance became a key topic, one which indeed provides a transnational motif in European cinema (Sorlin 1991: 52–80). Much has been written on both sides of the Channel about the representation on screen of these events. Historians of the Second World War and the Resistance such as Rod Kedward (1985 and 1993), Henry Rousso (1991) and Julian Jackson (2001) have examined at length the events and their legacy, especially on the French side, and touched on their media representation. Historians of French film under the German occupation, such as Jacques Siclier (1981), Evelyn Ehrlich (1985) and Jean-Pierre Bertin-Maghit (1989), have charted the cinema of the period, while Sylvie Lindeperg in her book *Les Écrans de l'ombre* (1997) has explored in depth the changing representation of the Resistance in French cinema until the late 1960s. The work of key directors and key films focusing on this period has also given rise to many studies, such as, among others, Judith Mayne on Henri-Georges Clouzot's *Le Corbeau* (2007), Kedward (2000) and Jacqueline Nacache (2008) on *Lacombe Lucien* and my own work on Jean-Pierre Melville (2003). On the British side, Antonia Lant (1991), Robert Murphy (2000), and Anthony Aldgate and Jeffrey Richards (2007), to name the most prominent, have studied British wartime cinema and British films' subsequent representation of the period.

I do not intend to revisit these analyses here, although I will inevitably refer to a number of them, as well as alluding to some of the classic Resistance films they focus on: *Against the Wind* (1948), *Odette* (1950) and *Carve Her Name with Pride* (1958) on the British side; *La Bataille du rail*, *Le Père tranquille*, *Jéricho* (all released in 1946) and *Le Silence de la mer* (1949) on the French side. Instead I shall turn to more recent cross-Channel work, namely two British productions that are entirely or almost entirely set in France: the notorious Resistance spoof television series *'Allo 'Allo!* and the 2001 film *Charlotte Gray*, based on Sebastian Faulks's 1998 eponymous novel. At first sight, this rapprochement between such different types of media products might seem surprising. However, within the overarching topic of this book, the desire to examine Resistance movies beyond French film prompted me to investigate whether common representations of the French Resistance from a British point of view could be identified across different aesthetic and ideological projects. In turn I am interested in how these might relate on the one hand to French views of the Resistance, and on the other hand to widely held notions and stereotypes of the French character in non-French productions.

From Burlesque to Heritage: Two Exemplary Resistance Texts

The BBC comic television series *'Allo 'Allo!* is one among several series revolving around the Second World War. It is the work of David Croft and Jeremy Lloyd, who also wrote and produced *Are You Being Served?* (a comic series set in a department store). In addition, Croft was involved, with Jimmy Perry, in the highly popular earlier series *Dad's Army*, about the Home Guard. *'Allo 'Allo!* is one of the longest running and most successful sitcoms in British television. It consists of eighty-five episodes of twenty-five or thirty minutes each in duration, spread across nine series between December 1982 and December 1992. In addition there was a stage show which toured several countries between 1986 and 1992, after fifteen 'record-breaking' months in London's West End (Search 1989: 12), a one-off reunion episode broadcast on 28 April 2007, and a range of merchandise. This included a cartoon, phone cards, a board game, a record of René and Yvette (Gorden Kaye, who

Figure 16.1: Gordon Kaye and Vicki Michelle in *'Allo 'Allo!* (1982–1992).
Image courtesy of the BFI stills department.

plays café owner René Artois, and Vicki Michelle, one of the waitresses) singing 'Je t'aime (allo allo)'[2] – a parody of Serge Gainsbourg and Jane Birkin's infamous song 'Je t'aime, moi non plus' – as well as two volumes of *The War Diaries of René Artois* (Haselden 1988 and 1989) and Gorden Kaye's *René & Me* (1989). *'Allo 'Allo!* was sold to fifty-six countries, including France (to the pay channel Canal +) and Germany. Series one to seven are available on DVD and there have been many reruns on cable and terrestrial channels. When Gorden Kaye was injured in an accident on 25 January 1990 and temporarily went into a coma, the event was treated as front-page national news by the British press.

Despite this extraordinary success, and the substantial pedigree of its writers and producers, *'Allo 'Allo!* has elicited revulsion from most critics – one typical remark ventured that, 'it is hard to find any saving grace in *'Allo 'Allo!*' (Morgan-Russell 2004: 49) – and there has been little attempt to reflect on its huge success. One exception is Andy Medhurst, who characterizes *'Allo 'Allo!*, not unreasonably, as 'politically incorrect, racist, homophobic, sexist, but very funny' (Medhurst 1988: 36). To my knowledge Medhurst is the only writer to engage properly with the series, that is to say as a piece of television that is *about* stereotypes, rather than simply complaining about its stereotypical nature. Nevertheless, he draws the line at the homophobia and I guess, taking a leaf from his book, I too will draw the line at certain French stereotypes. But more of this later.

Generically *'Allo 'Allo!* is a hybrid of at least three forms: first, the sitcom format, with its recurring characters and a narrative that embroiders on basic situations in a central studio-based location – here a café in occupied France; second, a Feydeau-like farce hinging on adultery, misunderstandings and mistaken identities, and third, a parody of earlier television programmes about the Second World War and the Resistance: in particular *Secret Army* (in which a café is also a key location) and *Dad's Army* (about the Home Guard), as well as a range of films. These include references to Conrad Veidt and allusions to Ernst Lubitsch's 1942 film *To Be or Not to Be*, perhaps *the* model for texts willing to joke about deadly serious Second World War issues ('So they call me Concentration Camp Ehrhardt?') as well as Michael Curtiz's 1942 film *Casablanca*. The nightclub run by Rick (Humphrey Bogart) in the latter film may be seen as a distant ancestor of René's café, and René's reluctance to take sides for the Resistance or Collaboration as a reference to Rick's famous motto, 'I stick my neck out for no one'.

As Medhurst says, *'Allo 'Allo!* is characterized by comprehensive derision. All recurrent characters are theatrically burlesque, with comic names like Yvette Carte-Blanche and Mimi La Bonq. Above all, the signature trait of the series is its use of caricatural accents – German, and especially French – by the British cast, working in tandem with the childish sexual innuendo of the dialogue (as in, 'I will give 'im one'; 'are you one of zem?' and so on). Central characters include two hopeless, upper-class British airmen (Fairfax and Carstairs), joined in the second series by an equally inept British officer, Crabtree, disguised as a *gendarme*; Crabtree is endowed with the most atrocious accent of all, and the source of one of the catchphrases of the series, 'Good moaning' (for 'Good morning'). Among the German characters there is the caricaturally sadistic Herr Flick of the Gestapo and Private Helga (both occasionally revealing kinky underwear); the genially ineffectual and corrupt German Colonel von Strohm and his sidekick, Captain Hans Geering, in pursuit of a painting of the 'fallen Madonna with the big boobies by Van Klomp' to be sent to Berlin; and the effete German Lieutenant Gruber. However, none are lampooned as much or as extensively as the French, if only because of the French setting and the fact that the French characters are more numerous. The 'hero' is René, a harassed, hen-pecked and womanizing café owner who alternates between reluctantly helping the Resistance and colluding with the Germans in exchange for black-market favours. He is surrounded by: his wife, Edith, who is 'ugly', bossy and an atrocious singer, Edith's senile mother, Fanny, permanently bed-ridden in the attic, and her elderly 'boyfriend', Monsieur Leclerc. Also prominent are the two 'naughty' waitresses, Yvette and Maria (later joined by Mimi), who are René's mistresses, and, last but not least, Michèle of the Resistance, the source of *the* most famous catchphrase from the series: 'Listen vairy cairefully, I will say zis only once'.

Directed in 2001 by Gillian Armstrong and starring Cate Blanchett and Billy Crudup, *Charlotte Gray* could hardly be more different. The high-profile international movie was a coproduction between the U.K., Australia and Germany; its crew included an Australian director, Australian and American lead players were surrounded by a mixed-nationality cast, and the film was largely shot on location in France. Nevertheless, *Charlotte Gray* has a firm British cultural identity derived from its source book, written by the British novelist Sebastian Faulks, and its topic – the story of a Scottish female Special Operations Executive (SOE) agent recruited by the British secret services for a mission to help the French Resistance. Despite this serious pedigree, the film relies on familiar types, less caricatural than in *'Allo 'Allo!*, yet nonetheless recognizable: the upper-class British SOE officers in London, the brutal German soldiers, the shifty French collaborationist, the bumbling gendarmes. While these are not presented as particularly comic, *Charlotte Gray* draws on them as stock characters, as well as on familiar narrative and iconographic motifs of the Resistance film (parachute drops, night-time landings, secret assignments, sabotage).

Despite Gillian Armstrong's assertion that she did not intend to produce a nostalgic view of the period, nor a film 'for women', *Charlotte Gray* fits within both the heritage genre and the romantic woman's picture. The film streamlines the book's narrative and set of characters, as is to be expected since Faulks's novel is long and detailed. But one of the key changes is the development of Charlotte's romantic involvements: first with Peter, an RAF pilot, and then with Julien, the local French Resistance leader. Moreover, shot in self-conscious heritage mode, on location in southwest France, *Charlotte Gray* displays a strong visual emphasis on period objects and especially costumes. Armstrong and the film's costume designer Janty Yates admit, for example, that Cate Blanchett's costumes were designed to fit their surroundings, especially the 'strong colours of the French countryside' (Armstrong 2002). It is also clear that at times visual design took precedence over verisimilitude; for instance, in the context of austerity-stricken occupied France, where there is no jam to put on children's bread, there are nevertheless ample opportunities to match Charlotte's

Figure 16.2: Cate Blanchett in *Charlotte Gray* (2001).
Image courtesy of the BFI stills department.

berets with the shades of her lipstick. Indeed, as Katja Hofmann put it, *Charlotte Gray* 'is a women's movie that seems to exist for its costumes' (Hofmann 2002: 10).

In their very different modes, *'Allo 'Allo!* and *Charlotte Gray* are thus united by the topic of the Resistance in occupied France, seen from an essentially British point of view, as well as by the cast of characters they draw on. Both were also made a considerable amount of time after the events. It is therefore interesting to look briefly at how they fit within the general pattern of films about the Resistance, on both sides of the Channel.

Unsurprisingly, while British cinema began to make films about contemporary events during the Second World War, such as *Pimpernel Smith* (1941) and *One of Our Aircraft Is Missing* (1942), the French could not, the film industry being under Vichy or German control (only coded and oblique representations of the times could get past the censors). In the immediate Liberation period a band of films exalting the glory of the Resistance was made, such as, as already mentioned, *La Bataille du rail, Jéricho, Le Père tranquille* and *Le Silence de la mer*. But with *Charlotte Gray* in mind, it is worth noting that whereas French films ignored or silenced women, the British movies of the 1940s and 1950s provided them with strong roles often based on real SOE activities – in particular *Odette, Against the Wind* and *Carve Her Name with Pride*. The Resistance disappeared from French screens in the 1950s, to flourish again when de Gaulle came to power in 1958, often in the form of gentle comedies in which, as Lindeperg discusses, initially mediocre characters became heroes almost accidentally (Lindeperg 1997: 363–74). This includes the Brigitte Bardot vehicle *Babette s'en va-t-en guerre* (1959) and one notable Anglo-French collaboration, the hugely successful *La Grande Vadrouille / Don't Look Now, We're Being Shot At* (1966). Generally absent from French screens were large-scale combat films such as those produced by British and U.S. cinema – for instance *The Guns of Navarone* (1961), *The Longest Day* (1962) and *A Bridge Too Far* (1977); *Paris brûle-t-il? / Is Paris Burning?* (1966) was a Franco-American coproduction.

The sway of the myth of the Resistance (in comic or serious mode) came to a brutal end in the early 1970s, when Marcel Ophuls's documentary *Le Chagrin et la Pitié / The Sorrow and the Pity* (1969) and Robert Paxton's book *Vichy France* (1972) opened the floodgates, revealing the less than glorious behaviour of a large section of the population. From then on, Vichy and collaboration came to the fore, famously fictionalized in Louis Malle's *Lacombe Lucien* (1974). There followed, in the 1980s, a period of cynicism and generalized derision, epitomized in France by the comedy *Papy fait de la résistance* (1983), while in the U.K., the series *'Allo 'Allo!* began. In the 1990s and 2000s, the challenging of the Resistance myth continued, finding its apotheosis in the film *Un héros très discret / A Self-made Hero* (1996), in which the Resistance has become a total fabrication. From a plethora of films portraying France as heroically resisting up to the early 1970s, films and television in France now depicted a dishonourable nation of collaborators. At the same time Jewish issues and especially the French responsibility in the 'final solution' increasingly took centre stage, as in Malle's *Au revoir les enfants* (1987). Finally, starting with François Truffaut's *Le Dernier Métro* (1980), the Second World War became a topic for heritage films, especially in France, with movies such as *Blanche et Marie* (1985), *Lucie Aubrac* (1997) and *Bon Voyage* (2003).

Interestingly, although made outside France, both *'Allo 'Allo!* and *Charlotte Gray* fit the wider trends characteristic of French depictions, attesting to the way these are determined not only by issues specifically located in the French past (the repression and retrieving of a shameful history) but also by wider, transnational issues – both historical (the querying of Resistance as a European rather than French phenomenon – see the Dutch film *Zwartboek / Black Book*, 2006) and cinematic, for instance the rise of the heritage film, with its dominant tropes of nostalgia and pastiche.

In this respect, *'Allo 'Allo!* is typical of the cynical derision of the 1980s in the way it reprises the motifs of earlier, serious films about the Resistance and turns them on their head. Parachute drops are botched and night-time aeroplane landings are used for absurd purposes (for instance, flying in a Savile Row tailor to France to take measurements for fake German uniforms); the Dunkirk episode is parodied in a series of increasingly ludicrous ways in which the British airmen attempt to cross the Channel; the clandestine radio is hidden in the mother-in-law's chamber pot and sabotage systematically misfires or hits the wrong target. Disguise and false identities are rampant and preposterous – in turn, all major characters are disguised, at some point, as German soldiers, French onion sellers, and Resistance women fighters. Courage and dignity become cowardice and abject corruption, while austerity and rationing are replaced by black-market indulgence.

If *'Allo 'Allo!* is typical of 1980s and 1990s indiscriminate ridicule, it nevertheless baulks at making fun of the Holocaust: the topic is virtually absent, except for the brief episode of the Savile Row tailor mentioned above. But in *Charlotte Gray* equally the emphasis on aesthetically pleasing surface cannot accommodate too much detail about the final solution. We witness the hiding of two Jewish boys, their arrest as well as the arrest of the older man with whom Charlotte hides (played by Michael Gambon), and we see them all being taken away by train. However, the film stops there and omits the horrific description of their plight in the death camps afterwards which is detailed in Faulks's novel.

Cross-Channel Stereotypes

'Allo 'Allo! and *Charlotte Gray* are thus products of their time, fitting both within French patterns of depiction of the Resistance and German occupation and within international modes of representation, in particular comic derision and the heritage genre. Yet at the same time their impact depends on their deployment of stereotypical visions of Frenchness seen from outside France. Indeed, in the piece cited above, Medhurst makes the point that the relentless bad taste and caricaturing of *'Allo 'Allo!* is intricately linked to its French setting:

> One reason why the series is such a success with British audiences is that it is all happening to the French. Not to gallant little Belgium, not to the Dutch (dangers here of stirring up Anne Frank connotations), but to our more traditionally abused neighbours – thus making available a whole repository of Francophobic humour, seized on by the writers with evident glee (Medhurst 1988: 36).

Sebastian Faulks, who signs his novel as written from Toulouse and London, made substantial research into French history, while Gillian Armstrong and her team took care to provide authentic detail, with location shooting, recourse to a local Resistance historian, Guillaume Agullo, and research into period costumes. And yet, fascinatingly, the image of the French Resistance in *Charlotte Gray* ends up as surprisingly close to that found in *'Allo, 'Allo!* in its adherence to stereotypes of Frenchness. To understand why this may be the case, we need to go back briefly into the history of the Franco-British relationship with regards to the Second World War and the Resistance.

Events connected to the Resistance during the German occupation of France appear to have exacerbated mutual Franco-British suspicion, starting with the notoriously stormy relationship between Winston Churchill and Charles de Gaulle, and aggravated by the attack on the French fleet by the Royal Navy at Mers-el-Kébir on 3 July 1940 and the Allied bombings over the French territory throughout the period. As Kedward argues, the existence of SOE networks whose task was to coordinate the French Resistance without reference to the Free French authorities also caused considerable tension and was perceived as a 'calculated insult' (Kedward 2004: 127). With notable exceptions (*Jéricho*, *L'Armée des ombres*, 1969) French films about the Resistance ignore or at best marginalize the substantial British participation in the Resistance, or complain of its limitations. Meanwhile British films relay a deep disappointment at the French collaborationist government and population and suspicion of the Resistance. Many heroic tales of SOE women in France were indeed told in *Odette*, *Against the Wind* and so on, but Robert Murphy also observes that during the war (as opposed to after) France tended to be ignored by British films about the topic, as opposed to Belgium, Poland or the Balkan countries (Murphy 2000: 102–103). And it is no accident that the more complimentary television series about the Resistance, *The Secret Army* (1977–1979), is set in Belgium.

'Allo 'Allo! and *Charlotte Gray*, if we abstract from their formal characteristics, are united in expressing derogatory views of the French Resistance. In doing so they have recourse to three main types of stereotypes of Frenchness, which, as we will see, echo wider stereotypes of France and the French, namely: France as a nation of cowards, France as a nation of peasants, and France as a nation of sex-obsessed, 'feminized' men.

The first of these stereotypes is the vision of France as a nation of cowards. In history books as in fictional representations, the crushing defeat of the French army in May/June 1940 became the ubiquitous motif of the 'Fall of France', in which the country not only collapsed from a military point of view but lapsed morally, prompting the need to be rescued by the U.K and U.S.A. After she has just been parachuted into France, Charlotte Gray acidly tells Julien, the Resistance leader, who speaks enthusiastically of fighting for a better future, that 'it would be a good idea to win the war first' – a line, incidentally, that does not appear in the book. Retrospectively, there is a tendency for the politics of prewar France to be seen as entirely characterized by fascism and anti-Semitism – and the politics and achievements of the Popular Front, for example, vanish. Similarly, the strong pacifist movement in the 1930s as a result of the World War I carnage that decimated rural France is perceived as weakness, or worse, cowardice. Although the military historian

Douglas Porch argues that 'the idea that France was too disorganized and defeatist to defend itself has been swept away' (Porch 2000: 160) and replaced by a longer-term understanding of French and British relative positions as declining colonial powers on the world stage, the view of France as a weak, cowardly and defeatist nation that brought defeat on to itself prevails.

Secondly, as historians such as Kedward and Jackson have shown in detail, the Resistance itself has been increasingly viewed with suspicion, that is when it is not deemed to have been simply useless. There is plenty of evidence that the population of occupied countries, including France, viewed Resistance activities with ambivalence, for reasons that ranged from fear for their safety to anticommunism, but in popular fiction, including *'Allo 'Allo!* and *Charlotte Gray*, this legitimate or at least understandable ambivalence becomes simply a sign of moral corruption.

According to Michael Gorman,

> Any student of British war films will soon learn that the British troops are portrayed as having respect for their German adversaries, whereas their French allies often provide the comic relief .... The British history and legends of the Second World War are full of negative images of the French. For every brave deed of the French resistance, there are stories of how 'stiff-necked' and 'difficult' the Free French and particularly Charles de Gaulle were, the craven behaviour of the Vichy French, and the cynicism of the likes of Captain Louis Renault in *Casablanca* (Gorman 2003: 9).

Consequently, in *'Allo 'Allo!*, René is the very image of cowardly French *attentisme* during the German occupation – always terrified, running away or physically cowering (he is literally often seen crouching, hiding under his bar), hen-pecked by wife and mother-in-law, in fear of the Germans, utterly devoid of bravery. One could cite many ways in which this is brought to the fore, but one particularly pertinent example is the episode that centres around a proposed duel with one of his wife's suitors, which he goes to incredible lengths to try and avoid.

At first sight, *Charlotte Gray* is, unsurprisingly, more nuanced, portraying a local Resistance group with whose leader, Julien, Charlotte falls in love. However, the only two actions we see the group of Resistants perform are either disastrous (an aeroplane landing) or semi-botched – a train sabotage which is, pointedly, done with Charlotte's help. The fact that the landing ends in disaster is due to London's political manipulation, but (unlike the book) the film does not make this clear to the spectator. Instead, we see Julien arriving too late and having to watch, helpless, his team mowed down by German machine guns; the image of the French Resistant is thus one of helplessness. True heroism, as in earlier classics like *Odette*, is embodied by the British heroine. She is the one who takes action, the one who truly 'resists'.

If France is seen as a nation of cowards in these two texts, it is also viewed as a nation of peasants. Indeed, in *'Allo 'Allo!*, the standard reprisal for any attack on the Germans is 'shoot ten peasants' or 'shoot twenty-five peasants', and a favourite disguise is that of the onion seller, with berets on their heads and strings of onions round their necks. In *Charlotte Gray*, the novel, the first mention of a French person is of an unkempt 'peasant'. It is revealing in this respect that novel and film are firmly anchored in rurality, whereas the main centres of Resistance until the end of the war (the book is set in 1942/3) were in cities, in particular Paris, Lyon and Marseille. This feature in any case is too ubiquitous to be a simple factual point about large numbers of French people living in the country. Something else is going on.

As a result of its long history as a rural nation, France has derived a countrified image, especially compared to urbanized Britain. From here it is a small step to a stereotypical view of France as a preindustrial country. This has negative connotations in foregrounding a backward image, divorced from any factual evidence about the achievements of French technology in areas such as, among others, medicine, nuclear energy and transport. Instead bad sanitation and dirty farmyards are stressed. The survival of this stereotype has been reinforced in a more positive light, through tourism, cookery writers extolling the virtues of French country cooking (from Elizabeth David and Jane Grigson to Rick Stein) and the widespread phenomenon of British people buying second homes or moving to France, mostly the rural west and south, where they do up picturesque ruins and eschew modern housing.

Charlotte Gray evidently cashes in on this with its setting in the pretty small town of Saint-Antonin Noble-Val in the Quercy area near Toulouse in southwest France, idyllically situated on the Aveyron river, among spectacular mountains (different from that of the book, which takes place in less picturesque Ussel and Clermont-Ferrand). The film thus feeds elegiac views of the French countryside as a leisure playground for the British middle classes. Gillian Armstrong speaks of the visual impact she wanted to create by showing German tanks running through the medieval streets of a 'typical' French village (Armstrong 2002), and many views in the film, including of the aesthetically decrepit *manoir* in which Michael Gambon's character lives, are straight out of a tourist brochure. The opening and closing images of the film make this point even more clearly, shot over lavender fields which are not, of course, native to the south west, but to Provence in the south east, the other major tourist location in the French countryside – as seen in Peter Mayle's book *A Year in Provence* (1989) and its 1993 television adaptation, and, more recently, *Mr Bean's Holiday* (2007) and Ridley Scott's *A Good Year* (2006), all of which feature Anglo-American stars but cast French characters as scruffy peasant extras (with the exception of Marion Cotillard in *A Good Year*). This portrayal of France as a backward, preindustrial country relates to the topic of the Resistance as it feeds the image of French ineptitude during the Second World War due to its lack of military heavy equipment (tanks, aeroplanes). This is seen as the main reason for the fall of France, in contrast to German tanks and British aeroplanes, as well as transmission technology – thus Charlotte Gray's only actual mission in the film is to deliver quartz for radio transmissions, a mission botched by her *French* contact (unlike in the book).

Of the various British stereotypes of the French, their reputation as immoral and over-sexed is probably the oldest, and the most enduring, cliché of all. Richard Abel in *The Red Rooster Scare* (1999) shows how, from the very beginning, French films were perceived in the U.S.A. as propagating an image of immoral conduct and debauchery. Fast forward to more recent times, and see Julie Delpy's *2 Days in Paris* (2007), in which she portrays her own French parents as over-sexed gluttons. Mark Twain's remark that 'there is but one love which a Frenchman places above his country, and that is his love for another man's wife' (in Rosenthal 1999: 901) could have served as inspiration for the character of René in *'Allo 'Allo!* The series is littered with jokes, such as 'only the French would have boys and girls in the same jail', while in one episode women sacrifice their silk knickers to make parachutes. In such a satirical series as *'Allo 'Allo!* such sexual stereotyping may appear very banal. Yet it is worth exploring a little further in relation to the Resistance.

In *'Allo 'Allo!* two things are striking. On the one hand there are no *young* French men – most (like René) are in late middle age or very old, like Monsieur Leclerc, Edith's suitor, and the customers in the background at the café. On the other hand, the Resistance is entirely represented by women. At the beginning of one episode in the second series, René enthuses wistfully about how wonderful it is that all the members of the Resistance are 'girls' with berets and little white socks and several scenes show them as a group of identically clad young women, in trench-coat, beret and, indeed, little white socks, pouting in red lipstick and kissing each other. It is no accident that at one point René is disguised as one of these women. In *Charlotte Gray*, Julien is good-looking and young but, as already mentioned, he is ultimately weak and ineffectual. When things come to the crunch, he is more concerned with saving his skin, whereas Charlotte bravely faces terrifying odds. One scene towards the end of the film makes this point vividly, especially as it takes place in a dramatic setting. Just after his own father and the two Jewish boys he was hiding have been arrested, Julien meets Charlotte at a small chapel on top of a hill with spectacular panoramic views. He tries to convince her to escape through the Pyrénées. Despite his entreaties, she decides to stay, at the risk of facing arrest. Although Julien's plan is sensible, since their Resistance network has just been blown, his haste in wanting to leave (enhanced by the fact that his friends in the car are getting impatient) looks like cowardice, while her stern resolve looks like courage rather than foolhardiness. We next see her in Julien's father's mansion holding a terrified gendarme at gunpoint.

The gender formation I have just outlined is the exact reversal of French Resistance films in which the Resistant is invariably portrayed as a virile young man wearing a leather jacket (this, in turn, has been caricatured in several films, such as in *Un héros très discret*). As analysed by Noël Burch and Geneviève Sellier (1996), the actual and symbolic blow to French masculinity dealt by the Fall of France is thereby exorcised, as it is also by the post-Liberation savage targeting of women who were deemed guilty of sleeping with the enemy, the *femmes tondues*. In *'Allo 'Allo!* Yvette and Maria, René's pouting waitresses, are forever performing jolly *collaboration horizontale* with the German officers in return for butter, eggs and paraffin. The fact that this is done with René's blessing, not to say encouragement, further underlines the point that from a British point of view, not only are French women guilty of sexual collaboration but by extension so are the men. This is also the point, within the series' homophobic sense of humour, of René being the object of Lieutenant Gruber's desire.

The accent on cowardice and lack of virility of French men in the Resistance fits also within more pervasive stereotypes of French men as 'feminized' by their excessive pursuit of sex and hedonism. In a study of gender-coded stereotypes of France and the French from an American point of view, Alan S. Rosenthal makes the following observation, which is worth quoting in full:

> For France as a country and a culture, the characterization is overwhelmingly feminine, so much so that even the masculinity of French men is open to question by more than a few Americans. There is evidence of a popular notion in the United States that France has qualities and faults that are 'characteristic' of the female gender and that compromise the virility of its men. There is evidence also that this perception owes much to the British view of the French, their traditional rivals, and is thus part of a heritage that goes back to the Middle Ages (Rosenthal 1999: 897).

This 'feminization' of the Frenchman derives from the association of France with luxury products (food, drink, perfume, fashion), with the refinements of culture, with frivolity and, paradoxically, then with sexuality. The French sociologist Michéle Sarde says of foreigners' views of Frenchmen: 'It is as if the Frenchman who so likes to pursue women is in turn contaminated by femininity' (Sarde 1983: 24). Thus relentless feminine conquest does not prove virility but on the contrary becomes evidence of weakness and feminization, as in the cases of René and Julien – in the case of the latter it is worth noting that in Faulks's novel, Charlotte is merely his friend (although they sleep together once), and that she goes back to her British first love. This gives Julien at first sight more importance in the film, especially in the climactic 'happy ending' (shot twice by Armstrong, with and without a kiss); however, as in the scene on the mountain top described above, his role as object of desire of a strong heroine could be seen also to 'weaken' him, and it is certainly the way the performances balance out, with Cate Blanchett more forceful (and of higher star status) than Billy Crudup.

It is relevant to the argument here that the male characters' feminization especially weakens masculinity in a war context, and therefore is part and parcel of the perceived lack, on the part of the French, of courage and prowess within the Resistance – reinforcing in turn the virility of both the Germans and the saviours, the Allies. It is true that in *'Allo 'Allo!* the British airmen are farcical upper-class idiots, but the humour concerns their class identity rather than their sexuality or their nationality as a whole. Crucially too, the parody has no real bite; it is literally 'harmless fun', since it is balanced by the knowledge of the heroic behaviour of the RAF in real life. Similarly the caricatural Germans exist, as representations, against the knowledge of other, more virile, images of German conquest, action and efficiency. On the other hand the French 'sissiness' can be, and is, equated with the actual behaviour of French soldiers during the Second World War, a myth more recently revived by the war in Iraq. As Gorman again puts it:

The British government (if not the British people) took the side of the US and participated in the invasion of Iraq while the French government and people opposed it. It was all too easy for the British gutter press to write about 'surrender monkeys' and portray Chirac as a latter-day Pétain (Gorman 2003: 9–10).

As if we needed further proof of how deeply entrenched this attitude is, in a January 2009 article about Czech artist David Cerny's controversial sculpture *Entropa*, representing the EU as a map of Europe with each nation bearing a national 'icon', journalist Marina Hyde in *The Guardian* mused how the icons could have been more insulting than they actually were: 'Instead of France being depicted by a strike banner, he might simply have flown a white flag' (Hyde 2009).

Undoubtedly the success of *'Allo 'Allo!* is largely due to its exaggerated farcical acting, burlesque accents and innuendo, and the fact that, in the words of Jürgen Kamm, 'it focuses on getting as much mileage as possible out of farcical constellations without ever touching upon the serious aspects of wartime experience' (in Morgan-Russell 2004: 49). Similarly, despite the background material for *Charlotte Gray*, which emphasizes 'The Real Charlottes',[3] it is clear that Gillian Armstrong had, in Geoffrey Macnab's words, 'no interest in making a latter-day counterpart to ... British flag-wavers such as *Odette* and *Carve Her Name with Pride*' (Macnab 2002: 41). Like most postmodern heritage films, *Charlotte Gray*, in the words of Katja Hofmann, 'eschews reality to let the viewer dream in the most corny way of being French (being sensual, elegant and seductive, doing exciting things, finding the "right man")' (Hofmann 2002: 11). But, however anodyne and/or seductive (or even affectionate) these representations of France may be, films about the French Resistance are also exploiting an undercurrent of less flattering, derogatory and occasionally hostile images of France and French people. Despite *'Allo 'Allo!* and *Charlotte Gray*'s postmodern loss of history (through parody on the one hand and nostalgia on the other), unexpectedly it is in their use of stereotypes of Frenchness that a more diffuse and normally buried history of ancient rivalry between Great Britain and France resurfaces.

Notes

1. The BCRA (*Bureau Central de Renseignements d'Action*) was a Free French secret service agency in charge of investigating the occupied territories, led from London by Colonel André Dewavrin.
2. *Je t'aime (allo allo)*, was a 7" vinyl single released in 1986.
3. Official website for *Charlotte Gray*, http://charlottegraymovie.warnerbros.com/cmp/real.html; accessed 24 August 2007.

Bibliography

Abel, R. 1999. *The Red Rooster Scare: Making Cinema American, 1900–1910*. Berkeley, CA, and London: University of California Press.

Aldgate, A. and J. Richards (eds). 2007. *Britain Can Take It: British Cinema in the Second World War*. London and New York: I.B. Tauris.

Armstrong, G. 2002. 'Interview with Gillian Armstrong', DVD *Charlotte Gray*, Film Four Ltd.

Bertin-Maghit, J-P. 1989. *Le Cinéma sous l'occupation: Le Monde du cinéma français de 1940 à 1946*. Paris: Olivier Orban.

Burch, N. and G. Sellier. 1996. *La Drôle de guerre des sexes du cinéma français: 1930–1956*. Paris: Nathan Université.

Ehrlich, E. 1985. *Cinema of Paradox: French Filmmaking under the German Occupation*. New York: Columbia University Press.

Gorman, M. 2003. 'How the English See the French', Lecture given to the Alliance Française, Fresno, 21 October 2003. Retrieved on 21 August 2007 from http://mg.csufresno.edu/PAPERS.HTM

Haselden, J. 1988. *'Allo 'Allo!: The War Diaries of René Artois*. London: BBC Books.

———., J. Lloyd and D. Croft. 1989. *'Allo 'Allo!: The War Diaries of René Artois – Volume 2*. London: BBC Books.

Hofmann, K. 2002. 'Does My Gun Look Big in This?', *Sight and Sound* 12(3): 10–11.

Jackson, J. 2001. *France: The Dark Years, 1940–1944*. Oxford: Oxford University Press.

Hyde, M. 2009. 'Thus Spoke Entropa: The EU Defined in an Airfix Model', *The Guardian*: 17 January.

Kaye, G. and H. Bonner. 1989. *René & Me*. London : Sidgwick & Jackson Ltd.

Kedward, H.R. 1985. *Occupied France: Collaboration and Resistance 1940–1944*. Oxford: Blackwell.

———. 1993. *In Search of the Maquis: Rural Resistance in Southern France, 1942–1944*. Oxford: Clarendon Press; New York: Oxford University Press.

———. 2000. 'The Anti-carnival of Collaboration: Louis Malle's *Lacombe Lucien* (1974)', in S. Hayward and G. Vincendeau (eds), *French Film: Texts and Contexts*, 2nd edn. London and New York: Routledge, pp. 227–39.

———. 2004. 'Britain and the French Resistance', in R. Mayne, D. Johnson and R. Tombs (eds), *Cross Channel Currents: 100 Years of the Entente Cordiale*. London and New York: Routledge, pp. 122–32.

Lant, A. 1991. *Blackout: Reinventing Women for Wartime British Cinema*. Princeton, NJ: Princeton University Press.

Lindeperg, S. 1997. *Les Écrans de l'ombre: La Seconde guerre mondiale dans le cinéma français (1944–1969)*. Paris: CNRS Editions.

Macnab, G. 2002. 'Charlotte Gray', *Sight and Sound* 12(3): 41.

Mayle, P. 1989. *A Year in Provence*. London: Hamish Hamilton Ltd.

Mayne, J. 2007. *Le Corbeau*. London: I.B. Tauris.

Medhurst, A. 1988. 'Race Riot', *The Listener* 120(3086): 36.

Morgan-Russell, S. 2004. *Jimmy Perry and David Croft*. Manchester: Manchester University Press.

Murphy, R. 2000. *British Cinema and the Second World War*. London and New York: Continuum.

Nacache, J. 2008. *Lacombe, Lucien, de Louis Malle*. Paris: Atlande Edition.

Paxton, R.O. 1972. *Vichy France: Old Guard and New Order, 1940-1944*. London: Barrie and Jenkins.

Porch, D. 2000. 'Military "Culture" and the Fall of France in 1940: A Review Essay', *International Security* 24(4): 157–80.

Rosenthal, A.S. 1999. 'The Gender-coded Stereotype: An American Perception of France and the French', *The French Review* 72(5): 897–908.

Rousso, H. 1991. *The Vichy Syndrome: History and Memory in France Since 1944*, trans. A. Goldhammer. Cambridge, MA: Harvard University Press.

Sarde, M. 1983. *Regard sur les françaises*. Paris: Stock.

Search, G. 1989. 'What Ees All Zees Zen?', *The Radio Times*, 2–9 September: 11–12.

Siclier, J. 1981. *La France de Pétain et son cinéma*. Paris: Henri Veyrier.

Sorlin, P. 1991. *European Cinemas, European Societies, 1939–1990*. London: Routledge.

Vincendeau, G. 2003. *Jean-Pierre Melville: An American in Paris*. London: BFI.

Filmography

Films

Against the Wind. 1948, Charles Crichton, U.K.

Armée des ombres, L' / The Army in the Shadows. 1969, Jean-Pierre Melville, France/Italy.

Au revoir les enfants. 1987, Louis Malle, France/West Germany.

Babette s'en va-t-en guerre / Babette Goes to War. 1959, Christian-Jaque, France.

Bataille du rail, La / The Battle of the Rails. 1946, René Clément, France.

Blanche et Marie. 1985, Jacques Renard, France.

Bon Voyage. 2003, Jean-Paul Rappeneau, France.

Bridge Too Far, A. 1977, Richard Attenborough, U.S.A./U.K.

Carve Her Name with Pride. 1958, Lewis Gilbert, U.K.

Casablanca. 1942, Michael Curtiz, U.S.A.

Chagrin et la Pitié, Le / The Sorrow and the Pity. 1969, Marcel Ophuls, France.

Charlotte Gray. 2001, Gillian Armstrong, U.K./Australia/Germany.

Corbeau, Le. 1943. Henri-Georges Clouzot, France.

Dernier Métro, Le / The Last Metro. 1980, François Truffaut, France.

Good Year, A. 2006, Ridley Scott, U.S.A.

Grande Vadrouille, La / Don't Look Now, We're Being Shot At. 1966, Gérard Oury, France/U.K.

Guns of Navarone, The. 1961, J. Lee Thompson, U.K./U.S.A.

Héros très discret, Un / A Self-made Hero. 1996, Jacques Audiard, France.

Jéricho. 1946, Henri Calef, France.

Lacombe Lucien. 1974, Louis Malle, France/West Germany/Italy.

Longest Day, The. 1962, Ken Annakin, Andrew Marton and Bernhard Wicki, U.S.A.

Lucie Aubrac. 1997, Claude Berri, France.

Mr Bean's Holiday. 2007, Steve Bendelack, U.K./France/Germany.

Odette. 1950, Herbert Wilcox, U.K.

One of Our Aircraft Is Missing. 1942, Michael Powell and Emeric Pressburger, U.K.

Papy fait de la résistance / Gramps Is in the Resistance. 1983, Jean-Marie Poiré, France.

Paris brûle-t-il? / Is Paris Burning?. 1966, René Clément, France/U.S.A.

Père tranquille, Le / Mr Orchid. 1946, René Clément, France.

Pimpernel Smith. 1941, Leslie Howard, U.K.

Silence de la mer, Le. 1949, Jean-Pierre Melville, France.

To Be or Not to Be. 1942, Ernst Lubitsch, U.S.A.

2 Days in Paris. 2007, Julie Delpy, France/Germany.

Zwartboek / Black Book. 2006, Paul Verhoeven, Netherlands/Germany/Belgium.

Television Series

'Allo 'Allo! (David Croft, Jeremy Lloyd)

Season 1 (7 episodes): 1982–1984; season 2 (7 episodes): 1985; season 3 (6 episodes): 1986–1987; season 4 (6 episodes): 1987; season 5 (26 episodes): 1988–1989; season 6 (8 episodes): 1989; season 7 (10 episodes): 1991; season 8 (7 episodes): 1991–1992; season 9 (6 episodes): 1992.

Dad's Army (David Croft, Jimmy Perry)

Season 1 (6 episodes): 1968; season 2 (6 episodes): 1969; season 3 (14 episodes): 1969; season 4 (14 episodes): 1970–1971; season 5 (13 episodes): 1972; season 6 (7 episodes): 1973; season 7 (6 episodes): 1974; season 8 (8 episodes): 1975–1976; season 9 (6 episodes): 1977.

Secret Army (Various writers credited)

Season 1 (16 episodes): 1977; season 2 (13 episodes): 1978; season 3 (14 episodes): 1979.

CHAPTER 17

'In the Ghetto': Space, Race and Marginalization in French and British 'Urban' Films *La Haine* and *Bullet Boy*

Jim Morrissey

In a 2007 polemic in which he proclaims 'the superiority of the French [universalist] model', philosopher Pascal Bruckner calls Anglo-American multiculturalism 'a racism of the anti-racists' because it means that 'we can turn a blind eye to how others live and suffer once they've been parked in the ghetto of their particularity' (2007). Concerns about how best to manage modern multiethnic societies came into sharp focus in Britain and France in 2005 following the London bombings in July and the rioting that spread through the French *banlieue* in November. While Bruckner opted for a confrontational approach, other commentators were more prepared to seek out flaws in their respective national systems. The sociologist and novelist Azouz Begag, who became France's first cabinet minister of North African immigrant origin in 2005, expressed his concerns about France's official blindness to race (2007: 117–21), while in Britain Timothy Garton-Ash wondered whether 'a more demanding civic-national identity, like that of the French Republic, has its advantages after all, giving a stronger sense of identity and belonging' (2006). This chapter will involve a comparative analysis of French and British versions of the 'urban' or 'ghetto' film – *La Haine* (Kassovitz, 1995) and *Bullet Boy* (Dibb, 2004) – undertaken to see what relevance they might have to these debates. Commentators have been keen to underline the debt these two films owe to the U.S. 'urban' model (French 2005; Vincendeau 2005: 31), established in works like *Do the Right Thing* (1989) and *Boyz 'n the Hood* (1991), and characterized by a particular configuration of cinematic space, place and race. Vincendeau has noted that while the French critical reception of *La Haine* prioritized aesthetic considerations (like cinematic space), Anglo-American critics paid more attention to sociological concerns including those pertaining to the film's treatment of race and ethnicity (2005: 95).

(Given the critical esteem in which 'Ken Loach-style' British social realism is held across the Channel ('Ken Who?' 2002), the French reception of *Bullet Boy* might have opened up interesting grounds for comparison here. Apart from a couple of festival screenings, however, Dibb's film was not released in France). This chapter will involve an effort to bring these strands together by examining *La Haine* and *Bullet Boy*'s strategies for the representation of ethnic difference alongside their divergent approaches to the depiction of space and place. Acknowledging the influence of the U.S. model, it will also foreground the respective national social-realist traditions within which these two films can be seen to sit; *La Haine* has much in common with French films known under the often overlapping labels '*beur*' and '*banlieue*', while elements in *Bullet Boy* suggest a lineage going back to the British 'kitchen sink' dramas of the 1950s. Overall, the chapter will ask whether the films at issue can be argued to provide particular insights into what are conventionally seen as the oppositional French and British approaches to multiethnic society.

Both *Bullet Boy* and *La Haine* are set in places whose reputations precede them. Filmed and set in the London Borough of Hackney, *Bullet Boy*'s very title reflects something of the notoriety of this part of the British capital. A series of fatal shootings in the early 2000s attributed to 'Yardie', or Jamaican, gangsters led to an area around the Lower Clapton Road gaining the media label 'the murder mile'. As a result, Hackney became virtually synonymous with gun crime in London (Ojumo 2005). *La Haine* sets its action in the Parisian *banlieue*, a place with a similarly unenviable reputation. Will Higbee explains that, 'as the cycle of youth riots continued in the early 1990s, the *cités* of the urban periphery were foregrounded in both media and political rhetoric as the emblematic site of *fracture sociale*; "no-go" areas of criminality and violence, inhabited by multiethnic gangs of disenfranchised, delinquent male youths' (2006: 67). Their settings' associations with 'criminality and violence' are evoked almost from the very outset in these films. *Bullet Boy* begins with the central protagonist, Ricky (Ashley Walters), being released from a young offenders' institution in the English countryside. Ricky's friend, the ironically named Wisdom (Leon Black), comes to drive him home to Hackney. As they enter familiar territory, Ricky and Wisdom are almost immediately drawn into two aggressive and potentially violent confrontations; one with a van driver concerning road etiquette and the other with Godfrey (Clark Lawson) over a broken wing-mirror. This dispute with Godfrey escalates over the course of the narrative and ultimately leads to the film's tragic conclusion. After its opening montage of social protest and unrest, *La Haine*'s diegesis begins with a news report concerning a riot in the *banlieue*. Kassovitz thereby foregrounds the media's role in perpetuating the image of the *banlieue* as a site of violence. In addition, in contrast to *Bullet Boy*, with the exception of Vinz (Vincent Cassel), *La Haine*'s protagonists are shown to be observers or, in the case of Hubert (Hubert Koundé) (whose boxing gym has been destroyed), even victims of the violence rather than active participants in it.

As Higbee notes, the media tend to present 'emblematic spaces', like Hackney or the *banlieue*, as 'exclusive site[s] of criminality, unemployment, delinquency and violence entirely removed from the rest of society' (2006: 73). Evidently, such a separation of social problems to 'another' place can work to reassure mainstream society. Not only are phenomena like violence and criminality presented as being geographically distant, the presumption is also that they can be confined to a ghetto. Such spatial and ideological distanciation has serious consequences for those who, by choice or by necessity, inhabit these places. While Ricky in *Bullet Boy* and Hubert in *La Haine* express their (ultimately frustrated) desires to 'get out', other characters like Wisdom and Vinz reflect what Begag has referred to as the tendency of marginalized youth to 'turn in on themselves geographically and mentally' (2007: 125). In *Bullet Boy*, after Ricky and Wisdom are seen at the sight of a shooting, in a scene that takes place in the dark and confined space of a lock-up garage, Ricky says that they have no choice but to run away. Wisdom responds: 'I ain't leavin the manor. I don't know nowhere else. I ain't got nowhere else.' Ricky's appeal – 'It's only a place, Rude Boy' – falls on deaf ears. Wisdom's inability to imagine an existence outside of Hackney exemplifies a state of mental confinement that confirms the success of the ideology that seeks to confine social problems to particular spaces. Wisdom's misplaced, though clearly logical, commitment to Hackney, the only place he knows, resonates with the territorial obsessions characteristic of gangs from economically deprived areas. A recent manifestation of this tendency is found in Britain in the 'postcode wars' in which gang members set themselves against those who come from different postal districts, a subject explored in Gordon and Mendoza's evocatively entitled documentary *North by Northwest Ten* (2007), which looks at gang violence in Harlesden in northwest London (Harlesden's postcode is NW10, hence the reference to 'Northwest Ten' in the film's title).

How these films choose to photograph their locations tells us much about their willingness to challenge the desire to marginalize the 'emblematic space'. Both *Bullet Boy* and *La Haine* make efforts to bridge the gap between the centre and the margins by presenting alternatives to more expected images of their settings as concrete-dominated wastelands. Kassovitz's decision to print *La Haine* in black and white makes his *banlieue* locations look not only 'cool' but frequently 'beautiful' (Vincendeau 2005: 48, 50). Meanwhile, *Bullet Boy* focuses on parts of Hackney that look almost rural in an effort to defy expectation; green spaces like parks and football pitches appear frequently while an extended sequence shows Curtis (Luke Fraser) and Rio (Rio Tison) playing in a wooded area around the River Lea. Some commentators have used the word 'bucolic' (Plunkett 2005) to describe the film's evocation of the rural. As Ben Walters points out in *Sight and Sound*, however, it is more correct to describe the film as 'mock-bucolic' (2005: 48) because urban elements (e.g. burnt-out cars) are shown so often to invade these 'natural' spaces.

Whatever one makes of the 'rural' aspects of *Bullet Boy*, its regular recourse to the extended establishing shot significantly problematizes its depiction of its marginalized setting. While the film, like *La Haine*, displays a debt to the U.S. 'urban' films, its use of these lingering shots suggests that its roots lie closer to home – in the British 'kitchen sink' dramas of the 1950s. Drawing on research by John Hill (1986), Julia Hallam states that the extended establishing shot, as featured in the 1950s social-realist films, 'accentuates a sense of place, which ... creates a visual spectacle of squalor and poverty of the working-class urban environment' (2000: 48). The shot works to separate the viewer from the social problems on display, or, as Hallam puts it, 'place is presented as an exotically realistic spectacle for consumption by those who do not have to inhabit it' (2000: 48). Andrew Higson states that 'the power of these images is their capacity to represent both the extent to which the protagonist is trapped within the city and the extent with which he or she desires to escape' (1996: 148). In *Bullet Boy*, as we have seen, Ricky expresses his determination to 'get out' of Hackney. One particular sequence cuts from an extreme long shot of an estate in Hackney to Ricky standing on his balcony with the towers of Canary Wharf looming in the background. The juxtaposition of downtrodden Hackney with London's soaring financial centres could be seen to make a point about inequality of opportunity. This reading is problematized, however, by the first long shot which places the viewer alongside Canary Wharf, 'outside and above' Ricky's predicament (Higson 1996: 152). In its frequent recourse to the extended establishing shot, *Bullet Boy* risks falling into one of the more serious traps of social-realist filmmaking; that identified by Martin O'Shaughnessy as 'the voyeuristic exploitation of social suffering held safely at a distance' (2005: 86).

As Vincendeau observes, this kind of shot is notable for its absence from *La Haine* (2000: 313). At the same time, Will Higbee suggests that because they rely on a '*cité*/city' binary that separates the protagonists and their *banlieue* from central Paris, films like *La Haine* 'perpetuate the very ideological modes of social and spatial division that identify the *banlieue* as the emblematic site of *fracture sociale*' (2001: 202). Higbee is clearly correct to highlight the prominence of this binary division in *La Haine*. I would suggest, however, that the way the film is shot involves significant effort to refuse the protagonists' separation into a delimited, objectified space. Characters in *La Haine* are regularly photographed from below: Kassovitz's use of low angles of framing can be seen to communicate a sense of confinement which, rather than distancing the spectator from the protagonists, aligns him or her with them. For example, in an early sequence when Saïd comes to collect Vinz, low angles of framing show the *banlieue* appartment buildings towering over the young *beur*.[1] These shots can be read to symbolize Saïd's confinement within the *banlieue* space. Significantly though, when Saïd converses with Vinz's sister and with a black neighbour, Kassovitz elects not to give us the counter images – high-angled shots that would provide the other characters' points-of-view of Saïd, from above. Thus, shots that would separate the spectator from Saïd's confinement and, arguably, objectify him in a similar way to the extended establishing shot are summarily refused. A similar point could be made about the 'Thoiry' scene in which the only high-angled shot is attributed to the television news crew. Kassovitz here marks the mainstream media's desire to objectify *banlieue* youth while refusing such objectification on his own part. As regards the *cité*/city binary, even though the average spectator is likely to feel more at home in central Paris than in the *banlieue*, one might argue, contra Higbee, that Kassovitz's use of increased focal length and mono sound in the 'city' section is designed, yet again, to align the spectator with the protagonists and thereby, to experience at least some semblance of their alienation in France's metropolitan centre. Something very different is happening in *Bullet Boy* where the frequent establishing shots can be seen as constantly working to reassure the spectator of his or her separation from the social problems on display.

This urge to separate social problems to an 'other' place clearly has a racial as well as a spatial dimension. As media representations of the 'emblematic space' tend to foreground its ethnic makeup, the way in which films set in these spaces choose to represent ethnic difference deserves careful attention. *Bullet Boy* tells a story of young black men with guns in Hackney and the film can be accused, therefore, of drawing on a preformed negative stereotype that associates the area with 'Yardie' violence. In the film's defence, it presents a number of black characters who reject criminality. Ricky's long-suffering mother Beverley (Clare Perkins) and her pastor-partner Leon (Curtis Walker) are shown to be at a loss to understand her son's involvement with guns. Shea (Sharia-Mounira Samuels), Ricky's girlfriend, shuts him out of her life when she hears of his presence at a shooting. And despite an initial fascination with his older brother's gun, by the end of the film when he throws it into the river, it is strongly suggested that Curtis will reject the criminal life. Though it ultimately proves impossible, even Ricky makes efforts to leave his criminal past behind. But in spite of the fact that many characters are shown to have other options, all of the young black men featured in *Bullet Boy* are involved in gun violence. One of the film's producers, Marc Boothe, is quoted as suggesting that its story 'will resonate and reverberate with different communities throughout the U.K.' He says that 'in terms of what it deals with, this story could have been set in Oldham or Toxteth; the characters could have been any colour' (in Ojumo 2005). So why are they black? As Akin Ojumo points out, '*Bullet Boy* is specifically about black boys because the image of a young black man with a gun is a powerful one' (2005). Donald Bogle has written of the stereotype of the 'brutal black buck' which has existed in cinema since D.W. Griffith's 1915 *The Birth of a Nation* (1997: 18–21). Stuart Hall suggests that there are 'many traces of this in contemporary images of black youth', specifically in those depictions of 'black urban youth "on the rampage"' (2002: 258) that tend to feature in 'urban' films like *Boyz 'n the Hood* or, indeed, *Bullet Boy*. The producers' decision to cast Ashley Walters in the lead role also raises questions here. Walters, otherwise known as Asher D, was a member of the South London rap group 'So Solid Crew', which achieved notoriety after shots were fired at one of its concerts in 2001. Walters himself famously served time in prison for possession of a loaded firearm (Walters 2005: 48). The conflation of the real and fictional in Walters's embodiment of Ricky is, then, fascinatingly contradictory. Walters's real life experience undoubtedly brings a weight of authority to the film. And while Ricky's inability to escape his criminal past would seem to represent a bleakly deterministic confirmation of a negative stereotype, Walters's own rejection of criminality and his self-reinvention as a successful multiplatform artist can be seen to refute that stereotype and offer a contrasting message of hope.

Overall, however, *Bullet Boy* exploits stereotype more than it challenges it. The film's title, combined with its marketing imagery, draws heavily on associations between young black men and guns. Ojumo recounts the reaction of a man who attended a special screening of the film in Hackney: 'It's a good drama, but I'm tired of seeing Hackney associated with gun crime. Why add to the body of stereotypes of men who look like me? ... This film could have been made about the same characters but they could have done something else apart from crime' (2005). In 2000, 'The Report of the Commission on the Future of Multi-Ethnic Britain', otherwise known as 'The Parekh Report', noted that the media play a central role in the perpetuation of negative racial stereotypes. The report states that coverage of minority 'communities and individuals ... is frequently negative, distorted or patronizing – or else the communities are simply invisible, not represented at all' (Parekh 2000: 161). The report goes on to speak of the damaging impact of the repeated appearance of words such as 'Islamic' and 'terrorist' or 'Afro-Caribbean' and 'criminal' side-by-side in newspapers: 'constant juxtapositions such as these have a cumulative effect on the consciousness of all readers, to the point where it is exceedingly difficult, for journalists and readers alike, to unlearn the assumptions and stereotypes they perpetuate' (Parekh 2000: 170). In this context, a film like *Bullet Boy*, which does foreground the experiences of Britain's ethnic 'others', bears a clear responsibility. Because of its recourse to preexisting racial stereotype, it seems to me that rather than working to reduce the separation between Britain's various ethnic groups, *Bullet Boy* runs a significant risk of what Yasmin Alibhai-Brown terms 'authenticating the prejudices which are bound to divide people and lock them in incomprehension' (2000: 125).

Questions of ethnicity are also central to the ideological construction of the 'emblematic space' in France. As Will Higbee reports, 'media attention often focuses on the disproportionate ethnic minorities within the *cités* – particularly those of North African origin – as a signifier of a more readily visible "other"' (2001: 199). Unlike *Bullet Boy* and unlike the U.S. 'hood' films which present their locations as largely monoethnic, *La Haine* is marked by 'its insistence on the *banlieue* as a multiethnic space' (Higbee 2006: 83). Although the Parisian *banlieue* has undoubtedly experienced a degree of 'white flight' (Dilday and Kuper 2007: 8), some areas remain extremely diverse as was demonstrated by the wide variety of ethnicities, including white French, shown to populate the Parisian *banlieue* of Montreuil in Bertrand and Nils Tavernier's documentary *De l'autre côté du périph'* / *The Other Side of the Tracks* (1997). The multiethnic makeup of *La Haine*'s three protagonists can be seen, then, to reflect a contemporary reality of the Parisian *banlieue*. However, the conveniently elegant 'black–*blanc*–*beur*' balance of the film's central trio has also attracted controversy. Writing of the French *beur* film, Carrie Tarr notes that it sometimes tends to foreground interethnic friendship in an effort to 'bridge the gap between *beur* and white French communities by offering French audiences a non-threatening and non-accusatory representation of ethnic differences' (2005: 45). This may work to counter negative stereotypes (Tarr 2005: 50), but the downplaying of difference can also mean that the realities of racial discrimination are glossed over. For Tarr, this is what happens in *La Haine*: 'Kassovitz provides a positive representation of inter-ethnic male bonding within an underclass youth culture ... but ... the question of racism and ethnic differences tends in the process to become marginalised, if not effaced' (2005: 68).

Figure 17.1: Vincent Cassel, Saïd Taghmaoui and Hubert Koundé in *La Haine* (1995).
Image courtesy of the BFI stills department.

One of the problems that Tarr identifies in *La Haine*'s presentation of ethnicity is the centrality of the white character. Because of this, *La Haine*, and, indeed, Kassovitz's previous film, *Métisse / Café au lait* (1993), 'rather than representing a multi-ethnic society *per se* ... serve primarily to work through the relationship of white youth to France's ethnic minority others' (2005: 62). Although Vincent Cassel's is the first name to appear in the credits and his (or more correctly, Vinz's) image is foregrounded in *La Haine*'s marketing material, I would argue that Hubert is a more important character and the central focalizer in the film.[2] The spectator is certainly allowed more access to Hubert's internal subjectivity, most obviously in the voiceover sequences that begin and end the film, but also during the young men's train journey to Paris. After the train passes the poster reading 'the world is yours', we are shown an extended close-up of Hubert's face. Separated from Vinz and Saïd who are animatedly reliving their recent encounter with the police, Hubert's grimace communicates his greater understanding of the challenges faced by young men from the *banlieue*, challenges that will not be overcome in individual confrontations with figures of authority. Overall, the film presents Hubert as a far more thoughtful and restrained character than Vinz. In this, *La Haine* can be seen to challenge what we have seen as one of the most long-standing racial stereotypes in cinema – that of the 'brutal black buck'. By comparison with *Bullet Boy*, *La Haine* demonstrates a much more sophisticated understanding of the dangers of racial stereotyping and of its own role as a representational vehicle. As Higbee notes, the film's foregrounding of the media's transformation of reality 'forces the spectators to question more deeply the "truth" behind the images they see on screen' (2006: 71). But, what of the other member of *La Haine*'s central trio – Saïd? As several commentators have observed, Saïd has a peripheral role in the narrative compared to Hubert and Vinz (Konstantarakos 1999: 166; Tarr 2005: 71). More importantly, while we as spectators are allowed access to Hubert and Vinz's homes and family backgrounds, Saïd's remain invisible. Given the fact that Islam is regularly cited as the main bar to the assimilation of France's sizeable population 'of Maghrebi origin or descent'[3] (Konstantarakos 1999: 166), its absence from the film would seem to support Tarr's contention that, in the end, *La Haine* proves itself determined to 'marginalize' or 'efface' the more challenging questions surrounding ethnicity and integration in contemporary France.

With mainstream media determined to explain marginalization in places like Hackney and the *banlieue* on the grounds of space and race, we should consider the extent to which the more intractable, though often less visible, causes of social exclusion are identified and explored in these films. Vincendeau's observation that 'contrary to the common perception of *La Haine* as a trenchant exposé of *banlieue* life, the social issues in the film are hinted at rather than explored' (2005: 68–9) is largely also true of *Bullet Boy*. The issue of inadequate housing does not arise in either film and though both suggest that education is failing or has failed their protagonists, this problem is never addressed in a sustained manner. In *Bullet Boy*, Curtis is seen wearing his school uniform for the majority of the film's running time, though, as Ben Walters points out, the boy seems to spend as much time out of school as he does in it (2005: 48). The first reference to education in *La Haine* is when we learn that the school building has been burned down. Later in the film, Vinz expresses an equally cynical regard for formal education when he proclaims that he learned more on the streets than he did in school. For the central protagonists of both of these films, issues of employment can be assumed to be more pressing than those of education. Interestingly, however, *La Haine* contains no reference to work in the legitimate economy. Writing of the employment prospects for young men in the French suburbs, Hargreaves says 'theirs is the flat horizon of teenagers who have seen their fathers and/or older brothers largely excluded from the labor market and can see little if any reason to suppose that better prospects await them' (in Begag 2007: x). In this light, it is not surprising that Saïd and Hubert should turn to the parallel economy to make money. The very banality of this choice is emphasized when Hubert hands over the money from a recent drug deal to his mother for the gas bill. If anything, *Bullet Boy* presents this choice between working in the legal and illegal spheres in even starker terms. Just after his release from prison, Ricky's announcement that he wants to get a job meets with general derision. Wisdom mockingly calls him a 'business man' and even young Curtis feels it reasonable to laugh at the thought of the thoroughly menial jobs that his brother, with a criminal record, will have a hope of obtaining – 'McDonalds? You're not even the manager! Can I have a cheeseburger please?' Although these scenes are played for laughs, there is a serious point at issue. With opportunities so limited (if they exist at all) in the legitimate economy, who would not be tempted to choose the greater rewards on offer elsewhere?

If such limited opportunities point to failures of state policy in marginalized communities, both films can be seen to level blame at what is often the most visible manifestation of the state in these areas – the police. As has been noted above, *Bullet Boy*'s focus is on black experience in Hackney. However, while Ricky, his family, his girlfriend, Wisdom and the opposing gang members are black, representatives of the state in the film are presented as almost exclusively white. Prison officers, Ricky's parole officer, Curtis' teacher, a morgue official and the police officers who appear at various points in the film are white. As we saw above, the separation of ethnic groups in this manner can be seen to play into firmly entrenched racial stereotypes. However, given the fact that 'the quintessential national institution embodying hostility towards the black population [in Britain] has been the police' (Korte and Sternberg 2004: 108), an alternative symbolic reading may be possible here. Presenting the police force as all white could be read as an effort to depict it as it is seen by many black British people, i.e. as institutionally racist and unrepresentative of their interests. Loosely based on the 1993 death of a young Zairean being held in police custody, *La Haine* is at least as concerned with issues relating to the police's role in marginalized communities (Vincendeau 2005: 12). By contrast with *Bullet Boy*, however, *La Haine* adopts what Vincendeau calls 'a non-Manichean, non-essentialist approach to ethnic difference' (2005: 64). Representatives of the state are portrayed, like the central trio, as ethnically diverse. This is most striking in the scene in which Saïd and Hubert are racially and physically abused by two police officers, one of whom (Zinedine Soualem) is a *beur*. Kassovitz here underlines what he sees as the institutional rather than the ethnic basis for police racism and the sequence highlights the undeniable complexity of racist attitudes in France (Vincendeau 2005: 64–5). At the same time, despite its brutality, by again downplaying the significance of ethnic difference, the sequence could be argued to sidestep difficult questions by failing to confront the instigator (France's white majority) with the historically established vectors of a racism from which it has benefited most.

These interrogations of the role of the state in marginalized communities bring broader questions of national identity into focus. National flags, of one form or another, make an appearance in both films. Near to the end of *Bullet Boy*, just after Ricky's body has been identified at the morgue, we are shown an English flag, the St George's Cross, being flown from a window in Hackney. The flag's association with the far-right BNP (British National Party) heightens the sense that Ricky's fate will be seen as something alien and incomprehensible, even by those that bear power in the country of his birth. This was virtually confirmed in a speech made by former Prime Minister Tony Blair just prior to his resignation in April 2007 when he suggested that 'the spate of knife and gun murders in London was not caused by poverty, but [by] a distinctive black culture' (Wintour and Dodd 2007). Although *Bullet Boy* seems to generally accept the spatial and ethnic ghettoization that Bruckner suggests allows us 'to turn a blind eye' (2007) to the social suffering of others, for this brief moment, Dibb's film can be seen to refuse the unthinking prioritization of difference that might represent Anglo-American multiculturalism's most serious flaw. *La Haine*'s investment in the French universalist ideal is further

Figure 17.2: Ashley Walters in *Bullet Boy* (2004).
Image courtesy of the BFI stills department.

evident in its musings on national identity. A sequence shot in the mirrored basement of a Parisian café arranges the characters into a black–*blanc–beur* triptych that evokes comparisons with the French flag, the *tricolore*. Kassovitz's reimagining of the national flag represents a challenge to those who would deny the multiethnic makeup of modern French society. Later in the film, the central trio find themselves on a rooftop in Paris. The young men proclaim the central motto of the French Republic – *Liberté, égalité, fraternité* – to be 'une phrase à la con': an idiotic, stupid phrase. They try and fail to repeat a trick they have seen in films – turning off the lights of the Eiffel Tower, another important symbol of France, with a click of the fingers. France, like Britain in *Bullet Boy*, is shown to be unresponsive to and fundamentally uninterested in these young men's plights. In much more direct terms than *Bullet Boy*, however, *La Haine*'s rooftop sequence places responsibility for social marginalization not at the feet of some geographically or ethnically separated other but, instead, on its nation as a whole. But does a universalist vision that can be seen to work towards the effective 'suppression of differences' (Tarr 2005: 50) really represent a more productive way forward for our multiethnic societies?

Overall, *La Haine* emerges well from the comparison undertaken here. Its treatments of space and race evidence resistance to the urge to confine social problems to a ghetto. Nevertheless, the film reflects problems with French universalism. Primarily, French Republican blindness to difference infects the film and can be seen to allow it to sidestep or gloss over the problems of discrimination faced by France's ethnic others. *Bullet Boy*, meanwhile, communicates little of the achievements of British multiculturalism but its failings in this regard may be attributed as much to broader institutional factors as to the film itself. In recent years, the number of home-based films released to cinema audiences in France has greatly exceeded that in Britain.[4] This could be argued to indicate that contemporary French film allows scope for a more diverse range of experience to reach cinema screens, although such a conclusion is, of course, debatable. Whatever the causes, the undeniable paucity of feature films dealing with black experience in Britain leaves each one struggling to bear a 'burden of representation' (Mercer 1994: 81) under which it is expected to embody the experiences of all black Britons. Furthermore, British film financing, like its U.S. counterpart, seems to have interiorized negative racial stereotypes to the extent that 'authentic' black experience has become equated with urban violence and gun crime (Smith 1997: 10). With money rolling in from films like *Kidulthood* (2006) and its more lucrative sequel *Adulthood* (2008) (see Gant 2008: 13), that present even more sensationalized pictures of multiethnic urban youth on the rampage than *Bullet Boy*, filmmakers complain that it is increasingly difficult to obtain financing for projects that would present alternative accounts of black British experience.[5] Both *La Haine* and *Bullet Boy* highlight flaws in their nations' respective approaches to multiethnic society – flaws that mean that their egalitarian ideals remain far from realized. However, as Garton-Ash suggests, the real debate is not about which model is superior but, instead, about 'which elements from each approach can best be combined' (2007). Also set in the Parisian *banlieue*, Kechiche's *L'Esquive / Games of Love and Chance* (2003), seems to incorporate a more productive synthesis of universalism and difference than *La Haine*. Despite the institutional barriers faced, we might hope that future filmic portrayals of Britain's multiethnic society will move in a similar direction, focusing more on the shared values that bring us together and less on the stereotypical and sensational factors that tend to pull us apart.[6]

Notes

1. I am conscious of the dangers of essentialism and simplification in my use of labels like 'black', 'white' and '*beur*'. In general, however, in the interests of legibility, I have decided neither to place them in inverted commas nor to use alternative phrases.
2. Vincendeau offers an alternative interpretation (2005: 58–64).
3. The phrase is Carrie Tarr's (2005).
4. For example, the Centre National de la Cinématographie (CNC 2008) reports that 262 French films came out in France in 2007, while the U.K. Film Council (2008) puts the combined figure for British releases (including U.K./U.S. and other coproductions) to the British and Irish markets during the same year at 107.
5. During group discussions held to mark Black Film Month in London in November 2008, filmmakers like Ishmahil Blagrove Jr repeatedly referred to these difficulties.
6. I am grateful to Guy Westwell, Tom Whittaker and Sue Harris for their helpful comments at various stages during the preparation of this chapter.

Bibliography

Alibhai-Brown, Y. 2000. *Who Do We Think We Are?* London: The Penguin Press.

Begag, A. 2007. *Ethnicity and Equality – France in the Balance*, trans. and intro. A.G. Hargreaves. Lincoln: University of Nebraska Press.

Bogle, D. 1997. 'Black Beginnings: From *Uncle Tom's Cabin* to *The Birth of a Nation*', in V. Smith (ed.), *Representing Blackness*. London: The Athlone Press, pp. 13–24.

Bruckner, P. 2007. 'Enlightenment Fundamentalism or Racism of the Anti-racists?' Retrieved 21 November 2008 from http://www.signandsight.com/features/1146.html.

CNC. 2008. 'Films en salles'. Retrieved 19 February 2009 from http://www.cnc.fr/CNC_GALLERY_CONTENT/DOCUMENTS/statistiques/par_secteur_FR_pdf/Film Salles_.pdf.

Dilday, K.A. and S. Kuper. 2007. 'Where French Muslims Struggle to Integrate', *The Financial Times*, 29 August: 8.

French, P. 2005. 'When Young Guns Go For It', *Guardian Unlimited*, 10 April. Retrieved 21 November 2008 from http://www.guardian.co.uk/film/2005/apr/10/philipfrench.

Gant, C. 2008. 'Street Smarts', *Sight and Sound* 18(8): 13.

Garton-Ash, T. 2006. 'What Young British Muslims Say Can Be Shocking – Some of it Is Also True', *The Guardian*, 10 August 2006. Retrieved 21 November 2008 from http://www.guardian.co.uk/commentisfree/2006/aug/10/comment.race

———. 2007. 'Better Pascal than Pascal Bruckner'. Retrieved 21 November 2008 from http://www.signandsight.com/features/1166.html

Hall, S. (ed.). 2002. *Representation – Cultural Representations and Signifying Practices*. London: Sage.

Hallam, J. with M. Marshment. 2000. *Realism and Popular Cinema*. Manchester: Manchester University Press.

Higbee, W. 2001. 'Screening the "Other" Paris: Cinematic Representations of the French Urban Periphery in *La Haine* and *Ma 6-T Va Crack-er*', *Modern and Contemporary France* 9(2): 197–208.

———. 2006. *Mathieu Kassovitz*. Manchester: Manchester University Press.

Higson, A. 1996. 'Space, Place, Spectacle: Landscape and Townscape in the "Kitchen Sink" Film', in A. Higson (ed.), *Dissolving Views*. London: Cassell, pp. 133–56.

Hill, J. 1986. *Sex, Class and Realism*. London: BFI Publishing.

'Ken Who?'. 2002. *The Economist*, 17 January. Retrieved 26 February 2009 from http://www.economist.com/world/britain/displaystory.cfm?story_idE1_JQDRDS

Konstantarakos, M. 1999. 'Which Mapping of the City? *La Haine* (Kassovitz, 1995) and the *Cinéma de Banlieue*', in P. Powrie (ed.), *French Cinema in the 1990s*. Oxford: Oxford University Press, pp. 160–72.

Korte, B. and C. Sternberg. 2004. *Bidding for the Mainstream – Black and Asian British Films Since the 1990s*. Amsterdam and New York: Rodopi.

Mercer, K. 1994. *Welcome to the Jungle*. New York and London: Routledge.

Ojumo, A. 2005. 'Loaded Questions', *The Observer*, 20 March. Retrieved 22 November 2008 from http://www.guardian.co.uk/film/2005/mar/20/features.review

O'Shaughnessy. M. 2005. 'Eloquent Fragments: French Fiction Film and Globalisation', *French Politics, Culture and Society* 23(3): 75–88.

Parekh, B. 2000. *The Future of Multi-ethnic Britain*. London: Profile Books.

Plunkett, D. 2005. 'I Didn't Want to Make Something Without Hope', *Guardian Unlimited*, 20 April. Retrieved 22 November 2008 from http://www.guardian.co.uk/film/2005/apr/20/hayfilmfestival2005.guardianhayfestival

Smith, V. (ed.). 1997. *Representing Blackness – Issues in Film and Video*. London: The Athlone Press.

Tarr, C. 2005. *Reframing Difference:* Beur *and* Banlieue *Filmmaking in France*. Manchester and New York: Manchester University Press.

U.K. Film Council. 2008. Statistical Yearbook 2007–2008. Retrieved on 19 February 2009 from http://rsu.ukfilmcouncil.org.uk/?pf&low&c1&y2007&s&low1

Vincendeau, G. 2000. 'Design on the Banlieue: Mathieu Kassovitz's *La Haine* (1995)', in S. Hayward and G. Vincendeau (eds), *French Film: Texts and Contexts*, 2nd edn. London: Routledge, pp. 310–27.

———. 2005. *La Haine*. London and New York: I.B. Tauris.

Walters, B. 2005. 'Bullet Boy', *Sight and Sound* 15(4): 48.

Wintour, P. and V. Dodd. 2007. 'Blair Blames Spate of Murders on Black Culture', *The Guardian*, 12 April. Retrieved on 21 November 2008 from http://www.guardian.co.uk/politics/2007/apr/12/ukcrime.race

Filmography

Adulthood. 2008, Noel Clarke, U.K.

Birth of a Nation, The. 1915, D.W. Griffith, U.S.A.

Boyz 'n the Hood. 1991, John Singleton, U.S.A.

Bullet Boy. 2004, Saul Dibb, U.K.

De l'autre côté du périph' / On the Other Side of the Tracks. 1997, Nils and Bertrand Tavernier, France.

Do the Right Thing. 1989, Spike Lee, U.S.A.

Esquive, L' / Games of Love and Chance. 2003, Abdellatif Kechiche, France.

Haine, La. 1995, Mathieu Kassovitz, France.

Kidulthood. 2006, Menhaj Huda, U.K.

Métisse / Café au lait. 1993, Mathieu Kassovitz, France/Belgium.

North by Northwest Ten. 2007, Richard C. Gordon and Danny Mendoza, U.K.

Notes on Contributors

Daniel Biltereyst is Professor in Film, Television and Cultural Media Studies at the Department of Communication Science, Ghent University, Belgium, where he leads the Centre for Cinema and Media Studies. His work is on screen culture and ideology, more specifically on film and screen cultures as sites of controversy, public debate and moral/media panic. His recent publications focus upon film censorship and the historical reception of controversial movies and genres. He is editing *The New Cinema History* (Wiley-Blackwell, with R. Maltby and P. Meers) and preparing a book on film censorship in Europe.

Ian Christie is Anniversary Professor of Film and Media History at Birkbeck College, University of London. He has published extensively on film and the visual arts. Recent publications include *A Matter of Life and Death* (BFI Film Classics, 2000) and, co-edited with Andrew Moor, *The Cinema of Michael Powell: International Perspectives on an English Filmmaker* (BFI, 2005). Ian is also a regular reviewer and broadcaster on film matters.

Jonathan Driskell has recently completed a Ph.D. at King's College London on female stardom in 1930s French cinema. He is now writing a monograph on the films of Marcel Carné, which is to be published by Manchester University Press as part of their French Film Directors series. He is also currently teaching part-time at King's College London.

Cristina Johnston is a Lecturer in the School of Languages, Cultures and Religions at the University of Stirling. Her research interests include contemporary French cinema, Transatlantic cinematic exchanges, and sexuality and citizenship in contemporary France.

Lucy Mazdon is a Reader in Film Studies at the University of Southampton. She has written widely on film and television. Her publications include *Encore Hollywood: Remaking French Cinema* (BFI, 2000), *France on Film: Reflections on Popular French Cinema* (Wallflower, 2001) and *The Contemporary Television Series* (Edinburgh

University Press, 2005), co-edited with Michael Hammond. She is currently leading an AHRC-funded project researching the history of French cinema in Britain from 1930 to the present.

Jim Morrissey teaches in the Department of Film Studies at Queen Mary, University of London where he is completing his AHRC-funded Ph.D. His thesis, theoretically underpinned by Bourdieusian insights into social distinction, focuses on the politics of French cinema since 1968. Jim's prize winning essay, 'Paris and Voyages of Self-discovery in *Cléo de 5 à 7* and *Le Fabuleux Destin d'Amélie Poulain*', was published in the journal *Studies in French Cinema* in 2008.

Robert Murphy is Professor in Film Studies at De Montfort University. His publications include *Realism and Tinsel* (Routledge, 1989), *Sixties British Cinema* (BFI, 1992), *British Cinema and the Second World War* (Continuum, 2000), *Directors in British and Irish Cinema* (BFI, 2006) and *The British Cinema Book* (BFI, 2009).

Geoffrey Nowell-Smith is Visiting Professorial Fellow at Queen Mary, University of London, where he is completing a research project on the history of the British Film Institute. He is the editor of *The Oxford History of World Cinema* (Oxford University Press, 1996). His most recent book is *Making Waves: New Cinemas of the 1960s* (Continuum, 2008).

Charles O'Brien is an Associate Professor of Film Studies at Carleton University in Canada and the author of *Cinema's Conversion to Sound* (Indiana University Press: 2005). In 2006–2007 he was appointed Ailsa Mellon Bruce Senior Fellow at the Centre for Advanced Study in the Visual Arts in Washington, D.C. He is currently writing a book on transnational musical films of the early 1930s from Britain, France, Germany and Hollywood, entitled *Musical Films for Export: Distribution, Technology, and Style*.

Vincent Porter is Emeritus Professor of Mass Communications at the University of Westminster and Visiting Research Professor in Film History at the University of Portsmouth. His recent film publications include *British Cinema of the 1950s: The Decline of Deference* (Oxford University Press, 2003 and 2007) (with Sue Harper) and *Walter C. Mycroft: The Time of My Life: The Memoirs of a British Film Producer* (Scarecrow Press, 2006), which he introduced, edited and annotated.

Cécile Renaud is currently completing a Ph.D. at the University of Southampton on the British exhibition of French films since 2001, as part of the AHRC-funded project on French cinema in Britain since 1930.

Melanie Selfe is an RCUK Fellow at the Centre for Cultural Policy Research, University of Glasgow. Her main research interests are in the cultural geographies of cinema exhibition, film policy, audiences, and the development of film cultures. She has published on the film society movement, amateur filmmaking and the Festival of Britain, the Regional Film Theatre programme, and the role of functional auteurism in responses to extreme cinema.

Justin Smith is Principal Lecturer in Film Studies at the University of Portsmouth. A cultural historian with a special interest in post-war British cinema, his research and writing cover film policy and finance, popular fandom, reception and exhibition cultures, and issues of identity and memory. His work on web ethnography has recently appeared in *The New Film History* (Palgrave/Macmillan, 2007). He is the author of *Withnail and Us: Cult Films and Film Cults in British Cinema*, published by I.B. Tauris. He is currently writing (with Sue Harper) *British Cinema in the 1970s: The Boundaries of Pleasure.*

Ingrid Stigsdotter is a freelance film and art critic, curator and academic with a Ph.D. in Film Studies from the University of Southampton. She currently teaches Film Studies at Gothenburg University and Visual Culture at Lund University and writes for the Swedish daily newspaper *Sydsvenskan*. Her publications include book chapters on British audiences for French and Swedish film and on the British television adaptations of Henning Mankell's novels about the Swedish detective Wallander. She has co-curated several silent film retrospectives for the London-based women's film festival Birds Eye View.

Sarah Street is Professor of Film at the University of Bristol. Her publications include: *Cinema and State* (co-authored with Margaret Dickinson, BFI, 1985); *British National Cinema* (Routledge, 1997 and 2nd expanded edition 2009); *British Cinema in Documents* (Routledge, 2000); *Costume and Cinema* (Wallflower, 2001); *Transatlantic Crossings: British Feature Films in the USA* (Continuum, 2002); *Black Narcissus* (I.B. Tauris, 2004) and (co-authored with Tim Bergfelder and Sue Harris), *Film Architecture and the Transnational Imagination: Set Design in 1930s European Cinema* (University of Amsterdam Press, 2007). She is currently working on a project on colour films in Britain, 1900–1955. She is a co-editor of *Screen* and of the *Journal of British Cinema and Television.*

Ginette Vincendeau is Professor of Film Studies at King's College London. She has written widely on French and European cinema and is a regular contributor to *Sight and Sound*. Among her books are *The Encyclopedia of European Cinema* (BFI, 1995); *Pépé le Moko* (BFI Film Classics, 1998); *Stars and Stardom in French Cinema* (Continuum, 2000); *Jean-Pierre Melville, An American in Paris* (BFI, 2003) and *La Haine* (I.B. Tauris, 2005). She recently co-edited (with Peter Graham) *The New Wave: Critical Landmarks* (BFI, 2009). She is currently completing a book on the representation of the south of France in film and television.

Catherine Wheatley is a Research Associate on the AHRC-funded project 'French Cinema in Britain, 1930–present' at Southampton University, working with Dr

Lucy Mazdon. She is the author of *Michael Haneke's Cinema: The Ethic of the Image* (Berghahn, 2009), as well as a forthcoming BFI Film Classics volume on Haneke's *Hidden*. She is also a regular contributor to *Sight and Sound* magazine.

Leila Wimmer holds a Ph.D. in Film and Television Studies from the University of Warwick and is a Lecturer in Film Studies at London Metropolitan University. She has recently completed a monograph entitled *Cross-Channel Perceptions: The French Reception of British Cinema* (Peter Lang, 2009).

Index